to 1

# Popular Religion in
Central Europe,

CW00351831

# THEMES IN FOCUS

*Published titles*

Jonathan Barry and Christopher Brooks
THE MIDDLING SORT OF PEOPLE: Culture, Society and
Politics in England, 1500–1800

Christopher Durston and Jacqueline Eales
THE CULTURE OF ENGLISH PURITANISM, 1560–1700

Paul Griffiths, Adam Fox and Steve Hindle
THE EXPERIENCE OF AUTHORITY IN EARLY MODERN
ENGLAND

Tim Harris
POPULAR CULTURE IN ENGLAND, *c.* 1500–1850

Roy Porter and Marie Mulvey Roberts
PLEASURE IN THE EIGHTEENTH CENTURY

Bob Scribner and Trevor Johnson
POPULAR RELIGION IN GERMANY AND CENTRAL EUROPE,
1400–1800

*Forthcoming*

Patrick Collinson and John Craig
THE REFORMATION IN ENGLISH TOWNS, 1500–1640

# Popular Religion in Germany and Central Europe, 1400–1800

*Edited by*

BOB SCRIBNER and TREVOR JOHNSON

MACMILLAN

First published 1996 by
**MACMILLAN PRESS LTD**
Houndmills, Basingstoke, Hampshire RG21 6XS
and London
Companies and representatives
throughout the world

ISBN 0–333–61456–9 hardcover
ISBN 0–333–61457–7 paperback

A catalogue record for this book is available
from the British Library.

| 10 | 9 | 8 | 7 | 6 | 5 | 4 | 3 | 2 | 1 |
|----|----|----|----|----|----|----|----|----|----|
| 05 | 04 | 03 | 02 | 01 | 00 | 99 | 98 | 97 | 96 |

Printed in Malaysia

Published in the United States of America 1996 by
ST. MARTIN'S PRESS, INC.,
Scholarly and Reference Division
175 Fifth Avenue, New York, N.Y. 10010

ISBN 0–312–12837–1

# Contents

# List of Illustrations

viii

*List of Illustrations*

# Introduction

BOB SCRIBNER

The purpose of this volume is to provide a collection of essays embodying recent research on popular religion within the boundaries of the Holy Roman Empire (Germany and Bohemia) in the later middle ages and early modern period. There has been a considerable efflorescence of research on the general theme of 'popular religion' over the past decade, although very little has been published on German topics, whether in English or German.[1] The work presented here represents a sampling of approaches and subjects that is distinctive in three ways. First, it reveals the extremely broad range of problems and issues that may be explored under the heading 'popular religion', encompassing female spirituality, the role of gender, the psychology of religious devotion, the creation of religious mythology and forms of religio-political discourse, attitudes towards the Jews, witchcraft, popular magic, the nature of Protestant 'popular belief' and the appropriation of popular religious phenomena by the Catholic Reformation. Such issues also encompass both the rural and urban worlds, and deal with intensively private as well as with overtly public manifestations of belief.

Secondly, these newer perspectives increasingly transcend the divide between the pre-Reformation and Reformation periods, showing how necessary it has become to view popular religion over a *longue durée* – not only despite the apparently radical break brought by the Reformation, but in many cases because of it, since the innovatory potential of the Reformation can only be discerned by a fuller understanding of the world of religious belief it sought to replace. We are now more than ever aware that a picture of dramatic change is misleading, that replacement of traditional religion was either partial or slow to take effect, so that it is necessary to explore not only innovations in religious forms, but also continuities, mutations and adaptations. The same

1

flexibility of perspective is evident in the geographical range of the material, which encompasses both north and south Germany, as well as lands with proximity or close political ties to it (Bohemia, Scandinavia, Austria). Developments did not confine themselves within neat geographical boundaries, but spilled easily from Switzerland into Germany and back, from north Germany into Scandinavia.

Thirdly, this collection presents original research by young scholars at the beginning of their careers, all combining fresh-ness of approach with significant new material that demands radical rethinking about the long-term popular impact of the Reformation. They were all produced within the framework of the Graduate Seminar for Early Modern German History at Cambridge University, but it could not be claimed that they repre-sent any unified 'Cambridge approach' in either their method-ology or subject matter. As with many recent studies of religious history, their hallmark is the thematic diversity and theoretical openness that now characterises the best analyses of social and cultural history in the late medieval and early modern period. It could also not be said that they address in any consistent way the problems associated with the onset of the Reformation, for each has its own distinctive set of questions and point of departure. However, the findings embodied in each of the chapters have considerable implications for our understanding of just what reli-gious change meant as a historical reality touching the lives of the masses of ordinary people. It is for this reason that the unifying theme around which they have been grouped has been given the label 'popular religion'.

It is necessary to comment further on the flag 'popular reli-gion' under which the volume sails, since it is one which arouses negative connotations among many scholars. For some the adject-ive 'popular' smacks too much of an artificial two-tier model of society, culture or religion, with an implied polarity between elite and non-elite, as though these were two hermetically sealed realms of experience. This objection certainly has some validity, although most who nowadays use the term could justify it in two ways. First, the word 'popular' is mostly used inclusively to mean the religion of the population in the broadest sense, while in no way excluding the participation of different kinds of elites, even if the ways in which they participated might be considered a problem for investigation. Moreover, recent attempts to introduce new terminologies have contained their own inbuilt polarities: 'official' and 'unofficial' religion, 'local religion', with the implied contrast 'non-local', i.e. centralised or universal, 'Herrschaft' and community, centre and periphery.[2] Even the notion of 'culture as appropriation' hides a bipolar conceptualisation, in that it tacitly presupposes a culture created by someone other than those who use it.[3] It seems, therefore, almost impossible to evade some kind of polarised conceptualisation, even if we can eschew the cruder versions of the two-tier model once in use.

It is not only the predilection of historians for such antithetical terms, mostly as a form of dramatised hermeneutic, that continually reinserts them into the discussion; they were also embedded in the mind-set of the age under discussion, which thought in polarities, inversions and contrarieties. Indeed, the history of the period is inescapably shot through with sets of oppositions used or recognised by contemporaries themselves: learned–unlearned, clerical–lay, powerful–disempowered (in the form *potens-pauper*, in German *die großen Hansen und der arme Mann*), privileged–disprivileged, elites–masses, rich–poor, male–female, orthodox–heterodox, religious–superstitious. It was the frequent bundling of sets of such polar opposites that constituted a discrete discourse about religion and enabled its deployment in instrumental and polemical ways, of which the evangelical discourse of the Reformation was only one example. These conceptual oppositions often created historical realities by drawing numerous overlapping boundaries between one thing and another, which then thickened up to mark out distinct territories from which certain types of person were excluded: Jews, heretics, witches, the ignorant lay person, the superstitious peasant. Essentially, this involved a separation into categories of the acceptable and the unacceptable, those who belonged and those who did not – the 'other'.

The point, therefore, is not that polarities of this kind did not exist, but that they existed as part of a complex dialectic between two sides of a dispute or power struggle, which is not even captured by contrasts between 'official' and 'unofficial', 'centre' and 'periphery', or even 'Herrschaft' and community. The chapter by Eric Wilson shows how a crucial stage in the creation of the witch paradigm involved a conflict between an overzealous inquisitor, Heinrich Institoris, anxious to cite papal legitimation, and local officials unconvinced by his arguments. Both sides sought to invoke an official papal authority which seems to have been comparatively uninterested in persecuting witchcraft on the terms presented by Institoris, leading the frustrated Dominican inquisitor to misrepresent the papal bull he had obtained to lend an appearance of official support to his campaign. The complexity and importance of such 'situational dialectic' is confirmed by Alison Rowlands' study of Rothenburg ob der Tauber. Here there was no absence of the accusations of witchcraft found in most other regions of sixteenth-century Germany, but the authorities were inclined to take a more sceptical attitude towards such accusations than the people who brought them. It was not that the Lutheran authorities in Rothenburg did not believe in the activities of Satan or that there might even be practices that the common folk described to them as witchcraft. It was simply that they held that Satan had created the notion of witchcraft as a diabolical illusion to distract people from the providential nexus that really ruled their lives. Misfortune was a divine punishment for sin rather than a consequence of witchcraft, and those who believed in either witchcraft or magic were deluded and superstitious. That is, the Rothenburg authorities saw themselves as primarily engaged in a struggle against popular superstition, and were therefore willing to punish the 'superstitious' practitioner of magic more severely than the person accused as a witch. Ordinary folk, however, believed in the importance of magic as a means to influence the exigencies of daily life and were therefore willing to seek out cunning folk to help them in their troubles. By virtue of the same logic, they were also willing to attribute misfortune to the work of witches and to invoke a stereotype of diabolical malevolence against which they expected their authorities to take decisive action. A stark contrast between official and unofficial belief certainly emerges in this instance, but also a complex underlying dialectic that was sometimes further complicated by divergence between secular authorities and the clergy – official belief was a far from cohesive or uniform matter.

Scott Dixon takes up a prototypical case of confrontation between the clergy, as representatives of 'official belief', and their rural parishioners in his discussion of Reformation campaigns against popular magic in the territory of Brandenburg-Ansbach in the second half of the sixteenth century. The clergy were here confronted not only with persistent popular beliefs but especially with practices they could not eradicate. This was, as Dixon shows, a clash both of belief systems and of forms of practice. It was also *par excellence* a confrontation between village culture and attempts to implement religious reform at the grassroots of society. Although the minor skirmishes and major battles of the struggle were catalogued in visitation records – the results of flying visits from outside officialdom – the front-line troops in the struggle were the village pastors, insiders who played the unenviable role of middlemen between local and central, official and unofficial, learned and unlearned. As I have commented elsewhere, it is through the experience of such middlemen that we see in as detailed a close-up as we are likely to find a direct encounter with popular belief.[4] Yet as Dixon emphasises, this is not an un-mediated popular belief but one refracted through the eyes of those who sought to change it, and what we see is a process of encounter, mediation and change. Dixon focusses upon this process to discern the dynamics by which Protestantism was 'inscribed' on the rural parishioners of Brandenburg-Ansbach. This was no mere writing on a blank sheet nor even a rubbing-out to create a palimpsest for official Lutheran ideas. It was a matter of exchange which led to a reconfiguration of views, rather than a substitution of them. One is reminded of the recent account given by Gananath Obeyesekere of the complex dialectical encounters between European explorers and aborigines in the South Pacific over the issue of 'cannibalism'.[5] Although Dixon's essay is written without knowledge of Obeyesekere's work, he has identified similar methodological principles and processes.

The older Reformation history tended to present the Reform-ation as something that arrived fully formed in the moment that Luther allegedly posted the Ninety-five Theses, or at the very least when he refused to recant before Charles V at the Diet of Worms. Such historiographies owe more to piety than to history, although it is still possible to find historians using the terms 'Lutheranism', 'Protestantism', 'Calvinism' in extremely anachronistic ways as a form of conceptually sloppy historical shorthand. The work of Johannes Wolfart on the Reformation in Lindau provides an important and radical corrective to that practice. Lindau is one of those interesting anomalies which defy traditional categories of

'Reformation'. Sometime in the early 1520s, the city experienced an evangelical reform which led it away from traditional Catholicism, although the Lindauers refused to be squeezed into the corset of Lutheran Protestantism as represented by the Confession of Augsburg, subscribing instead to the equivocal Tetrapolitan Confession alongside Constance, Memmingen and Strassburg. As Wolfart shows here and elsewhere, just what 'the Reformation' meant in Lindau was not a cut-and-dried matter, of some moment of collective conversion.[6] Strikingly, there were no church statutes issued in Lindau before 1573, and even in the seventeenth century Lindauers squabbled over the exact nature of their form of 'Protestantism'. Their understanding of 'the Reformation' was an ongoing process of definition and redefinition in which questions of religious and confessional identity became entangled in political discourse. That discourse was intensely pragmatic and sensitive to the wider political context of the given moment, in keeping with the city's border position, which made it economically and culturally more inclined to the Swiss, but necessarily politically involved with German princes and the Emperor. Every moment of decision-making about religion thus involved the city in potentially dangerous internal divisions – joining the Schmalkaldic League, timely reconciliation with the Emperor and acceptance of the Interim, adopting the Formula of Concord of 1576, its stance during the Thirty Years War.

Wolfart chooses to view this process of definition and redefinition through the prism of private confession, a practice with a central place in any discussion of popular religion because it was a crucial point where private piety and official control confronted each other. Understandably it was a key issue of the early Reformation, since it represented in early evangelical polemics the epitome of papist tyranny over souls. Yet in one of those theological somersaults characteristic of the Lutheran Reformation, it became a defining feature of Lutheran as opposed to Zwinglian/Reformed confessional identity. As Wolfart shows, even this apparently neat distinction is very misleading in the Lindau context. Wolfart's highly original study opens up a vast array of issues about the nature of confessionalism, how religious identity was defined and the ways in which it became so enmeshed with local political identity that the categories currently used to define the process of 'confessionalisation' look crude and inadequate. Wolfart's work can be placed alongside recent studies of Catholic confessionalisation by Forster and François that show how far we have yet to travel before we can claim to have adequate analytical categories for understanding what it meant to be Catholic, Calvinist or Lutheran in early modern Europe.[7]

A major conclusion of Wolfart's article is the impossibility of separating religious and political discourse, especially once these became a matter of public polemic and propaganda. A comparison at this point with the work of Thomas Fudge is informative for a number of reasons. Fudge deals with a very distinctive form of religio-political discourse, the creation of popular Hussitism in the first third of the fifteenth century, although the ways in which that discourse was created stand comparison with similar processes occurring after 1500. Much recent discussion about the interplay of religion and politics in the Reformation over the *longue durée*, especially that about the so-called 'Second Reformation', has operated with a woefully foreshortened perspective of the phenomenon of 'reformation', whereby what was undoubtedly the 'first' Reformation (if we must number them like Schwarzenegger films), that carried through by the Hussites in fifteenth-century Bohemia, simply takes place unnoticed off-stage. Recent research on the Bohemian Reformation, including that of Fudge himself, has done much to establish this as a major variant of religious reform and not merely a forerunner of the 'real' Reformation of the sixteenth century.[8] The Hussite reformation and revolution undoubtedly had its own distinctive defining characteristics, but there are many valuable points of comparison with the reformation of the sixteenth century, indeed far beyond the like phenomena of iconoclasm and the demands for the vernacular Bible and the cup for the laity. Parallels can be found in the nature of the mass movements involved, in the combination of religious legitimation and social upheaval, the religious roles ascribed to common people and especially (as Fudge points out in some interesting examples) the roles taken by women; the potency of the politics of religious commitment and militancy; the mobilising force of eschatological feeling; and the creation of a very distinctive form of politico-religious discourse, forged in the crucible of polemics and propaganda.

Highly original in Fudge's account is the dimension of 'popular religion' discernible in Hussite practice. This phenomenon was

8     *Popular Religion in Germany and Central Europe*

created in two ways, through creative popular adaptation of the
more learned ideas of Hussite theologians, and through an
appropriation of traditional popular religious notions such as liturgical innovation, sainthood and apotropaic magic. Far from being
an aberration or marginal phenomenon, the popular religious elements became central to Hussite practice, a case of situational dialectic in which the 'unofficial' assimilated the 'official' to become
the 'legitimate' form of popular Hussitism. Surprising to the historian used to viewing the Hussites as proto-protestants is the creation of a myth of St John Hus, the manipulation of visual symbols,
popular communication and visual propaganda (on all of these
points the parallels with the Reformation of the sixteenth century
are striking). In some respects, the formation and trajectory of
such popular Hussitism invites comparison with the movements of
direct action in German and Swiss towns in the 1520s, with the
evangelically-inspired rebellion of the German Peasants' War, and
with the liturgical and social radicalism of sixteenth-century
Anabaptism. Clearly, there is much to be explored here in further
comparative research.

   The manner in which the Hussites reworked traditional sacred
charisma finds an echo in Jürgen Beyer's work on Lutheran
popular prophets of the early modern period. Beyer's discovery of
the phenomenon of the Lutheran prophetic visionary is surprising not only in itself, but above all in the astonishing number of
these figures who were abroad in north Germany. They represent
a creative adaptation for Protestant purposes of the medieval
saintly apparition, usually part of the legitimation of a sacred
shrine, although sometimes simply as a means of communicating a
penitential message. The most obvious pre-Reformation example
of such prophecy is Hans Boheim, the Piper of Niklashausen,
whose revelations came close to having social revolutionary consequences. The Lutheran prophets were a protestantised version of
this tradition, admonishing their contemporaries to repentance
lest divine anger befall them. The message was, as Beyer shows, im-
peccably Lutheran in its theology, but depended for its effect on
ongoing Protestant belief in a sacralised world in which supernatural power could still intrude into human affairs. Indeed, it depended on the notion of a moralised cosmos, in which
relationships with the supernatural were determined by the quality
of human moral action. Such popular phenomena drew on the

Protestant doctrine of providence, although that doctrine was in itself ill-suited to cope with such irregular manifestations of the supernatural as occurred in apparitions, miracles or demonic possession. Protestant doctrine had disarmed itself of the traditional means (sacramentals, blessings, exorcisms) used to deal with such intrusions of the supernatural. The only recourse open to Protestants was prayer and reliance on God's inscrutable will, which was all too often insufficient to allay human anxieties. For this reason, early modern Protestants turned willingly to popular magic, to the frustration of pastors and theologians alike. Providentialism was increasingly seen, even among the devout, as a doctrine that had failed.[9] In response to Catholic evidence of divine support through apparitions and miracles, Protestant polemicists were frequently tongue-tied, or else attempted to redefine sainthood in ways appropriate to their own doctrines. It was perhaps a sign of their awareness of the insufficiency of this strategy that they also promoted what they could by way of their own official miraculous saint's cult, that of St Luther, with incombustible images and the alleged preservation of Luther's remains uncorrupted by the grave.[10]

Beyer's work shows that there was an alternative popular strategy, one which found more ready resonance among the less theologically educated. The Lutheran popular prophets, with their angelic apparitions (more biblical than traditional Catholic apparitions of the Virgin Mary or the saints, less theologically dubious than eucharistic miracles) and messages of repentance provided a more direct, personal channel to the supernatural than vague recommendations about the power of prayer or trust in God. Above all, they were closely related to their local context, to immediate causes of anxiety and distress, and presented a message that undoubtedly struck home with their audience. The affront to official Lutheran belief and its representatives, local pastors, churchmen and secular magistrates, was multiple. As ministers of the Word, the Lutheran clergy had since the early 1520s fulfilled the function of controlling and policing access to the sacred, especially in the face of the challenge from religious radicals such as the Anabaptists. Direct revelations undermined that control and opened up the Pandora's box of subjective judgement. Not inconsiderable was the fear of losing ground to Catholic confessional opponents, since Lutheran self-confidence was easily shaken by their continual failure to overcome the manifest errors of papal religion and the church of the Antichrist, a weakness Catholic controversialists did not fail to exploit.[11] The instinctive strategy adopted by Lutheran churchmen was that of demonisation, explaining such apparitions as the direct work of Satan himself, a difficult task indeed, given the generally impeccable Protestant credentials of the prophets. An alternative response was to stigmatise the prophets as mentally ill, as melancholics, or better still as downright frauds. The lack of success of such strategies is attested by the continued existence of the phenomenon until the eighteenth century.

In the case of the Lübeck prophet David Frese, Beyer has also chosen an example that touched another neuralgic point for early modern official Protestantism, relations with the dead. Early modern Protestantism, despite its official doctrine and practice, proved unable to eradicate traditional popular concerns about the spirits of the dead, and there continued to be, well into the twentieth century, a thick sub-stratum of Protestant popular belief about spirits, ghosts, poltergeists, restless souls, and above all the untimely or 'dangerous dead', those for whom the rites of separation had been imperfectly performed. Here official behalf could do no more than exercise a passive tolerance of what it could not eradicate.[12] That such an issue appears in the context of a popular prophet such as Frese shows how closely such persons could feel the pulse of Lutheran popular belief.

The final affront to official Lutheranism was to secular authority, so anxious ever since the disturbing events of the German Peasants' War to detach charismatic religious phenomena from social criticism. The argument used by secular authority to justify days of prayer to seek God's grace was that all were collectively responsible for the state of sin that had occasioned divine wrath. However, in the mouth of a popular prophet such a statement had another, more ominous ring to it: that the authorities were also responsible through their own failings. In the case of one of the most notable prophetic apparitions in south Germany, the 'angelic apparition at Dürrmenz' in 1567, part of the supernatural message concerned the neglect of the poor by the rich, for Lutheran churchmen a sure sign that this was indeed a false prophecy![13] The possibilities of using prophecy as a stick with which to beat negligent or oppressive authorities was only too well understood, as Beyer shows in his example of the cowherd in the Palatinate in 1659, who wished to scare district officials into treating their subjects more humanely. Beyer's article does not deal with all the ramifications of his vast array of popular prophets, but he has certainly opened a window on the as yet unexplored world of popular Protestantism, a fruitful field of research to be tilled in the years ahead.

The relationship between official and popular religion in Protestantism generally seems to have been one of official reluctance to countenance popular misapprehensions, although this often amounted to no more than turning a blind eye to the 'superstitions' of folk belief. By contrast, Catholic official religion seemed only too ready to interact with popular belief, especially if this provided a confessional advantage in the struggle against Protestant heresy. An older tradition of Counter-Reformation historiography sought to distance the religion promoted by Catholic reform from pre-Reformation 'pagan superstitions', painting a picture of a Tridentine reform which introduced a more interiorised, spiritual and theologically sound religion among the people.[14] A much more differentiated picture has emerged in recent studies by Châtellier, Forster, Gentilcore and Soergel, revealing a far more complex relationship between Tridentine and traditional Catholicism, and between official religion and popular belief.[15] Trevor Johnson's work contributes substantially to this newer view of the Counter-Reformation, revealing that Tridentine Catholicism certainly did not replace older forms of 'superstition', but revived traditional pilgrimages, holy places, saints' cults, thaumaturgic holy men and sacramentals.[16] Most surprising in Johnson's account is the willingness of the Jesuits, assuredly part of the Counter-Reformation intellectual elite, to make blatant use of popular religious belief in their missionising strategies. Theatricality and the invocation of emotional excess is perhaps not surprising for the 'baroque mentality', although the promotion of Ignatius-Water as an apotropaic sacramental somehow seems very unjesuitical. The use of the miraculous as a catholicising strategy has been mentioned above, and the apparent success of cures using Ignatius-Water must have infuriated Protestants anxious to counter Catholic claims to such manipulations of sacrality. Here, of course, we are dealing once again with the complex dialectic between official and unofficial, elite and popular that saw accommodation between two religious worlds to the point where they seemed to merge. Successful exorcisms, healing miracles, even levitating Jesuits (the extraordinary Jakob Rem!) may have had even more impact on the popular mind than theatrically staged rural missions and penitential strategies. Clearly, the traces of pre-Reformation popular religion were strongly inscribed on both Protestantism and post-Tridentine Catholicism. Just as the story of popular Protestantism remains to be told, so too does the full story of Counter-Reformation Catholicism.

As both Trevor Johnson and Philip Soergel have shown, Bavaria and the Upper Palatinate were replete with holy places and sacred landscape. These were largely marked during the Reformation and Counter-Reformation as a form of defensive boundary against the 'confessional other'. There was, of course, a longer tradition of defining orthodoxy by expelling and excluding the 'other', as Ronnie Hsia pointed out in his study of the discourse of Jewish ritual murder.[17] Perhaps the most well-known case of such exclusion of the religious and ethnic 'other' occurred in Regensburg, with the expulsion of the Jews in 1519. The purification of the former Jewish quarter and dedication of the site of the demolished synagogue to the Virgin Mary provides a classic case of the definition of sacred space and its miraculous legitimation by divine intervention. Mary Minty's fascinating study of how Jewish ghettos were converted to Christian quarters provides further powerful evidence for the continuities in ritual and sacral life across the centuries of the 'long early modern period'.

As in so many of the chapters in this volume, religious events prove impossible to separate from political discourse and secular interest. Political and economic factors played their undoubted part in the conversion of Jewish quarters, but, as Minty shows, there were also inescapable elements of popular belief, embodied in the preconceptions Christians held of exactly what went on in the Jewish synagogue – witchcraft, host desecration, ritual murder – giving incredible emotive power to the term 'the synagogue of Satan', which was to resurface in anti-papist as well as in witchcraft discourse. Yet the rituals of Christian purification and consecration of such formerly nefarious places had the effect of neutralising them for Christian use, indeed perhaps analogous to the ways in which evangelical rites of image-breaking purified the Christian churches for Protestant use. Minty has much to say on the complex symbolism associated with all these actions, reminding us of the 'semiotic universe' that enveloped popular and official belief alike and which could bind it into a plausible and powerful unity. There is a close affinity between the processes analysed here by Minty and those presented to us by Soergel in his fascinating study of the constitution and reconstitution of sacred landscape in Bavaria. The geographic spread discovered by Mary Minty for the Christian reconstitution of sacred space across the length and breadth of the Holy Roman Empire shows that this was a phenomenon almost of general European significance.

The last major theme to mention in this introduction brings us to the first contribution in the volume, that by Ulinka Rublack. Her essay falls into a field which, although relatively young, has proved to be one of the most fruitful and challenging for new research, the importance of gender in the construction of religious belief. The chapter is concerned with a commonplace of late-medieval religion, the relationship between the devotional image and the interior piety of the devout believer, in this case a doll of the Infant Jesus of a kind commonly given to nuns when they entered the convent. The role of the image in late-medieval personal devotion was both intense and existentially important, especially devotion to the image of Christ, which was to place his redemptive, suffering humanity at the heart of late-medieval religion. Although the Reformation was to reject much of this kind of piety, its own christocentric message was but a development of this late-medieval emphasis, and unthinkable without it. Images of the Infant Jesus were also intimately associated with a wide range of visionary experience, combining intense individualism with unmediated access to the sacred. The subject in itself represents an important corrective to the view that late-medieval religion was essentially collective, while highly subjective, interiorised, individual religious experience was a product of the Reformation and Counter-Reformation. Indeed, Margaretha von Ebner's devotion to her Infant Jesus doll has transcended both the late-medieval and early modern period, and become itself an object of popular piety, another proof of the tortuous ways in which popular religion has been transmuted from one kind of precious metal into another across the ages.

Rublack's major focus, however, is on the gender-specific aspects of such devotion and of female spirituality in general. The mystical experiences of late-medieval nuns have always excited historical and scientific interest, producing academic analyses which in themselves were an engendered discourse. Eighteenth and nineteenth-century attempts to grasp the phenomenon simply saw it as a sublimation of repressed sexual desire or a compensation for the motherhood denied the nuns by their celibacy. As always, Freud was willing to pronounce on such matters from an a priori judgement which placed them in the realm of hysteria. This kind of interpretation has even been followed by some recent feminist historians, albeit from within a different form of discourse about female religiosity, seeing the nuns' experience as a compensation for hidden but real female desires for motherhood and genital sex. Rublack, however, seeks to recover the authenticity of the nuns' experience within its own terms, to discern a psychology of spirituality that is not dependent on Freudian ideas or similar products of a nineteenth-century bourgeois (and patriarchal) mentality. On Rublack's reading, mystical relationships between nuns and the Infant Jesus are indeed to do with powerful images of motherhood, mother–child relationships, sexuality, the fragility and permeability of the body, the salvific meaning of pain and the shedding of blood. However, she places these phenomena within a symbolic universe where many more meanings may be ascribed to them than is conceived in one-dimensional twentieth-century understandings of sexuality, motherhood or even of gender. We are reminded of Caroline Walker Bynum's discovery of the gender-ambivalent or even non-gendered views of Jesus in medieval spirituality that enabled relationships with the Saviour to be constructed in more complex ways than merely male-to-female or male-to-male.[18] Such explorations open up a rich field of enquiry not only about religious subjectivities, but about a wide range of engendered experiences and their psychologies, as recent work by Lyndal Roper has shown.[19]

We are vividly reminded by work such as Rublack's or Roper's of how far the official religion of both Reformation and Counter-Reformation flattened out the multi-dimensionality of much medieval popular belief. As the essays in this volume show, it refused to accommodate itself to one-dimensionality, continually bursting out of official and disciplinary constraints, acculturating official belief and creating syncretic forms of the traditional and the new, the orthodox and the heterodox, the medieval and the early modern (as if such terms had meaning for most people in the centuries under discussion), combining religious experience and appropriated theologies, practices and meanings, symbols and semiotic systems into a phenomenon which defies the taxonomies often used in academic discourse. It sometimes seems that modern secular historians react to pre-modern religious phenomena as one might expect the crassest utilitarian scientists to respond to beings from another galaxy. For this reason, many historians since the 1970s have turned to the discipline of social anthropology as a paradigm of how to approach such forms of otherness. But even here we have now been made aware of the fragility of such forms of endeavour, which often construct the image of the other merely as the antithesis of the explorer, embodying his (sic!) deepest fears and anxieties, and in the process destroying the culture under observation until it is no longer the same as that met on first encounter.[20]

This is not a counsel of methodological despair, a claim that the historian will never know the religious belief of the past in ways that might have been recognisable to the people concerned. It is simply to argue that we should avoid cruder ways of merely laying a conceptual stencil over the period and without further reflection running across it the thin watercolour of modern perceptions. What is required in formulating heuristic concepts is the kind of sensitivity to context, to local experience, to the connections made from within the period itself that we see in these essays. Perhaps for this very reason they succeed in recovering, in dialogue with people of the past, much of the distinctiveness of the period – but it is a dialogue which listens to the past more than it shouts at it. For this reason, such work should form the vanguard of the next historical generation.

# 1. Female Spirituality and the Infant Jesus in Late Medieval Dominican Convents[1]

ULINKA RUBLACK

## I

A visitor coming today to the beautifully situated convent of Maria-Medingen in Bavaria will find a doll of the infant Jesus proudly displayed in a glass shrine. It is in a chapel dedicated to the fourteenth-century nun to whom the doll once belonged, the mystic Margaretha von Ebner. In the rear of the chapel the visitor will also find about sixty ex-voto images donated to Margaretha von Ebner in the seventeenth and eighteenth centuries.[2] Some of them depict her praying or meditating in front of her doll. Others show her at the bedsides of sick babies for whose health the parents were supplicating. Yet most show her in intense contact with the doll, mediating between the donor's concern and Jesus's grace. Through her relationship to Jesus, mediated through the doll, Margaretha von Ebner gained a spiritual power which the laity could recognise. In her own time, the doll enabled her to bypass structures of clerical authority as it responded to her questions about people's salvation and told her about God's attitude towards individual saints and male mystics. But why did her devotion focus on an infant Jesus doll? We can only regard this as bizarre. The question takes us back to the context of medieval piety.

From the twelfth century onwards devotion was directed less and less towards a God who ruled as a judge and king, and increasingly towards a 'human' and loving God, with whom fusion was possible because of the likeness between God and the believer. The centre of religious experience came to be located

16

within the self. Christ's love and sufferings were experienced through contemplation, dreams, visions, illnesses, and bodily pain.[3] An experience of the infant Jesus's humanity became characteristic of female piety.[4] During the thirteenth century women increasingly turned to a religious life in poverty which was devoted to serving the sick and needy. At the same time preaching and other clerical services were turned into male privileges, so that the institutional spaces in which religious women held offices contracted. Intense spiritual experiences became the only way women could forcefully direct their journey towards God or mediate between God and the laity.

By the fourteenth-century, therefore, female devotion in Dominican convents was firmly linked to an 'experiential' spirituality and to physical, visionary, and intimate interactions with the infant Jesus. The readiness to envisage Christ's life more corporeally had also changed the status of devotional art. Until the thirteenth century images had only been accepted as aids to help lesser minds remember key religious narratives. During the fourteenth century, images were increasingly used to facilitate and focus visionary experience.[5] Devotional objects such as the cross and Christ's dying body were complemented by infant Jesus figures and cradles.[6]

This chapter investigates the symbolic meanings of these infant Jesus figures and Dominican devotion to the Infant. It explores in detail the meaning which Margaretha von Ebner's doll had for her spiritual life. It is argued that a doll, as a material object which gained its lifelikeness through an attribution of speech-acts and gestures, could become the source of a nun's socially acknowledged spiritual power and deepen her understanding of God's being. The meanings of such a doll, and hence the relation to the infant Jesus, were multilayered, but it is not suggested that dolls compensated for non-existent husbands and (male) babies. This would be to overlook the fact that nuns experienced real love, desire, and motherly care on a complex spiritual and emotional level, within an eroticised spirituality now alien to our understanding and imagination. What needs to be emphasised in nuns' emotional responses to the infant Jesus is the historical specificity of the psychological processes involved – their meaningfulness in their own time, in other words, and not their meaningfulness merely as 'displaced desire'.

Herbert Grundmann has drawn attention to the large number of visions experienced by medieval nuns in which the infant Jesus played a central role. In these visions the nuns carried him in their arms, played with him, suckled him, or even had the illusion of being pregnant with him.[7] His interpretation of these as 'crazy notions' can be regarded as the stereotype of explanations offered for a long time: the women wanted to identify with Mary and act out their maternal instincts. Recently, Christiane Klapisch-Zuber reformulated this interpretation while presenting a more feminist version of the thesis. She argued that the behaviours of the nuns 'echo the hypermaternal attitudes that the devotional texts attribute to the Virgin herself'.[8] Drawing mainly on fifteenth-century Italian examples of 'holy dolls' she concludes:

> the infant Jesus allowed the recluse her primary social function – the maternal function – and put her desire and frustrations within limits that her male confessors recognised and could accept. The child-husband allowed these women an experience that their secluded life condemned them never to know.[9]

During the past ten years research on medieval female spirituality has slowly moved away from the view that visions are best understood as sublimations of worldly experiences inaccessible to nuns. Recent research has evaluated how religious women actively positioned themselves in the mystical search for the divine.[10] Individual self-definitions and institutional frameworks have been explored in order to assess how far their experiences derived from common secular or spiritual beliefs and brought new meanings to them.[11] This chapter similarly investigates how nuns related to the paradoxical construct of Jesus as a human and divine child, and gave meaning to it within their spirituality.

## II

Margaretha von Ebner was born in 1291 in Donauwörth. When she was twenty years old she entered the nearby Dominican order of Maria-Medingen, founded by the Duke of Dillingen in 1246 for daughters of the Donauwörth patriciate. There she lived for forty years until her death in 1351. In her *Revelations*, which she started writing when she was fifty-three, she summed up her life at home thus: 'how I lived for twenty years before this, I cannot put down, as I did not perceive myself'.[12] She went back to her family only once, in the years 1324/25 at the approach of war. Only mutual alienation was felt. Margaretha remained in the convent for the rest of her life. She was the best friend of one prioress, but only once held a minor official position herself. In 1332, when she was forty-one, she got to know her future confessor, close friend and admirer, Heinrich von Nördlingen. Their correspondence is the first in the German language to be preserved. After several experiences of God's grace, in 1344 von Nördlingen asked Margaretha to record her spiritual experiences for him. During the next four years she both dictated and wrote the 166 pages of the *Revelations* in the vernacular.[13] The writing turned into a spiritual experience when God put visions in her head and words in her mouth. Margaretha revealed that especially while she wrote she felt 'great desire for the childhood of our Lord' and his circumcision.[14] She sent parts of the *Revelations* to Heinrich for correction. The extent of his corrections and whether the text aimed at a wider audience remains unclear.

### III

I first wish briefly to discuss some characteristic features of Margaretha von Ebner's religious life before clarifying how attitudes towards the infant Jesus differed by gender. Central to her piety were the birth and the passion of Christ, in short the series of events which expressed both his human nature and his love and accessibility. This is clear from God's answer to her decisive question: how might the believer experience God most directly? God referred first to Mary's pregnancy, and secondly to the birth of the Christchild; then followed Christ's sufferings, the reception of the Holy Sacrament, and finally the daily experience of Christ's love.[15] In view of these answers, she felt the highest certainty about God's presence in the Eucharist: 'the living power of God is in me, his holy blood and flesh'.[16] After the Eucharist, God powerfully expressed the mutuality of their love, telling her:

As I am beloved by you, so you are beloved by me. As your desire is in me, so I am in you with all my power, and I never want to depart from your soul and from your heart, except if with your soul to eternal life. ... I am the Truth, which lives in you and emanates from you, and I want to work many things with you to my eternal honour.[17]

In these terms Margaretha demonstrated how it was possible to imagine the equality of God and the believer in their mutual desire for each other. This notion formed the basis for religious practices in which contact with the infant Jesus was easily achieved, because no spiritual hierarchy had to be overcome. Hence her experiences with the infant Jesus (as with most nuns) were characterised by joy, playfulness, spontaneity, comfort, mutual dependence, care, and fidelity.

Dominican nuns typically saw the infant Jesus as a child with whom they played, joked, and kissed; who accompanied them when they were ill or dying, and who in turn received their care during Advent. Apart from these visions their experiences varied widely. Some nuns wanted to see him as a newborn baby, others as a little child or an eight-year-old boy, yet others as a friend or spouse. Thus Gertrude von Helfta's *Herald of Divine Love* (1289) records her observations one night shortly before Christmas:

Then she understood, that God gives to each according to his desire, as if each possessed him alone. And some embrace him as a tender little child who became human through us; others as their most dear friend; and others as their sole spouse. Thus he was given to each, that he might bring joy and pleasure in them according to his will.[18]

The gender-specific differences in the relationship to the infant Jesus are striking. When von Nördlingen and Heinrich Suso meditated on the infant Jesus, they concentrated on the baffling contradiction that God's son became human. In doing this, unlike the nuns, they tacitly emphasised his distance from mankind. In his sermon *How he celebrated Candlemas*, Suso described what happened when Mary gave him the child Jesus at Christmas:

And when she kindly passed the child to him, he stretched out his arms into the infinity of the wide world, received, and embraced the loved one, a thousand times in an hour. He gazed into his pretty little eyes, he beheld his tiny little hands, he greeted his tender little mouth, and he touched all the infant limbs of the heavenly treasure. And then he lifted up his eyes and exclaimed in his heart over the great miracle, for the one who carries heaven is so great and yet so small, so magnificent in the kingdom of heaven, and yet so childlike and so poor on earth. And then he played with him, just as he suggested, singing and crying and doing spiritual exercises.[19]

In Suso's vision it is difficult to feel that he is relating to a natural, living child. The vision became less personalised as he used the third person to talk of himself. The main characteristic of the baby Jesus lay in the paradox that he was divine and human; Suso tried to adore the child's divinity and engage with its naturalness at the same time. The distance between him and the baby remained central to his understanding of Jesus's presence. Heinrich von Nördlingen's experiences were similarly contradictory. Even while the believer was himself bound within his own humanity, the infant Jesus embodied the possibility of glimpsing divinity. As Heinrich wrote to Margaretha at Christmas in 1341:

I wish you to be small and great in him, rich and poor, lowly and yet exalted, sick and strong, lost and found, pale and yet beautiful, dark and yet glowing, blind and yet seeing in him, hungry and yet satisfied, sorrowing and yet full of joy, and daily to die with him and yet to taste eternal life. Oh! What strangely contradictory things he does, until he makes his own become like him![20]

Men were unlikely to indulge in corporeal images in letters and sermons. Dominican Christmas sermons, however, encouraged their audiences to becomes 'mothers of Christ' and to let their souls give spiritual birth to Christ. A rare reflection of how this could lead a man to have corporeal visions of motherhood and union with the Infant can be found in the revelations of Friedrich Sunder. He was chaplain of a female Dominican convent near Nuremberg, and died when Margaretha was twenty-seven years old. His intense contact with the infant Jesus began when the child joined with his soul one Christmas. He now frequently asked Mary for her permission to let his soul give birth to the Infant before the Eucharist. This, he explained, turned Mary into Jesus's physical and him into his spiritual mother. When Jesus had once fed him in the Eucharist, the Infant demanded reciprocity. He wanted to be fed by Sunder. He said 'give me your right breast, so that I can suckle and be spiritually fed by it'.[21] Sunder used equally concrete images to describe the Infant's wedding with his soul in a bed of flowers arranged by Mary after he had once read the third Christmas Mass:

> Then Jesus advanced to the little bed, and Mary ... joined the holy soul with the little Jesus. And they had such loving joy and pleasure with one another of embraces and kisses, with laughter and all divine pleasures.[22]

Like women's experiences, Sunder's emphasised closeness through the Infant's childlike spontaneity and through their mutual joy and nurturing. His experience was, however, not free from ambiguities. Once when Sunder spontaneously welcomed the infant Jesus as 'my child', the Infant implausibly said that he was not his child, but his brother.[23] When on the other hand Mary once came to Sunder and talked to him about Jesus as 'my and your child' (implying that he was a spiritual mother) he coyly rejected the notion of his motherhood.[24] He elaborated on the spiritual meaning of the suckling-scene. The senses, he explained, had to be shown what the suckling meant 'with bodily things', since the *mind* by itself was unable to understand the meaning of the Infant's union with the soul.[25] This obscured whether he himself had experienced the suckling physically, or whether he merely preferred to use corporeal metaphors for their greater impact on the readers' senses.

Yet ambiguity also formed part of Margaretha's experiences; these were not wholly gender-specific. She too emphasised that intimacy always had to be balanced by respect for Jesus's divinity. If there was a gender difference, it lay in Sunder's emphasis that any contact he described in corporeal images involved the relationship between the Infant and his soul. In other words, his experience was tied to an intellectualised spirituality. Nuns, by contrast, somatised their spiritual experience, making it physical (for example, by the giving of the breast).[26] This led to less intellectually structured, but not therefore less complex, experiences with the infant Jesus, as we must now see.

## IV

Margaretha did not recall any significant encounters with the infant Jesus during her first thirty-three years in the convent. She was either merely joyful at Christmas, or empathised with his poverty and need as an exiled child. Then at Christmas 1344 she received a carved figure of the infant Jesus (shown in Figure 1). From then on their interaction became more individualised and intense.[27] The doll was sent to her from Vienna, probably ordered by her confessor Heinrich von Nördlingen. It came with a richly decorated cradle, with an angel fixed on each post.[28] Made of wood, the figure was only eighteen centimetres high, and, unlike most of its Italian equivalents, it was not in swaddling-clothes. It represented the naked body of a genital-less child with a bird in the left hand symbolising the soul.[29] Because it could not stand on its own feet, it had to be laid in the cradle, stood on an altar, or cradled in the arms. It clearly permitted several perceptions, because it had neither a baby-like expression nor the expression of the suffering and wise adult Jesus. It had slightly opened lips, so that it was easy to imagine him talking. From surviving examples we can assume that many nunneries possessed an infant Jesus figure of this kind, usually about thirty-five centimetres high, with or without genitals. In Sarnen, in the early fourteenth century, the doll was given Queen Agnes of Hungary's marriage-gown as a present.[30] In the sixteenth century it became customary for a novice or her family to donate a figure to her convent, often with whole sets of clothes and jewellery. When the Swiss doctor Felix Platter visited a convent in 1561, the abbess showed his wife her private infant Jesus doll in a cradle.[31]

The figures came alive in the nuns' visions when they touched the dolls' feet or bodies. Margaretha von Ebner picked up her figure from the cradle, put it on her lap, 'and thereupon it became a real bodily child'.[32] The Infant himself offered his feet

**Figure 1**  The Dominican mystic Margaretha von Ebner's infant Jesus doll, carved in Vienna in 1344, now in the Bavarian convent of Maria-Medingen

to the sister Adelhait Oethwins: 'the child offered her his little feet, and she took them in her hand, and at once the little feet became flesh and blood and the child withdrew them'.[33] When a sister in St Andrew's cloister in Sarnen was too ill at Christmas to attend the service, she asked whether she could have the convent's infant Jesus doll at her bed instead. While she was meditating the infant Jesus suddenly began to move, pressing his hand on his heart. She was terrified and cried out that she did not deserve the figure. These stories were passed on in convents orally or though written accounts of spiritual experiences, thus encouraging similar visions among other nuns. For the medieval believer it was accepted that an image was not just a material object but was linked with the spiritual energies of the person depicted.

## V

Margaretha von Ebner experienced her relationship to the infant Jesus in three dimensions. First through the spontaneous *physical contact* which was initiated through the desire of both the infant Jesus and Margaretha and expressed in embracing and kissing, breast-feeding and rocking. She experienced it secondly in her *dialogue* with the infant Jesus, which began mostly with her questions or with his telling her about his childhood. She wrote in direct speech, even through she was aware that he did not use real human language in communicating with her. Thus: 'I had a great desire that he should speak with me in human bodily words; but I was answered: "Is it not sweeter and more tender to you, that it is in your soul and heart, and that you should truly acknowledge it, than that you should be spoken to in your ear?" ' Thirdly, there was the *meditative* dimension, where there was no active interaction, as in Margaretha's 'thinking of our Lord's childhood' and her imagining one special event, the circumcision. Each of these dimensions will be discussed in turn.

Soon after she had received the doll Margaretha described two scenes in which their physical contact was made central and in which she negotiated her relationship to him as to a needy child. She first imagined how he forced her to give him her breast by saying: 'if you will not suckle me then I will depart from you when you most love me'.[34] Here Margaretha allowed the infant to manipulate her love by threatening withdrawal. This reflected the everyday language Margaretha imagined a mother and child would use to negotiate attention and love playfully and pleasurably, the mother pretending to surrender to a demand she enjoyed. On another occasion, similarly, the infant Jesus played in his cradle at night so noisily that Margaretha could not sleep. He demanded that she pick him up, because he did not want her to sleep. She responded with pleasure, and continued the game by saying that if he kissed her, she would forgive him for disturbing her. After this verbal prologue the emotional peak was reached:

> Then I said to him: 'why won't you be good and let me sleep? This certainly isn't how I ought to bring you up!' Then the child said: 'I will not let you sleep: you must take me on to you.' Then I took him out of the cradle with great desire and joy and put him on my lap. Then he was a darling child. Then I said: 'If you kiss me, I'll forgive you for disturbing me.' Then he threw his arms around me and held me and kissed me.[35]

Margaretha's notion of motherhood thus played with the idea of reversing her dependence on Jesus's love by making the infant dependent on her. He needed her and asked for closeness which she could decide to give or not. On the other hand she loved and needed what upon her touch and gaze turned into a 'darling child'. His threat to withdraw from her as a bad, unsatisfactory mother when she most loved him exposed the inextricable dependence between mother and child. This imagined relationship, in short, 'naturalised' her belief in the equal need and desire which she and Jesus had for each other, and which she regarded as the basis for a complete, positively dependent, and faithful love.

Nuns negotiated the meaning of motherhood in different ways. Their encounters with motherhood were commonly facilitated by spiritual exercises during Advent, which required them to help Mary care for the Infant. Adelhait von Frauenberg's vision, for example, violently expressed her own need for motherly love, a sense of unworthiness as mother, and the anxiety of having to sacrifice herself completely in order to give or receive:

She desired with a loving desire of her heart that all her body might be martyred to serve the sweet child; she desired that her headcloth might be taken off and used as a napkin for Our Lord; her veins woven to make a little dress for him; and desired that her blood might be poured out to make a little bath for him and her bones burnt to make a fire; and desired that all her flesh be used up for all sinners; and she conceived a great misery in her heart, for she wanted to receive just a little drop of the milk that fell from Our Lady when she suckled Our Lord.[36]

This offer of limitless self-destruction won Mary's attention. Adelhait later received Mary's 'pure, tender breast' and the milk the Infant himself had suckled.[37]

In these different ways nuns' mystical experience depended on an intense experience of love and desire, linked to feelings of dependency, longing, unworthiness, and union. God's love always hurt. Once experienced, it opened a wound that would never heal thereafter; once known, it could not be forgotten. God commonly expressed his experience of love to Margaretha in terms of pressure and compulsion. She repeated three times what God once said to her:

You are a grasper of the truth, you are the one who feels my sweet grace; you are a temptress of my holy pleasure; and a lover to my love. I am a husband of your soul, and that is joy to my honour; I have a work of love in you that is a sweet game to me. Your sweet pleasure *finds* me, your inner desire *forces* me, your burning love *binds* me, your pure truth *maintains* me, your stormy love *protects* me; I shall receive you joyfully and embrace you as a lover in the one and only, that I am. This will I give to you, the kiss of love, of which your soul is desirous, a sweet inner touch, a loving union.[38]

We find a very similar expression in a dialogue written by Mechthild von Magdeburg. It was Heinrich von Nördlingen who translated her *Flowing Light of the Divinity* into High-German, and he read extracts of it to Margaretha von Ebner when he visited her. In this dialogue, which takes up metaphors of courtly, love poetry, love ('minne') speaks to the soul, and the relationship is akin to that between God/Jesus and the believer:

*Love*: You have hunted me, caught me and bound me, and
you have given me deep wounds, so that I can never be
again.
*Soul*: That I hunted you was my lust, that I caught you my
desire, that I bound you my happiness; when I wounded you,
we joined.[39]

The reverse image of this mutuality of love and desire was
expressed in a typical vision of nuns. In this, Jesus withdrew
suddenly and unintelligibly, causing them anguish when he never
returned. Sister Anna's experience in the convent in Töss is only
one example:

And one time at Christmas she sat in the choir thinking upon
the childhood of Our Lord, and then she saw her Dearly
Beloved going as a child to the altar, and as he walked his little
curly locks shimmered, and a great radiance shone forth from
his eyes so that it seemed to her as if the whole choir rose up
and went up into the heights where the altar was, and he came
to her and sat down upon her dress which she spread out, and
then, when full of desire, she wanted to embrace him, she saw
him no more.[40]

The biblical background for this experience was probably the
Song of Songs 6:2–9, in which the beloved knocks on the door at
night, but has gone when his bride, glowing with love, opens it for
him.[41] The pain of this experience is strongly conveyed in the
story of sister Irmgard in Kirchberg to whom the infant Jesus
came while she was cold and ill. While she enjoyed his company
Mary came in and took him to the convent's Eucharist. Irmgard
missed the infant Jesus so strongly that she continually shouted
for him. When the nuns visited her she cried for weapons. She
accused them of having stolen the child from her. Irmgard even
told her nurse to get some special food to attract the Infant back,
but she never saw him again.[42] Likewise a hundred-year-old nun
in Adelshausen kept shouting and moaning 'little son, little son'
until she died, after she had once seen the eight-year-old Jesus
playing and singing next to her bed.[43] This was not an abstract
experience, comparable to the 'wondrous contradictoriness' von
Nördlingen writes about. The paradox of his childlike accessibility

and divine withdrawal was experienced directly. The fidelity of the nuns longing secured their redemption in heaven.

Visions of the Infant's withdrawal could on the other hand also demonstrate that not everybody was able to cope with the strength of God's love. Bechte von Oberriet in Adelshausen felt that God had filled her soul with so much grace that it needed to be wider than anyone else's in the world. She wanted to see the miracle of her soul. It turned out to be the infant Jesus. Her joy with him as a living child became even more unbearable. She asked God to let her return to the former experience of grace. But that did not happen either, nor did she ever see the infant Jesus again.[44]

These visions illustrate how nuns did not simply relate to the infant Jesus as to a natural child. They always signified an encounter with divine humanity which was related to their spiritual concerns. For Margaretha the infant Jesus doll gave an important sense of Jesus's presence and accessibility. Thanks to the doll she did not fear his complete withdrawal and her lonely, ascetic phases devoted to the imitation of Christ's sufferings were always followed by experiences of union and joy. God kept reassuring her of the mutuality of their love and desire, while the infant Jesus assured her that he loved her and everyone she loved, so that she could forcefully pray for their after-lives.

## VI

It was unusual for a nun to pursue a desire for Jesus's presence as much as Margaretha did. She once woke at night and had such 'a great desire for the childhood of our Lord' that she went to the choir and took the statue of the infant Jesus to her breast. Then she felt a human mouth at her breast and the infant Jesus kissed her. She was shocked at first, but then delighted. Shortly afterwards the sister Elsbeth told her that she had had a dream about Margaretha: 'I offered you your child this very night in a dream. And it was a living child, and you took it from me with great desire and laid it on your heart and wanted to suckle it; and that astonished me, since you are so shy, that you were not embarrassed.'[45] Most nuns would have been embarrassed by behaviour which might have seemed so unchaste.

Other mystics often achieved intimacy with the infant Jesus by imagining Mary's presence and approval. Mary, for example, came to Adelheit Langmann one night and 'carried the child in her arms and he was so beautiful that never was there his equal, and he sucked at her breast and was beside her until the bells rang for matins.'[46] When Margaretha was insecure about her intense contact with the infant Jesus she too sought guidance from Mary. For example she asked the infant Jesus 'whether Our Lady could satisfy all her desires in kissing and in other pleasures with him'. He replied in a rather abstract way that Mary always feared the enormous power she received from him. She asked Mary 'that she might help me, so that I should know what holy joy there was with the child. Then I was answered by her so lovingly: "you ask me such strange things that I do not know what I should do with you"'.[47]

For Margaretha, however, Mary did not have a privileged access to the feelings of the infant Jesus. Only once did she feel uncertain about her relationship to Mary as the real mother. She said to herself that 'no one could be more worthy than his tender mother'. But even then the infant Jesus answered: 'Whoever does my father's will, he is my father and my mother.'[48] This established Margaretha's equality with Mary. What she did worry about was whether the intensity of her love for Jesus was at odds with Mary's more chaste love. Once, after the Infant had kissed her breast, she wondered whether 'it was he himself in truth, or whether it was the great desire of my Lord' which did so. One must assume in this rather mysterious phrasing that the blurred barrier between spiritual and physical desire disturbed her. But the infant Jesus replied that there was no dichotomy between truth and a desire for God.[49] Distrust became unnecessary: desire led to truth.

## VII

One feature of the dialogues between Margaretha and the infant Jesus doll is that Margaretha was granted foreknowledge of the death and after-life of people. This was a tremendously important spiritual power. Margaretha thus seems to have occasionally become a mediator between God and people who wanted to know about their death. This acquired a political dimension when she asked the infant Jesus whether Ludwig of Bohemia could rely on having God on his side (despite the fact that the king opposed the pope). After Ludwig's death she wanted urgently to know 'how things had gone with him', and was glad to hear that he had gained eternal life.[50] She quizzed the Infant about how close individual spiritual figures and saints were to God, and gained his promise to cure Heinrich von Nördlingen once when he was sick.

The longest dialogue she recorded was about Jesus's birth. As in the later visions of Bridget of Sweden, it was of central importance for Margaretha to hear that the birth occurred without pain and in greatest 'purity'. She imagined that Mary's body was like a crystal, and that Jesus was light as a feather in her womb. (In her own experience of a mystical pregnancy Margaretha felt unlike Mary: her body was swollen and she had strong pains reminding her of labour pains.[51])

She had also an intense interest in the facts and details of Christ's early infancy. In her dialogue with the infant Jesus she wanted to know about Mary's and Joseph's poverty at the time of the birth. She shared the popular belief that it was so cold and Mary and Joseph so poor that Joseph had to make swaddling-clothes out of his garments.[52] Margaretha thought that this was highly unlikely, but the infant Jesus replied that this was all Joseph could have done. She then wanted to know about the circumcision, and he replied that Joseph performed it because Mary was too weak and cried, and that he, Jesus, also cried, experiencing great pain and losing large amounts of blood. At points her curiosity brought her close to impertinence. Her final questions were whether or not he had to use human language to talk to his mother, and what had happened to the valuable goods they received from the three wise men, since the holy family remained so poor afterwards.

Margaretha von Ebner's most intense spiritual longing for connection with an event in Jesus's childhood focussed on the circumcision. This is how she described her longing:

Then I had a great desire for the childhood of Our Lord, and his most sweet circumcision, that I wanted to enjoy his most powerful holy blood welling up with love. And this desire stayed with me, following me powerfully day and night, so that I could not sleep during these attacks because of the true holy lust and desire which I experienced in the choir for the presence of the grace of God which was given to me.[53]

In the Bible the circumcision took place eight days after Jesus's birth when his name was also given to him. So it was not only the circumcision that mattered to Margaretha. The name 'Jesus' also had a central role in her spirituality. During certain periods she was simply able to repeat his name again and again in her prayers, as if she could only understand their love by pronouncing his name.[54] It gave her 'joy and humility' to meditate on his name and the circumcision. In the only dream she had of the heavenly kingdom she dreamed that she stood at Christ's coffin, and watched a group of people at a well with holy water in it. She wanted to splash the people with the water, and when she did so

> they all ran up to me very joyfully, and I was glad and I thought I would speak the words 'Jesus Christ'. And now I felt a great grace and joy and began to sing the sweet name of Jesus Christ and they sang after me. And I said 'Let us dance'; and they answered 'Let us dance and eat and drink with each other.' Now I had a great desire to know who they were, and I asked my child about them, and he said 'To you are revealed the great joys of heaven and the love which there abides.'[55]

In this dream about the heavenly kingdom she gathered people to celebrate a feast through the power of her words 'Jesus Christ': the very name signified love and salvation for her. The very fact that Jesus was given his name on the day of his circumcision was important for her spiritual feelings about the circumcision itself. But the event was also significant as the first time he experienced pain and showed his humanity through his willingness to suffer.

As an image, the drinking of blood was familiar through belief in transubstantiation. The laity, however, could only drink Christ's blood during the Eucharist after it had been consecrated. Visions circumvented dependence upon the priests. In one of Margaretha's early visions, she and St Thomas drank blood from Jesus's heart and were strengthened through his sufferings. His blood stood for the pains he had to endure like every human being. The amount of blood shed and the amount of pain were important not only for Margaretha, who questioned her infant Jesus about it, but for other sisters as well. Margaretha recorded that one of her sisters saw the circumcised Jesus during the service the convent held eight days after Christmas. She saw him kicking out with his hands and feet, bleeding so much that the blood streamed from his little body.[56] Heinrich von Nördlingen venerated relics, and in one of his letters to Margaretha we learn that the blood of Christ's circumcision was associated with them. He wrote:

> With this I send you a holy Marian bath, which is given to us by him in these eight days: this is the chaste maidenly milk which he sucked, the infant tears which he wept, and the most tender milk-coloured blood, which he shed. Herein he shed his sweet name of Jesus, that he might flow in us and we in him.[57]

Milk, tears, and milk-coloured blood were the fluids which signified the humanity and pain of the infant Jesus. For Margaretha an exchange of fluids was part of a close union; just as she suckled him, she wanted to drink his purifying blood.

Bernard of Clairvaux's *Speech on the Feast of the Circumcision of Our Lord* illustrates that the meaning she attributed to this event was shared.[58] Bernard had been the first to point out the connection between the circumcision and the fact that it was then that Jesus was given his name.[59] He praised Jesus as the mediator between God and human beings. The pain of the circumcision proved that he had really taken on a human nature. Jesus was not just the shadow of his name, wrote Bernard, but its fulfilment. His name, in other words, signified the presence of love and salvation. Jesus was finally purified through the circumcision, as sinful desire was cut off. How important this event was at high levels of the church is indicated by a council debate on whether the foreskin was retained at the resurrection. Likewise the nun Agnes Blannbekin tasted the foreskin several times, and found it as sweet as eggskin on her tongue. Each time she tried to swallow it, it returned, and only when she tried to touch it with her fingers did it disappear.[60] Catherine of Siena received Christ's foreskin as wedding ring.[61] However alien this may seem to us nowadays, we must realise that the circumcision was commonly understood as a wholly spiritual event at the time. This was where Jesus gained his name. Next to the Passion it was the event at which he most strongly demonstrated the pains he bore for the believer.

We are now better equipped to understand why Margaretha thought about Jesus's childhood and circumcision when she wrote. Through the linkage between the circumcision and his naming she sought images and words which would signify his presence as strongly as the mere calling out of his name signified in her spirituality.

### VIII

*The Freethinker*, published in 1783 in Freiburg, announced in its third volume:

> The over-intimate involvement with Jesus as child, bridegroom, brother, etc., comes without doubt, like most superstitions, from the convents. In a certain convent which has now been dissolved, the nuns used to lead around a little Jesus doll in a cart on a red string through all the passages of the convent. The female sex has a natural, irresistible instinct to have children. If it has no living children, it makes them out of wood or rags. Even at fifty, nuns remain children, as happy to play with a holy doll as a thirteen- year-old girl is to play with a profane doll.[62]

In the view of this eighteenth-century author, a doll could only be a material and profane object. To deal with it in a religious context was no more than a compensation for the nuns' sterility.

A century and a half later the Zurich parson Dr Oscar Pfister, interested in the connection between ecstatic piety, sexuality, and female hysteria, contributed to the first volume of Sigmund Freud's journal *Zentralblatt für Psychoanalyse* (1911) an article on 'Hysteria and Mysticism in Margaretha Ebner'. In this he followed Charcot, Freud's teacher, who had studied artworks as a kind of 'historical clinic' in order to prove that the ecstasies of mystics and the attacks of the demonically possessed revealed symptoms of hysteria similar to those of his patients.[63] The link between these 'attacks' and the visions supported Charcot's view that hysteria was a nervous disease, caused by imagination and fantasy. This meant that he had discovered more than the modern symptoms of hysteria. Demoniacs and mystics proved 'the final validity and incorruptibility of a scientific law'.[64] Pfister turned from visual to literary evidence. He concluded that the *Revelations* of Margaretha von Ebner were nothing but 'a chronicle of her primary and sublimated hysterical symptoms'.[65] The *Revelations* recorded for him 'the martyrising and lustful, and ethically inferior history of piety of a nun, sickening from an unfortunate sexual repression'.[66] He concluded with the judgement:

> But the fact that her libido is in no way satisfied by a platonic relationship with Jesus is betrayed not only by the nun's interest in the circumcision of Jesus, but also by the steamy description of the stormy, most sweet feelings awakened by love of the holy Beloved. The fifty-three-year-old virgin certainly does not surrender herself to sensuality, she simply projects this onto the heavenly spouse instead. Very severe acts of repression must have taken place to bring about such a stormy enthusiasm for the renunciation of earthly eroticism.[67]

Even though Freud had just invented the new paradigm that the hysteric was not the degenerate woman, but merely the intellectual, sensitive, bisexual woman with artistic talents who had to act out a traumatic sexual experience in infancy by sexualising her body,[68] Pfister sought to show, with at times compassionate, at times morally condemning undertones, that the inferior spirituality of a nun was determined by her sublimated sexual passion. Her ecstatic behaviour seemed to mirror every aspect Freud had, *pace* Charcot, described as visible signs of hysteria: her movements and language were disturbed, she suffered from attacks, and she could not control acts and thoughts consciously.

What if anything has changed in our interpretation of the ecstatic piety of mystics? Many interpretations have argued that female spirituality was often merely an image of hidden but 'real' female desires and served a compensatory function. Even Klapisch-Zuber seems to assume that nuns' desire was ultimately directed onto a real husband and genital sex.[69] These interpretations dismiss the spiritual climate of the late middle ages, in which

erotic metaphors could meaningfully serve to express devotion to
Jesus. It may be a modern sensibility which regards this as either
pervertedly or tragically displaced, but it was certainly not a medieval one. Female mystics are often fitted either into an idealised
stereotype of the devotional woman, or into a view (nowadays)
that women were victims of a patriarchal society in which only
certain groups could escape from marriage into a convent, there
to suffer unconsciously from their desires. But this overlooks the
fact the practices of the nuns were not simply symbolically
structured self-gratifications. They have to be understood as a
language of desire directed at an utterly paradoxical but real
lover: omnipresent, nurturing, and equal, a child even, and yet
also absent, demanding, and almighty. This led to direct, physical,
and intense encounters with the notion of divine humanity and
the possibility of a mystical union. There is no reason why
historians should attribute greater value and dignity to those
mystics who intellectualised their experiences with divine love
than to those who experienced their spirituality through complex
emotions.

## IX

Female piety was characterised by nuns' ability to engage easily
with the vision of a child and to enjoy Jesus's childlikeness as one
of the dimensions of his humanity. Caring about him meant
reciprocating protection and love for a needy little human being
who came into this world to save them. Perhaps this was to
change. By the fifteenth century the psychological structures
exposed in the mother–child relationship could be exploited for
a sacrificial, disciplined faith. We can see such tendencies in a
fifteenth- or sixteenth-century spiritual guide of the Clarissas in
Eger. This guide devalued physical experience and laid out the
spiritual significance of every exercise instead. When at Advent,
for example, the nun had to prepare for the birth of Christ, she
was informed that the hay signified her obligation to suffer from
pain; not to oppose, to want punishment. When his napkin had a
hole, she had to ask Mary for help to knit it together again, and to

repent and improve her life.[70] In this directive the experience with the infant Jesus was channelled into a one-dimensional faith.

We cannot speak in this way of a one-dimensional spiritual experience in the case of Dominican nuns before the late fourteenth century, however. This chapter has argued that spiritual understandings, religious attitudes, and psychological processes, however strange they may seem to us now, and however 'hysterical' they may seem to some, had a historical specificity to them. Furthermore it has opposed the thesis that the ecstasy of mystics served a compensatory function for the absence of 'real' experiences of sexuality and motherhood. Though it was imaginary, mystics' spiritual experience of Jesus was real in its own terms, entailing a wide range of emotional experiences: love and desire, need and frustration, anxiety about loss and possessiveness. Margaretha experienced conflicts about chastity, platonic and true holy love, and her wish for physical union, which streamed out of the language of spiritual desire developed in the twelfth and thirteenth centuries. No less complex was the spiritual meaning of her desire to confront the circumcision, again something to which the compensation-thesis is blind, because it construes it only in terms of misplaced sexual desire. Her experiences with the infant Jesus were meaningful both within her spirituality and in her social situation as a nun without clerical office. A compensation thesis simply fails to accommodate this rich diversity of meaning. By the seventeenth century her doll was worshipped by the 'pious folk' from surrounding villages. Her status came close to that of a local saint.[71]

# 2. The 'Crown' and the 'Red Gown': Hussite Popular Religion

THOMAS A. FUDGE

[After the execution of Jan Hus in 1415] ... *the Bohemians and Moravians were filled with indignation and a number of priests both in Prague and throughout Bohemian and Moravian towns began to give the body and blood of Christ, under both kinds, to the ordinary people. They elevated the host in monstrances and it was customary for the multitudes of people to march behind the elevated host in praise to God. When the common people began to celebrate Holy Communion under both the elements of the body and blood of Christ, they were ridiculed as Husses, Wyclifites and heretics. Then the people were divided, both priests and laypeople, into two groups. There were many adherents to both sides. These two groups ridiculed and fought the other to such an extent that even the king was unable to prevent it.*[1]

*All songs introduced in a prejudicial manner concerning the position of the holy council and the living Catholic Church, with regard to the Wyclifites and the Hussites; or all songs commending the condemned heretics Jan Hus and Jerome, are prohibited in all cities, villages and towns, and whatever singing [of these songs] remains, is under severe penalty of punishment.*[2]

## POPULAR RELIGION AND ITS ROLE IN HUSSITISM

The formation of Hussite religion was a multi-faceted ideological evolution occurring simultaneously within a social maze. Early

38

ideas of reform from the learned world – the university in Prague and the pulpit of Bethlehem Chapel – were but one source fuelling the rise of Hussitism. The interpretation and appropriation of developing Hussite ideas in the backrooms of Prague taverns, in the marketplaces of rural Bohemian towns and amongst the peasants in the fields gave impetus to an equally important stimulation for the Czech Reformation. The convergence of marketplace discourse and tavern theology with university polemics and ecclesiastical preaching helped define the contours of Hussite religion.

Hussite religion, especially in its more radical expressions, was a popular religion. That is to say, it encompassed elements of what might be called 'official' and 'non-official' religion.[3] Even though Hussitism was separate from the institutional church it none the less had its own internal 'official' religiosity. The resulting divergent popular piety and de-institutionalised expressions of faith came to denote the cutting edge of the Bohemian Reformation and the concomitant Hussite revolution. In other words, Hussite popular religion was the expression and practice of faith as espoused by the masses of those called Hussites, especially that piety which appropriated a folkloric interpretation of 'learned' ideas. For example, all Hussites perceived Jan Hus as a founder of Hussitism and martyr of truth. Jan Roháč of Dubá was known as a supporter of radical Hussite thinking, a military captain and a martyr. Hussite popular religion developed a significant variation of these and other Hussite themes. Jan Rokycana, Hussite enthusiast and later archbishop, brought Hus and Roháč together into a mystical configuration with Christ, reminiscent of the trial of Jesus. 'They laughed at Master Jan Hus and put a crown on his head and they put a red gown on Roháč'.[4] The efficacious sufferings of Hus and his devoted disciple are but one example of the development of ideas within Hussite popular religion.

Alongside the crown and red gown were the popular religious Hussite notions of the sainthood of Master Jan Hus,[5] the ubiquitous chalice which appeared proleptically and prophetically literally all over Hussite Bohemia, actual and symbolic destruction of the wicked (warfare and iconoclasm), religiously motivated social experiments,[6] an active programme of proselytisation and a combining of pious sentiment with folk superstition.[7] In other words,

the 'popular religion created a system of ritual and of belief that
fulfilled the expectations that could not be met by evangelical
religiosity based on the principles of *communitas* or by the "elite
culture" of Church Christianity'.[8]

Hussite popular religion neither existed nor functioned as a
sub-culture within the constellation of 'official' Hussite religion.
Instead it became the flagship of a popular movement based
upon the three principles: 'St' Jan Hus, the chalice for all
believers and a steadfast conviction of the Hussite agenda as the
authentic law of God (*boží zákon*). The symbols of the crown and
the red gown were thus indicative of a profound piety and spirituality which constituted a continuing dynamic religiosity. The
element of popular religion within the Hussite movement, at least
from 1410 to 1437, may be considered one of the factors for
Hussite resilience, longevity and attraction to the socially dis-
possessed and ecclesiastically disinherited of the Czech lands. The
representatives of status quo Hussitism – Křišt'an of Prachatice
(+1439), Jan Příbram (*c.*1390–1448), Petr of Mladoňovice
(*c.*1390–1451), Prokop of Plzeň (*c.*1383–1457) and, later,
Jakoubek of Stříbro (*c.*1373–1429) – cast one particular
image into the mortar of the times, while the popular movement
within Hussitism forged its own identity on the anvil of
Central European religious history. By the time the crown and
the red gown had become transformed into icons, Hussite
popular religion had become part of the evolving Hussite
tradition.

## HUSSITE RELIGION AND THE ROAD TO TÁBOR

The progression of the Hussite movement and the coalescing of
'official' and 'popular' religious ideas served to direct the Czech
Reformation into a wider orbit, encompassing more than Jan
Hus's concern for moral reform. Priest Jan Želivský, through his
sermons at the church of St Mary of the Snows in the New Town
of Prague, attacked the oppression of poverty, called both clerics
and civic administrators to task and denounced the current socio-
ecclesiastical structure as spiritually and morally bankrupt.[9]
Želivský attempted to take sides aggressively with the Prague

urban poor in their struggle for identity and social stability. As 'the preacher of poor, deprived and oppressed people'[10] Želivský's emphases gave Hussitism another dimension and added credibility to the popular progressions of the movement. The social aspect of Hussite history should neither be ignored nor minimised.

As early as 1412 Jan Hus's preaching in Prague, together with the agitations caused by Jerome of Prague and Nicholas of Dresden, served to facilitate popular involvement in the reform movement and caused the Hussite ideas to come out into the streets in open defiance of civic authority and ecclesiastical proto-col. Street demonstrations took place, complete with propagan-dist banners, signs and pictures which grew to proportions of exceptional notoriety. Several incidents in the year 1414 which in-volved the smearing of crucifixes with excrement in Prague churches were traced to the influence of Jerome.[11] The death of Hus in 1415 and that of Jerome the following year, both at the hands of the Council of Constance, brought a deep sense of in-dignation and urgency to the Hussite cause and only added to the Czech sense of persecution. Jakoubek of Stříbro, Hus's replace-ment in the Bethlehem Chapel, took a more radical tack than his predecessor, and the innovations of utraquism, infant commu-nion and widespread radical preaching began to strike a chord in the collective Czech consciousness which then began to reverber-ate in an ever-increasing concentric fashion across Bohemia. A decade later the fervour was unabated. The courtbooks of the Rožmberk family in southern Bohemia reveal that in 1423 two Hussites, Jan of Prague and Dietle the Cook, were part of a plot to poison Oldřich Rožmberk, the Hussites' powerful opponent.[12]

Despite the clear position of clerics in the radical Hussite move-ment, popular involvement became a highly visible aspect of Hussite religion. Laypeople began to preach and engage in icono-clastic activities. This latter action was both a release of frustration with the institutional church and the beginning of the Hussite of-fensive. Ondřej of Brod noted that the Hussites innovated the liturgy by refusing to sing the introit, the gradual and other worthy songs, and instead introduced their own songs sung in the Czech language by women and children![13] Priest Želivský gave impetus to the gathering momentum of the popular movements with his own fiery denunciations of the perceived wickedness of the church: 'O good Christ, what immense idols the authorities have erected in Prague, endowed priests; what great idols are in the church, images, vestments!'[14] The constituency of the burgeoning Hussite popular religion went further. With the sermons of radical preachers like Želivský ringing in their ears, the popular movement began to interpret and appropriate the ideas of the Bohemian reformers. When Hussite priests from Prague attempted to celebrate the sacrament of the Holy Eucharist in Říčany, clad in ecclesiastical vestments, they were accosted by a group of men and women who belligerently demanded an explanation: 'What are you doing with those sheets on? Take them off and conform to Christ and his apostles when you say Mass, or we'll do it for you!'[15] On another occasion, Hussite women from the north-west Bohemian towns of Žatec, Louny and Slany converged on the Convent of St Catherine in the New Town and, after chasing the nuns away, burnt the cloister to the ground. In collusion with the 'mentally-deranged priest', Václav Koranda of Plzeň, another group of women attacked the Church of St Michael in the Old Town, ransacking the nave and destroying much of the interior.[16]

The percolation of learned ideas into the popular religion of the Hussite movement was met by a dynamism within the popular religion itself. Radical priests like Želivský denounced the perfidious infidels, traitors and criminals who 'killed our beloved preacher', Hus. At the same time others began to meet in Prague taverns to hear Scripture taught and Hussite ideas explained. The Hussite chronicler Vavřinec of Březová asserted that a number of the leaders of the early popular movement – Martinék Húska, Václav Koranda of Plzeň and others – received expert theological instruction from Václav, a biblically literate bartender in his Prague tavern.[17] More than that, to the scandal of many, Štěpán of Dolany, an anti-Hussite polemicist, claimed that women had begun to preach in Prague as early as 1416,[18] while Ondřej of Brod made the charge that the Hussites actually hired women to preach![19] A popular anti-Hussite song summed up the notion of preaching in popular Hussite religion: 'They make preachers out of cobblers, millers, butchers, bakers, tanners, barbers, and other craftsmen. Even women are allowed to preach'.[20] This sharp divergence from the orthopraxis of the medieval institutional church was accompanied by an entire battery of radical ideas. The early growth of Hussite popular religion seemed unstoppable as it ground inexorably on its way across Bohemia.

As noted earlier, the heat created from the intense friction between the Hussites and their opponents became so overwhelming that even the king, Václav IV, could not endure it. Soon Prague itself was unable to contain the intensity of Hussite popular religion and the mass movement began to spill out into the Bohemian countryside. The summer and autumn of 1419 proved to be the decisive turning point in the progression and establishment of Hussite popular religion within the parameters of the Crown of St Wenceslas. On 22 July a mass gathering occurred on Mount Tábor near Bechyně. Sources report that more than 40,000 people congregated from the immediate area, Prague, Domažlice, Hradec Králové in eastern Bohemia and from as far away as Moravia.[21] 'More than 40,000 people received the sacrament of the body and blood of the Lord under both kinds, both in bread and wine, with great devotion, according to the tradition of Christ and practised and observed by the early church.'[22] Eight days later the Prague government fell to the popular movement in what has now been termed the first defenestration of Prague.

This event marks clearly a decisive transition in the shift of Hussite popular religion from aberration to legitimacy. On the morning of 30 July, Priest Želivský preached an inflammatory sermon in the Church of St Mary of the Snows. At the conclusion of his discourse, Želivský, holding a monstrance, led his parishioners through the old cattle market to the Church of St Stephen. There the mob broke down the bolted doors, evicted the Roman priests and worshippers and Želivský began promptly to preach his second sermon of the day. Urging his hearers to promote righteousness and take action against sin, Želivský celebrated the Eucharist again. The mob of Hussites, fuelled with the energy of two sermons and two celebrations of the utraquist sacrament, now marched to the New Town Hall where Želivský demanded the release of prisoners who had been incarcerated for practising utraquism. His request was denied and the town councillors barricaded themselves in the tower. The assault on the Town Hall was obviously premeditated as the pious Hussites had come to worship that morning armed with 'pikes, swords and clubs'! Using these weapons the crowd broke into the Town Hall, defenestrated the civic officials from the tower window, elected four captains representing the revolutionary government and occupied the seat of local authority.[23] It had been a *coup d'état*, a popular revolt by the people in the interests of Hussite popular religion.

On 17 September the crowd again congregated near Plzeň on a hill called Bzí Hora. Koranda and Mikuláš of Hus were the main organisers. This hilltop gathering had all the signs of political action and aggressive religious activity. This meeting produced a manifesto called 'The Pilgrims' Declaration of Bzí Hora' wherein the Law of God, free preaching and utraquism were lauded, the latter being termed necessary.[24]

A third rally took place on 30 September at Na Křížkách (at the Crosses) near Benešov not far from Prague. Jan Žižka, Mikuláš of Hus and Václav Koranda were on hand again. The climax of the gathering was well summarised in a fiery speech by Koranda: 'Brethren, the time has come to lay down the staff of the pilgrim and to take up the sword. God's vineyard is flourishing but goats are threatening to destroy it.'[25] The multitude then headed for Prague and though arriving after dark marched through the streets by torch-light to the clanging sounds of church bells. The following day church property lay destroyed throughout the city. Hussite popular religion was now a force to be reckoned with. But it lacked a friendly environment within which to incubate and flourish. Prague was divided along ethnic and religious lines. To the north were the ever hostile Germans. In the west lay strong Roman opposition to Hussitism as well as the later powerful anti-Hussite Plzeň Landfríd. Eastern Bohemia beckoned, but it was south Bohemia where popular religion had flourished in the fourteenth century and it was here where the radical Hussites found a home.

The road to Tábor was a radical road and the popular religion that travelled that road became, in the process, even further divergent from orthodoxy. However, it is erroneous to perceive Hussitism at Tábor as mere fanaticism, blind revolution, religious and social excesses, confused other-worldliness, or a simple extension of 'official' Prague Hussite religion. It is also only a partial picture which interprets Hussite religion at Tábor in the categories of traditional theological thought.[26] The gulf between Tábor and her allies and the institutional Roman church on one hand and the 'official' Hussite church on the other was a considerable chasm. The road to Tábor was lined with the cobblestones of the Hussite myth.[27] In 'official' Hussite religion Jan Hus was a martyr and such was to be the destiny of Jan Roháč of Dubá. In Hussite popular religion the same was true, but there was an added stress on the crown and the red gown.

The unity of Hussite popular religion was tied up in the person of Jan Hus and the cult of the chalice.[28] Hus's transformation from humble parish preacher to patron saint of a radical popular religious movement will be discussed below. Concomitant with 'St Jan Hus' was the observation of the cult of the chalice. All believers, or all the baptised, were communed under both kinds (*sub utraque specie*). Jakoubek of Stříbro referred to utraquism as the great *revelatio* of Hussite religion,[29] and some sources allege that certain radical Hussites in the New Town of Prague at the house called At the Black Rose (*U Černé růže*) had been driven out of German territory because they had practised utraquism.[30] Sermons of Jakoubek of Stříbro during 1414 also pointed to the growing emphasis on communion in both bread and wine.[31] Eschatological overtones present in the thought of fourteenth-century Czech reformers, namely Jan Milíč of Kroměříž and Matěj of Janov, were also to be found in Hussite popular religion. 'With the chalice the Hussite movement created not only its own liturgy...[but] transformed a movement into a church'.[32] The chalice began to function as the trigger of transformation within Hussite popular religion, socially, theologically and eschatologically.

If the chalice was the visible entity, the Law of God (*boží zákon*) was the invisible force active within the evolving mentality of Hussite popular religion. Despite Jan Příbram's charge that Tábor operated on the sole authority of Scripture,[33] a suggestion Frederick Heymann construes to mean that *boží zákon* referred to the fundamental biblical teachings,[34] the rule of faith within Hussite popular religion was not so easily defined. While Heymann and Příbram are correct in one sense, it is more accurate to modify the definition to one which relates the Law of God to the Hussite ideas based upon or extracted from Scripture. Jana Nechutová has shown that Wyclif, Hus, Matěj of Janov and Nicholas of Dresden all used the idea of the Law of God as did the sectarian ideology of the

Waldensians.[35] The motif came to function centrally in Hussite popular religion from the earliest days to long after the decline of Tábor.[36] As the birthplace of Hussitism, Prague became the handmaiden of the Law of God. The importance of the Law of God is nowhere better stated than in Jan Želivský's sermon for 13 August 1419: 'O that the city of Prague would now be the example for all believers, not only in Moravia but in Hungary, Poland, Austria ...!'[37]

From this point on, Hussite popular religion at Tábor took two decisive turns: liturgical and social. Zdeněk Nejedlý has pointed out that in contrast to 'official' Hussite liturgy, the Táborites espoused a simple format centred around preaching and an utraquist Eucharist. Congregational singing was accentuated and the entire liturgy was celebrated in the vernacular.[38] All liturgical vestments and most ecclesiastical fixtures were ignored. The Sacrament was sometimes celebrated outdoors and frequently tables rather than altars were utilised. Chalices were often used but any vessel whether clay, tin or wood could be employed. It is also reported that women were permitted to consecrate the Sacrament themselves.[39] Needless to say, the entire Hussite liturgical rite, as performed in the radical wings, came under criticism by 'official' Hussite religion.[40] There were also further aberrations within Hussite popular religion. Martinék Húska and his followers allegedly divided the Sacrament amongst themselves.[41] Convinced of the notion that the Eucharist was not truly, physically, the body of Christ, some of those at Tábor emptied monstrances and broke open the pyx, dumped the host on the ground and trampled it under foot.[42] Adherents of Hussite popular religion in Hungary in the 1430s went about carrying the blood of Christ in containers for the purpose of communing.[43]

The second significant development within Hussite popular religion at Tábor was a thorough-going social experiment. In 1420 a declaration was proclaimed:

> Henceforth, at Hradiště and Tábor there is nothing which is mine or thine. Rather, all things in the community shall be held in common for all time and no one is permitted to hold private property. The one who does commits sins mortally. ... No longer shall there be a reigning king or ruling lord; for

there shall be servitude no longer. All taxes and exactions shall cease and no one shall compel another to subjection. All shall be equal as brothers and sisters.[44]

People flocked to Tábor from all over Bohemia and Moravia and placed their money at the feet of the priests.[45] Communal chests were set up at Písek, Tábor and Vodňany[46] and the chest at Písek was under the administration of a layman, Matěj Louda of Chlumčany.[47] The intention of this programme was to eliminate social inequality,[48] but the idea of communal goods posed a significant threat to the stability of hierarchical society and the medieval social structure. Governed by the Law of God, united in a common commitment to St Jan Hus and the chalice for all believers and inspired by an apocalyptic–chiliast vision, Hussite popular religion created a significant chapter in the dawning of modern Europe.

Both liturgical and social innovations were directed against the perceived corrupt institutional church. The interpretation and appropriation of ideas within popular religion found expression in a number of ways. There was, of course, the ongoing radical iconoclastic campaign. The cloister of Smichov was attacked, wooden statues in Litoměřice had their noses hacked off, in Prachatice pictures were destroyed, images and statues defaced.[49] Other Hussites showed their contempt for ecclesiastical tradition by washing their boots with chrismal oil.[50] The Hussite delegates to the Council of Basel were suspected of throwing snowballs at crucifixes,[51] while Hussite religion in other quarters was accused of employing magic in its practice.[52] The response to Hussite popular religion came in a variety of ways. The choirboys who lived on Hradčany in Prague would ambush Hussites and thrash them unmercifully with sticks.[53] In more drastic cases, Hussites by the hundreds were thrown alive into the mine shafts at Kutná Hora.[54] The Hussites in various instances responded in like fashion.

The Hussite myth and religion certainly transformed the lives of its adherents in many ways. One of the most interesting is the case of Jan Žižka. In 1421 Žižka acquired a small castle in north Bohemia and named it Chalice (*Kalich*). He changed his own name from Jan Žižka of Trocnov to Jan Žižka of the Chalice and replaced the crab on his coat of arms with a chalice.[55]

After Žižka's death his followers called themselves orphans (*sirotci*)[56] and, as we shall see below, Žižka became part of the evolving Hussite popular religion.

Hussite religion in its popular context went well beyond Master Jan Hus to the crown and the red gown, and popular religion in Hussite Bohemia eventually became a significant force in its own right. While Hus called for a moral reform, the Hussites forced morality on the country; while Hus insisted on living by the Law of God, the Hussites demanded that the Law of God should rule the land; while Hus eventually advocated the chalice, the Hussites elevated it to the keystone of their theological thinking and practice; while Hus was generally cautious in his approach to religious and liturgical novelty, the Hussites practised thorough-going innovations. The road to Tábor was not simply a sideline within the Hussite phenomenon. Indeed, Tábor was neither a political nor a geographical term, it was an idea[57] which became, in the first half of the fifteenth century, intrinsically related to Hussite popular religion.

## THE HUS OF HISTORY AND THE HUS OF MYTH

Hussite popular religion, in terms of the Táborite idea, has its own symbolic foundation in the figure of Jan Hus. The dramatic metamorphosis of Hus into a symbol of popular religious culture is an essential link in the evolution of the Hussite chain. The creation and use of this symbol demonstrates the amorphous nature of nascent population religion.

Jan Hus (*c.*1372–1415) was a faithful parish priest. In his own mind, he was a loyal son of the Roman church. However, this idea is entirely foreign to Hussite popular religion. His transformation from 'the persecuted' to saint via martyrdom was not long in coming. Records of his *passio* were read from the first anniversary of his death.[58] The same year, the Council of Constance protested to Sigismund that Hus was being referred to as a saint in certain Bohemian churches[59] and Štěpán of Dolany, a Carthusian abbot in Moravia, wrote indignantly to the Council that pictures venerating Hus were in circulation in the Czech lands.[60] By 1420 Vavřinec of Březová was reflecting the common popular Hussite opinion that Hus was among the heavenly saints.[61] Earlier, an incident in Písek in 1418 revealed that Hus was being venerated[62] while anti-Hussite opinion inferred that the Hussites perceived Hus as a prophet and apostle[63] and were calling for the punishment of all those who were against 'Holy Jan Hus'.[64] Hence, within a short period of time the Hus of myth replaced the Hus of history and the reformer of Prague was transmuted into the patron saint of a sectarian popular movement.

St Jan Hus soon began appearing in liturgical texts. David Holeton has recently discovered an utraquist antiphonary containing the 'Office for the feast of St Jan Hus'.[65] This Hungarian codex is the only known liturgical text containing the aforementioned office. There were certainly others. A mutilated manuscript in Prague undoubtedly once contained the same liturgical text.[66] The canonisation of Hus is further reflected in other sources. A fifteenth-century gradual now housed in St Mark's Library, General Theological Seminary in New York, has Hus's name added to specific texts. For example, *De Sancti Johanne* has been changed to *De sanctissimo Johanne Hus*.[67] The Rackovsky *kancionale* in Prague lauds *sancto Johanne Hus*.[68] Another gradual has the office text *De martyribus* dedicated to Hus, while a Hussite *kancionale* makes detailed reference 'Concerning St Master Jan of Husinec' (*O swatem Mistru Janovi z Husynce*).[69]

Two final examples of the Hus of myth will suffice. The Gradual of the Lesser Town (*Malostranská Graduále*) in Prague contains an illuminated folio devoted to Hus.[70] The heading reads 'Concerning the Holy Master Jan Hus' (*O Swatem Mistru Janowi Husy*) and a song about Hus follows. The bottom quarter of the folio shows Hus in the flames at Constance. The right margin has the interesting feature of Wyclif rubbing two stones together, followed by Hus lighting a candle and finally Luther holding a flaming torch. The engulfing influence of the Protestant Reformation is unmistakable in its attempt to portray Wyclif and Hus as mere forerunners to the reformer *par excellence*, Luther.[71] Finally, the Litoměřice Gradual (*Litoměřicky Graduále*) reveals in striking fashion the apotheosis of Jan Hus.[72] In one moment and one illustration the Hus of history is transformed into the Hus of myth. At the bottom of the folio Hus is bound to the stake in the flames. A large crowd has gathered to 'burn Jan Hus'. The suffering of the reformer is evident. It is not insignificant that Hus's 'paper crown' has fallen from his head.[73] At the top of the stake the smoke parts and Hus ascends through the flames and smoke into the heavenly realm where he is received by angels and cherubim. Hus's plain white gown is replaced with a heavenly robe while a crown of glory is placed upon the martyr's head, effectively replacing the ignoble paper one. Henceforth, the Hus of myth and Hussite popular religion overshadowed the reality of the Hus of history.

The Hus of myth allowed Hussite popular religion to develop the conviction that Hus is still living (*Hus stále žiný*). Even in the sixteenth century Hus seemed alive.

> John Hus was condemned ... and they supposed that his name was obliterated forever. Yet now he is shining forth with such glory that his cause and his teaching have to be praised before the whole world, while the pope's cause lies ignominiously in the manure.[74]

'Hus ... is again coming to life!'[75] In the popular movement his image appeared on Hussite banners and his spirit, interpreted and appropriated, inspired the popular movement. The man was significant, the crown all-important. It was this perception of Hus which caused this shout against the institutional church during a procession in Prague: 'We will obey Master Hus and not that gang of adulterers and simoniacs!'[76]

As a symbol of Hussite popular religion, St Jan Hus became a valuable commentary on religious culture in Hussite Bohemia. For between 'the image and the reality'[77] stood the Hus of history and the Hus of myth, and both, depending on the perspective, were authentic portraits.

## POPULAR RELIGION CAUGHT IN THE ACT?

Is it possible to define and explicate popular religion in specific terms? Michel Vovelle has posed the intriguing query as to whether or not popular religion can be caught in the act.[78] Obviously, the whole enterprise is fraught with numerous difficulties and bedevilled by scarcity of records and lacunae in those records which are extant. One possibility, however, is to analyse how piety was recorded and transmitted. In the Bohemian context, Hussite propaganda – oral, visual, literary and dramaturgic – is a rich mine in the quest for understanding popular religion in fifteenth-century Bohemia. Much of popular religion was oral. Of course the oral form has long disappeared. But certain records remain. These written records must be treated in terms of their original aim; i.e., preservation of an oral form of communication or popular piety. Quite clearly, in this context we are left not with actual popular religion but rather with the active mediation of popular religion. None the less, such mediation does provide significant information about both popular religion and popular culture. What follows is an attempt to demonstrate that propaganda in the Hussite movement was in part the product of Hussite popular religion.

Popular songs in Hussite Bohemia functioned as a means of communication, a vehicle for expressing faith, as well as mass propaganda. Even after the rise of the press the primary mode of communication remained oral.[79] Hussite popular religion used songs as a medium to transpose the message from the proverbial pages of the book to those conventionally illiterate. The praises of Master Jan Hus were sung almost from the beginning of the movement following his death. 'A song about Hus and about Communion in Both Kinds' (*Píseň o Husovi a o přijímání pod obojí*) asserted that Hus and Jerome suffered because they opposed sin.[80] The 'Song About Master Jan Hus' (*Píseň O M. Janovi Husovi*) claimed that Hus was burned by a treacherous 'gang of bishops' (*roty biskupské*) because he defended God's truth. Despite the false witness of that 'gang of priests, monks and Canons', Hus was received into heaven.[81] Another popular song underscored Hus's role in Hussite popular religion: 'And you, dear Hus ... Czechs must love you, because they have no other preacher so honest'.[82] Hus's preaching and his activity at the Bethlehem Chapel were also featured in Hussite songs: 'If you want to know the Bible you must go to Bethlehem and learn it on the walls as Master Jan of Husinec preached it'.[83]

Indeed Hussite popular religion was played out on several
stages, including the theatre of war. When the Hussite warriors
went into battle, in defence of Hussite religion, their songs went
along with them. The most famous song, 'Ye Warriors of God'
(*Ktož jsu boži bojovníci*), includes this verse:

> Thus ye shall shout exultant:
> 'At them, hurrah, at them!'
> Feel the pride of the weapon in your hands
> And cry: 'God is our Lord!'[84]

After the Hussites won the Battle of the Vítkov in Prague in 1420,
they celebrated their stunning success in another popular song
written by Jan Čapek.

> Children, let us praise the Lord,
> Honor Him in loud accord!
> For he frightened and confounded,
> Overwhelmed and sternly pounded
> All those thousands of Barbarians,
> Suabians, Misnians, Hungarians
> Who have overrun our land.
> With his strong protecting hand
> To the winds He has them waved,
> And we children are now saved.
> Faithful Czechs, let's sing our love
> To our Father high above
> With the older folks along,
> Praising God in joyous song![85]

Hussite songs also tended to be polemical. 'A Song About
Archbishop Zbyněk' (*Píseň o archibiskupu Zbyňkovi*) calls the
'knights of God' to battle against 'Antichrist' and 'an arrogant
clergy' who 'ridicule the apostles' and 'suppress the truth of
Christ'. The 'law of Christ' must be promoted, 'let Hus instruct
you how'.[86] When Zbyněk resisted the Hussite advances he was
caricatured as an ignoramus.

> Bishop Zbyněk, ABCD
> Burned books not knowing

What was written in them.
Zbyněk burned books
Zdeněk kindled a fire
He brought great shame on all Czechs;
Woe to all bad popes.[87]

The faith of Hussite popular religion also found expression in the sung conviction 'that it was both proper and good for all people to eat the body of Christ and drink the blood of Christ'.[88] The song 'By the Certain Times' (*Časy Svými Jistými*) repeated over and over the refrain, 'We ridicule those who refuse Communion'.[89]

From the wider corpus of songs relating to Hussite popular religion it is possible to delineate Hussite piety and some of the implications of the Hussite movement: the Roman church is an abomination, the Hussites are God's warriors, God defends the Hussites, Jan Hus is a saint, the Germans should be expelled, God sanctions the Hussite military force and 'truth' resides in the Hussite faith. Hussite songs, then, functioned both as expressions of popular religion and as a vital instrument in the promotion of that faith.[90] The songs reinforced Hussite identity, imposed conformity within the ranks and by natural consequence identified the enemies of the growing popular religion.

The religious fervour behind the crown and the red gown did not remain confined to the sometimes pleasant poetry of popular tunes. After Hus went into exile in 1412 demonstrations began occurring in the streets of Prague.[91] The most famous of these events was an anti-indulgence demonstration in 1412. Voksa of Valdštějn and Jerome of Prague organised a procession in which a person, dressed as a whore, rode on a beast. From her bared breasts hung imitation papal bulls. She was covered with little silver bells which rang with her every move in the same manner as the church bells during Mass. Imitating the soft voice of the harlot and the enticing sales-talk of the indulgence hawker, she offered her indulgences to the crowd, who roared their delight and approval. With leers and lewd gestures the whore blessed the congregation as if she were pope. As the mob passed the residences of the king and the archbishop, the people in one accord denounced the pope's bulls and indulgences. The parade finally reached the open expanse of the horse market in the New Town and the bulls were burnt.[92]

Events such as this were propagandist in their orientation but also pious in their origin. In these and other demonstrations the world was turned upside down. The lecherous whore played the virgin or pope, the fool became bishop, the criminal donned the king's crown, the ass brayed at the altar, while everyone ran leaping through the cathedral singing uproariously the drunken liturgy. It was not simply the glorification of foolishness. Hussite popular religion was an attempt, however modest, to subvert medieval ecclesiastical order.

Hussite popular religion, in its attempt to throw off the yoke of 'official' religion, promoted the crown and the red gown as examples of genuine piety in contrast to the perceived forces of antichrist. Following Jan Hus, who agreed with the notion that pictures are the books of the illiterate,[93] propagandist art became part of the legacy of the Hussite tradition.[94] As early as 1412 Nicholas of Dresden, a Hussite supporter, produced an illustrated work contrasting the primitive church and the Roman church.[95] The antithetical tables, for example, showed Christ carrying his cross while the pope rode a horse, and Christ washing the feet of the disciples while monks kiss the feet of the pope. Another portrait showed the pope as antichrist surrounded by whores. Howard Kaminsky has noted that the pictures of this work were carried in street demonstrations.[96] Similar motifs were also displayed on the walls of Bethlehem Chapel.[97] Together with inscriptions on the walls in the vernacular, these pictures form the point of reference for the popular song noted above: 'If you want to know the Bible you must go to Bethlehem and learn it on the walls as Master Jan of Husinec preached it', as well as Hus's own reference, 'and if you will not believe it, learn it on the wall in Bethlehem'.[98]

These ideas gained momentum among the adherents of Hussite religion. The Hussites used the language of the Bible, transmuted biblical characters into Hussites and managed to get other Hussites into the Bible itself. The earliest portrayal of Jan Hus at the stake appears in the margin of a Bible from around 1430.[99] A Czech Old Testament shows a battle between Hussites and crusaders.[100] More interesting is the portrayal of the biblical King David as a Hussite warrior triumphing over his foes.[101] As noted earlier, portraits of Hus began appearing in liturgical manuscripts. Even the Hussite captain, Jan Žižka can be found in religious books.[102]

Some of the most profound examples of Hussite popular religion caught in the act, as it were, can be found in related illustrated manuscripts in Prague and Göttingen.[103] The pictures illustrate what the Jena Codex on fol. 1ʳ calls the *antithesis Christi & Antichristi*. The last supper of Jesus and his disciples is an ultraquist celebration in contrast to 'the New Mass' (*Nová mše*), which shows monks dancing with girls, host adoration and the inspiration of a demon.[104] While the Ethiopian eunuch of the canonical Acts of the Apostles is baptised by the Apostle Philip, a monk slays a newborn baby, in reality his illegitimate son, while the mother looks on. In the foreground is a recently dug grave, shovel still in place, and a baptismal font.[105] While St Laurence is subjected to the torture of a bed of hot coals, two monks recline in a bath-house attended by four seductive women.[106] With his moneybag hanging from his waist-belt, Judas Iscariot kisses Jesus as armed hoodlums move in. The companion portrait shows the pope kissing a woman while two others look on.[107] Another picture portrays Hussite religion and the church of Rome being weighed in the balances. The former, represented by a chalice, prevails over the latter, represented by the papal tiara.[108] Elsewhere, a drollery of a monk in a Hussite Latin gradual bears this inscription: *'Ha ha, Monachus, Veritas Vincit'*.[109] The mocked monk represents the decline of Rome and the expression 'truth triumphs' was a reverberating slogan of the popular movement. The portrayal of the pope in the flames of hell in a Czech Bible is a stark expression of popular Hussite sentiment.[110] The centrality of the chalice is a regular feature in Hussite art but nowhere as clearly represented as in the hand holding a chalice appearing from heaven to a group of people.[111] The caricature of a monk bound in fetters and shrieking in pain[112] is connected to the 'magnificent ride'[113] of the Hussite movement typified by the illumination of Jan Žižka leading the Hussite warriors of God, behind a monstrance-bearing priest, into combat.[114] The best example of Hussite popular religion in art is the portrait of the heavenly court. Saints and angels alike join the Almighty. On the right hand of Christ, however, St Peter has disappeared and in his place stands the blind Jan Žižka! Žižka holds a red Hussite banner displaying a gold chalice in one hand, and in the other the keys of the kingdom!. Next to Žižka is John the Baptist and beside the Baptist a figure holding a chalice who iconographically could either be St John the Evangelist or St Jan Hus![115] In the popular mind, the Hussites were God's chosen people, empowered to rescue the righteous and destroy the wicked. The Hussites are the defenders of the Law of God and the porters of the heavenly gate.

'Official' religion regarded Hussite popular religion with suspicion. Such posture was only natural. 'That base fellow' Žižka[116] was in heaven holding the keys of entrance, pictures in the heretic Hus's church ridiculed Rome, monks were denounced as wicked, clamped in chains and left to scream. The forbidden chalice had appeared from heaven as *revelatio* and had then defeated the tiara. Even little children were marching to the beat of Hussite piety.[117] These pictures conveyed the Hussite faith and provoked an irrepressible reaction. In the end, Hussite popular religion utilised 'art in the service of an idea'.[118]

Directly or indirectly, Hussite popular religion helped to establish institutional heresy in Bohemia. At Tábor an independent reformed church was founded apart from Rome. The archbishop of Prague embraced Hussite religion. Civil authority in large sectors of the country was under the control of Hussite sympathisers. Roman parish priests were replaced with Hussite clerics. Bohemia had its own militia, the Warriors of God. Later they had their own Hussite monarch, Jiří of Poděbrady. This phenomenon stretched at the very least from the defenestration in 1419 until the deaths of King Jiří and Jan Rokycana in 1471, well over half a century. Whether or not they were espoused fully, Hussite values, norms and traditions can be located throughout Bohemia in the fifteenth century. Where Hussite manifestos were not sent, Hussite songs were sung. Where the songs were not heard, Hussite slogans resounded. Where the slogans were unknown, the Warriors of God marched. Where the Warriors were unseen, tales of their exploits were told from generation to generation.

In 1420 Jan Roháč of Dubá was clad in a coat of mail. By 1437 that coat of mail had become a red gown. Jan Hus wore a paper crown in 1415, but from then on he wore the crown of a saint. As motifs and metaphors of Hussite popular religion the crown and the red gown provide us with a brief glimpse into the conceptual world of popular religion in pre-modern Europe.

# 3. *Judengasse* to Christian Quarter: The Phenomenon of the Converted Synagogue in the Late Medieval and Early Modern Holy Roman Empire

J. M. MINTY

In 1519 the artist Albrecht Altdorfer produced two finely detailed woodcuts depicting the entrance hall and interior of the Regensburg synagogue (Figures 2 and 3). The conspicuous dates on each are most significant; on 22 February 1519, shortly after Emperor Maximilian's death on 12 January, the city council of Regensburg decreed not only the expulsion of the Jews but also the demolition of the synagogue and much of the *Judengasse*.[1] Obviously, Altdorfer, who was a member of the Outer Council of the city of Regensburg,[2] hastened to record the synagogue before it and much of the *Judengasse* vanished (Figure 4).[3] The synagogue was promptly razed and a wooden church 'Zur Schönen Maria' (Figure 5) quickly erected on the site and consecrated about a month later on 25 March 1519, the day of the feast of the Annunciation;[4] this hastily constructed building was soon replaced by a lavish stone church (Figure 6).[5] The destroyed *Judengasse* is represented in the backgrounds of these latter two images,[6] both woodcuts by Michael Ostendorfer.[7]

The fate of the Regensburg synagogue, specifically, the conversion of its site to consecrated Christian ground, was hardly unique in the late medieval and early modern Holy Roman Empire. In

the course of altering *Judengassen*, synagogues met a wide range of
fates other than this one: they were replaced by religious edifices

PORTICVS SINAGOGAE
IVDAICAE RATISPONEN
FRACTA. ZI DIE FEB.
ANN. 1519.

**Figure 2** Albrecht Altdorfer, 'View of Entrance Hall of Regensburg
Synagogue', etching 1519

ANNO · DÑI · D · XIX
IVDAICA · RATSPⁱ·ⁿ
SYNAGOGA · IVSTO
DEI · IVDIGO · FVⁿ
EST · EVERSA·

**Figure 3** Albrecht Altdorfer, 'View of Interior of Regensburg Synagogue', etching 1519

other than chapels and churches;[8] they were simply destroyed;[9] they entered private hands;[10] they were converted for secular use, e.g., granary,[11] brewery,[12] or flour mill.[13] In a significant number of cases, however, a church or chapel was established on a

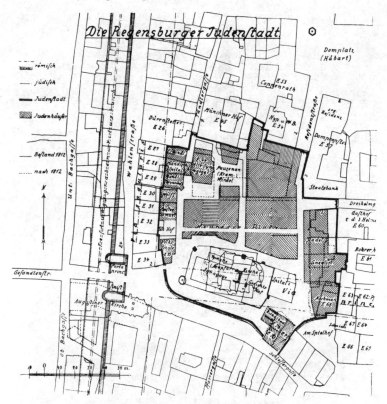

**Figure 4** Topographical reconstruction of Regensburg, *c.* 1519, showing the destroyed *Judengasse* and synagogue

synagogue site. Between 1390 and 1520, including the example of Regensburg, churches or chapels were consecrated on at least twenty-seven synagogue sites: Heidelberg;[14] Amberg;[15] Ingolstadt;[16] Rothenburg ob der Tauber;[17] Linz;[18] Iglau;[19] Cologne;[20] Deutz;[21] Eger;[22] Jauer;[23] Graz;[24] Munich;[25] Mainz;[26] Coburg,[27] Landshut;[28] Schweidnitz;[29] Striegau;[30] Bamberg;[31] Trent;[32] Passau;[33] Erfurt;[34] Magdeburg;[35] Wiener-Neustadt;[36] Budweis;[37] Regensburg;[38] Rothenburg ob der Tauber.[39]

These conversions mark a pattern, already evident in the fourteenth century, and perhaps even earlier; in 1124 a Prague synagogue was converted to the Church of the Magdalen;[40] in the mid-fourteenth century, synagogues and synagogue sites in Nuremberg,[41] Bamberg,[42] Würzburg,[43] Rothenburg ob der

**Figure 5**   Michael Ostendorfer, 'The Old Church of the Schöne Maria, Regensburg', woodcut, *c.* 1520

CHAEL OSTENDORFER

**Figure 6** Michael Ostendorfer, 'The New Church of the Schöne Maria, Regensburg', woodcut, *c.* 1520, after a design by Hans Hieber

Tauber,[44] Landshut,[45] and Wertheim[46] are known to have been consecrated.[47] These earlier examples bring the total number of converted synagogues I will be considering to thirty-two.

Apparently, then, the phenomenon of the converted synagogue was widespread, both chronologically and geographically within the Holy Roman Empire. Although most of the these examples are found in Bavaria, they are also found in Hesse, Baden, Brandenburg, Bohemia, Silesia, Hungary and Styria.

Although the case of Regensburg has been a focus of scholarship,[48] to my knowledge, the phenomenon of the converted synagogue in the late medieval and early modern Holy Roman Empire has been noted only summarily.[49] The present chapter is drawn from incipient research devoted to more thoroughly documenting and studying it.[50] Consequently, rather than concentrating on one of these thirty-two cases, it focuses on identifying distinguishing characteristics of the phenomenon as suggested by these thirty-two cases, a principal goal being to place the well known case of Regensburg in some sort of context.

Three questions therefore structure this investigation: (1) what circumstances prompted these conversions?; (2) what were some key political and economic factors involved in their implementation; (3) how did medieval Christians respond to the converted synagogue and synagogue site, and what does their response reveal about their attitudes to Jews and Judaism?[51]

Turning now to the first of these questions: what circumstances prompted the conversion of synagogue to chapel or church? Synagogues were replaced by chapels and churches in the course of destroying, relocating and transforming *Judengassen* to Christian quarters. Scholarship on expulsions,[52] a key factor effecting the transformation of a *Judengasse* into a Christian quarter, demonstrates that pinpointing key economic, social, political and religious causes of the relocating, razing and conversion of *Judengassen*, let alone determining the dynamics between them, is difficult. However, five principal stimuli to the transformation of *Judengassen*, usually occurring in various combinations, may be identified: (1) expulsions; (2) pogroms; (3) the ritual murder charge; (4) the host desecration charge; (5) urban growth and town planning. Expulsion figured in many of these alterations; between 1338 and 1520, it is estimated that roughly ninety cities in Germanic-speaking lands expelled their Jewish communities,[53] and in twenty-two of these thirty-two cases, the transformation of synagogue site to consecrated Christian ground occurred in the aftermath of expulsion decrees.[54] This indicates that in at least a

quarter of the ninety expulsions effected between 1338 and 1520
a synagogue was replaced by a Christian ground. Pogroms figured
in at least seven cases,[55] urban growth and town planning in at
least four cases,[56] and the ritual murder[57] and host desecration
charges[58] were clearly responsible for two cases.

In the present chapter, I will not elaborate further on the first
four of these stimuli – expulsions, pogroms, ritual murder and
host desecration charges – as it is clear what they involved. I will
instead concentrate on the fifth, urban growth and town planning, as its role in setting the pace and tone of a number of these
*Judengassen* conversions needs clarification.

Many *Judengassen* had originally been established in the twelfth
century or earlier on the peripheries of towns, i.e., near city
walls[59] or limits.[60] Over time, urban growth caused some to end
up in the central parts of towns, often adjacent to what had
become focal points of Christian civic and religious life.

Urban growth and town planning were clearly paramount in
the relocation of the Rothenburg ob der Tauber *Judengasse* in
1404. In 1353, in the second half of the fourteenth century, a plan
had been devised to enlarge the town; it was finally implemented
in the early fifteenth century.[61] It in part required the relocating
of the *Judengasse*, which had been founded at the beginning of the
thirteenth century near the city wall,[62] and which by this date had
come to occupy a central rather than a marginal position in the
town. After tearing down the old city wall near it, filling in the
moat, and constructing a new city wall further out, the *Judengasse*
was relocated on land created by the filled-in moat near the new
city wall.[63]

Urban growth and town planning may be identified as having
played a major role in the conversion of at least four other
*Judengassen*: Nuremberg (1350); Landshut (*c.*1350–1410);
Cologne (1424); Frankfurt (1462).

The circumstances and sequence of events leading up to and
governing the destruction and transformation of the Nuremberg
*Judengasse* in 1349–50 have been much discussed.[64] It here suffices
to stress how important a role urban growth and town planning
played in these events. The combination of Charles of
Luxemburg's machinations about the Jews during his battle for
the throne, and the town of Nuremberg's ambition to gain
control of and reorganise the centre of Nuremberg, were in large

part responsible for the destruction and transformation of the Nuremberg *Judengasse*. His fight for the throne had forced Charles IV to use his rights to Nuremberg Jewry as bartering power; in 1349 he pawned his rights to Jewish taxes (*Judensteuer*) to the bishop of Bamberg and the Nuremberg Burggrafen.[65] He also made gifts of valuable *Judengasse* properties:[66] for instance, on 27 June 1349 – months before the December pogrom – he promised the Margrave Ludwig von Brandenburg three Jewish houses of his choice in the Nuremberg *Judengasse*.[67] Meanwhile, the city of Nuremberg had its own agenda for the area of the *Judengasse* once it was emptied of Jews. Charles IV's and the city of Nuremberg's building and design plans for the emptied *Judengasse* are essentially spelled out in a document of 16 November 1349 known as the *Markturkunde*; Charles IV, now king, both granted Nuremberg permission to raze the walled *Judengasse* (located just north of the Pegnitz river) in order to lay out a new market area,[68] and ordered 'a Marian church to be made' out of the synagogue (*judenschul*).[69] Shortly before the December pogrom, which claimed the lives of 562 Jews, the city of Nuremberg had connected the two separate unwalled quarters of St Sebald and St Lorenz,[70] in preparation, it seems, for the transformation of the *Judengasse*. The razing of much of the *Judengasse* occurred around 31 May 1350.[71] This choice land was then partitioned between the town and Charles IV; the town proceeded to lay out two central market areas, the *Hauptmarkt* and *Obstmarkt* (Figure 7),[72] which were connected to the Lorenzkirche side by two bridges across the Pegnitz;[73] Emperor Charles IV asserted his claim to the site of the razed synagogue for a royal *Hofkapelle* and the Frauenkirche was erected between *c.*1350 and 1358 on what had become the north side of the *Hauptmarkt* (Figure 8).[74] Building costs of the Frauenkirche were in large part met by the estates of the murdered Nuremberg Jews,[75] which had been seized by the Nuremberg town council after the December pogrom.[76]

In Landshut, where the *Judengasse* had been founded in 1200,[77] its destruction in 1410 was intimately connected to design plans for Landshut which had nothing to do with any policy about the Jews. At this time, two architectural projects, the building of the Martin's and Holy Ghost churches, had introduced a larger, grander scale to Landshut and stimulated Duke Heinrich the Rich to continue the recreation of Landshut, his city of residence, on this more

67

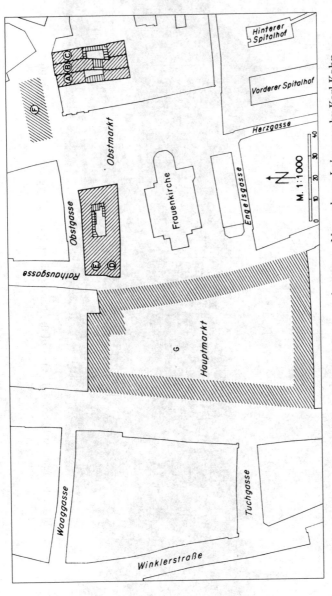

**Figure 7** Topographical reconstruction of the mid-fourteenth century Nuremberg *Judengasse* by Karl Kohn

68

**Figure 8**   Lorenz Strauch, 'Earliest Panoramic View of the Hauptmarkt, Nuremberg', oil on panel, c. 1599

monumental scale; he destroyed the *Judengasse* in order to lay out the wide street today known as the Dreifältigsplatz.[78]

In Cologne, expulsion in 1424 was key to the altering of the *Judengasse* at this time.[79] However, it is also clear that the town council had long coveted the synagogue site. The synagogue, first established in 1000, and three times rebuilt on the same site, in 1096, 1270 and 1370,[80] faced the town hall (*Rathaus*),[81] which had also long occupied the same site,[82] and was technically situated in the *Judengasse*[83] (Figure 9). Town ordinances passed in 1341[84] and 1404 and chronicle accounts indicate that the synagogue's proximity to the town hall (Figure 10) had long been viewed as an irritant and an embarrassment, a 'religious' eyesore; Jews were not to

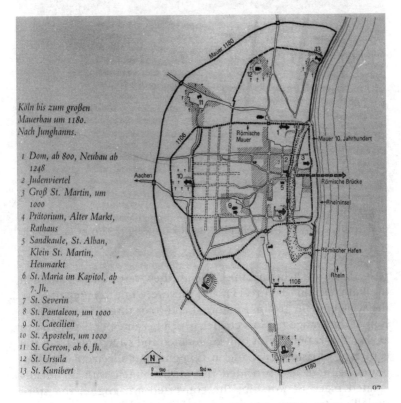

Köln bis zum großen Mauerbau um 1180. Nach Junghanns.

1 *Dom, ab 800, Neubau ab 1248*
2 *Judenviertel*
3 *Groß St. Martin, um 1000*
4 *Prätorium, Alter Markt, Rathaus*
5 *Sandkaule, St. Alban, Klein St. Martin, Heumarkt*
6 *St. Maria im Kapitol, ab 7. Jh.*
7 *St. Severin*
8 *St. Pantaleon, um 1000*
9 *St. Caecilien*
10 *St. Aposteln, um 1000*
11 *St. Gereon, ab 6. Jh.*
12 *St. Ursula*
13 *St. Kunibert*

**Figure 9** Topographical reconstruction of Cologne, *c.* 1180, as determined by Junghanns. (1) Cathedral, built *c.* 800, rebuilt *c.* 1248; (2) Jewish quarter.

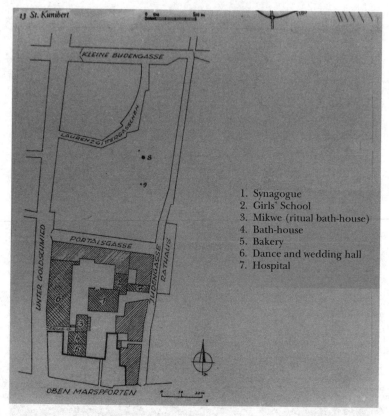

**Figure 10**   Topographical reconstruction of medieval Cologne *Judengasse* as determined by O. Doppelfeld, 1958, ink drawing (1980) by G. Grosch

pass, stand or sit before the *Rathaus*; they were not to gather in the Rathausplatz (Figure 11), and they were not to enter or leave the synagogue in groups of more than two or three.[85] The conversion of the synagogue to a chapel, which became popularly known as the 'Ratskapelle', not only eliminated the synagogue from the centre of Christian civic life in Cologne, but spectacularly eliminated it, and also provided the town council with an ideally located place of worship; the converted synagogue, the spire signalling its conversion, appears in Figures 11 and 12.

It is critical to consider identification of urban growth and town planning as a key stimulus to the destruction and transformation of *Judengassen*, for one reason in particular. In combination with the

**Figure 11** View of the Town Hall and St Maria in Ieruslame (Ratskapelle), Cologne, lithograph by G. Grösch

**Figure 12**  View of St Maria in Ieruslame (Ratskapelle), Cologne, coloured ink drawing (*c.* 1870) by W. Grohns

facts that many Jewish communities soon re-established themselves in towns from which they had been expelled,[86] and that Christians are known to have lived in some active *Judengassen*,[87] it suggests that a primary motive in transforming *Judengassen* was not the desire to banish Jews and Jewish space, but to acquire rights to *Judengasse* properties in order to implement plans to enhance or enlarge towns. In these four cases – and there are probably more – the altering of *Judengassen* was more contingent on policies concerned with town expansion and growth than it was on policies about the Jews. These four cases therefore suggest that to identify and assess principal factors motivating the destruction of *Judengassen*, it is essential to look very closely at the general evolution of the town, and to identify the urban planning strategies of individual towns which required the destruction and/or relocation of *Judengassen*.

Having briefly looked at key causes of the transformation of *Judengasse* to Christian quarter, we may now focus on our second question: what were the key political and economic factors involved in implementing the conversion of a synagogue? Perhaps the main point to be made about these conversions is that unlike the case of Regensburg in 1519, where the synagogue was hastily and dramatically destroyed, and a church hastily and dramatically erected on its site in a matter of weeks, most of the thirty-two conversions were not undertaken in an atmosphere charged with drama and religious fervour, but were undertaken in one of economic and political pragmatism created and controlled by machinations and transactions over Jewish properties.

One factor in particular governed these transactions: two interrelated pieces of legislation about the Jews – 'Chamber serfdom' (*servitudo camerae/Kammerknechtschaft*), and rights to the property of Jews slain in a pogrom. The first, 'Chamber serfdom', has been defined by Guido Kisch as the 'complete "appertainment" of the Jews, with their persons and possessions, to the imperial chamber', and as having developed in its final legal form at the summit of the Middle Ages.[88] It simply meant that the Emperor owned the Jews, and it is no exaggeration to say that it shaped all Jewry legislation.[89] The second concerns rights to the property of slain Jews; according to a late fourteenth-century compilation no one was allowed to appropriate the possessions of slain Jews, 'because the Jews with their possessions belong to the Reich chamber.... The property of Jews, movable or immovable, is forfeited property and falls to the Reich chamber, when one kills them.'[90] Evidence suggests that this legislation was applied to the property of expelled as well as murdered Jews.

This Jewry legislation conspired to create the following situation. In most cases in the course of dismantling a *Judengasse*, a series of property transactions over synagogue ownership,[91] and the prevailing politics and power struggles between town, church and empire over rights to particular Jewish communities, occurred. In most of these thirty-two cases a pattern prevailed; first, the owner, or strongest claimant to ownership, of a Jewish community repossessed the properties of murdered or expelled Jews; secondly, this party then gave or sold the buildings to individuals or towns; thirdly, the town then sought ecclesiastical permission to turn the site into consecrated Christian ground.[92] In three of the thirty-two cases, an emperor or noble ordered the conversion themselves.[93] It is notable that cases where ecclesiastical powers exercised control of synagogue sites directly or relatively quickly were few; only Bamberg (1349), Passau (1478), Brühl (1491) and Regensburg (1519) seem to fall into this category.[94]

In summary, in most cases, towns were not free to convert the synagogue buildings without first securing the rights to the site from whoever held the rights to the Jews (*Judenrechte*). When in a position to do so, emperors and nobles used it to make money or consolidate power by giving or selling Jewish properties to towns or individuals. From a town's point of view, it seems that the converted synagogue was one of the more cost-efficient solutions to the need for an additional chapel or church. According to recent scholarship on the medieval synagogue, the typical medieval synagogue plan was 'close or even identical to those of aisleless chapels',[95] and two examples suggest that this facilitated these conversions and made them appealing; the conversion of the Cologne synagogue to the Ratskapelle, not only eliminated the long-standing synagogue from a strategic site in the town centre, but also solved the town council's problem of the lack of a centrally located place of worship; the plan of St Barbara's church – the transformed Striegau synagogue (*c.*1453) – suggests that the synagogue building had been easily adapted to Christian worship.[96]

Perhaps the most striking consequence of this pattern of property transactions was its effect on not only the pace but also the mood of these conversions. Unlike the case of Regensburg (1519), where the transformation occurred in a matter of weeks, typically there was a much greater time lag between the dismantling of a Jewish community, emptying of the *Judengasse* and establishing of a chapel or church on a synagogue site. For instance, in Cologne, although the Jews were expelled in 1424, the synagogue was not consecrated until 1426.[97] In Passau, where a most dramatic and incendiary event – the host desecration charge of 1478 which was believed to have been planned in the Passau synagogue[98] – triggered the conversion, it was not until 16 August 1479, the day after the feast of Mary's assumption, that Bishop Ulrich III of Nusdorf laid the first stone of the church of St Salvator.[99] Perhaps the slowest conversion occurred in Jauer, Silesia; after the expulsion of the Jews in 1420, the synagogue sat abandoned for eighteen years until the city sought and secured permission from Emperor Albrecht II to convert it.[100] From the point of view of pace and tone, the Regensburg conversion, then, was extraordinary.

This brings us to our third question: how did Christians view and respond to the converted synagogue site? Before looking at their response to the converted synagogue, it is useful to note first what they believed the synagogue meant to Jews, and secondly, the response of Christians to the intact, active synagogue.

Unlike a church, a synagogue is not consecrated and its sanctity derives strictly from the activities occurring within the building in distinction from the space and object of the building; for Jews the synagogue was not a sacred object and it did not create sacred space.[101] A key ritual Christians required Jews to perform, however, suggests that Christians did not make this distinction and believed that Jews viewed the synagogue as sacred; the fact that Christians required Jews to take the Jewish oath (*Judeneid*) either within or in front of a synagogue[102] suggests that they did so. This in turn suggests that Christians probably understood the act of converting a synagogue to a church as signifying the conversion of sacred Jewish space to sacred Christian space.

Predictably, the reputation of the medieval synagogue building with Christians was overwhelmingly negative. However, more moderate views may be distinguished from more extreme views. More moderate views are found in medieval Christian synagogue legislation, which contained both positive and negative stipulations about synagogues: it restricted the maintenance, height and enlarging of existing synagogue buildings, and the construction of new synagogues, but it also protected the medieval synagogue,

thereby legitimising and encouraging respect for it.[103] It seems
that both types of legislation were only erratically enforced; new
synagogues were certainly built and towns possessed more than
one synagogue;[104] medieval Ashkenazi synagogues were repeatedly destroyed. More extreme views were expressed in diverse
sources: often cited biblical and theological texts described the
synagogue as the scene of evil doings, the 'synagogue of Satan';[105]
it was believed that witches congregated in synagogues;[106] it was
believed that Jews plotted and committed the ritual murder of
Christians[107] and host desecrations[108] in synagogues; it was believed that Jews sought every opportunity to torture, in various
forms, Mary and Christ in their synagogues;[109] it was known that
individual Jews or Jewish communities had perished in their synagogues by their own hand, in fires started by themselves,[110] or by
Christians.[111]

Despite the overwhelming negative reputation of the synagogue
building, however, evidence does not suggest that chapels and
churches consecrated on synagogue sites were stigmatised by their
distinctive origins, which indeed could be remarked and enter
town lore; in Bamberg, where the synagogue had first been converted to a Marian chapel in the fourteenth century,[112] expulsion
in the 1470s prompted the replacement of this now dilapidated
chapel with an elaborate Marian church which became popularly
known as the 'Juden-Kapelle'.[113] Furthermore, it is significant that
most of these synagogue buildings were not dramatically razed
and replaced by brand new buildings but simply altered and consecrated.[114] So far, only one negative response to a converted synagogue building has come to light. In the case of Rothenburg ob
der Tauber in 1520, the preacher Johannes Teuschlein[115]
opposed plans to renovate the synagogue building. Complaining
that one should not offer Mary 'wässerigen wein', he demanded a
brand new building.[116] He wanted the synagogue to be demolished and joyfully replaced, regardless of cost.[117] However,
Teuschlein's plea was not successful; on 10 April, a little over a
month later, the renovated synagogue was consecrated.[118]
Imperviousness to the negative reputation and superstitions embodied by the medieval synagogue building is strikingly demonstrated by the case of Rothenburg ob der Tauber: the
consecrating bishop's first directive for the preparation of the
Rothenburg synagogue for consecration was that the cellar of

the building must be checked for bodies, which must be moved.[119]

Perhaps the most important evidence that these buildings were not stigmatised by their origins is that indicating that some clearly played important roles in the lives of towns and powerful individuals: in Würzburg in 1377, Prince Bishop Gerhard destroyed the 'too small' Marian pilgrimage chapel which had replaced the razed synagogue in the aftermath of 1349 and laid the first stone of a larger, more lavish Marian church,[120] which the city celebrated as its own church;[121] in Heidelberg, the converted synagogue became the University chapel;[122] in Rothenburg, on 21 March 1416, the mayor, the council and the burghers made an arrangement with the chaplain of the chapel created on the site of the Rothenburg synagogue in 1404 to use the chapel;[123] in Cologne the synagogue became the prestigious Ratskapelle; in Graz it became the parish church;[124] on 24 April 1443, the new Munich chapel was granted to Archbishop Friedrich of Salzburg and Cardinal John of Bavaria by the papal legate of the Council of Basel;[125] in Nuremberg, on 11 April 1361, Emperor Charles IV had his son baptised in the Frauenkirche.[126]

It seems that Christian symbolism and ritual employed to effect the conversion of a synagogue not only played a key role in preventing the buildings from being stigmatised by their origins, but even made the origins work to advantage. This is certainly suggested by literary imagery generated by the act of converting a synagogue or synagogue site, and the rituals this typically involved.[127]

Miscellaneous comments celebrate these chapels and churches as victories for Christianity over Judaism. The replacement of a house of Jewish worship with one of Christian worship is celebrated as the architectural embodiment of the victory of Christianity over Judaism, the superseding of the Old Law by the New. The 1421 University of Vienna report on the fate of the demolished Vienna synagogue, whose stones were given to the university for building material, triumphantly states: 'and behold the miracle, the synagogue of the old law is wondrously transformed into the virtuous school of the new law'.[128] This sense of triumph is also expressed in a document for the conversion of the Cologne synagogue in 1426: on 7 September 1426, the provost and archdeacon of Cologne officially granted the Cologne magistrate permission to convert the building, which is described most negatively:

For many years those same Jews who refused to recognise our
dear lord Jesus Christ as God and man had a synagogue next to
the town hall of the said city of Cologne and behaved therein in
ways which good Christians would never tolerate in such a holy
town. And so that, in place of the damned Jewish customs and
practices, fitting praise and honour might be given to Almighty
God, Christ Jesus his only son and the blessed Virgin Mary on
that same site, the said mayor and council have informed us [of
their intention to convert the building to a church].

Two chroniclers of events in Cologne comfortably mention 'the
consecration of the synagogue [*Judenshole*]',[130] which, they stress,
had been standing for some 414 years.[131] The conversion of the
Mainz synagogue in 1440 is imbued with the same triumphal symbolism in a papal letter granting the town of Mainz permission to
found a Marian chapel in the former synagogue 'ad omnem illius
tenebrarum expiationem, ac laudem et gloriam Dei omnipotentis,
et gloriose Virginis Marie'.[132] Pope Pius II praises the conversion
of the Landshut synagogue (1452) as the noble act of Ludwig,
King of the Palatinate and Duke of Bavaria.[133] A poem written in
about 1490 to commemorate the alleged host desecration in
Passau (1478) celebrates the establishing of a church on the site
of the evil Jewish deed as most fitting:

> And on the site where the oven stood,
> in which the Holy Sacrament had been thrown,
> a beautiful church was built,
> where many joyous Masses held,
> and praiseworthy services with great devotion
> to the suffering of God and our beloved Virgin.[134]

The destruction of the Regensburg Synagogue in 1519 is sanctioned by the weighty inscription 'according to God's just judgement' (*iusto dei iudicio*) prominently featured in one of Albrecht
Altdorfer's woodcuts of the doomed building (Figure 3), and a
local chronicler celebrates the erection of the new church 'on the
site where the synagogue of the blasphemous, usurious and cruel
Jews had stood'.[135]

The rituals of consecration and dedication may be seen as
having reinforced the already powerful symbolism of these

chapels and churches as architectural embodiments of the superseding of the Old Law by the New. The medieval consecration
liturgy, for instance, stressed the concordance of the Old and New
Testaments; Psalm 23 and its imagery of procession to the temple
on Mount Zion typically appeared at the beginning of medieval
consecration liturgies,[136] and the Old Testament lesson used in the
Roman consecration rite is the account of Solomon's dedication of
the first temple.[137] Most significant is the fact that the ceremony of
consecration used for medieval synagogue sites stressed exorcism
and purification.[138] It has been remarked that a special consecration liturgy existed for the consecrated medieval synagogue; a copy
of the *Liber Sacramentorum Romanae Ecclesiae* includes special
prayers to be added to the consecration service when the building
has been a synagogue.[139] These prayers were to ensure purification
of the site or building from the presence and spirit of Judaism:
they called for the 'expulsion of old Jewish error' (*Vetustate Iudaici
erroris expulsa*) and the 'cleansing of hideous Jewish superstitions'
(*Iudaicae superstitionis foeditate detersa*).[140] The final prayer is addressed to the audience – 'As your people, we ask you, Lord to
repel bad spirits and free the air of evil powers.'[141] Research on
the liturgies used for these thirty-two converted sites is likely to
reveal that these, or a similar set of prayers, were probably added
to the standard consecration liturgy.

It is notable that the consecration of some synagogues was lav-
ishly celebrated. The construction of the Frauenkirche in
Nuremberg began on St Afra's Day in 1355,[142] and it took six years
before it was completed and consecrated in 1361;[143] relics included the bones of Abraham, Isaac and Jacob.[144] On 26
December, St Stephen's Day, 1391,[145] the bishop of Worms consecrated the Heidelberg synagogue (sited on the south-east of the
crossing of Dreikönigs- and Unterstrassen), now displaying many
relics,[146] as the new University chapel in honour of the Mother of
God,[147] in the presence of the Palatine, his son, and university
officials. In Cologne, the synagogue was consecrated as Mary of
Jerusalem,[148] on 8 September, Mary's birthday,[149] and, following
the consecration, High Mass was held in the chapel with much
singing.[150] The anniversary of the consecration was celebrated an-
nually by the city fathers with High Mass in the chapel and a
banquet.[151] Like the Frauenkirche in Nuremberg, the Ratskapelle
was richly endowed with relics.[152]

The ritual of dedication in turn often reinforced the symbolism of the Old Law being usurped by the New and the ritual of purification by bringing the powerful presence of Mary into play. Although churches established on synagogue sites were dedicated to a variety of saints,[153] evidence suggests that the majority were dedicated to Mary. Most of the examples dating to the mid-fourteenth century presently known to this author were dedicated to Mary,[154] and between 1390 and 1520 at least ten of the twenty-six churches established on synagogue sites were dedicated to her.[155]

The difficulty of assessing the significance of a Marian dedication – a most common medieval dedication – is obvious. However, Marian chapels and churches founded on synagogue sites may be safely identified as a corpus of Marian churches with particularly distinctive origins, warranting examination of their significance and repercussions.

There has been some discussion of the Marian dedication of so many churches of this origin; it has been attributed to three factors: (1) Mary as symbol of the New Eve[156] and of *Ecclesia*;[157] (2) the general popularity of the Marian cult;[158] (3) the desire to retaliate for Mary's persecution by the Jews, who were perceived as her worst enemies.[159]

The Marian dedication of chapels and churches of this origin in the Upper Palatinate has been interpreted as an expression of the classic Marian symbolism of Mary as the 'New Eve', as embodied by the image of the *schöne Maria*, a dominant Marian iconography in this region since the middle of the fourteenth century, the period when it first appeared.[160] Marian dedications of Bavarian synagogue sites have been interpreted as reflections of the general importance of the veneration of Mary in Bavaria;[161] apparently, in southern Germany the Marian cult was particularly strong.[162]

Marian churches of this origin in Bavaria have also been interpreted as representative of a more militant anti-Jewish Marian symbolism. For instance, Lionel Rothkrug proposed that Bavarian churches created directly on synagogue sites or elsewhere in *Judengassen* were dedicated to the militant image of Mary as symbol of *Siegerin aller Gottes Schlachten* (Lady Victor of all God's Battles) as well as to the more neutral image of Mary as symbol of 'Queen of Heaven'.[163] He also asserts that in Bavaria–south Germany, where he claims the type of the *schöne Maria* did not appear on the south German religious scene until about 1490 (the year of the Blutritt),[164] the *schöne Maria* appeared 'only at pogroms, to avenge Jewish assaults on the living body of the saviour'.[165] In short, Marian churches of this origin have been defined as manifestations of a generally unexplored phenomenon labelled 'Marian antisemitism' (*marianischer Antisemitismus*).[166]

The role of the classic symbolism of Mary as *Ecclesia* warrants further comment as it seems that this symbolism helped to make the conversion of a synagogue site not only desirable but natural. The view that the conversion of a medieval synagogue to a Marian chapel or church embodied the victory of *Ecclesia*/Mary over *Synagoga* is clearly expressed in documentation on the fate of medieval Ashkenazi synagogues: for instance, the *Urkundenbuch* of the Würzburg Marian chapel, which was erected on the site of a razed synagogue (*c.*1350), states that the chapel was dedicated to Mary to express the replacement of the synagogue by the 'new' *Ecclesia*.[167] The symbolism of Mary as *Ecclesia* therefore made the Marian dedication of the consecrated synagogue or synagogue site particularly suited to express not only the image of the *Ecclesia Triumphans* but also the concept of concordance of Old and New Testaments; *Ecclesia* is synagogue's natural and rightful successor. The Marian dedication of a synagogue site not only signalled the victory of *Ecclesia*, but also firmly acknowledged and drew attention to Mary's ancestry.[168] The missionary activities of the Franciscan preacher John of Capistrano in Nuremberg in 1452 in fact suggest that he used the Marian church, the Liebfrauenkirche, built on the site of the synagogue razed in 1350, to do just this; he delivered the majority of his twenty-seven sermons – which Jews were forced to attend[169] – with this Marian church of Jewish origins as backdrop,[170] and, during his second sermon, he pointedly reminded his audience of the Jewish origins of Christ, Mary and the apostles: 'When I do not love the Jews, I am not a good Christian. Was not Christ a Jew, and the blessed Mary? Were not the apostles Jews?'[171] It is hard to believe that Capistrano did not gesture towards the impressive structure of the Frauenkirche (Figure 8) as he delivered these words.

Together, then, the image of the superseding of Old Law by the New and the symbolism of Mary as *Ecclesia* made the conversion of a synagogue natural. More than any other Christian symbolism, it seems that Marian symbolism muted the powerfully negative reputation of the synagogue building.

Predictably, the Marian dedication of synagogue sites generated a range of anti-Jewish tales celebrating in various ways these transformations as great Marian victories over the Jews; they stressed Mary's imperviousness to the revengeful attacks of the Jews; they told of Mary experiencing new and miraculous powers because of the banishment of the Jews. A late fifteenth-century Nuremberg chronicler begins an account of the founding of the Nuremberg Frauenkirche in the mid-fourteenth century by explaining that until its establishment, Mary had had no church of her own in Nuremberg because she could not bear to be near so many Jews:

> It was a great lack in Nuremberg that the Queen of Heaven, the noble Virgin Mary, who gave birth to God, had no church of her own. In my opinion, the mother of the crucified fled the murderers who had killed her beloved child, and wanted nothing to do with a place where so many of them lived.[172]

By explaining that Mary 'wanted nothing to do with a place where so many of them lived', the author of course implies that Mary approved the banishing and murder of Nuremberg Jews in the mid-fourteenth century, that these actions pleased her and persuaded her to permit a Nuremberg church to be dedicated to her at that time, and again to permit the Jews to be expelled at the end of the fifteenth century.

The Marian chapel in Ingolstadt, converted in the 1390s, generated the following miracle tale:

> Enraged by their expulsion, the Jews stole a wondrous image of Mary known as the *Schuttermuttergottes* from the chapel built on the site of their synagogue. They then hid it, cut off Mary's head and threw the pieces in the Danube upstream at a spot hidden from the city. But not long after, Mary, still in pieces, swam downstream into the Schutter which lay next to the chapel. Then a jubilant cry arose throughout the city... .[173]

Whether this tale may have in fact been circulated to counter rumours about the presence of lingering Jewish spirits and their harmful effect on the chapel's reputation cannot be ascertained without concentrated research on the fortunes of this Marian chapel.

The drama of the swift razing of the Regensburg *Judengasse* was heightened when workers suffered accidents in the process of dismantling the synagogue,[174] and one *Judengasse* house.[175] Their recoveries were treated as some of the first miracles performed by Mary upon the destruction of the Regensburg Jewish community and the erection of the wooden chapel 'Zur Schönen Maria' on the site of the razed synagogue. These incidents were publicised in a pamphlet entitled *In dysem buchlein seind begriffen die wunderbarlich zaychen beschehen zu Regensburg zu der Schönen Maria der Mutter gottes.*[176] This tract suggests that by expelling the Jews, destroying the *Judengasse* and dramatically transforming the *Judengasse* into Christian space, Regensburgers had both liberated and empowered Mary – made it safe for Mary and her child to occupy what was perceived to be the most notorious and sacred site of her bitterest enemies:

> ... their synagogue, where daily they disgraced,
> slandered and severely blasphemed our lord Jesus
> Christ, his honourable mother the Queen and
> *schöne Maria,* was smashed and destroyed, the
> paving stones too, and on this spot the
> establishment and erection of a church was begun
> in which the most laudable Virgin Mary is now
> honoured and the most wonderful signs occur....[177]

Obviously, Mary saved the lives of those hurt in the act of demolishing the *Judengasse* in approval of and gratitude for the destruction of her enemies, The converted Rothenburg synagogue is similarly celebrated in a song written by the poet Kunz Has in about 1520–25 to commemorate the expulsion of Rothenburg Jewry; it recounts miracles wrought by Mary with the help of her child in the new chapel.[178]

In summary, the conversion of a synagogue site to church site constituted an event which would have been witnessed by many and probably would have become known to most, if not all, town occupants; the erection, renovation and decoration of a chapel or church automatically required the participation of a wide variety of people, and was obviously bound to be noticed by many more; in Aldo Rossi's words 'One can say that the city is the collective memory of its people.'[179] The conversion of the Jewish house of worship to a Christian house of worship provided an explicit and public symbol of the banishing and vanquishing of Judaism by Christianity. The publicity generated by a building project, especially one occurring in the midst of a town, was sure to have been amplified by the pomp of the dedication and consecration ceremonies. The converted synagogue dedicated to Mary defines a chunk of material Christian culture which simultaneously asserts Mary's victory over and liberation from Jewish persecution, and her Jewish origins.

## CONCLUSION

Further insight into the significance of the phenomenon of the converted synagogue for medieval Christian culture will of course be gained not only through a comprehensive treatment of these thirty-two cases, but also by comparing the phenomenon as manifested in the realm of the Holy Roman Empire with its manifestation in other parts of Europe, in particular, France and Spain, and by comparing and contrasting it with related phenomena – earlier and later examples of iconoclasm, for example.

At present, the following conclusions may be drawn. First, for a number of reasons, it is clear that these thirty-one other cases demonstrate that the form and tone the phenomenon took in Regensburg in 1519 was extraordinary. In most cases, this type of transformation did not occur in an atmosphere created and dominated by some sort of pro-Christian or anti-Jewish religious fervour, but instead occurred in an atmosphere determined and dominated by two interests, political and economic wrangling over rights to immovable and movable Jewish property, and the urban planning ambitions of individual towns and rulers.

The thirty-two examples provide a significant body of evidence that urban Christians had no compunctions about creating sacred Christian space, not only on the site of a building with a reputation ranging from dubious to dreadful, but in such a building. In most cases extant synagogue buildings were converted to chapels and churches rather than being dramatically razed and replaced by consecrated Christian ground. It is significant that the Rothenburg preacher Teuschlein's comment equating the dedication of a former synagogue building to Mary to offering her 'watery wine' is the only objection voiced to converting an extant synagogue building to consecrated Christian ground so far discovered in the course of researching the phenomenon of the converted synagogue.

In fundamental terms, the act of transforming a synagogue into a church expresses confidence that Jewish space could be truly transformed into Christian space. At this point, the evidence suggests that a combination of two factors was responsible for the ease with which towns transformed Jewish space to Christian space: (1) the attitude that the converted synagogue building was a cost-efficient solution to a need for additional chapels and churches; (2) the perception of the converted synagogue as a natural event, meaning that it was perceived as the architectural embodiment of the superseding of the Old Law by the New. Insight into which factor really prevailed may be gained by comparing the treatment of the synagogue with the treatment of the other key type of Jewish space – the Jewish cemetery.

Evidence repeatedly indicates, that, rather than fearing the Jewish cemetery and its contents as tainted by evil or bad luck, medieval Christians not only vandalised them (in violation of legislation protecting the cemetery from such actions, it may be stressed[180]), but used the tombstones for building materials for both secular Christian spaces, i.e. houses,[181] city walls,[182] bridges[183] and clock towers,[184] and sacred spaces, meaning of course, churches.[185]

The incorporation of Jewish tombstones into churches – especially during the *Angst-* and disease-ridden mid-fourteenth century – suggests that, rather than fearing that the presence of Jewish cult objects might damage, inhibit or corrupt consecrated Christian space, Christians approached them in one or a combination of three ways: (1) they did not believe them to be imbued with any negative powers; (2) they understood the act of consecrating a synagogue site as expressing the superseding of the Old Law by the New; (3) they believed that consecrated Christian space overpowered and subjugated sacred Jewish space. In light of the fact that Christians readily incorporated Jewish tombstones into unconsecrated Christian space, it seems that the first of these attitudes – that they did not believe them to be imbued with any negative powers – really prevailed over the others. This suggests that the rhetoric about the triumph of the New Law over the Old was evoked because it suited or enhanced the occasion, not because it was vital to do so. The description cited above of the use of the dismantled Vienna synagogue for building materials for the University of Vienna, found in a University report of 1421, is a perfect example of this.

Viewed from this perspective, the phenomenon of the conversion of Jewish space to sacred Christian space is revealing about the nature and expression of urban anti-Judaism and anti-Semitism in the late medieval and early modern Holy Roman Empire. Above all, it suggests that medieval Christians did not believe Jewish space to be in any way irrevocably contaminated by Judaism. This is most evident in the case of Rothenburg ob der Tauber (1520), where the consecrating bishop's first instruction for the preparation of the synagogue building for consecration required that the cellar of the building be checked for Jewish bodies, which must be moved before consecration can occur.

There is very little evidence that Christians viewed consecrated Ashkenazi synagogue sites as plagued by evil spirits of dead or expelled Jews, or devils and witches for that matter. This is significant in light of the fact that medieval German Christians did fear places of execution as the haunts of evil spirits.[186] The miracle tale of the Marian Ingolstadt chapel, which tells of expelled Jews stealing and assaulting an image of Mary from it in revenge for their expulsion and the destruction of their synagogue, is the sole example of a tale of Jews seeking revenge for a consecrated synagogue.

Above all, the phenomenon of the converted synagogue suggests that although medieval Christians chronically suspected and feared both unconverted and converted Jewish persons, they did not chronically suspect and fear Jewish space. It suggests that they only perceived Jewish space to be problematic when it was inhabited or being used by the living Jewish dweller; that once the Jews had left the premises, Jewish presence and powers effectively left too. Unlike Jewish persons, Jewish space could be 'truly' converted, especially, it seems, with the Virgin Mary's help and powers, which were liberated and activated upon the transformation of Jewish to Christian space.

Apparently, then, the phenomenon of the converted synagogue as it occurred throughout the medieval and early modern Holy Roman Empire suggests that superstitions about Jews and Jewish space were quite different matters, and should be treated accordingly.

# 4. Institoris at Innsbruck: Heinrich Institoris, the *Summis Desiderantes* and the Brixen Witch-Trial of 1485

ERIC WILSON

The grossly exaggerated importance normally ascribed to the *Summis Desiderantes*, also known as the 'Witch Bull', promulgated by Pope Innocent VIII on 5 December 1484, makes it perhaps the most overrated document in the entire history of European witch-craft persecutions.[1] The document is clearly a *Fakultät*, a formal papal authorisation for a specific office to be fulfilled by a specific person for the indefinite future. Although it is exceptional in being issued 'ad perpetuum rei memoriam', the *Summis* fully belongs in that long series of *Fakultäten* issued throughout the fourteenth and fifteenth centuries which empowered numerous inquisitors and instructed them in their duties.[2]

While many historians have traditionally regarded the *Summis* as the crucial document indicating the willingness of higher eccle-siastical authorities to engage in the extensive prosecution of witches,[3] closer examination reveals that it is, in fact, a wholly con-ventional account of papal views regarding diabolic magic. The entire notion of witchcraft is hardly touched upon, and the very word *maleficium* is actually never used.[4] Even the most cursory reading of the previous major papal decrees concerning the threat of satanic magical practices, most notably the pronounce-ments of John XXII[5] and Eugenius IV,[6] shows the total absence of any substantial structural or thematic differences between these earlier texts and the *Summis*. Regarding its actual theological content, the Bull appears surprisingly meagre. It is primarily a po-litical document, issued by Innocent in response to Heinrich

Institoris's and (possibly) Jakob Sprenger's petitioning the Papal Curia for a declaration of support in the face of deeply entrenched regional ecclesiastical and lay opposition to their inquisitorial practices.[7] In this capacity, the *Summis* is an outstanding example of a *Reskript*, a specific form of papal authorisation issued in response to a petition, previously sent to the Curia, which seeks papal instruction on politically and/or ecclesiastically sensitive issues.[8]

A careful examination of the *Summis* also reveals its essentially political nature. After lamenting the reported (by uncited sources) spread of heretical depravity, 'haeretica pravitas', throughout the dioceses of Mainz, Cologne, Trier, Salzburg, and Bremen – that is, all the metropolitans of Germany west of the Elbe – the Bull provides a short account of the satanic machinations of the alleged heretics. Although Innocent explicitly mentions demonic intercourse ('cum daemonibus incubis et succubis abuti'), his listing of customarily popular concerns with witchcraft – namely, the supernatural infliction of sexual impotency and sterility, deformed births, agrarian blight – replicates in succinct fashion the way in which lay concerns with harmful magic were actively assimilated into and re-interpreted within the context of 'high' scholastic and judicial concern. There is no reference to nocturnal flight and the only suggestion of either the satanic pact or the Sabbath is a very indirect one:

> They blasphemously renounce that Faith which is theirs by the Sacrament of Baptism, and at the instigation of the Enemy of Mankind they refrain not from committing and perpetrating the worst excesses to the peril of their own souls, whereby they outrage the Divine Majesty and are an example of scandal and danger to many.[9]

After this rather tenuous identification of *haeretica pravitas* with diabolism,[10] Innocent discusses in extended detail the judicial plight of the apparently hapless inquisitors, Institoris and Sprenger. More than half of the remaining text is devoted to the 'vexing problem' of local opposition to the two Dominican inquisitors.[11] After naming Institoris as the fully empowered inquisitor for heretical depravity in Upper Germany ('Alamaniae Superioris') for all those aforementioned territories and dioceses and Sprenger for certain parts of the Rhineland ('certas partes linae Rheni'), the Pope makes a highly revealing comment concerning the insolence of certain local clerics within these regions. Although both members of the Order of Preachers had received full recognition through earlier papal letters:[12]

> Nonetheless, not a few clerics and laymen of those countries, seeking too curiously to know more than concerns them, since in the aforesaid delegatory letters there is no express and specific mention by name of these provinces, towns, dioceses and districts, and further since the two delegates themselves and the abominations they meet with are not ashamed to contend with shameless effrontery that these enormities are not practised in those provinces, and consequently the aforesaid Inquisitors have no legal right to exercise their powers of inquisition in the provinces, towns, dioceses, districts and territories which have been mentioned, and that the Inquisitors may not proceed to punish, imprison, and penalise criminals convicted of the heinous offences which have been detailed,[13]

Innocent declares it his duty to remove all hindrances blocking the actions of the inquisitors and goes on to state that,

> the aforesaid Inquisitors be empowered to proceed to the just correction, imprisonment, and punishment of any persons, without opposition or hindrance, in every way as if the provinces, townships, dioceses, districts, territories, even persons and their crimes in this kind were named and particularly designated in Our apostolic letters.[14]

Furthermore, Institoris and Sprenger are both fully authorised to:

> proceed, according to the regulations of the Inquisition, against any persons of whatever rank and high estate, correcting, imprisoning and punishing as their crimes merit, those whom they have found guilty, the penalty being made suitable to the offence; moreover, they shall enjoy a full and perfect faculty of expanding and preaching to the Faithful as often as opportunity may offer and it seems good to them, in each and every parish church of the designated provinces, and they shall

freely and lawfully perform any rites or any business which appears advisable in the aforesaid cases. By Our Supreme authority we grant them anew full and complete faculties.[15]

The *Summis* thus clearly demonstrates that the opposition to the inquisitors was based upon those perceived legal restrictions inherent within the previously issued documents; hence, the *Summis*'s declaration that the inquisitors were to have full power over all people at all times and in all places almost certainly reflects papal responsiveness to Institoris's own pleading.[16] After commending the two Dominicans to the protective care of the archbishop of Strassburg, Albrecht of Bavaria,[17] the Bull concludes with a dire threat. Innocent instructs the metropolitan:

Not to suffer [the inquisitors] in disobedience to the tenor of these presents to be molested or hindered by any authority whatsoever, but he shall threaten all who endeavour to hinder or harass the Inquisitors, all those who oppose them, and rebels of whatever dignity, status, position, preeminence, nobility, or any condition there is, or whatever privilege or exemption they claim, with excommunication, suspension, interdict, and even more terrible censures, penalties, and punishments as seems appropriate to him, and if he so chooses, he may by Our authority increase and renew these penalties as often as he will, calling upon, if it suits him, the help of the secular arm.[18]

What is most striking about the text is not its marginal concern with the nature and reality of witchcraft, but rather the exceptional political powers that it grants the two inquisitors against all possible opponents, including members of the aristocracy – all of which is indicative of the tremendous amount of opposition the author(s) of the *Malleus* must have encountered during his/their career(s) as witch-hunters. As Sigmund Riezler has pointed out, the *Summis* does, at least in its formal pronouncements, in some way imply a degree of papal commitment to the prosecution of witches far greater than evidenced in any previous curial edict.[19] Nevertheless, rather than being placed within a quasi-teleological framework, the end-product of a steadily intensifying papal concern with malefic subversion stretched out over the course of several centuries, the *Summis* can be most profitably interpreted as a document of bureaucratic expediency, structured in such a way as to undermine the ground of juro-political opposition encountered by Institoris while active in the field. The modicum of historical significance the *Summis* does possess is derived almost entirely from its incorporation by Institoris into the original edition of the *Malleus Maleficarum*, which guaranteed that the Bull would be reprinted into every subsequent re-issuing of the text. This highly self-promoting manoeuvre proved successful in securing Institoris's objective of obtaining greater papal approval for his inquisitorial activities, an ambition manifested by Institoris entitling the document 'Bulla apostolica adversus haeresim Maleficarum'.[20] By the end of the sixteenth century, the *Summis* was commonly cited as the most authoritative papal pronouncement guaranteeing the ecclesiastical and judicial propriety of witchcraft trials.

The essentially political nature of the *Summis*, and the political uses to which it was put, can be best exemplified through a study of Institoris's career as an active hunter and prosecutor of witches. Despite Institoris's own claims to widespread inquisitorial activity,[21] extant records exist for only two trials that he personally conducted: the proceedings at Ravensburg in October 1484 and those in the diocese of Brixen, from August 1485 to February 1486. For the purposes of this discussion, the Ravensburg trials shall be omitted, as they took place at least two months prior to the issuance of the 'Witch Bull'.[22] It is important to note, however, that Institoris's comparative success at Ravensburg – the condemnation and execution of at least two accused women, Anna of Mindelhym and Agnes Baderin – seemed to be due almost entirely to the absence of what so effectively stymied his efforts at Brixen, namely entrenched episcopal opposition.

The origins of the Innsbruck witch trials, the greatest judicial proceeding of Institoris's entire career, appear somewhat obscure, as does the precise nature of the inquisitor's initial involvement in the affair. Historians have traditionally tended to emphasise the role played by Archduke Sigismund of Austria in encouraging the trials as well as enlisting Institoris's services. Karl Müller has pointed out that the chancellor of the ducal court during the 1480s, Landislaus Sunthaim, was a distant relation by marriage to Elisabeth Frauendienst, one of the seven accused women at the earlier Ravensburg trial, and could therefore have plausibly served as the 'middleman' in drawing Sigismund's attention to the possible utility of Institoris as a witch-hunter in the archduke's employ.[23] In truth, however, the evidence we possess concerning Sigismund's personal involvement is highly circumstantial, the most important bit of which is a laudatory, and highly self-serving, reference provided by Institoris at the end of his summation of the Innsbruck trial in the *Malleus* – 'These details are recorded not to the shame but for the praise and glory of the most illustrious Archduke, since he has striven considerably as a Christian prince and zealous leader to eradicate witchcraft, with the assistance of the most reverend bishop of Brixen.'[24] Although Sigismund undoubtedly harboured concerns about the reality of malefic activity – his letter to the mayor of Ravensburg, as well as his instigation of a limited hunt during the *Landtag* of August 1487 when his former mistress Anna Spiess ('die Spiessin') feigned demonic possession,[25] both attest to the fact – there is virtually no hard evidence implicating the archduke in any direct involvement in the proceedings at Brixen. On 18 June 1485 Innocent VIII dispatched a letter to Sigismund thanking him for the support which he had provided the two inquisitors and commended him to Abbot Johann of Weingarten in the diocese of Constance, who had also apparently provided some services to the Dominicans,[26] but the precise nature and scope of the supposed assistance is never specified. The famous dialogue contained within the *De Pythonicis Mulieribus* of Ulrich Molitor (1489), often cited by commentators as conclusive evidence of archducal approval of witch hunting[27] is, in fact, highly ambivalent, as Sigismund is portrayed as a sceptic concerning the value of the persecutions, and it is the avowed intent of the other two participants, Ulrich Molitor and Konrad Schatss, to convince him otherwise.[28] Furthermore, the fact that Institoris openly commends Bishop George Golser of Brixen for his aid in the persecution of witches at Innsbruck,[29] when the bishop was the one primarily responsible for thwarting the inquisitor's efforts there, should certainly cast suspicion upon the veracity as well as upon the sincerity of Institoris's positive assessment of Sigismund's activities.

Whatever the precise course of events preceding Institoris's involvement at Innsbruck, by July 1485, the inquisitor, equipped with the *Summis desiderantes*, had taken up residence in the diocese of Brixen. It was this papal Bull, in fact, that was to play the crucial political role in the course of the events that followed: the Dominicans' attempts to secure convictions, as well as the bishop's efforts in opposing inquisitorial gains, both centred upon a subtle negotiation of the papal power provided by the *Facultät*. The inherently ambiguous political nature of the *Summis* revealed itself from the very beginning. On 23 July 1485 Golser issued a promulgation of the *Summis*, granting a forty-day dispensation to all who would actively comply with the inquisitor's efforts.[30] Although too lengthy to include here, two features of this text deserve comment. The first is that the bishop pointedly fails to specify the punishments to be administered to the confessed and convicted witches. The second is that he refers to witchcraft as something illusory – 'demonum illusiones' – indicating that he understood the *maleficia* mentioned in the Bull within the context of the earlier theological pronouncements of the famous *Canon Episcopi* of the tenth century.[31]

It is evident that Golser understood Institoris's function as an inquisitor of heretical depravity to have been exclusively within the capacity of a preacher, at no point evincing his belief in any malefic occurrence within the Innsbruck region that warranted an inquisitorial investigation.[32] After his customary procedure of delivering sermons denouncing the omnipresent evil of *maleficium*,[33] Institoris initiated a series of hearings, which lasted from 9 August to 14 September and resulted in the collection and examination of depositions given against more than fifty suspects, all but two of whom were women.[34] So great was the total number of accused that the investigation, although originally intended to be restricted to the town of Innsbruck, must have expanded to incorporate neighbouring parishes as well.[35] Altogether, at least forty people from Innsbruck and nearby Wilten were accused; likewise, at least ten more from the immediate vicinity and numerous others from various surrounding localities whose names do not appear to have been recorded.[36] The clear majority of the accused came from the local peasantry, although a few were of artisan status. No such lines of demarcation were noticeable with the self-proclaimed victims of magical assault, who traversed the entire social spectrum of the community, from labourers to the household of Archduke Sigismund himself.[37]

Golser's increasing scepticism concerning the legitimacy of the proceedings is clearly indicated in a number of letters he issued during their final phase. On 21 September he sent an epistle to Archduke Sigismund which, although acknowledging the binding quality of Institoris's authority as established by the papal *Summis*,[38] requested that the archduke exert his influence on the inquisitor compelling him to restrict his efforts to those guilty of the more heinous offences of malefic bodily harm and, as befitted a German bishop, blasphemy, with penance to be employed as the main disciplining corrective in the milder cases of bewitchment.[39] That same day he issued a formal letter of episcopal recognition to Institoris, stipulating that the Dominican respect existing legal norms, including the constitution of Boniface VIII, which forbade withholding the identities of their accusers from the accused,[40] and that he should observe the opinion of the territorial princes in every instance, and apply the full force of the law only to those guilty either of the desecration of holy objects or of murder through the employment of malefic techniques.[41] Through these statements, Golser reveals himself as a rather typical representative of orthodox episcopal opinion, demonstrated by his sceptical attitudes concerning the illusory nature of witchcraft as well as his emphasis upon the offence of blasphemy as opposed to *maleficium*. It is apparent, however, that the bishop's efforts at moderation met with little success. The records of the depositions and interrogations clearly indicate that Institoris blatantly violated established ecclesiastical procedure on a number of occasions, including the gratuitous employment of torture.[42]

By the beginning of October, Institoris was prepared to bring formal charges against seven of the suspected women – Helena Scheuberin, Barbara Hufeysen, Agnes Sneiderin, Barbara Pflieglin, Barbara Selachin, Rosina Hochwarin and her mother Barbara Rosalin – all of whom were subsequently incarcerated.[43] Scheuberin was the first to be formally accused, on 4 October, and from that date until 21 October, a total of thirty interrogatory sessions of the women took place. Only Institoris and the papal notary, Johann Kanter of the diocese of Utrecht, appear to have been present at all sessions. On various occasions, however, the inquisitor was joined by a number of his fellow Dominicans from the immediate vicinity, including Wilhelm Behringer, Heinrich Hoffman, Wolfgang of Basel, Caspar of Freiburg and Magister Johann of Roesbach. He was also aided at times by the Minorite Johann of Rosenbart, the court chaplain to Sigismund, as well as Paul Cael Schrmaister.[44]

On 7 October, the archduke wrote to Golser informing him of the imprisonment of the seven women and, perhaps out of concern about an undesirable escalation of the judicial proceedings, requested him to appoint a special episcopal commissioner to advise Institoris and to supervise the investigations.[45] Golser duly appointed Sigmund Saumer, a parish priest at Axams and certified *Licentiat*, as investigator and empowered him to serve as his representative on the episcopal commission to be drawn up to judge the accused, the bishop excusing himself on grounds of ill-health. In a noticeable departure from Institoris's inquisitorial method, Golser also instructed the priest to urge the convicted to return to the body of the Holy Mother Church – 'ut redeant ad gremium sancte matris ecclesie'.[46]

On 14 October, Saumer commenced his inquiries[47] despite Institoris's attempts to thwart him by conducting inquisitorial sessions in his absence[48] – the only interrogation during which Saumer was recorded as being present was the session on 14 October with Helena Scheuberin.[49] A crisis point was reached during the initial trial proceedings against the accused. A potentially tragic situation rapidly degenerated into a farce. The first meeting of the episcopal tribunal took place on 29 October in the town hall, and consisted of the seven commissioners – in addition to Heinrich Institoris, who also served as prosecutor, three local representatives of the Dominican order,[50] as well as Sigmund Saumer, Christian Turner, *Licentiat* and general commissioner of the church at Brixen, and Magister Paul Wann, doctor of theology and canon law from Passau – aided by the two public notaries Johann Kanter and Bartholomaeus Hagen.[51] Scheuberin was the first to be presented before the court, where she was interrogated by Institoris concerning her moral status within the community and her sexual practices. This provoked an immediate response from the other members of the commission, who overruled this kind of questioning as irrelevant and threatened to remove Institoris from the session if he continued with this line of inquiry. At the same time, Saumer, acting within his capacity as episcopal commissioner, accused Institoris of severe procedural irregularities during the previous phases of the investigations and called for a short recess until Institoris had formally drawn up an official set of questions. During the interim, Golser's agents made their move, recruiting the services of Johann Merwais of Wendigen, a doctor of medicine and a *Licentiat* of canon law, to act in defence of the accused.[52]

Merwais proved his worth at the reconvention of the commission. His first act was to call for an indefinite postponement of the trial, allowing him time to acquire the official certification he needed in order to serve as defence lawyer of the accused, who by this time, both individually and collectively, consented to transfer the conduct of their defence to the *Licentiat*. Merwais pressed his case, declaring all proceedings hitherto null and void, Institoris having undermined his own position on five points of gross procedural misconduct. The inquisitor had failed to obtain a public notary certified by the bishop to supervise and record the conduct of the interrogations as was specified by the *Summis*. Further, Institoris had brought accusations against the defendants that technically lay outside his jurisdiction and which were not explicitly described in the Bull. In addition, he should have asked each of the accused about the nature and contents of the depositions against them, but had failed to do so because he had neglected to formulate a standard questionnaire. The Dominican had also imprisoned the seven women even before any official judicial procedures had been initiated. Finally, Institoris had conducted all phases of the investigation, including the procurement of testimony from the accused, in the absence of the aforementioned public notary authorised by Golser.[53]

There followed a long verbal duel between the defendant and the prosecutor, Merwais openly rejecting Institoris's status as a judge on the grounds of partiality and calling for his replacement by the bishop as well as the deacon and the vicar-general of the diocese of Freising. Basing his opposition upon Institoris's apparent deviations from the stipulations of the *Summis*, Merwais requested that Institoris be placed in custody and the accused released. Following Institoris's strenuous protests, Merwais accepted the commission's decision to subject the accused to less stringent conditions of imprisonment. Merwais then continued his efforts to further undermine Institoris's position by instructing the accused to ignore the questions of the prosecutor altogether, and to reply only to the queries put to them by the episcopal commissioner himself. While Merwais called for a direct appeal to the papal chair, thereby circumventing the political status bestowed on Institoris by the Bull, Institoris vigorously defended his right to remain as judge. Clearly recognising that they had failed altogether to halt Institoris's initiative during the first session of the trial, episcopal representatives on the committee agreed with the Dominican faction to reconvene several days later at a different locale to review the validity of Merwais's objections.[54]

The second, and final, session met on the morning of 31 October in the house of Conrad Gunther, a prominent burgher. Taking advantage of the unexpected interlude, Golser had subtly strengthened his hand by appointing two new members to the commission, Ulrich Puchter, chaplain of Innsbruck and priest of the diocese of Naumburg, and Johann Blanckenhayn, a 'Cooperator', both of whom must certainly have been strongly sympathetic to the bishop's position. A direct clash between the prosecutor and the defendant began the new session, Merwais reiterating his demand for an appeal to the Curia in the face of Institoris's strenuous opposition. Merwais finally relented and offered a compromise solution which the committee found acceptable. The commission was to postpone the trial indefinitely until it had extensively reviewed the legality of the inquisitor's actions. Although failing in his grander ambitions, Merwais had succeeded in securing a minimal objective, the recognition of the impropriety of Institoris's handling of the proceeding, thereby releasing himself from the more formidable task of proving the innocence of the accused. In his capacity as general commissioner, Turner declared the trial invalid – 'invalidatum seu invalidandum' – on the grounds of the inquisitor's misconduct and released the women, but, significantly, only after they had declared their willingness to appear before a future court that might be convened to investigate the charges against them. Turner officially nullified the episcopal recognition bestowed upon Institoris by Golser and demanded the return of the original copy of the notice. So vigorous was Institoris's protest that Turner consented to confine himself to lodging a formal complaint against the inquisitor through the public notary, Bartholomaeus Hagen. The final matter that related to the trial, financial remuneration, was quickly resolved by the archduke himself, who promised to subsidise the cost of the proceedings as well as rewarding Institoris for his services, but refused to guarantee financial support for any further investigations or trial.[55]

Although down, Institoris was by no means out, refusing to leave Innsbruck even after his humiliation in court. It was only at this point, after his men had effectively undermined Institoris's position, that Golser took direct action against him. Raising fears concerning the possibility of a popular uprising following the witchcraft proceedings, the bishop wrote to Institoris on 14 November, urging him to quit Innsbruck, as he could no longer guarantee his safety.[56] The first of the bishop's not-so-subtly-veiled threats obviously failed in its purpose, however, as Institoris continued to reside in the Tyrol, purportedly busying himself with the collection of new evidence for another round of witchcraft accusations. By 8 February 1486, Ash Wednesday, the bishop felt the need to take further action. In a letter addressed to a priest named Nikolaus, Golser lamented the deterioration of Institoris's intellectual faculties.[57] He then instructed the priest to convey to the inquisitor an additional missive blatantly informing him of the acute undesirability of his continued presence.[58] This letter produced the desired effect, as Institoris withdrew immediately, apparently to Salzburg.[59]

Several features of the Innsbruck proceedings deserve comment. One that has already been touched upon is the extreme ambivalence of the role played by Duke Sigismund. Several factors indirectly attest to Sigismund's general lack of support for the trials: the close ties between the archduke and bishop as displayed in the September correspondence; his apparent silence following both the commission's annulment of Institoris's episcopal authority on 31 October and Golser's attempts to evict the inquisitor in November and February; and his refusal to finance any further trials. It seems the most plausible conclusion that while Sigismund did not agree with the manner in which the investigations were conducted, his detachment from the proceedings was the result of his reluctance to become directly embroiled in an ecclesiastical dispute between warring parties of papal and episcopal authority.[60] Such transparency is unfortunately not the case concerning the role played by Bishop Golser. Certainly, the non-Dominican members of the episcopal commission could have acted neither as effectively nor as blatantly against Institoris as they did, without the bishop's tacit support. Within this context, Golser's own intellectual attitudes towards *maleficium* acquire some interest.[61] There are sufficient indications that he was harbouring some scepticism, if not concerning the reality of *maleficium* as such, then at least against the specific connotations given to it by the scholastic demonology propagated by a Realist Dominican such as Institoris. As we have already seen, Golser largely reaffirms the position of *Canon Episcopi* concerning the illusory nature of supposed demonic magic.[62] Furthermore, even though he specifies that bodily harm or death resulting from *maleficia* should be severely punished, he does not explicitly advance a view on the presumably demonic causal agency underlying such occurrences, the theological lynchpin of the emergent witchcraft ideology. The crucial point is that Golser never identifies magic with heresy.[63]

Theological concerns – the nature and status of occult transgression – thus neatly dovetailed with more conventional political factors, in this case a subtle and sustained negotiation of the power contained within the papal *Summis*. In some ways the witch trial of Innsbruck seems almost to duplicate in miniature certain crucial features governing the general relationship between episcopal and papal–inquisitorial authority. The entire ground of resistance offered to Institoris was not centred on a denial of the reality of malefic supernatural agency as such but rather on the inquisitor's infringements of canonical jurisprudence perpetrated in the pursuit of his own conception of the nature of the demonic threat. The distinguishing characteristic of the Innsbruck affair was the tremendous and unique political status granted to Institoris through the *Summis Desiderantes* and the conflicting ways in which this authority was interpreted by the rival parties. Golser's oppositional efforts, mirrored in his basic scepticism concerning the particularities of the scholastic paradigm of demonic agency, were therefore based upon a strategy of neutralising Institoris's political authority: that is, by illustrating the inquisitor's own deviations from the prescriptions of the Bull, the keystone of his apparently unassailable authority. It is significant that at least two of Merwais's accusations of procedural misconduct were, in fact, groundless. The *Summis* does not specify that a duly appointed episcopal notary must be present during interrogations. Furthermore, the evidence reveals that, whether officially empowered by Golser or not, the notary Johann Kanter was in fact present at most sessions.[64] What was at issue, of course, was the desperate pursuit of the only strategy of resistance available to the episcopal authorities that could eventually prove to be politically efficacious: the demonstration of Institoris's own flagrant abuse, and thus the nullification of that very authority with which the Curia had invested him. Supporting this interpretation is the intriguing fact that even though the seven accused were ultimately released, they still had to promise to appear before any future court of inquiry. This indicates that the episcopate was more concerned with countering the danger of inquisitorial excess than with denying the possibility of diabolic deviancy, a possible threat which it obviously preferred to handle on its own terms within its own capacities.

Although a clear victory for Golser, the fiasco in the Tyrol produced the unexpected result of convincing Institoris that he should continue his pursuit of demonic transgressors by other means.[65] The Brixen ordeal left its mark upon Institoris, and through him, the *Malleus*, not only with regard to the original impetus to compose the text so as to negate the baleful effects of sceptical clerics, but also concerning the development of certain key features of the basic argumentative structure of the treatise itself.

Not only are many of the initial depositions of the Innsbruck trial reproduced within the *Malleus*,[66] but their subsequent reworking by Institoris clearly reveals the manner and the extent to which the inquisitor sought to perpetuate the diabolic heretic stereotype by demonising the notion of magical causality through the introduction of the principle of diabolic agency, a central feature of the discursive apparatus infusing the text.[67] The legacy of Institoris's failure to implement the political authority of the *Summis* at Brixen was two-fold. It compelled him to undertake the composition of a text which would in future enable him and other inquisitors to circumvent local opposition, and this text would be composed in such a way as to maximise the potential of the heretical–demonic threat inherent within *maleficia* so as to make its vigorous persecution that much more imperative. The results speak for themselves.

# 5. Witchcraft and Popular Religion in Early Modern Rothenburg ob der Tauber

ALISON ROWLANDS

## I

In his stimulating article 'Protestant Demonology: Sin, Superstition, and Society (*c.*1520–*c.*1630)', Stuart Clark highlights the existence of an early modern Protestant pastoral demonology qualitatively different from that of its Catholic counterpart. It was a demonology which downplayed the significance of maleficent witchcraft and the power of witches and instead reserved its ire for popular magic, or the wide range of rituals used for healing, divination, detection and counter-witchcraft. This emphasis, Clark argues, sprang from a pastoral concern to persuade the layperson that to regard misfortune as the work of witches 'undervalued the spiritual function of misfortune as a retribution for sin and a test of faith, and questioned God's providential control over affairs'. To counter misfortune with beneficent magic 'ignored the need for repentance ... and attributed specious powers to the supposedly protective or curative properties of persons, places, times, and things'.[1]

This chapter seeks to test the validity of Clark's theory – that moderation towards witches on the part of educated, literate Protestant elites was paralleled by severity towards popular magic, its users and purveyors – in early modern Rothenburg ob der Tauber and its rural hinterland. It will do this by examining legal and religious records involving cases of witchcraft and magic for the period 1544–*c.*1630. This examination aims to show not just what the Rothenburg authorities said, but what they actually did when dealing with such cases, and also aims to gain an insight into what popular attitudes in such cases were. In this way Clark's theory will be significantly nuanced as well as tested.[2]

## II

Rothenburg ob der Tauber was an imperial town in Franconia of about 6,000 inhabitants. It was ruled by a patrician sixteen-man council which also had jurisdiction over a large rural hinterland containing a further 10,000–11,000 subjects. Though Lutheranism was adopted in 1544, Rothenburg's reformation did not gain an institutional basis until 1559, when a *Church Ordinance* was published and a Consistorium established to oversee religious matters.[3]

A trawl through Rothenburg's legal records for the years 1544–1630 provides a meagre enough catch of witchcraft cases to suggest that the town's elites did in fact embrace a distinctly moderate approach towards witches and witchcraft. During this period the town council investigated only some nine cases involving suspicions of witchcraft in any great depth.[4] None of these cases escalated into the sort of large-scale hunt which typically occurred in areas where witchcraft was treated as *crimen exceptum* and where all legal safeguards on use of torture and admissibility of evidence were abandoned.[5] Only one case ended with an execution and that was more for infanticide than for witchcraft.[6]

There is also evidence in the Rothenburg cases to support a connection between mild treatment of suspected witches and a particular Lutheran perception of witches as creatures who were not only powerless, but in fact non-existent, the product of diabolic illusions. In 1582, for example, a woman named Margaretha Seitzin claimed that three of her village neighbours, Gertraud Durmenin, Anna Wehin and Anna Schneiderin, were witches who had transported her against her will to their nocturnal feast. Two jurists commenting on the case argued that Seitzin's experience had probably been an illusion (*Spiegelfecht*) created by the Devil to endanger her three neighbours and to corrupt other villagers by encouraging them in their superstitious belief in witches. Seitzin's claims were investigated no further.[7]

This idea was developed further in a report written in 1627 by Rothenburg's foremost religious official, Georg Zyrlein, on a case

in which thirteen-year-old Margaretha Hörberin claimed to have
had sex with Satan and attended numerous witches' sabbaths.
Zyrlein's approach was to divide those who had had dealings with
the Devil into two categories. In the first came the magician
(*Zauberer*), necromancer (*Schwarzkünstler*), exorciser of devils
(*Teuffelban[n]er*), poisoner (*Gifftmischerin*), sooth-sayer (*Warsager*),
and astrologer (*Zeichendeuter*). These individuals gave themselves
to Satan willingly, made pacts with him by means of oath or blood
signature, and did harm by magic with his help. The Bible condemned them to death. Witches (*Unhold*, *Hexe*, *Drutte*) made up
the second group. They did not enter willingly into associations
with Satan but were forced or deceived by 'fantastical imagination' into so doing. They did not confirm pacts in writing and did
no magical harm to man or beast. They should go unpunished:
that the Devil had already plagued them was bad enough. Zyrlein
felt that Hörberin came into this second category.[8]

Here then was an elite tendency to see witchcraft not as reality
but as diabolic illusion or deception. A witch did not really fly
through the night astride a fire iron or dance at sabbaths or cause
any harm, but was merely deluded by Satan into thinking that she
could do so. And if witches were not real, then there was no need
to be terrified of them or of what they might do and no need to
orchestrate a ruthless campaign to root them out and destroy
them.

It seems likely, therefore, that this perception of witches helped
fashion and sustain the extremely scrupulous and sceptical legal
approach which Rothenburg's council and the jurists advising it
took towards individual cases of suspected witchcraft. This approach was characterised by two features which made the execution of witches and development of witch-hunts highly unlikely:
the treatment of witchcraft as an ordinary crime, subject to all
legal safeguards, rather than as *crimen exceptum*, and the assumption that a suspected witch was innocent until proved guilty, not
vice versa.[9]

Contrary to the impression sometimes given, Germany's early
modern imperial code of legal procedure, the *Carolina*, did not
constitute a licence to burn witches indiscriminately,[10] but made it
quite hard to prove that someone was a witch if its precepts were
strictly adhered to. A person could be convicted of witchcraft only
by the testimony of two witnesses or by his or her own

confession.[11] Someone could be taken into custody and questioned under torture if suspected of witchcraft in the first instance only on the basis of the testimony of one witness or of other 'sufficient indications' of guilt, one of which was the possession of a bad reputation for witchcraft.[12] To safeguard the suspect the *Carolina* decreed that both witnesses and those who testified to a person's bad reputation had to be good, upright and impartial sources.[13]

In Rothenburg these precepts were interpreted almost entirely to the advantage of those women unfortunate enough to be called witches.[14] For example, in 1582 a jurist advising on the Seitzin case argued that Seitzin was unfit to testify as the sole witness against her three neighbours because she herself was the party interested in proving her story true and because she was a woman.[15] Rothenburg's council in fact took a generally dim view of a single person's testimony in such problematic cases. In 1602 a young man named Leonhardt Brandt concluded that five women of Steinach unter Endsee were witches after he claimed to have seen them gathered round a strange fire on Walpurgis Eve (30 April). The flimsiness of his evidence was exposed by a jurist who referred to the dictum that 'one man's testimony is half a testimony', a dictum which was important enough to be written for all to see on a board in the council chamber.[16]

A bad reputation, or ill-fame, for witchcraft likewise did not necessarily seal a woman's fate in Rothenburg and its rural environs. Whilst investigating the Seitzin case it emerged that a rumour had been circulating in Oberstetten for at least seven years which maintained that one of the three supposed witches, Gertraud Durmenin, had once transported her husband back to the village on a goat.[17] This potentially damning piece of evidence was treated with disdain by two of the jurists advising on the case, who pointed out that it was impossible to pinpoint who had started the rumour to see if they were honourable, credible people. One jurist also noted that it was the habit of common people to accuse old women of such things on the slightest pretext.[18] The problem of tracing ill-fame to its original sources was likely to crop up in most cases of supposed witchcraft, as it was usually of several years' standing.[19]

Not only did Rothenburg's council and the jurists advising it tend to interpret what constituted a 'sufficient indication' of witchcraft with great scrupulousness, they also tended towards caution and scepticism in their general handling of witchcraft cases. Again the Seitzin case illustrates this. One of the jurists, named Renger, advised general caution in the investigation of Seitzin's claims, telling the council that it was better to proceed too slowly and cautiously than with too much haste and zeal.[20] Jurist Hardessheim echoed these sentiments, citing Wiesensteig, where sixty-three women had been executed as witches in 1562–3, as a salutary example of what could happen if witch trials got out of hand.[21] The jurists also suggested other, more 'plausible' explanations to account for what Seitzin had experienced without recourse to witchcraft, the most popular of which proved to be that she had been blind drunk and imagined the whole thing.[22]

This same desire to prove that things could not have happened as a result of witchcraft was apparent in other cases. In 1627 young Margaretha Hörberin was examined by the town midwives to see if she had lost her virginity, while the girl with whom she shared a bed was asked whether Margaretha had ever disappeared at night, to disprove once and for all her claims that she had had sex with Satan and flown to witches' sabbaths. Both investigations proved negative, thus vindicating official scepticism.[23]

The Hörberin case illustrates a similarly sceptical and legally scrupulous approach towards people named as sabbath-attenders by supposed witches. Margaretha named nineteen women and three men she claimed to have seen at sabbaths.[24] In an area where witchcraft was taken more seriously this list of names might have provided the next batch of witches to be hunted. In Rothenburg the jurists advising on the case noted that the girl's statement alone was insufficient evidence on which to arrest and torture any of those named. Additional proofs, such as the possession of bad reputations or evidence of harm done to neighbours or their animals, were needed and it was up to the council to investigate further. None of the twenty-two was taken into custody, thereby forestalling any self-perpetuating hunt.[25]

Perhaps the key legal factor ensuring that none of the Rothenburg witchcraft cases escalated into a hunt was the council's relatively mild application of torture. In six of the nine witchcraft cases torture was not applied at all, because there was insufficient legal indication to justify its use. When torture was used, it tended to be in moderation, to see whether people would

stick to their stories or not, rather than to excess, simply to force
them into confessing they were witches.[26]

Especially significant in this regard was a case from 1587 in
which fairly severe torture was inflicted: thumbscrews and two
floggings on a six-year-old boy and strappado on his mother.
However, the jurists advising on the case were at pains to point
out that torture of a minor was justified only by the inconsistency
of his statements.[27] Ultimately the case simply petered out, apparently on the advice of jurist Prenninger, who had concluded that
'one cannot hope to get anything at all certain out of the boy',
who was the chief witness. The case should therefore be dropped
'because one cannot get onto certain ground, nor discover what
the truth is'.[28] Here then was a belief that no amount of torture
would produce the truth, as opposed to the conviction that anything confessed under torture was true.

All in all, and unlike certain of their Franconian neighbours,
Rothenburg's elites showed greater zeal in defending a person's
good name, or 'honour', than they did in following up the slightest aspersion of witchcraft cast against it.[29] And their subjects
seem to have recognised this. It was in fact her three neighbours
who brought Seitzin's story to the attention of the council in
1582, for the express purpose of having their names cleared of
the suspicion that they were witches, and this pattern was repeated in at least three of Rothenburg's other eight witchcraft
cases.[30] Once this had happened the person who had made the
accusation of witchcraft risked suffering punishment for defamation if they could not prove their claims. That six of Rothenburg's
nine witchcraft cases ended with the accuser suffering more at the
hands of the law than the suspected witch underlined how
difficult this was and suggested that the Rothenburg authorities
regarded the slanderer as more socially disruptive than the
witch.[31]

### III

So far only the attitudes of Rothenburg's elites – councillors,
jurists and churchmen – towards witches and witchcraft have been
discussed. This might suggest an image of elite scepticism versus

popular credulity, of elite legal scrupulousness limiting the potentially damaging effects of a popular thirst for the blood of hapless witches. However, what is striking about Rothenburg and its rural hinterland is the high degree, not only of elite, but also of popular disinterest in hunting witches. That this may have helped fashion a moderate witch-hunting profile is a possibility which finds no place in the schema of Clark's Protestant pastoral demonology, yet without it Rothenburg's legal records might well have told a different story.

Two things are conspicuous by their absence from Rothenburg's legal and religious records from the popular point of view: the frequent and widespread naming of specific women as witches and the frequent and widespread connection between such women and specific acts of harmful magic. Crops must have failed, goods and objects must have gone missing, people and animals must have fallen ill, had accidents and died in Rothenburg and its rural hinterland during this period. Yet relatively few women were named as witches, and those that did appear in the records tended not to have a whole catalogue of *maleficia* attributed to their evil machinations over the years. In sum, particular witches were scarce and physical manifestations of their malevolence scarcer still.

How can this paucity of evidence be explained? One set of possible explanations revolves around the importance of honour and the relationship between Rothenburg and its rural hinterland. It may have been the case that villagers were aware of the council's dislike of slanderers and rumour-mongers and were therefore unwilling to make accusations, voice suspicions and confess to being the source of a witch's ill-fame, since to do so and then fail to prove one's claims meant risking punishment for defamation. This suggests that an element of the pre-inquisitorial law of talion remained in Rothenburg.[32] Or it may have been the case that the emphasis on the value of the individual's good name was so deeply instilled into people that they rallied on principle to the support of the accused witch rather than the accuser.[33] This happened in 1629 when Anna Dieterichin, the aged, widowed herdswoman of Untereichenroth, was accused of witchcraft by fifteen-year-old Margareta Härterin. Although seemingly a classic candidate for such an accusation, Dieterichin was fully exonerated, thanks to her protestations of innocence and the testi-

monies to her good character and faithful service given by the
men of Bovenzenweiler and Untereichenroth.[34]

Rallying to the defence of the accused may also have been connected with a dislike of town interference in village affairs. In the
second half of the sixteenth and early part of the seventeenth centuries a stream of council ordinances sought to regulate the lives
of its subjects in the rural hinterland, while church visitations introduced a hitherto unheard of level of official surveillance into
village life.[35] The council also attempted to increase control over
the political life of the villages.[36] These policies may have considerably decreased enthusiasm for taking suspicions of witchcraft to
the council in the first place and for helping the council to
convict as witches the women of one's village thereafter.

In addition to these possibilities, however, there seems to have
been a strong streak of genuine popular scepticism about witches
and what they were supposed to be able to do, a scepticism which
might more plausibly account for the sparse and tame nature of
popular witchcraft suspicions. Inhabitants of Rothenburg and its
villages did not necessarily see witches as particularly frightening,
nor did they necessarily make a strong connection between misfortune and the machinations of witches. In other words, and in
striking parallel with elite ideas, witches were creatures of the
imagination rather than actual beings who caused real harm.

Extracts from two witchcraft cases support this idea. In 1629 a
troop of Schönburgische cavalrymen quartered in Rothenburg's
rural hinterland during the Thirty Years' War did its best to
incite the villagers of Untereichenroth, Obereichenroth and
Bovenzenweiler to start burning witches, beginning with the
herdswoman Anna Dieterichin. They also suggested to one man,
Veit Georg, that his wife was a witch responsible for the deaths of
his horses. Far from following the cavalrymen's lead, Georg re-
torted that his horses had died of natural causes, while other
village men admitted that yes, they might have called Dieterichin
a witch in the past, but that this had been done to tease, as a joke,
and in the way that old women were usually called witches. Unlike
the cavalrymen, they did not want to take the accusation seriously
and instead rallied to Dieterichin's defence.[37]

Even more significant in this regard was the evidence given by
innkeeper Lorentz Dolman in a case of suspected witchcraft from
the village of Hilgartshausen in 1587. Witches had supposedly

taken wine from his cellars and ridden his horses on their nocturnal visits to the inn, so the authorities asked Dolman whether he
had recently lost any wine or livestock in suspicious circumstances. Under questioning Dolman showed an initial tendency
not to blame witches for curious occurrences and misfortunes and
the susceptibility to being 'educated' about the activities of
witches in various ways.[38]

In response to the query about loss of wine, Dolman said that
yes, wine had disappeared from his cellars over the past two years
with no money to show for it. His servants had, however, pointed
out that he sold most of his wine on credit and it had never occurred to him to think that the wine could have been taken by
witches.[39] On the question of livestock, Dolman explained ailments and deaths which had occurred a decade or so before quite
matter-of-factly.[40] More recent problems were described with
more ambivalence. One of his horses stood wet with sweat some
mornings and he thought this 'strange'. His cattle also had recently become thin and were afflicted with sweating and fearful-
ness, especially at night. Again Dolman said that he had not
thought of attributing these afflictions to the actions of witches,
but had learned that this was possible on a recent trip into
Württemberg when he had heard that several women had been
burned there for harming livestock.[41] Dolman's initial scepticism
about what witches could do was thus being tested and perhaps
re-fashioned by news of witch trials from other territories and also
by the council's investigation into the case in his village.

It is important to stress that the argument being advanced here
is not that nobody believed that witches could cause actual harm
in Rothenburg and its rural environs in the early modern period.
Far from it. Peasants still thought that witches could harm their
livestock and sought protective remedies from cunning folk.[42]
Georg Rigel's wife Ursula, from the village of Hilgartshausen,
thinking she might be attacked by witches at night, planned to
protect herself by hammering the walls of her house full of nails.[43]
Endris Schmid of Oberrimbach thought that he had been rendered impotent by a witch and visited the town prostitutes in the
hope that they could restore his manhood.[44]

It does seem clear, however, that these beliefs were not necessarily universal, but rather that they were part of a spectrum of
popular beliefs about witches in Rothenburg and its rural hinter-

land; a spectrum ranging from a belief in witches as genuinely capable of harm, to a belief in witches as something of a joke. And it would appear that occupying the broad middle ground of this spectrum was a belief in witches in general, without any corresponding belief in specific witches and their connection with specific acts of misfortune. What the Rothenburg records of witchcraft cases illustrate, then, is a relatively high degree of both elite and popular scepticism on the question of witchcraft which may well have been mutually reinforcing.

IV

To turn now to the second half of Clark's Protestant demonology theory, did Rothenburg's elites regard popular superstition as a greater problem than witchcraft in the early modern period? Evidence from two witchcraft cases would suggest that they did. In 1582, after he had argued that Margaretha Seitzin's nocturnal experience had probably been an illusion created by the Devil to encourage other inhabitants of Oberstetten in their superstitious belief in witches, jurist Hardessheim recommended that the council try to establish exactly where Seitzin's three neighbours really had been that Shrove Tuesday evening. This was suggested not so much to prove their innocence, but to make it clear to the 'common people' that Seitzin had been deluded and that witches did not really exist. In other words, what was needed was more faith in God and less willingness to believe in witches.[45]

Similar comments were made in the course of the Hörberin case in 1627. A report had been sent to the council describing the peculiar behaviour of the old shepherd of Gebsattel. This could have had damaging consequences for the shepherd, as he had been named as a sabbath-attender by Hörberin. Jurist Seuter, however, commented scathingly on the report. He pointed out that the old man's antics – chiefly running about in the fields before and during spells of cold weather – was hardly evidence of witchcraft. He then criticised the villagers of Gebsattel for being so superstitious – they believed that Walpurgis Night (1 May) was the night of the witches and blamed Satan for the misfortunes God visited upon them for their sins! The village pastor should preach against such superstition, rather than encourage suspicion against the shepherd.[46]

If popular superstition was perceived as a greater problem than witchcraft, was it also deserving of harsher punishment? Again the Rothenburg evidence would suggest that this was the case. If one considers Superintendent Zyrlein's report on the Hörberin case of 1627, most of the people he assigned to his first category as willingly in cahoots with Lucifer and deserving of death according to God's word were exactly the sort of people who were most usually found offering their services to the 'superstitious' villager or town-dweller – the astrologer, the soothsayer, the worker of magic, the exorciser of evil spirits.[47] In fact the only person missing from Zyrlein's list of enemies of the faith was the *Segensprecher*, the person who literally 'spoke blessings' as a means of healing, protecting and endowing objects with 'magical' power and significance and who was an especial bugbear of the Lutheran establishment thanks to this impious misuse of God's word.

The 'speaker of blessings' did make an appearance in an ordinance issued by the council in 1612 to curb popular resort to cunning folk (amongst other acts of popular ungodliness). According to the ordinance, the council had realised with deep regret that people in both town and rural hinterland were running for help to astrologers, speakers of blessings, exorcisers of devils and purveyors of magic (*Zeichendeuter, Segensprecher, Teufelsbeschwörer, Zauberer*) on account of the slightest misfortune, in search of good health and because they had lost things. And this despite the fact that God had ordered that such people should not be suffered to live! Such behaviour constituted the most infamous blasphemy of God's beloved name and majesty and was prohibited on pain of (unspecified) corporal punishment. Furthermore, villagers were to look out for any purveyors of magic trying to sneak into the rural hinterland and were at once to capture and give into council custody any they encountered.[48]

As well as rhetoric like this there are examples in Rothenburg's legal records of cunning folk actually suffering fairly severely at the hands of the law. In 1582, for instance, Georg Kissling, the smith and cunning man of Ergersheim, was set in the pillory, flogged and banished for activities which included using a crystal ball to retrieve stolen goods and special herbs to protect animals

from worms and witches.[49] A year earlier, travelling quack Anna
Gebhartin had also been banished after being set in the pillory
and having a cross burned into her forehead and two holes
burned through her cheeks. She had claimed that she could
make bad marriages good, restore male potency and find hidden
treasure with the help of a spirit.[50]

A cursory glance, then, would seem to support the idea that leniency towards witches on the part of the elites was accompanied
by severity towards popular superstition in Rothenburg and its
rural environs. However, a closer look reveals that, in actual fact,
as far as popular superstition was concerned, the bark of
Rothenburg council and its advisors was far worse than its bite,
and that there was little in the way of a particularly active, systematic, or punitive campaign against popular superstition between
1544 and 1630.

Take the 1612 ordinance as an example. What is most
significant about it was not so much what it said but the fact that it
was very probably the *earliest* piece of legislation designed
specifically to deal with the problem of popular superstition and
popular resort to cunning folk.[51] This is strange, given that some
of the earliest ecclesiastical visitations of both town and rural hinterland brought popular use of magic to the authorities' attention.[52] Before 1612 the council may well have hoped that its
general ordinances against blasphemy would have covered the
popular superstition problem, or that patient exhortation and instruction from men of the cloth would be sufficient to persuade
the misguided to see the error of their ways. Whatever the case,
the authorities had not exactly been making huge efforts to eradicate the problem.

As for the legal records, there is no gainsaying the fact that
Georg Kissling, Anna Gebhartin and others like them were quite
severely punished for their activities. However, they were hardly
the targets of any sustained campaign against purveyors of magic.
Georg Kissling and another cunning man named Leonhardt
Geüder from Gattenhofen came to the attention of the authorities in the first instance for crimes other than their trafficking in
magic – Kissling for defamation, Geüder for adultery, bigamy, and
threefold perjury – and the final summaries of their cases focussed mostly on these major transgressions.[53] Anna Gebhartin's
mistake seemed to have been plying her trade so obviously in

Rothenburg itself, giving herself the maximum chance of arous-
ing the council's suspicions about what she was up to and the
minimum chance of making a speedy getaway once the council
had decided to act against her.

In addition, the authorities were by no means convinced that
cunning folk were worthy of death nor willingly in league with the
Devil, whatever the rhetoric of the 1612 ordinance or Zyrlein's
pronunciations on the matter might suggest to the contrary.
Geüder was beheaded, but this was far more for his other crimes
than it was for being a cunning man. Anna Gebhartin *was* asked
whether she was a witch who could transport people on a goat
and, because she claimed she could conjure a spirit which would
find hidden treasure for her clients, whether she was allied with
the Devil.[54] These questions, however, formed only a fraction of
her lengthy interrogation and the council was quite happy to
accept her explanation that she had invented all her grandiose
claims the better to persuade people to part with their money.
Her final punishment was for fraud, not for consorting with the
Devil.[55]

These findings are not altogether surprising. The authorities of
any early modern jurisdiction simply did not have the resources to
police and punish any crime particularly effectively, especially one
as widespread as the use of magic and resort to cunning folk.[56]
The problem was exacerbated for Rothenburg's council by the
fact that its rural subjects could quite easily visit cunning folk
outside the hinterland and therefore beyond its jurisdiction, and
by the fact that it had to rely on the very people who used the services of cunning folk to apprehend them and hand them over
into its custody. That cunning folk and quacks were punished
more for their other crimes or for fraud than for being in league
with the Devil was commensurate with the council policy described above for cases of suspected witchcraft. Without a strong
belief in the reality of diabolic machinations and a willingness to
torture to extract specific confessions, defamation, bigamy, or
fraud were simply far easier to prove.

So while Rothenburg's council in the second half of the sixteenth and early part of the seventeenth centuries could refer in
disapproving tones to 'improper physic with the saying of blessings and other forbidden means' and to 'forbidden, devilish
magic and saying of blessings',[57] while pastors and visitors in both

town and rural hinterland dutifully reported and took to task the
'ungodly' members of their flocks,[58] and while an example was
made of the occasional cunning man or quack, this was about as
far as action against popular 'superstition' went. Little headway
appears to have been made towards either persuading or forcing
people to stop using magic and to rely instead on God's mercy
and the solace offered by Rothenburg's Lutheran establishment
before the events of the Thirty Years' War plunged all council
attempts to impose its will into disarray.[59]

## V

As far as the 'common people' were concerned, what
Rothenburg's council condemned as 'superstitious' practices were
an integral part of everyday life, providing a whole range of ways
of coping with or protecting against misfortune. These practices
fell into three main categories: pre-emptive protection against
misfortune; healing or curing injury or disease; and retrieval of
missing objects or people.

The first category included ways of guarding against attack from
witches. We have already seen Georg Rigel's wife Ursula of
Hilgartshausen planning to hammer her walls full of nails to catch
or scratch any witches who might fly into her house at night.
Cunning man Georg Kissling had a less violent method of protecting peasants' cows against witches, which consisted of putting
herbs grown from seeds brought all the way from Hungary into
holes bored into the barn-lintels under which the cattle went in
and out.[60]

Kissling also offered a type of root, dug up on Good Friday, to
cure horses of worms, and a healing salve for people who came to
him with 'bad legs and other damages'.[61] Other ailments, like
pains in the head and throat, might be dealt with in Rothenburg
and its environs by the speaking of blessings over the afflicted
person.[62] A cure for aching toes was described by an old woman
called Kulssheimerin during a visitation of the town in 1560. She
had been given 'something' to hang round her neck by a woman,
over which she had to pray five Our Fathers and five creeds, then
throw it into running water to be rid of the pain.[63]

Finally there were the methods of retrieval. Kissling offered a reassuringly complicated process involving a Hungarian crystal, a bucket of water and three nails made before sunrise on Good Friday, which was guaranteed to make thieves return stolen goods – with the proviso that the theft had not taken place more than four days ago and that the thief was no more than two miles away when the ritual was performed. Kissling had apparently returned a horse and a coat to their grateful owners using this method.[64] Other cunning folk offered ways of forcing people – usually a missing spouse or fiancé – to return home.[65]

The official records also give some clue as to the identity of some of the purveyors of magic who offered their services to the inhabitants of Rothenburg and its hinterland at this time. As well as the smiths Leonhardt Geüder of Gattenhofen and Georg Kissling of Ergersheim, there was the herdsman of Gammesfeld and his wife, and Els, the herdswoman and sorceress of Detwang.[66] There was Jorg Fronhöfer, the magician of Oberbreitenau, who claimed to travel far and wide to collect the herbs he needed for his work and boasted that his skills were greater than those of any doctor or barber-surgeon; the magicians of Aib and Feuchtwangen, who figured in a late sixteenth/early seventeenth-century list of notorious users and purveyors of magic; and a man named Müllerlin of Buch, whose notoriety was such that he was singled out for attention in a council ordinance issued in 1639.[67]

Such well-known cunning folk would have been able to attract custom from a wide catchment area and could make a good profit from their trade. Georg Kissling, for instance, claimed to have charged up to ten gulden for the protection he offered cows against witches, six for his healing salve, and one for finding lost or stolen property.[68] They also provided an interesting link between the town of Rothenburg and its rural hinterland. Ordinances and visitation records complained that both urban and rural subjects used the services of cunning folk, yet most of these cunning folk seem to have lived in the villages of the hinterland, if not further afield. This suggests that as well as providing the townsfolk with daily necessities in the form of grain and livestock, the hinterland supplied the equally essential resource of beneficent magic.

While the elites condemned this magic as superstitious, popular attitudes towards it were utilitarian. With little or nothing in the way of medical help available or affordable and with an unsystematic legal system and non-existent police force, it made a lot of sense to those of the lower orders to do what they could to cope with misfortune. And the emphasis was very much on doing something, on taking action to resolve a problem – which was no doubt why the Lutheran line of coping with misfortune by means of repentance and prayer was less enthusiastically received. Popular concern was not with whether a practice was superstitious or a cunning man ungodly, but with whether the practice worked and whether the cunning man gave value for money.

The perceptual gulf between popular and elite views on the issue of beneficent magic can be seen in cases where the two clashed. On being told to stop misusing God's word in the attempt to cure her aching toes in 1560, old Kulssheimerin had apparently said that she would use the blessing again if she were in pain, even if she ended up in Hell for it.[69] In 1570 Anna Lösin described a method, involving three leaves of wintergreen, a pan of fat and God's name, which she used for retrieving stolen goods, adding that she had not thought it was a sin.[70] In 1611 another woman excused the fact that she had put objects under the altarcloth in the hospital chapel to be blessed by explaining that she had done it 'with good intentions' ('bona intentione').[71] All three women obviously failed to see how the authorities could possibly object to something done with good in mind.

## VI

The example of Rothenburg ob der Tauber and its rural hinterland, then, does lend support to Clark's theory of a distinctive early modern Protestant pastoral demonology. Rothenburg's literate, educated elites *did* adopt a moderate approach towards witchcraft, an approach born of legal scrupulousness and a particular conceptualisation of witches which made the development of large-scale hunts virtually impossible. The same elites *did* express themselves as more concerned with the problem of popular magic than with that of maleficent witchcraft, branding it 'devilish' and 'superstitious'.

However, this was by no means the whole story. Two things emerge as especially significant in the case of Rothenburg to nuance these findings. The first was the fact that although they expressed greater concern with the problem of popular superstition, the authorities did not really *do* a great deal to try and stamp it out. The second was the fact that, despite their differing opinions on the merits of beneficent magic, the elites and at least some of their subjects seem to have shared a streak of scepticism with regard to witches and their activities. There was therefore far less of an elite attempt to discipline popular behaviour and far more harmony of belief between the authorities and their subjects in Rothenburg and its rural hinterland than the Protestant pastoral demonology highlighted by Clark could have led one to expect.

# Appendix: Witchcraft Cases Investigated in Depth 1544–*c.*1630

(For more details of these cases, see chapters 1 and 2 of my 'Women, Gender and Power in Rothenburg ob der Tauber and its Rural Environs, 1500–*c.*1618' (Cambridge University Ph.D. dissertation, 1995).

(1)   In 1561 **Barbara Brosam** of Wettringen was accused of being a witch by Hans Lautenbach. Lautenbach was set in the pillory and banished for defamation. See RStA A858 fols 14r–25v, 28r–31v, 33v, 34r–6r; A846 fols 433v–35v, 435v–38v, 438v–41v, 452r–55v.

(2)   In 1563 **Appolonia Kellnerin and her daughter Anna** of Finsterlohr were banished with two other members of their family for calling each other witches and disrupting village life with their quarrels. See RStA A860 fols 497r–502r, 504r–508r; A847 fols 353v–55v.

(3)   In 1582 Margaretha Seitzin accused **Gertraud Durmenin, Anna Wehin and Anna Schneiderin** of Oberstetten of being witches. Seitzin was cautioned for defamation. See RStA A875 fols 186r–88v, 192r–98v, 199r–200r, 202r–6r, 209r–v, 211r–15r, 217r–219r, 221r–23v, 225r, 226r–28v; A853 fols 393r–94r.

(4)   In 1587 a six-year-old boy from Hilgartshausen claimed that he had flown to a sabbath with his mother **Magdalena Gackstattin** and four other village women; the case was dropped because of the boy's inconsistent statements. See RStA A877 fols 533r–35v, 537r–40r, 543r–44r, 545r–53r, 555r–58v, 560r–66v, 568r–69r, 570r–74r, 577r–79v; A855 fols 447r–v.

(5)   In 1602 Leonhardt Brandt accused **the wives of Frantz Kupper, Michel Lientschner, Daniel Krafft, Leonhardt Holenbuch and Jörg**

**Stehl** of Steinach unter Endsee of being witches. Brandt was cautioned for defamation. See RStA A739 fols 441r–44r, 446r–53v, 456r, 458r–59r, 462r–v, 463r–v, 464r–65v, 468r–69v, 471r–72r, 473r–76r; A857 fols 499r–500v.

(6)  In 1627 **Margaretha Hörberin** of the Siechen mill confessed that she had had sex with Satan and had flown to several witches' sabbaths. She was kept in council custody for several months while her case was investigated, but this was to thwart her overlord, the Catholic monastery of Komburg, from encroaching on council jurisdiction and sending Hörberin to almost certain execution for witchcraft in Würzburg. See RStA A886 fols 268r, 269r–72v, 273r–76r, 277r–78v, 279r, 280r–81v, 282r, 283r–86v, 287r, 289r–90v, 291r–92r, 293r–97r, 298r–300r, 301r, 302r–v, 303r–4r, 305r–5v, 306r–7r.

(7)  In 1628 Barbara Röestin, a maidservant in Rothenburg, claimed that her mistress, **the wife of former Bürgermeister Georg Bezold**, was a witch. Röestin was banished for defamation. See RStA A888 fols 1r–3r, 5r–v, 7r–9r, 13r–v, 15r–v, 17r–23v; B665 fols 21r–23v.

(8)  In 1628 **Magdalena Dürrin** of Standorf was taken into custody on suspicion of infanticide. She freely confessed to having killed her baby and to various acts of witchcraft and was beheaded and then her remains burned. See RStA A887 545r–47r, 548r–50r, 551r–54v, 555r–60v, 561r–66r, 567r–71v, 572r–73v, 574r–75r, 576r–80r, 581r, 582r, 583r–86v, 587r, 588r–v, 589r–91r, 592r–94v.

(9)  In 1629 Margareta Härterin of Bovenzenweiler was forced by the Schönburgische cavalrymen into accusing **Anna Dieterichin** of Untereichenroth of being of a witch. The council investigated and Härterin was flogged and banished for defamation. See RStA A888 fols 595r–600r, 601r, 603r–v, 609r–12r, 606r–8r, 614r–16v, 618r–19v.

# 6. Popular Beliefs and the Reformation in Brandenburg-Ansbach

C. SCOTT DIXON

In 1589 the pastor Jacob Graeter gave an extended sermon to his parishioners in Schwäbisch Hall entitled (to cite the preamble) *Hexen oder Unholden Predigten*. Graeter spoke on the subjects of magic and witchcraft. The words 'witch', 'fiend', or 'sorcerer' were laden with significance for the sixteenth-century mind and Graeter used them to advantage. But it is doubtful whether the average parishioner induced the range of meaning implied by the clergyman: 'What we say here of sorcerers should also be understood of magicians, necromancers, purveyors of black magic, soothsayers, crystalball readers, and others of the Devil's brood.'[1] Graeter's homily was intended to make an impression on his audience; he warned against the wiles of the Evil One, and how easily man may forswear his trust in Christ and fall prey to Satan's promised 'mountain of Gold'.

In recent years, Reformation historiography has concerned itself more and more with the reception and appropriation of the ideas in sermons like *Hexen oder Unholden Predigten*, rather than with the subtleties of their invention. This has entailed a study of popular culture, which has problems of its own. According to scholars in the field, representations of popular culture were distorted or manipulated as they were set down by the observer. Written accounts of the thoughts and behaviour of the parish populace are not transparent windows on the past. In response to this textual bias, historians have begun to focus on the mediating process itself, the flow of cultural influences, and the contact between traditions of thought. And yet this new concern with the transmission and mediation of traditions has not abolished the dichotomy familiar to most studies of early modern popular culture. Two cultural traditions did exist in this period, and to distinguish

119

between a 'great' and a 'little' tradition does not necessarily elide the fact that the relationship was fluid, or that one tradition shaped or modified its counterpart. Popular culture was part of a wider context of beliefs; it was not fixed and uniform, impervious to influence.[2] With this renewed emphasis on cross-cultural inter-action in mind, the following chapter will address two aspects of popular culture and the sixteenth-century Reformation move-ment. The first section will portray manifestations of popular or 'parish' culture, the type of activity Graeter termed 'Crystalball reading', soothsaying, fortune telling, and popular magic. What was the nature of popular belief? The second section will examine the relationship between the Reformation and this stratum of local beliefs. Did the Lutheran authorities undertake a 'reform of popular culture?' If they did, how profound was its influence and how resonant was its effect?

In 1581 the pastor of Berg, Andreas Schaller, a Wittenberg-educated clergyman described in 1560 as 'pious and industrious', was brought before the chancellery officials. The charge against him was as follows: his wife, together with her maid, had sought aid from a wisewoman in Baiergrün, a neighbouring parish. The main concern for the Lutheran officials was that Schaller's traffic with this woman would look bad for the clerical estate, for it was well known (*ein gemein geschrey*) in the parish. Schaller faced the interrogations of Johann Moninger, a doctor and archivist in Kulmbach, together with the assembled clergy.[3] The pastor of Selbitz was able to get Schaller to confess that his wife had visited the Baiergrün woman, purchased herbs (*kreutter*), and fed them to the cattle. But it had all occurred without his knowledge, or so claimed Schaller. Doctor Moninger was not convinced. If Schaller knew of this woman in Baiergrün, why had he not reported her to the authorities? Moninger, twenty-one years in the service of the margrave, was certainly right. It was Schaller's clerical duty to report repeated offenders to the visitation commission. But it would have taken more than the efforts of a single pastor to banish the wisewoman of Baiergrün.[4]

For many years the pastor of Kirchleus, Pancratius Feindtel, had been instructing his parishioners to place their trust and hope 'in no one else than solely in the true eternal and omniscient God'. But in practice the opposite was happening: 'In times of pressing need many of my parishioners seek help and salvation not (as instructed) with God in Heaven, but rather from a woman and a man in Baiergrün. They hold these people in their hearts as a God.'[5] Recourse to the Baiergrün wisewoman was widespread. In the 1580s alone, parishioners from Schauenstein, Bischofsgrün, Stammbach, Harsdorf, Hof, Münchberg, Selbitz, Ködiz, Berg, and Kirchleus were cited as making the trek (or 'pilgrimage') to Baiergrün – a thirty-five mile radius. And when they got there, who did they find? Reports vary. Pancratius mentioned a woman and a man. The visitor of Hof simply mentioned 'a woman in Baiergrün'. The Schauenstein pastor cited two women: one, Margaretha Hohenberger; the other, the wife of a soldier who had died in France. And the pastor added: 'to the one, no less than to the other, a great pilgrimage has emerged'.[6]

Parishioners sought the help of the wisewoman in times of illness, to seek remedies to ill-fortune, to procure abortions, to recover stolen goods, or to learn of the future. As the Hof visitor made clear, many people believed 'that the woman of Baiergrün can advise and help with all kinds of bodily afflictions; therefore, as at other places, without doubt there are many here as well who seek her counsel and advise'.[7] In Kulmbach a clergyman re-marked that not only was she consulted 'during the sickness of men and animals' but she was often persuaded to visit many parishes (*an vil Ende geholet*) in the hope that she would bring remedies to their door. Such a housecall was a relative luxury; most people would have been faced with the situation con-fronting an official of Köditz. When his son fell sick in 1587 he rushed him to Baiergrün to seek aid, but the child died on the journey.[8] There was no scarcity of soothsayers and wisewomen in the parishes of Ansbach and Kulmbach, nor a paucity of home remedies, so the popularity of Margaretha Hohenberger of Baiergrün must have been well-earned. As late as 1603 Margaretha Vießman, answering to charges that she was a sooth-sayer, confessed that she had inherited her crystal ball (*Cristallen*) from her aunt, and her aunt in turn had received it from 'the woman of Baiergrün'.[9]

There seems to have been a fairly comprehensive network of practitioners of popular magic in the parishes of Kulmbach (cunning people, soothsayers, white witches, etc.) singled out as effective in their craft. It was difficult for the visitors to root them out, for, as the superintendent of another Lutheran principality

remarked, they often befriended one another in a fellowship of
silence.[10] Despite this silence, the source materials do offer examples of people similar to Margaretha Hohenberger of Baiergrün.
The superintendent of Hof noted that there were two people in
the district of Hof who were suspected of purveying magical remedies. They had a crystal ball and seventy-two species of herb
at their disposal.[11] The visitation protocols listed a cunning man
in Dottenheim, another in Unternesselbach, Hans Scheffer
in Heidenheim, Michael Igel of Thuisbrunn, a woman
(*Sägensprecherin*) in Equarhofen, another in Pfofeld, the cunning
woman (*weis fraw*) near Würzburg, the soothsayer of Absberg, the
soothsayer of Plech (whose reputation was widespread), a woman
in Münchberg, the barber's wife in Aha, and the shepherdess
near Köditz who blessed the people and their children in times of
illness.[12] These are just some names that failed to escape detection. No doubt the visitor of Hof was correct in assuming that
these 'Devil's vermin' worked in secret in many parishes.[13]

The same Hof visitor made another observation worth note: not
only were the 'simple, superstitious people' in the countryside
flocking to the cunning people in droves, but the prominent
(*fürnembsten*) city burgers also held 'everything they say, advise, or
do' as correct.[14]

> Last summer [wrote the pastor of Weißdorf in 1576] Junker
> Hans Eitel of Sparneck housed a public magician at his
> Weißdorf estate, maintaining him for a long time, and letting
> him soothsay for him [Hans Eitel] and other people. And when
> the pastor, as befits his office, preached against it (which
> annoyed the magician or soothsayer) he not only abused [the
> pastor] horribly, but threatened to harm him. And all of this
> was heard and tolerated by the said Hans Eitel of Sparneck.[15]

Noble women sought the services of the Köditz shepherdess. In
1569 a noblewoman sent her maid to the sexton's wife in Birk (a
soothsayer) bearing considerable gifts.[16] Barbara Fleißmann, resident of Kulmbach and wife of Johann Thomas Fleißmann, a man
on familiar terms with Imperial counsellors, was herself accused
of dealings in magic. She denied the charge, referring instead to
her German books of astronomy, and asked that she be treated
lightly 'on account of her good name and lineage'.[17]

Perhaps even more surprising than the involvement of the secular elite is the number of clergymen associated with the magical arts. Doctor Moninger's doubts about Pastor Schaller's (non)relationship with the Baiergrün wisewoman were not necessarily ill-placed. The pastor of Windsfeld, Georg Schneider, promised the Absberg soothsayer one thaler for her services after an infamous drinking bout.[18] In Oberferrieden, the clergyman's wife was also accused of treating with cunning people to heal her husband's illness, going so far as to invite them into the house.[19] Caspar Gunther of Neudrossenfeld was valued for his talents with herbs, but he had to be careful lest he fall suspect of alchemy.[20] For the clergy, there was a fine line between indulgence of popular magic and abetting unwanted superstitions. Clerical reactions were correspondingly varied. Faced with the suspicion of the consistory, the incumbent in Kairlindach decided to throw all of his arcane books into a fire.[21]

In view of the fact that recourse to prophesy, soothsaying, divining, adjurations, blessings, protective healing, or any other form of 'magic' was outlawed by both the ecclesiastical and the secular authorities, it needs to be explained why these popular remedies remained so dominant, and just what it was they were thought to accomplish. A contemporary scholar has concluded that popular magic was 'undoubtedly a form of cultural practice concerned with mastering the exigencies of material and daily life, and specifically the processes of production and reproduction, the maintenance of physical and spiritual well-being, the preservation of property, and the management of social relations'.[22] This definition chimes with the comments of contemporaries. A return form Neudrossenfeld (1575) offers a summary:

> Magic and recourse to soothsayers have become very common on account of [the frequency of] theft; and it follows from this that many use magic in times of illness, and bring these soothsayers to themselves. These same people [*teüffels banner*] teach the parishioners many kinds of unpleasant arts for the cattle's food and health; many times they make innocent people suspect, and show how they can cause people to die.[23]

Other clergy, in their assessments of the purpose of magic, included the desire to recover stolen goods, to locate a lost person, to bewitch or correct the mind of an acquaintance, to still pain, to deaden remorse, to purge melancholy, to liven the crops, to tempt the weather, to save the life of a child, or to catch a thief. The function of popular magic was to answer those urgent needs of the parishioner that could not be met in any other way. The common denominator was the need. In a pre-industrial society, this might apply to even the most basic situations and desires confronting man. The sheer reach of its claims reveals magic's centrality in the parishioners' lives.

In general, the nature of popular beliefs in Ansbach and Kulmbach, in so far as they are preserved in the source materials, corresponds to the popular practices common to medieval and modern Europe.[24] Some talents – healing for instance, or the power to foresee – might be the preserve of local cunning people and soothsayers, but recourse to popular magic remained an overarching means by which the average parishioner dealt with the exigencies of sixteenth-century parish life. According to a Kulmbach official in 1592, not a single day passed in his district without a complaint about magic coming to his notice.[25] The Reformation did not cleanse Ansbach and Kulmbach of popular magic and its practitioners, despite the fact that it was a conscious goal of the movement and its leaders. Lutheranism did not seduce a people into betraying their traditions of belief. Such popular beliefs, and the 'superstitions' attendant upon them, were the manifestations of a parish mentality which remained unchanged throughout the first century of reform.

For the Lutheran clergy, it seemed that their preaching was in vain. Pastors repeatedly gave sermons on the evils of magic, the wiles of the Devil, and (more to the point) the vanity of a trust in powers other than those of Christ.[26] But the people would not surrender their beliefs.[27] In the final decades of the century, it was not uncommon for the higher clergy in Kulmbach and Bayreuth to refer to this stubbornness as *Sicherheit* – denoting security, certainty, confidence, a trust in alternative powers, and all at religion's expense. The physician and demonologist Johann Weyer (1515–88) thought the root cause of such 'foolish work of the Devil' was just this lack of belief in Christ, an *Unglaubigkeit der Menschen* (admittedly, he adds, less widespread in lands where the Gospel was preached), which left man predisposed to favour magic (and thus Satan) over the salvation-including faith in

Christt.[28] No compromise was brooked between religion and magic; the superstitious man, as Weyer wrote, was a man without faith. 'It is startling to hear', concluded the Ansbach council in 1569, 'that despite the pure preaching of the efficacious and salvation-inducing word of God, people should be found who are dependent upon magic and superstitious things.'[29] Recourse to magic, as the 1533 church ordinance observed, remained a panacea for the 'simple peasants' whose weak powers of reasoning could not think of any other explanation for the strange or unusual.[30]

Thus it was left to the Lutheran authorities to mark the boundaries between popular magic and religion. In doing so, the reformers not only drafted a catalogue of forbidden beliefs, unprecedented in its intimacy, they also asked the parishioners to betray their deepest convictions. Historians have labelled this process 'the reform of popular culture' or the 'acculturation of the rural world'. Unlike earlier medieval attempts at reform, which were sporadic, localised, hampered by primitive networks of communication and law enforcement, both the sixteenth-century Protestant and the Catholic drives to enforce a unified faith were guided by a much more systematic and articulate programme. Robert Muchembled views the emergence of the modern state as the essential engine behind this process.[31] The intrusion of the state, going so far as to effect a 'destructuration' of the traditional social context, shattered the relative peace enjoyed by the practitioners of popular beliefs.[32] Other historians see the process as a more static intellectualisation: the process of reform, in this instance the Counter-Reformation, represents the actual 'Christianisation' of the rural masses through indoctrination.[33] These are sibling ideas of the more general view of confessionalisation and the multifaceted influences seen as engendered or accelerated by the Reformation (or Counter-Reformation) movement.[34] Here, for our purposes, the consequences may be seen as twofold: the extension of the influence of the state to the realm of parish practice, and the subsequent indoctrination of the faith.

There is no doubt that the Reformation in Brandenburg Ansbach-Kulmbach presented the broad stratum of popular beliefs with a threat. And although, as has been implied above, the first century of reform did not eradicate these beliefs, there is reason to believe that some parishioners felt themselves to be under siege. In 1536, with the second visitation, the visitors were instructed to examine the midwives to determine whether the women were employing 'superstitious charms and words' in order to facilitate birth. By 1578 this concern had extended beyond this traditional subsection of the village population (known for their suspect remedies) to include the specialists of popular magic (*zauberer, segensprecher, wahrsager*) or indeed any member of the parish.[35] Secular injunctions followed suit. The 1516 Brandenburg Criminal Court Ordinance called for an investigation of the type of magic used by the defendant (*mit was wortten oder wercken*) and whether the magic could be reworked. In 1582, when it was reissued, the same section – *So der Gefragte Zauberey bekennet* – was appended with the order. 'So should also be asked: From whom such magic was learned, how it came to be known, whether such magic has been used against more people, and whom, and what harm occurred as a result.'[36] Hopeful of banishing the Baiergrün wisewoman, the Hof superintendent issued the following orders:

> Therefore it should be investigated, and notice should be taken, whether there are many, and who, and in what instances people seek her advice, and what means she uses. Otherwise it could well be that charmers and witches and similar people are secretly in the parish. Thus the strictest observance should be kept; and in the case that one or more is accused and found, they should be made known to the authorities.[37]

The Lutheran clergy worked in more subtle ways as well. As Stuart Clark has noted, Protestant demonology placed greater weight on the theological implications of recourse to magic. Lutheran authors stressed that demonic agency could only work within the limits determined by the divine. Unpleasant events were 'allowed' by God to test the faith of the people.[38] 'So that He tests the pious and Godfearing in their faith, whether they remain steadfast in misery as well as bliss.'[39] Two corollaries follow: first, to trust in magic is to abandon faith; second, all forms of magic necessarily imply the intervention of the Devil. Protestant pastors began to focus on the episodes of daily life and see the Devil at every turn.

One hears daily [wrote Ansbach clergyman Andreas Althamer] of the hideous deeds effected by the Devil. There many thousand are struck dead; there a ship goes down with many people beneath the sea; there a land perishes, a city, a village; there someone stabs himself to death; there someone hangs himself; there someone drowns himself; there someone loses his head ...[40]

Common and uncommon misfortunes that had previously been countered and explained by recourse to the realm of popular beliefs were now invested with notion of diabolism. Scholars speak of the 'theologisation' of traditional folklore.[41] Magic, misfortune, and the mysterious were attributed to the Devil and his tireless allies: witches, sorcerers, soothsayers, and cunning men.

The parishioners grew wary of recourse to magic, but not because the 'reform of popular culture' convinced the peasantry it was wrong in principle; rather, they soon began to recognise that the forbidden practice of magic (*Zauberei*) – now strongly equated with the Devil – might elicit the attention of the authorities. Very few people were safe from accusation. Practitioners of blessings and spells were brought before the clergy on a regular basis and told to abandon their crafts. Often they replied that 'they did not know it was wrong' along with the promise 'to abstain from such things'.[42] Other parishioners, realising that they were dabbling in forbidden matters, either defended their actions (such as a reference to the 'natural' power of their herbs) or distanced themselves from the clergy.[43] The old soothsayer in Dottenheim simply refused to enter the church.[44] The shepherd of Mönchsondheim did not attend communion 'on account of his blessing'.[45] Sixteenth-century parishioners understood that the church represented a real menace to the autonomy of their beliefs. 'Say nothing to the clergyman (*Pfaffen*)', was how a Franconian shepherd, learned in the craft, advised his clients, 'don't confess and don't take communion, otherwise [my] art will not help.'[46] But the church would not go away, and so the people were forced to take shelter from the threat.

The 'reform of popular culture' in the sixteenth century thus induced an unprecedented process of dissimulation.[47] Feeling themselves under attack, the parishioners began to look for ways to deflect the threat without abandoning their beliefs or implicating themselves. In many ways this was a 'functional' or a social process, with a scapegoat, such as a witch, bearing the brunt of transition. The strategy is analogous to the dissimulation exercised by sixteenth-century scholars who, when addressing contentious issues, would take shelter in the ambiguity of their writing and look for scapegoats in their texts. [48] The range of dissimulation was no less complex at the parish level. Historians have noted for some time that the static model of popular versus elite culture (to use two applicable terms) and the emergence of the latter at the expense of the former is too reified. [49] As Carlo Ginzburg has recently demonstrated in his work on the witches' sabbath, many conceptual inheritances form the early-modern period might be seen as 'the hybrid result of a conflict between folk culture and learned culture'. [50] Parish beliefs were not passively altered by the encroaching state. Popular culture was willing to adapt to the religious environment in order to survive.

Here, in a study situated in a single century, it is not feasible to assess the impact of the Reformation on the popular mind with any real authority. All that can be said with certainty is that in Brandenburg Ansbach-Kulmbach the Reformation did not purge the parishes of popular magic. The actual influence of the Reformation is a rather more complex matter and deserves a broader study. Nevertheless, by using materials that amplify the conflict between traditional parish culture and the church, it is possible to illustrate aspects of the initial impact of the reform movement on the parishioners' expressed beliefs. The most detailed accounts of this process are found in trials against witchcraft; and one of the most detailed witchcraft trials of sixteenth-century Brandenburg Ansbach–Kulmbach was the process against the sexton's wife of Birk, Katherina Hoser.

In the face of the emergent Lutheran church, no one was more at threat, especially as the sixteenth century passed into the seventeenth, than the noted wisewoman, the sorcerer, or, as she came to be categorised, the witch. Compared with the neighbouring dioceses of Bamberg and Würzburg, Brandenburg Ansbach-Kulmbach did not prosecute a large number of women, but the principality was not immune from the 'witch-craze' which swept through the Empire during this period, even if it kept its fear in relative check. The laws against maleficent magic were extracted from the *Bambergensis* and, as embodied in the 1582 reissuing under Georg Friedrich, called for punishment equivalent to that for heresy – death by fire. (Magic without harmful intent was to be punished 'according to the circumstances of the case'.) Thus the authorities did have the legal writ to try suspected witches and burn them at the stake, though the instances appear to have been few.

Nevertheless, the threat of witchcraft was serious enough to encourage the margrave to assemble his leading secular and ecclesiastical authorities at Heilsbronn in 1591 to discuss the matter. During this gathering, the titular abbot Adam Francisci drafted his *Generalinstruktion von den Trutten*, wherein a call to arms against the 'curse' of witchcraft was sounded. Citing the authority of the Old Testament, Francisci called for increased prosecution of such people, 'big or small', and entreated the margrave to warn his subjects of the dangers of the art. In that same year, twenty-two witches were executed in Bayreuth.[51] As in other territories in the Empire, the late sixteenth and early seventeenth century marks the apogee of the campaign against witchcraft in Brandenburg Ansbach-Kulmbach; but the glut of trials was in part only a belated affirmation of steps that had already been taken, if only on a smaller scale. In Kulmbach, processes against the local witch began many years before.

On 7 April 1569 Georg Nürnberger, an official in Creußen, informed the Kulmbach council that Katherina Hoser, wife of the Birk sexton Bastian Hoser, had been cited before the authorities because of the suspicion that she was a soothsayer.[52] She had already been summoned before the clergy on one occasion, where she was told to renounce her 'superstitions' and surrender her soothsaying stone (*wetterstein*) to the superintendent.[53] And indeed, this is what Katherina did. But she did not hold fast to her promise to abstain and so she was again taken into custody. In fact, if the report of the clergyman Nikolaus Friederich is correct, Katherina was somewhat audacious on her return to the parish. At the inn, she is claimed to have boasted that: 'recently she had overcome nine clergymen at the chaplain's house in Creußen. She could overcome other people as well.' Kunigund Streber, as she sat cutting fabric, said to Katherina that she had heard of the confiscation of her stone. To this, Katherina replied: 'as you might have guessed'.[54] But this boldness did little to help her case, and she was forced to answer to the clergy.

It seems that Katherina had amassed a considerable reputation as a wisewoman, or soothsayer, and was consulted by the neighbouring parishioners in times of crisis. A maid from Goldkronach, for example, was sent to Birk by her noble patron (bearing gifts) in the hope that Katherina could fathom if a woman friend, big in body, was expecting. 'She wants to see', explained the maid, 'whether or not it is a child.' After a quick look into her stone Katherina declared that, although it looked like a child, it was not. On another occasion a neighbour asked what could be done with her sick cow. Katherina suggested that the animal should drink from a skull. She purveyed a multitude of remedies for humans as well. Hansen Hoffner's wife, 'swollen and sick' in body, was told that she was ill from too much cold water and a cure was prescribed. Other women were advised to smear themselves in wine. Hans Grebner, suffering from gout, was once blessed by Katherina; in fact underwent a four-week diet of wine in place of water to ensure that the cure would take effect.[55] She could also probe less manifest mysteries. She had a necklace of shiny stones used to discern 'what was sin and what not' in a manner comparable to *ein priester in den Buch*.[56] And she could locate lost people – or such was the hope of Barbara Raüben, who was worried over the disappearance of her husband and turned to Katherina for help.[57]

There is no clear indication how Katherina's activities first came to the attention of the authorities. The diversity of her clientele, coupled with the breadth of her expertise (hinted at by the types of problems brought her way), would suggest that it was not difficult for the clergy to find her. In later inquisitions the examiners often coloured a factual statement with the prologue: 'Since she is held to be (*beschrait*) a soothsayer and sorcerer in Creußen and other surrounding places ...'. But it may have been the case that social tensions gave rise to the accusation. Often the village witch had close ties with her accusers, or at least there was usually a more intimate connection – beyond the supposed act of maleficent magic – between the victim and the witness.[58] Later testimony from Katherina herself seems to single out Barbara Raüben, who turned to her after Katherina's meeting with the clergy.

In the process of consulting three different soothsayers over the whereabouts of her husband, Barbara Raüben received three different answers: 'The first had said, he lies under the town hall in a well; the second, he lies in a storage room [*Kemmath*]; the third, he lies in a cellar and old wall.' Finally, desperately, she turned to Katherina, who in turn informed her (with some misgiving) that she could indeed see Contz Raüben in her weatherstone: he was at the house of Georg Prebitzer settling an account with the maid. Then, said Katherina, he disappeared: 'He must have used magic, so that she could no longer see him in the stone.'[59] But she could see other things in the stone, in particular the vision of Barbara Raüben hitting her husband with a kitchen spoon. She also claimed that Contz, as he would not appear in the stone, might be dead by his own hand. What was worse, she added, he may have been spirited away by the Devil. In any case, were Katherina to see him, she would inform the town officials. No doubt all of these unwanted images caused a rift between Katherina and Barbara, for soon after the latter left Katherina began to cry, and told her child and husband the reason:

> When her daughter and husband asked her what was wrong, she said to them that she had seen in her stone, that because she had recently promised the gathered clergy at Creußen she would no longer soothsay, she fears now that Barbara Raüben would betray her, and that they would have cause to place her under arrest.[60]

In this instance her prophecy was correct.

Georg Nürnberger was instructed by the Kulmbach councillors to interrogate the now incarcerated Katherina using a résumé of questions sent to him for that purpose.[61] Katherina Hoser's period of imprisonment, the number of hearings to which she was subjected, the questions put before her, and the torture used to elicit the wanted response, were in part a consequence of the 'learned' stereotype of the witch that beset continental Europe in the sixteenth century. The learned notion of witchcraft focused on the pact with Satan and the nocturnal Sabbaths.[62] Katherina insisted at the outset that she did not exercise maleficent magic, that she did not harm people or animals, and, more significantly, she denied the accusations, as couched in the questions, that she was in fellowship with the Devil or that she had inherited her talents under his tutelage. Rather, Katherina said she found the stone under the grass on a hillock and that 'perhaps God had given this luck to her'. She was able to see in the stone the cure for her ailing father, for she was a 'Sabbath daughter' (*güldes süntags kindt*).[63] But the authorities thought she was hiding the truth, so the trial continued, though now with the application of torture to loosen her tongue.

The questions drawn up for the first interrogation (12 April 1569) and sent to Georg Nürnberger were true to the logic of the learned view of the witch, taking for granted the demonic pact and thus tautologically worded, always trying to uncover the particulars and the motives of the covenant. This appears to have worked its way into Katherina's fears. She began to speak of devils, and she soon realised that she was seen as a danger to the church. One night in April while Katherina was in jail, (according to a story she told the wife of a Creußen official [*Statknechtin*]), some tiny black devils appeared in her stone, as they had before, and told her that the clergy were on their way to see her. Katherina asked the woman whether it was true. 'And when the woman answered yes,' recounted Justus Bloch, the Bayreuth superintendent, '[Katherina] had responded that she knew it well, for the little black men had said it to her.'[64] Justus Bloch had indeed been informed of this case by the authorities, who feared that Katherina's actions (and perhaps denials) occurred 'from the blinding of the Evil One, [who] can easily seduce the poor women'. Bloch was ordered to travel to Creußen with other clergy in order to interrogate her.[65]

During Bloch's first session with Katherina, she spoke of her maltreatment at the hands of her demons in her cell.[66] It is clear at this stage that Katherina was suffering from her exposure to torture and was willing to confess to Bloch's accusations to escape the pain. After Bloch's repeated insistence that 'such could not happen without a pact with the Devil' she succumbed to his charges: 'That she spoke with the Devil; that the arts which she knew were promised by him; and that he had asked her to be his, which she also agreed to.'[67] She also confessed that the Devil forbade her to attend communion or to pray. Her only reservation was raised when it was suggested that the man who appeared to her in the stone had a cloven foot (*Geißfuß*). Bloch, however, had no such uncertainty – 'we knew full well beforehand that it was the Devil, were he to have these or any other feet.'[68] Finally, on the Thursday sitting, after persistent questioning designed to expose her dealings with the 'Evil One', Katherina looked into her stone as she sat in the presence of Bloch, the pastors of

Creußen and Gesees, the city scribe, and Georg Nürnberger. The scribe recorded reactions:

> When she looked in the stone she began to shake, shiver, and grow pale. She threw the stone away on the table and cried: 'Ah, Margaretha, he has a cloven foot! I want my life long never to look in the stone again. Oh, Oh, that God in Heaven should be merciful, I am a conjurer of demons [*Teüfels bannerin*].'[69]

Bloch tried to console the woman in his own way: 'You see Katherina, as you did not know you were in league with the Devil, we had to convince you with your own art.'[70] Katherina confessed to a confederacy with the Devil; all the other implications of the demonological stereotype followed in train.

It is worth stressing the extent to which Katherina was manipulated, both physically and mentally, to extract her confessions. A letter from the Kulmbach council (4 May 1569) advised the executioner to be wary of too much torture, since she was weak in body.[71] But this did not exempt her from bouts of torture (*Taümenstockh und Zügkh*). The executioner was once reprimanded for leaving Katherina strapped to the rack for several hours while he drank wine at the inn.[72] Such torture, in train with the unremitting references to the Devil in the interrogations, the leading questions and the learned sophistries – all of this forced Katherina to admit to anything that was asked. But when she had recovered, and when it seemed safe to recant, she denied her previous statements. In a letter signed Katherina Adlerin (her maiden name) she 'revoked and retracted' all she had confessed about her relations with the Devil. Her words were, she claimed, the product of torture.[73] She could not bear that she had to betray what she perceived as her exoneration of a higher power:

> 'Oh, woe my poor soul', cried Katherina one night from her cell, 'a holy angel from Heaven has come and whispered in my ear and said I have not answered correctly. It is not true and I do myself a wrong. I should recant, otherwise it will not go well with me.'[74]

It would be wrong to abstract from this isolated case of supposed witchcraft fixed laws governing the interchange of ideas, much as if an anthropologist were to describe a global ethnology based upon a single clan in a single village. The subject of witch-craft in the early modern period, however, is hardly suffering from a poverty of research, and there is nothing especially unusual about this case.[75] The trial of Katherina Hoser does not speak in a vacuum. And although a witchcraft trial was specific event following a predetermined logic, in many ways it was no more than the process of reform situated and accelerated, with a 'popular' offender and an 'elite' jury. As Serge Gruzinski has written (in similar circumstances though a different context):

> it remains true that only these individual experiences enable the historian to reconstruct the hazards of, the trial and error experienced in, an acculturation; to grasp the emergence of syncretisms and the sudden or progressive reorganization of a complex of cultural characteristics – in short, to analyse a dy-namics that is generally obliterated by the static description of a symbolic system or of a mentality.[76]

The process against Katherina Hoser can be used to illustrate the relationship between the Lutheran church and parish beliefs in the sixteenth century. In what follows, the trial of Katherina Hoser will be analysed to show the response of a parishioner faced with the learned stereotype of the witch and the gradual sedimen-tation of this notion in her mind.

Central to the concerns of the inquisitors was the provenance of the stone. Question 2 of the 15 April examination made clear their intention to know: 'From whom she received the stone which she used for her magic.' Under a small patch of grass on a hillock in the village where she was her original answer. She found the stone at a propitious moment, as her father was quite ill; and she was able to see in the stone the reason for his misfor-tune along with the possible cure.[77] When pressed, she claimed that God had given her the luck to discover the stone. As a later deposition read, 'such was given to her by God, and not from the Devil'. By May, following upon her subsequent recantation, the story changed, but essentially it was true to her claim that she came upon the stone in all innocence. A woman named Anna Hörlin had given her a stone, in addition to a verse used to conjure its powers, many years before.[78] But she rejected all hints of association with the Devil.

After the initial April interrogations, the application of torture, and the recurrent impression of the demonological theme, Katherina changed her story. She confessed to visitations by 'little black devils' in her Creußen cell. And, more significantly, when told it was impossible for her to have found the stone unaided, without danger to her soul, Katherina answered: 'At first there was a small dark man who appeared and said she should lift the grass. She would find the stone there.' When asked who she thought this man was, she answered that: 'she did not know, [and] does not think it the Devil, but rather God'.[79] As she told Bloch and the pastor of Gesees, this diminutive man had advised her: 'Look under the tuft of grass beside where you sit, there is a stone. Grab it, and you will see what your father has, where he got it, and how he can be cured.'[80] For Bloch, this was clearly the Devil; it was not possible that this little man would have appeared to her 'without explicit confederation or union with Satan'.

When this tiny devil reappeared, he was no longer external to the stone, working as an advocate, but in the stone, part of the stone. A report of her statement, drawn up by a secular official (27 April 1569), continues her story about the discovery of the stone on the hillock: 'In which stone, a small black man (*Menlein*) stood, who had a body, and hands, like any other man.' She added that she did not know whether he had a cloven foot (since she had not looked), nor whether 'such black man was the Devil ... she does not know'. And she denied the (implicit) accusation of having conjured the man to the stone. He had been there when she found it.[81] Katherina now attributed her powers of foretelling and prophecy to the man in the stone. It was at this stage that Bloch forced her to look at the man's feet, and they were, as everyone expected, cloven. 'She had not considered that this man was a devil,' is how the report was worded. 'She had thought it was God.'

In the final version, the presence of God was altogether resigned and Satan himself took full stage, thus replacing the little black demon. In a later report (5 May 1569), written by the secular authorities, and subsequent to a bout of torture, Katherina spoke of the Devil's appearance. In 1563, on her way to Creußen, 'at first a small dark man had come toward her, and he grew ever longer and ever bigger until finally he was as big as her husband. This was the Devil'.[82] Here, quite literally, the figure of

Satan evolves from the smaller demon and approaches her on numerous occasions, with 'black clothing, also dark and big like her
husband' and seduces her into a covenant. Katherina confirms
the learned stereotype: She agreed 'to be his'; she had sexual relations with him, finding his body of 'a really cold nature'; he
promised to teach her maleficent magic, how to harm people and
animals; and he admonished her to stay clear of the church.
Moreover, he takes pains to protect her from the clergy. He
warned against a trip to Creußen, where he believed she would be
imprisoned, tortured, and burned; and when his forecast was partially realised, he visited her in her cell, offering to free her from
the chains and 'fly out through the window' into the night air.
Katherina looked to God (she claimed) and his power was
undone. She then looked to her captors for guidance.

Modern historiography is still coming to grips with the concept
of *mentalité* and the grounds for assuming a uniformity of thought
when a multiplicity is, historically, more the norm.[83] Some scholars, most notably anthropologists, have moved away from the
'history of ideas' approach to the past – which isolates certain intellectual trends for analysis – to investigations of how ideas were
actually used, how they were reproduced and modified, and what
sort of factors might influence their composition, transmission,
and codification.[84] An approach of this nature, more concerned
with ideas in context than the study of ideas through time, seems
most suited to an investigation of the effect of Lutheran thought
on the rural populace. The reform of popular culture was a long-
term fluid process; it included the birth of some ideas and the
conflation of others. Rather than simply substituting one belief
system for another, one vernacular *mentalité* for a more learned alternative, the effect of the reform of popular culture on the
parishioner might be seen as more dynamic, more of an exchange. The case of Katherina Hoser lends itself to just such an
investigation. While her confession was told in different drafts at
different times, and the narrative was not so ordered as it is represented above, a gradual variation in the story does unfold, and it
does so around the object of scrutiny: Katherina's stone.

At the beginning of her testimony, Katherina claims she found
her stone by chance, rather good chance, and when this is
doubted it becomes a moment of chance, she suggests, engin-
eered by God. Under further scrutiny, and further accusations

that the powers of the stone must implicate its user with the Devil, Katherina distances herself from its discovery and instead surrenders herself to the clerical notion that she was entrapped in a realm of (demonic) power in strict opposition to the church. The idea is at first still alien; the demon must cajole her, trick her, dupe her into discovering the stone. But Katherina does not yet think she acted improperly and the stone is still a neutral object. With time, however, the stone itself takes on the substance of their accusations: it becomes the property of the Devil, and indeed the Devil (or perhaps a minion) resides within it. The world of the forbidden, the prohibited, a world in strict opposition to sanctioned Lutheran beliefs, is seen in microcosm, and it dwells in Katherina's stone. Once this is conceded, the full implications can no longer be denied, and Katherina confesses to a confederacy with the Devil. The demon in the stone grows to full size, meets her at times she can remember, assumes the likeness of her husband, wears clothes she can describe, and she is – literally – seduced. Katherina now imagines herself in a world created by the clergy.[85]

Scholars have traced a similar process at work in the conquered lands of Mesoamerica. Christianity was only assimilated (and never completely) through a gradual acculturation. In the first instance, alien concepts – such as an omnipotent, benevolent God – were only adopted in so far as they could be embodied in the religious system. The Devil, for example, was overlaid upon those gods with malevolent characteristics, and thus a degree of syncretism took place; following this, the knowledge of prehispanic religion ebbed, and the Devil assumed a more 'European' significance; finally the old religion evaporated almost completely, leaving nothing but 'disjointed structural residues' and the devils of old shorn of their former meanings. Not only did such a 'slide toward Christianity' – viewed over the course of centuries – divest Indian beliefs of their original significance, but by the eighteenth century popular (Indian) piety went so far as to express itself through the written word, and so order was imposed upon a world of heterogeneous beliefs.[86] This process of acculturation is similar to the model suggested by the Hoser trial: in both examples the people were not converted, beliefs were not abandoned. Aspects of popular belief were simply invested with different values until the original context of thought was shattered.

Unlike the reform of morality, which relied upon the imposition of restraint and on displays of power, the Lutheran campaign against popular beliefs found its forum in the parish mind. As has been demonstrated above, the Reformation did not eradicate recourse to magic; but with the threat of punishment ever present, the parishioners gradually integrated the ideas of the church and began to consider their own beliefs in relation to the ideas of the 'elite'. Rather than consider their tradition of thought as at odds with the church, the parishioners first assimilated the idea of demonic intervention to explain away their reasons for recourse to popular magic. It was only later, when popular magic could not avoid the brush of diabolism, when each rite or gesture had a corresponding tie with the Devil, that magic and religion could no longer be held in separation. Popular beliefs were slowly invested with a changing set of values as the parish mind was drawn into a more systematic context of thought. This is not the erasure of one tradition of beliefs by another, but its gradual distortion. By the seventeenth century, there is reason to talk of 'Protestant forms of magic', as this process of reconfiguration occurred.[87]

The very practice of investigation, the rules and logic of inquiry, forced order on the eclectic world of popular beliefs. Again the witchcraft trial is the archetype of the process. In seventeenth-century Franconia each trial pursued an equivalent end: to discover where the magic was learned – whether from the Devil or one of his brood – how it was facilitated, with what words or things, how many other people were implicated, and what reasons led a soul to witchcraft.[88] The authorities were in search of tidy answers to sorted questions and they forced the parishioners to organise their thoughts. 'It is not appropriate or fitting to answer here "it must have been" "it must have been",' was how the inquisitors advised their victims, 'rather you should just answer yes or no.'[89]

For the parishioners, in the face of this reforming threat, the most immediate defensive reaction was that of social accusation. In the search for a first cause, for the source of the magic, the parishioners turned to one another in order to deflect the attention of the authorities. In the case of Katherina Hoser, the final days of her inquisition unearthed hitherto unmentioned names and thus the reach of the investigation broadened. But it is likely that over the course of time select practices were signally discredited or considered suspect, and so the parishioners were then forced to view certain forms of magic in relation to others. Gradually a template of order – from the forbidden to the allowable – emerged, and the two worlds of magic and religion were given firm boundaries.[90] This is a process that would need a long-term investigation in order for the historian to prove the point, but a glimpse at the events in sixteenth-century Brandenburg Ansbach-Kulmbach would suggest that a start had been made. The Reformation did not put an end to the diversity of parish culture, but it was the death knell for private beliefs.

# 7. Why was Private Confession so Contentious in Early Seventeenth-Century Lindau?

J. C. WOLFART

## I

Auricular confession[1] was instituted officially by the Fourth Lateran Council. Canon 21 compelled all Christians to make a full confession of all sins once a year; only after hearing the full extent of a parishioner's sins could a confessor assign penance and grant absolution. How strictly these instructions were followed in the south German imperial city of Lindau is unknown; however, it appears that by the late fourteenth century the local clergy considered the administration of auricular confession one of the defining powers of their office. In 1395 it was the last of the parish priest's powers to be shared with the recently arrived Franciscans.[2]

Lindauers almost certainly abandoned the practice of auricular confession some time in the early 1520s. By 1532, when the reformers Wolfgang Capito (Strassburg) and Johann Zwick (Constance) came to Lindau to regulate church practices, a relatively formal 'general confession' (*Allgemeinbeichte*) was already in use. It was marked by (i) a pastoral warning of the dangers involved in the 'unworthy' reception of the sacrament;[3] (ii) a general acknowledgement of sins; (iii) a general absolution of the whole congregation.[4] From 1555 onwards church registers (*Kirchenbücher*) give a clear idea of official practice. By this time Lindauers took communion every Sunday – unlike the neighbouring Swiss, who only took it once a year – and the celebration of

140

the sacrament was preceded by two 'open confessions' (*öffentliche Beicht*). The confession formula consisted of (i) the warning against the 'unworthy' reception of the sacrament; (ii) the actual self-examination and 'confession' (*Beichtfrage*); (iii) a collective affirmative response; (iv) a general absolution.[5] This mode of general confession remained much the same throughout the rest of the century.[6] In the early seventeenth century, however, there developed considerable ministerial pressure on the government, which resisted vigorously, to institute 'individual confession' (*Einzelbeichte*), also known as 'private confession' (*Privatbeichte*). For example, in 1620 the only printer in Lindau, Hans Georg Brem, had his press confiscated for publishing an unsanctioned pamphlet by the minister Marcus Zangmeister, the main thrust of which was to advocate private confession.[7] And then, in 1626, the government reversed its position and, in the face of staunch popular opposition, tried to introduce Lutheran-style confession, 'a private confession in the church'.

What was this 'Lutheran-style' confession, and how, if at all, did it distinguish itself from previous Lindavian practice and from other evangelical doctrines? Luther himself had initially attacked auricular confession because of its connection with the papal claim to the power of the keys, and, according to contemporary accounts, attendance of auricular confession at Wittenberg dropped dramatically after 1521.[8] By 1523, however, Luther was advocating individual doctrinal examination as a precondition for receiving the sacrament and, although technically distinct from auricular confession, the practice was soon recognised as a compulsory 'private confession'.[9] Nevertheless, the Lutheran distinction between 'open' (*öffentlich*) and 'secret' (*heimlich*) sins undermined the compulsion to confess each and every sin. Thus article XI of the Augsburg Confession specified private confession but stated that one needed only to tell one's confessor those sins one could remember in order to receive absolution from Christ.[10]

The Zwinglian position on private confession was rather more straightforward than the Lutheran one. Zwingli, and after him Bullinger, maintained that since there was no scriptural basis for private confession, one should not tolerate it.[11] Moreover, private confession did not enjoy the legitimacy of past use or custom; there were no obvious advantages over general confession; and, finally, potential corruption and communal disruption far outweighed any of the conceivable advantages of private confession.[12] Lastly, the office of the confessor presented Zwingli with certain problems since, in contrast to both Luther and Calvin, he did not recognise any form of spiritual office. On earth all authority was temporal and resided solely in the magistracy; ideally a pastor was a prophet to the people and in practice he was the magistrates' advisor.[13] It was here, too, that Zwinglian doctrine distinguished itself from that of Butzer and Calvin. Both Butzer and Calvin held that a guardian/pastoral office (*Wächteramt*) existed to administer and enforce the first five commandments. Moreover, they found some scriptural basis for their conception and favoured private confession over general confession because they anticipated some advantages for the execution of their *Wächteramt*.

The question remains, however, how is one to assess early seventeenth-century Lindauers' interest in the mode of confession practised in their church, especially since theological debates appear to have been marginal to that interest? E. Roth and C. Klein, both studying the Reformation in Siebenbürgen, have identified private confession and absolution as a 'doctrine of distinction' (*Unterscheidungslehre*), much like predestination or eucharistic teaching.[14] Private confession had been a key issue in the Reformation, remained a shibboleth for confessional identity, and could be used for confessional identification.[15] For example, in Siebenbürgen in the 1570s and 1580s private confession was increasingly associated with access to the sacrament and the power of the keys. Since 'the keys are an instrument more suited to the purification of the commune than to the comforting assurance of personal salvation',[16] church discipline (Butzerian/Calvinist) was evidently winning out over (Lutheran) pastoral care. In the first quarter of the seventeenth century in Siebenbürgen Cryptocalvinism was a major force; its hallmark was the abandonment of private confession.[17]

Where did Lindauers position themselves in relation to this 'doctrine of distinction', private confession? First of all, accusations of Calvinism were indeed levelled at the senior minister Alexius Neukomm, when he resisted the introduction of private confession. On the other hand, Neukomm similarly denounced individual officials and the whole government as Calvinists.[18] Early on in his career the government had denied Neukomm and the other ministers the right of excommunication;[19] later they had ruthlessly pursued Zangmeister (and the printer Brem) for advocating private confession. Moreover, the government was making efforts to enforce strict moral discipline.[20] In 1624 the consistorium or marriage court had been elevated to the exalted status of Church and School Council (*Kirchen- und Schulrat*, henceforth referred to as CSC),[21] not without opposition. While Neukomm was criticised for leniency (and high-handedness) for readmitting adulterers to communion,[22] he berated the authorities for their inflexibility in the expulsion of those guilty of sexual misdemeanours. While the government argued the necessity of such measures for the prevention of rampant sinning and the maintenance of public peace, Neukomm was concerned for the transgressors' souls: expelling them from the church and the city, he insisted, merely drove them into the waiting arms of the Catholics.[23] So who was actually 'Cryptocalvinist'? On balance, it seems the government was, especially when viewed against Neukomm's 'Lutheran' emphasis on pastoral care.

And yet, it was the government who decided to introduce private confession. Why? According to Roth, the first generation of reformers targeted private confession because it served to preserve spiritual jurisdiction in evangelical regions.[24] Was it possible that, in the ongoing process of Reformation, or 'second Reformation',[25] private confession represented a partial restitution of distinct or semi-distinct spiritual authority, albeit under the ultimate control of the magistrates? That is, I suspect, how Neukomm saw it, although, as will be seen, many Lindauers simply feared recatholicisation.

The specific example of private confession relates to many wider questions in the historical interpretation of local religion and politics in early modern Germany. Above all, our case illuminates the striking inability of Lindauers to reconcile, in thought or in action, the triangular contraposition of amateur magistracy, clergy and administrative officials. By Alexius Neukomm's own count he had engaged in open confrontation with the government or its officers on no fewer than sixteen occasions since his appointment to the Lindau ministry in 1599; the official count was fifteen.[26] In 1624 Neukomm had publicly confronted the lawyers retained by the government, Dr Funk and Dr Heider, over the extension of their influence into church matters by means of an expanded CSC.[27] The process by which the government established control over the devotional lives of Lindauers – and, unless one is reserving the term for some purported early sixteenth-century cataclysm, that process is the Reformation – was still far from complete in the 1620s. It is in this context, for example, that the otherwise striking resemblances of seventeenth-century anti-lawyer invectives to sixteenth-century anti-clerical arguments become banal.[28] Similarly, there was a great deal of continuity in the constitutional and political structure of Lindau throughout the so-called 'long sixteenth century'. The constitutional reforms imposed on the imperial cities by Charles V in the mid-sixteenth century proved rather ineffective.[29] In fact, the guilds survived in Lindau, despite a nominally patrician consitution. Moreover, a pre-reform tension between the Council and the City Court, rivalry between 'old families' and more recent arrivals, and a certain guild-based political radicalism all endured. Most importantly, bourgeois republican ideology,[30] which played no mean role in the contest over private confession, remained potent in Lindau.

## II

**Key Figures (in order of appearance):**

| | |
|---|---|
| M. Alexius Neukomm | (Lindau's senior minister and chief opponent of private confession) |
| Dr Daniel Heider | (lawyers retained by the city; both are personal enemies of |
| Dr Ulrich Funk | Alexius Neukomm and strong proponents of private confession) |
| Andreas Neukomm | (Alexius's brother and Lindau's *Stadtamman*; as head of the City Court he is a leading figure in the Neukomm party) |
| Caspar Mezler | (a cordwainer who reported the events of 7 November 1626 from a rebel perspective) |

| Dr Georg Zaeman | (theologian from Kempten frequently consulted by the Lindau Council) |
| Dr Conrad Dietrich | (Superintendent of Ulm with family connections to Lindau) |
| Hugo of Montfort | (local count; as such he is Lindau's traditional rival and in 1627–8 he was one of two Imperial investigators into Lindau's affairs) |

My interest in private confession was first aroused by work on an anti-government uprising in the imperial city of Lindau.[31] This chapter proceeds from the position that, in German early modern urban politics, issues mattered.[32] That uprising, on the morning of 7 November 1626, was related to debates over certain issues including whether or not to introduce something called 'private confession'. Several contemporary accounts of the uprising specifically identify government plans to introduce private confession in the Lindau church as being a source of citizen ire. On the other hand, other significant narratives cite a variety of political disputes, none over private confession, as the cause of the uprising.[33] Similarly, reports of the rebels' demands do not all concur, but most of them mention that the government was forced to promise either to retain the old church constitution (*Kirchenordnung*[34]) or to shelve the planned introduction of private confession.[35] Documents produced in civic administration several months prior to the uprising reveal that there was indeed widespread unrest over the issue of private confession as early as June of that year.[36]

On 4 April 1626, the CSC had debated the introduction of private confession and, despite the anticipation of some resistance, had adopted a plan for its gradual introduction.[37] The following day the city Council decided that one of the city's five ministers should be available in the church to instruct communicants at all times. Henceforth no first-time communicant, particularly youths and servants (who were presumed to have been raised in a foreign church), was to receive the sacrament without first having been examined by a minister.[38] Unfortunately Lindau's senior minister, Magister Alexius Neukomm, who had absented himself from the previous day's CSC meeting, vehemently opposed any amendment of the church constitution and withheld his endorsement. In fact he was perceived as the instigator of a popular outcry against what the citizens and peasants believed was an attempt to reintroduce *auricular* confession; and indeed, rumours of compulsory sacramental confession and of recatholici-sation soon reached official ears. When the CSC was reconvened on 27 April to discuss measures to quell the unrest, Neukomm was again absent. When he finally did appear, by express order of the Council, he maintained his opposition to the planned intro-duction of private confession. Continued popular unrest led the Council to seek the advice or endorsement of the other two branches of civic government, the Court (*Gericht*) and the Commons (*Gemeinderat*). On 11 June the citizenry was presented with a proclamation (*Fürhalt*) from the pulpit designed to pacify them and to assure them of the government's good intentions.[39] Further attempts to muzzle Alexius Neukomm – on 21 June, 13 October and 25 October – proved fruitless, and the authoritative advice of theologians from neighbouring cities did not, as the Council had hoped, soothe tempers. Finally, on 6 November, the morning after Neukomm had delivered himself of a particularly incendiary sermon, the Council suspended him from office and banned him from the pulpit. For some reason they had failed to anticipate that popular support for the preacher and resistance to the Council could lead to violence.

To understand what the Lindau government's proposal meant, and to see why they met such fierce opposition, one must first look at what the Lindauers had practised, or thought they had practised, prior to 1626. According to one official source, private confession had been abolished along with the Catholic religion (in the 1520s). Since then the practice had been that those who wished to take the sacrament would assemble in the church prior to the Sunday sermon where a minister would read them a 'con-fession and absolution'.[40] The formula used was established in the Lindau church constitution of 1573, drawing heavily on Württemberg's 1553 church constitution. According to E. Sehling, Lindau distinguished itself from Württemberg precisely because there was no provision for the pastoral examination of individual communicants.[41] Nevertheless, thirty years prior to 1626 ministerial pressure had led to the establishment of private examinations for first-time communicants in Lindau. The practice was secured, however, not in an amendment to the church constitution, but rather in an instruction manual by the Lindau minister Samuel Lins.[42] Moreover, the private examination did not take place in the church but in the house of a minister.[43]

The official reason why it was necessary to change the practice outlined above was as follows: it had come to pass that some people, especially women who were busy with their children, came to church so late as to miss the reading of the confession formula; sometimes they did not appear until well into the pronouncement of absolution. Furthermore, not all parents and masters actually sent their children and servants to the ministers for instruction.[44] It was widely accepted that, according to scripture, people who received the sacrament in a state of unworthiness faced eternal damnation. Scripture also condemned those who administered the sacrament indiscriminately.[45] Clearly, it was important to ensure that only the worthy received the sacrament in Lindau.[46]

But how significant were such 'theological' arguments in the course of the dispute? While it is true that several authorities were cited,[47] there is no evidence for debates on the theological soundness of what was practised and what was planned. Only Alexius Neukomm argued his position with direct reference to the scriptures, two days before his suspension, when he preached the efficacy of general confession (*allgemeine Beicht*) and claimed it was equivalent to private confession. In fact, the ignorance of his opponents is revealed by the inability of various witnesses to properly identify the passage cited in Neukomm's last sermon.[48] Nevertheless, many of the arguments deployed by both proponents and opponents of private confession allude to questions of religious doctrine or even belief. It seems likely that such allusions constitute a mingling of prevalent confessional rhetoric with indigenous political culture. Before turning to a discussion of these, however, it is useful to provide a brief sketch of who in Lindau was involved.

Of the five ministers retained by the city, only Neukomm opposed the plan to introduce private confession; in fact his own colleagues had first tabled the matter in the CSC. Neukomm's arch-enemies, the advocates Daniel Heider and Ulrich Funk, were also strongly in favour of the plan. Judging by the proceedings against the rebels, all the members of the Council were either in

favour of private confession or remained prudently neutral. On
the other hand Neukomm's brother, *Stadtamman* Andreas
Neukomm, and other members of the Neukomm family, formed
the core of what was identified as the 'Neukomm party'.[49]
Generally the narratives of the dispute do not differentiate
Neukomm supporters from opponents of private confession. They
were 'recalcitrant plebs' (*widerspenstigen Pöbel*), or simply 'the
common man' (*gemaine Man*). While the measure was still in its
early CSC phase, it was opposed by the 'citizens and peasants'; apparently anyone who was not actually in government was in opposition.[50] Of course, some groups were already at loggerheads with
the authorities. According to one source, Neukomm was quick to
exploit the dissatisfaction of the bakers, tanners, butchers and
boatmen of Lindau.[51] There are also indications that the Tailors'
Guild, to which Neukomm had family connections, was particularly radical.[52] One of the few extant non-official narratives, that
of the cordwainer Caspar Mezler, describes the conflict in con-
ventional terms, as citizen resistance against the Council; the so-
called 'lost protocol' suggests that the authorities' chief concern
was citizen resistance to private confession.[53] The only key to the
position of individual citizens comes from the punitive proceedings against the rebels. While only one of those punished,
Andreas Neukomm, held public office, nine of the seventeen
family names mentioned appear in the lists of public office-
holders. Nevertheless, only three of these families had ever controlled a seat in the Council.[54] Finally, there is an inherent danger
in assessing who may or may not have opposed private confession
on the basis of records concerned with the uprising of 7
November and mostly written after that date. For example, while
Mezler and official accounts agreed that Neukomm enjoyed the
especially strong support of Lindau's female population, the
pastors' reports to the Superintendent at Ulm claimed that
women as a group had remained uninterested in the whole
affair![55]

Returning now to the role played by confessional rhetoric in
the contest over private confession: any attempt to assess that role
must first take account of the extraordinary range of rhetorical
moves employing confessional categories. Nothing better illustrates that range, often bordering on the comical, than the
various accusations levelled at Neukomm by his colleagues. He

had at one time been employed at the court of Baden-Durlach, until the Count embraced Calvinism. Consequently, Neukomm had been an easy target for charges of Calvinism since the day he returned to Lindau. For example, in the course of a bitter conflict between Neukomm and the advocate Daniel Heider, the latter had simply denounced Neukomm as a Calvinist.[56] Ironically, in 1620 a former colleague, Marcus Zangmeister, had complained bitterly to the Council that Neukomm and his wife had defamed him as – among other things – a Calvinist.[57] At the other extreme there were those who saw fit to decry Neukomm as a papist. For example, in 1610 the city physician Dr Peter Eggolt had reportedly accused Neukomm of delivering 'a lying, godless, heretical, unconstructive, fomenting, disgraceful, bothersome *Jesuit* sermon'.[58] In 1626 Neukomm was still being denounced in some quarters as a 'sacrament priest' (*Sacraments Pfaffen*).[59] For its part the CSC, in the face of Neukomm's assurances of allegiance to both the Augsburg Confession and the Formula of Concord, intimated that he was not 'properly evangelical Lutheran Christian'; in lieu of hard evidence they maintained that an orthodox Lutheran never would have opposed their plan to introduce private confession.[60] Of course such charges were relatively mild compared with the expert opinion of a consultant theologian, Dr Georg Zaeman of Kempten, that Neukomm was an Anabaptist, motivated by both the spirit of Münster (the city) and Müntzer (the heretic).[61] Finally, the Superintendent of Ulm, Dr Conrad Dietrich, a man who certainly knew something of theology but who had also experienced personal and professional disagreements with Neukomm, impugned Neukomm's orthodoxy. In answer to the charge that he was a practising Calvinist, and indeed kept a Calvinist church, Neukomm showed Dietrich 'the two painted glass crucifixes in the chancel and drew his attention to the images on the organ'.[62] We are not told if Dietrich was convinced.

While this freewheeling approach to confessional categories might appear humorous, confessionalism was also, of course, a deadly serious business. After all, by 1626 Lindauers had gained first-hand experience of a war considerable confessional elements.[63] In the weeks prior to the uprising of 7 November, there was a virtual panic over rumours that the Jesuits were going to establish themselves in Lindau under imperial patronage.[64] It is no small wonder, then, that confessional rhetoric and the threat of recatholicisation did much to anathemise private confession to Lindauers. After the uprising, popular suspicion and sensitivity to 'popery' remained such that the government prudently purged a draft letter of reconciliation between the Council and citizenry of all Latin words.[65] The spectre of recatholicisation had been raised by Neukomm immediatedly following the CSC meeting of 4 April, that is, the moment he got wind of plans to introduce private confession. It did not take long before the population at large was convinced that the authorities wanted to re-introduce *auricular* confession (*Ohrenbeichte*),[66] and they quite naturally assumed that they would thereupon be forced to practise Catholicism. Moreover, Neukomm claimed – and Lindauers apparently believed him – that ministerial support for the measure stemmed from their desire to pocket the anticipated confession fee (*Beichtpfennig*) of three kreuzer for young people and six kreuzer for old folks.[67] Official assurances that nobody would be coerced and no compulsory fees levied apparently fell on deaf ears.[68] Neukomm's final sermon of 5 November shows that these issues retained their rhetorical puissance. In a reminder to his audience that sins were remitted solely by the grace of God, Neukomm stressed that penance, as implied in his representation of private confession, would have no efficacy. Thus he actually alluded to a major Lutheran theological principle before proceeding to a devastatingly lightfooted ridicule of Catholic doctrines on penance and good works.[69] By skilful deployment of confessional rhetoric Neukomm created an unbearable tension in the Lindauers' confessional identity. This move, which was more than a simple denunciation of private confession as bad Lutheranism or neo-Catholicism, is exemplified by Neukomm's characterisation of private confession as 'Lutheran indulgence sales' (*Lutherischer Ablaß Kram*).[70]

### III

While confessional rhetoric would seem to have outweighed genuine theological questions, that does not mean conflict over private confession was all sound and fury. From the very begin-

ning, evangelical preaching had complicated Lindau's already
awkward diplomatic position. The city, although small, was of
strategic importance, perched on the edge of the Empire. While
the threatening proximity of Austria and the neighbouring Count
of Montfort made good relations with the Emperor and the
German princes a priority, Lindau's economy relied largely on
trade with the Swiss. Culturally and politically the city had more in
common with Swiss towns than with German territories. This
meant that Lindau governments were forever walking a diplomatic tightrope, and that Lindau's population was usually divided
over policy. The Tetrapolitan Confession, submitted by Lindau,
Constance, Strassburg and Memmingen in 1530 as an alternative
to the Augsburg Confession, was a supreme example of fence-
sitting, placing Lindau exactly between the German protestant
princes and the Swiss.[71] Unfortunately, many later observers, even
Lindauers, perceived the Tetrapolitan Confession as 'Zwinglian'
and, from the mid-sixteenth century, one of the main objectives
of Lindavian diplomacy centred on living down the city's 'Swiss'
past. When Dr Zaeman advised the Lindau government on how to
handle private confession, he pointed out that the abolition of
private confession had been a Zwinglian measure in the first
place, ascribing to Zwingli the pronouncement that 'a confessor
could, by granting absolution, no more assure a confidant of
divine mercy than he could turn a mosquito into an elephant'.
For good measure, Zaeman intoned that those who had no
private confession were as bad as 'Anabaptists, Schwenkfelders,
enthusiasts and other apostate fantasts'.[72]

Lindau's policy in the Schmalkaldic War, like its initial attitude
to the Augsburg Confession, had been cautious and pragmatic.
Lindau was a member of the League, but when the fortunes of
war changed, the town had thrown itself on the mercy of the
Emperor, thereby escaping the harrowing fate of nearby
Constance.[73] Behind every such compromise, however, there was
an internal split between radicals and moderates. Thus the *Interim*
was accepted only after a bitter dispute which ended in the emi-
gration of many prominent citizens.[74] Likewise, Lindauers had
disagreed sharply over the Formula of Concord, and its acceptance had necessitated the expulsion of two pastors, Sebald
Scheffler and Tobias Rupp, in defiance of considerable popular
support for the two.[75] Clearly, as confessional ideologies solidified

and battle lines emerged, local compromises like the Tetrapolitan Confession became more difficult, and ambiguity very dangerous. By 1626 many citizens considered unquestionable confessional status a prerequisite for Lindau's survival, and the clarification of Lindau's confessional status was one of the major points in favour of private confession. Lindau should introduce private confession, it was argued, to keep pace with the other evangelical estates of the Empire who subscribed to the Augsburg Confession.[76] Even Neukomm believed in the importance of uniformity among the evangelical estates.[77]

When the plan to introduce private confession was first tabled in the CSC, its strongest proponents opened their case with claims that private confession (i) was in accordance with the Augsburg Confession and the Formula of Concord; (ii) was advocated by commentators and theologians, even in those places were private confession was not practised; (iii) was currently practised in Pomerania, Mecklenburg, Saxony, Meissen, Thuringia and many Upper German churches; (iv) had been recently introduced in Ulm, Memmingen, Kempten and Isny.[78] Other sources identify a 1568 pronouncement by the theological faculty at Rostock, the church ordinances (*Kirchenordnungen*) of Lower Saxony and the works of Luther as the major authorities in favour of private confession.[79]

It was also argued that if Lindauers did not heed these authorities and follow other Lutheran churches, it would provide Catholics with ammunition against Lindau. Lindau was, after all, surrounded. The Catholic argument, that Lindau's inability to conform to the other churches of the Augsburg Confession constituted a breach of the Religious Peace, was threatening indeed.[80] The CSC had heard that Lindau's enemies claimed that she had never been properly Lutheran, which meant that Lindauers had remained true to their original inclination, Zwinglianism. It is evident from Neukomm's response to supporters of private confession that other external critics of Lindavian religious practice represented the absence of private confession as a hallmark of Calvinism, an accusation which recalled Lindau's divided approach to the Formula of Concord. In any case, Neukomm flatly rejected this view and roundly ridiculed those who feared such insinuations; their grip on reality was, according to Neukomm, tenuous.[81] Nevertheless, when the events of 7 November rendered private confession in Lindau a very remote possibility, observers feared the worst. Dr Zaeman, writing to Lindau at the end of November, pronounced that, since they had disdained Christian confession and absolution, it would serve Lindau's citizens right if the Jesuits took over.[82]

## IV

The drive to confessional uniformity was countered in Lindau by an extremely powerful localism, the sources and mechanisms of which cannot be discussed here.[83] While this localism was deeply embedded in the political culture of imperial free cities in general, Lindauers may have been particularly susceptible. The peculiar confessional history mentioned above, along with the development of a city church (*Stadtkirche*) which paralleled local legal and political culture, can only have reinforced localism or chauvinism. Thus Neukomm, when charged with deviation from the Augburg Confession, insisted on his duty to uphold Lindau's own church constitution. In any case, he argued, the Augburg Confession and the church constitution made much the same provisions for private confession and differed only in their modes of application. The other members of the CSC did not agree: Neukomm's appointment in Lindau had entailed an oath to uphold the Augburg Confession and the Formula of Concord and Neukomm was not sworn to defend the church constitution. Indeed, they pointed out, Neukomm had himself contravened the church constitution on several occasions in the past.[84] Nevertheless, localism remained an important factor, especially when the question was raised: who was competent to interpret Lindau's church constitution? For example, Neukomm responded to the official censure of 21 June by asserting that he alone understood the content and function of the church constitution since his colleagues were not only young, but also foreigners (*Frembde*).[85] Similarly, Neukomm rejected the recommendations of the Superintendent of Ulm on the grounds that while Neukomm was a 'native born preacher and citizen', Dr Dietrich was an alien (*Außlender*).[86] As the crisis of 7 November approached, the native/foreign distinction would help determine who among the population at large supported Neukomm's hard-headed resistance to private confession. One particularly emotive argument from Neukomm's sermon of 5 November (see below) had an exclusive appeal for members of old Lindau families.[87]

In the light of this localism, and in the context of the Lindauers' 'constitutional' view of their church, the vehemence of their resistance to private confession makes sense. Lindauers were not so much attacking private confession as mounting a general defence of their church constitution. Thus, although the actual exactions of the rebels – as deduced from the capitulation document extracted from the government – included a demand that the government abandon all attempts to introduce private confession, very few narrative accounts presented the rebel grievance that way.[88] In fact many analysts made no mention of private confession whatsoever, stating instead that the rebels had forced the government to preserve the old church constitution (*Kirchenordnung*), at least for the time being.[89] This 'constitutionalist' resistance to private confession had been part of the conflict from the start. The initial 'citizens' and peasants' outcry', noted by the CSC, centred on fears that the government was planning to abolish the old church constitution along with the form of confession currently in practice.[90] The government's strategic response to this outcry attempted to establish that the *Kirchenordnung* simply was not a constitution in the sense that it was understood by early modern Lindauers. The nature and power of a constitution lay in its stability, its age and its immutability. The authorities argued, however, that Lindau's *Kirchenordnung* was actually a 'frequently interpolated Upper German work', implying – among other things – that it did not possess the requisite immutability of a constitution. In this context, even the government's insistence that they did not wish to deviate from the *Kirchenordnung* but merely to supplement and improve it, served to undermine its nature as a constitution. The authorities also drew attention to recent modifications, endorsed by Neukomm, to the formula for the celebration of the Eucharist.[91] Moreover, as already mentioned, Neukomm himself had been responsible for several innovations over the years.[92]

For his part, Neukomm responded with a pedigree of 'our old church constitution', and defended it on the following grounds: (i) it was established in Württemberg many years ago; (ii) it was printed in Tübingen several times, not without the approval and permission of the theological faculty; (iii) it was confirmed by Dr Jacob Andreae and a full Council, Court and Commune in 1575;[93] (iv) until now nobody had found any shortcomings and everyone had been happy and content with it.[94] Furthermore, when Neukomm mounted his full-scale assault on private confession and its proponents (as well as other personal enemies) on 5 November, he insisted that the commune (*Gemeinde*) should remain true to 'the old and good church constitution', and then he gave the argument a powerful twist. Changing the constitution would mean, claimed Neukomm, that previous practices had been inefficacious (*ohncräfftig*). It followed, therefore, that everyone who had received the sacrament according to the old constitution had done so unworthily (*unwürdig*) and would be damned and lost forever. It was also clear what this meant to native Lindauers: by accepting private confession and undermining the church constitution, they would retroactively condemn 'our deceased ancestors'.[95] It was certainly a peculiar argument, but the idea that they might inadvertently consign their relatives to eternal damnation somehow struck a chord with the Lindauers.[96] Hence the authorities reacted with uncharacteristic swiftness. They relieved Neukomm of all further duties, claiming he had willfully perverted the facts and that the government had no intention of abolishing the church constitution.[97] The draft proclamation (*Fürhalt*), which the government had planned to issue to the assembled citizenry on 7 November, concentrated heavily on Neukomm's claim that the church constitution was going to be overturned and the Lindauers' ancestors damned.[98] The proclamation was never issued and there is no way of knowing if it would have worked.

V

One of the more puzzling questions arising out of the whole conflict is why the government, in the face of steadily mounting opposition and no sign of cooperation from Neukomm, pursued its plan so doggedly? What was private confession to them? Not much, probably, but as the documents generated in the clean-up operations of late 1626 and early 1627 show, governmental authority was at stake.[99] What had started out as a 'foreign policy decision' to amend church practice, and possibly to add one tool of government to what was already a good selection, quickly became a test of governmental authority itself. Given the 'constitutional' view of the established church discussed above this is not actually that surprising. The question of a government's relation to the authority by which it exists is necessarily a difficult one, even if one assumes that everyone shares the same view of that constitution, an assumption which is not valid for Lindau. While a considerable number of Lindauers viewed their relationship to government and governmental authority in accordance with what might be called 'bourgeois republican ideology', in government circles many, especially recent arrivals like Dr Heider, were beginning to think and act in terms of a 'sovereign authority' (*Obrigkeit*). For a variety of reasons they perceived a fundamental distinction between the rulers who wielded that authority and their 'subjects' (*Untertanen*). The greatest burden of an *Obrigkeit*, even if it was no longer directly responsible to the citizenry, was that failure to govern effectively (i.e. exercise its authority) implied an immediate loss of authority; *Obrigkeit* was an all-or-nothing proposition.[100] Hence, maintaining good order and public peace (in a real rather than an ideal sense) was the Lindau government's chief preoccupation. The minutes of the Council show that the government expended remarkable energy on the resolution of petty disputes. In this the *Obrigkeit* government actually differed very little from previous governments, which had operated under more 'democratic' precepts. It is in this context that one must see the government's hope that private confession would ultimately establish a uniformity (*durchgehende Gleicheit*) of worship among its subjects.[101] Unfortunately, in matters of religion, the government lacked, and was seen to lack, competence and legitimacy. For both of these, therefore, it relied on the expertise of specialists in the form of the CSC. One could say the trouble started when the government tried to use the CSC to establish private confession, but undermined the body's legitimacy by failing to secure Neukomm's vote. It was an easy thing for Neukomm to portray the government and the CSC as usurpers; they had acted without legitimacy and had in fact misappropriated authority.[102]

The government's response to Neukomm's challenge reveals much about their complex mutual relationship. Most striking is the injured tone with which the authorities criticised Neukomm's failure to support them. Instead to pacifying the citizens, he had indulged in superfluous digressions in his sermons, justifying collective confession and absolution with the example of John the Baptist, who had baptised all of Judea in a single act, and St Peter, who had converted three thousand souls at once. This was not the first time the government had chastised Neukomm for siding with the common man rather than reporting to the government on the nature and source of popular displeasure.[103] Moreover, the government actually claimed that it wanted to introduce private confession not only for the spiritual benefit of Lindauers, but specifically to alleviate the consciences of the pastors, who would no longer be burdened with responsibility for administering of the sacrament to unworthy parishioners. When both enticement and exhortation to duty failed to secure compliance, the government simply ordered Neukomm to appear before the CSC.[104] Of course, such a move entailed the risk that Neukomm would stand in open defiance of the Council. Therefore, the authorities had tried previously to coerce Neukomm in more subtle ways: for example, by the exertion of economic pressure. Since the early sixteenth century Lindau's pastors' meagre salaries had been supplemented with discretionary awards (*Verehrungen*), usually of grain or wine, and, while the salary could not be withheld without a formal suspension, the *Verehrung* could. Moreover, in Neukomm's case, the authorities simply passed legislation which prevented the conversion of the produce into ready cash.[105] As was his habit, Neukomm did not take it lying down and devoted considerable energy to denouncing the authorities' use of financial pressure, especially in his sermon of 5 November.[106]

Under normal circumstances Lindau's pastors might well have accepted that, for all intents and purposes, they had become government employees. The contest over private confession, however, exposed profound ideological differences, strongly reminiscent of the early Reformation, on the subject. For example, the one extant narrative of the 7 November uprising by a known Neukomm sympathiser, Caspar Mezler, states that the citizens rose against the Council because they tried to prevent, 'our, the citizens', pastor and preacher', from preaching.[107] Other reports agree that Neukomm defied the government's attempt to dismiss him with references to the authority of the commune (*Gemeinde*).[108] When the authorities interrogated Conrad Stärck about events at Neukomm's house on the evening of 6 November, he testified that Neukomm had met news of his dismissal with a speech in which he asserted that the dismissal of a Lindau pastor required three votes: that of his colleagues, that of the Council and that of the *Gemeinde*.[109] The issue remained very 'hot' and some weeks after the uprising, the Council proceeded against one Augustin Miller for circulating a book in his guild 'from which he purported to prove that no sovereign authority (*Obrigkeit*) has the power to appoint ministers, unless it has been endowed for that purpose with special privileges'.[110] From the government's point of view, any limitations on governmental authority affected its sovereignty and called into question its status as an *Obrigkeit*.

It was precisely this fundamental deficiency of (protestant) *Obrigkeit* which Neukomm targeted time and again. One observer even claimed that Neukomm was not particularly interested in private confession, but that he used it as a pretext 'because he long had been pregnant with a desire to foil the *Obrigkeit*'.[111] While Neukomm claimed no desire to challenge his proper *Obrigkeit*, he did attack members of the CSC with a sharp reminder of the separation of secular and spiritual offices.[112] On the other hand, Neukomm certainly was given to liberal interpretation of his own sphere. Technically, and on this Neukomm and the government agreed, his office (*Predig- und Straffambt*) entitled him to coerce and punish parishioners.[113] Nevertheless, the government, on the advice of legal experts retained by the Council, had occasionally felt the need to curb Neukomm's enthusiasm. For example, as early as 1603 Neukomm and his colleagues had been pressing for the power to exercise a ban and excommunicate parishioners. The official response of the syndic Dr Heider was that the pastors 'were trying to get a foot in the door of City Hall and were making to grab for secular jurisdiction'.[114] Needless to say the government followed Heider's recommendation and did not concede any further power to the pastors.

In fact, the spiritual authority of the Lindau government, which claimed control of the *Stadtkirche*, was highly questionable. For example, in 1617 the authorities had felt compelled to proceed against one Philippina Cawazin, because she had taken her case to the marriage court of the bishop of Constance. Lindau had its own marriage court which competed for the jurisdiction in matrimonial cases. Attempts to exert its authority backfired on the government when the notary Hans Georg Brem made public speeches to the effect that the government had no jurisdiction in matrimonial cases and was not permitted to establish its own marriage court. Hence, he argued, the citizens were under no obligation to render obedience to the Lindau government in such cases.[115] Clearly this was a severe blow to a government which increasingly claimed legitimacy on the basis of unqualified, sovereign authority. Here was a chink in the government's armour and Neukomm could not resist a few well-placed strokes. Obviously, when the Council commanded both spiritual and secular obedience from Neukomm, they were challenged. Although he granted them secular authority, he firmly denied that he had to answer to anyone in spiritual matters.[116] Neukomm also took the initiative himself, undermining government claims to effective spiritual authority with sharp ridicule. 'Since the authorities meddled in the church, despite the fact that it was improper for them to do so,' he said, he had 'no choice but to point out that convicted adulterers were announcing their intentions to take communion elsewhere.'[117] In other words, the government was not only unjustified in claiming authority in religious matters, but it was also incapable of exercising it effectively. The breadth of the gulf separating the arguments of Neukomm or Hans Georg Brem from the authoritarian position of the government is best illustrated by the comments of a Lindau advocate, Dr Funk. In discussions in mid-December, Funk expressed the guiding principle of government policy throughout the conflict. As an *Obrigkeit* they could command obedience in all things, religion included: 'even if the *Obrigkeit* had wanted to introduce the Turkish faith, it would have been wrong for the subjects (*Underthonen*) to rebel'.[118] Evidently Funk was a theorist.

## VI

While knowing that many Lindauers had an interest in preserving their church constitution, and that the authority of the government was fragile, provides a context for the contest over private confession, it does not address the question of why this particular political contest, one of many conducted every year, ended in violence. What was it about private confession *per se* that so incensed the Lindauers? As already mentioned, confessional rhetoric played no mean part in forcing Lindauers to declare themselves either for or against the measure; however, one more important factor, Lindavian political culture and ideology, demands attention. When their plan met with swift and determined popular resistance, the authorities blamed Alexius Neukomm, who, they claimed, had 'anathematised' private confession. Certainly, many citizens supported 'their pastor' once the government tried to suspend him, but had it really been in Neukomm's power to set Lindauers against private confession with a single sermon? Neukomm himself certainly bemoaned his lack of influence and power in other cases.[119] In fact it is possible that Lindavian sensibilities were most offended by the idea of *private* confession itself. The terms 'public' and 'private' were ideologically loaded by their association with local political thought,[120] as is evidenced by their use, as a pair or separately, to denounce the 'unofficial' political activity of individuals. Strictly speaking, the pair of terms *heimlich* and *öffentlich* were considered equivalent to *privatim* and *publice*, as is indicated by their use in translations of legal texts.[121] Yet the Lindau terminology contains significant cultural aspects which go beyond the classical public/private distinction between an individual's actions on behalf of the office or offices held and his personal interests or actions. The original meaning of *heimlich* had to do with the sphere of the house, the 'domestic', which was shielded from public view; *öffentlich*, by contrast, was that which was conducted in plain sight of all eyes.[122] The crux, however, is the issue of accessible and inaccessible arenas of action and the use of the inaccessible for concealment. R. F. E. Weissman has noted that in Renaissance Florence houses were indeed retreats and there was a certain inviolability connected with the fact that they offered shelter from the public eye. It was a privilege and an honour to be admitted to someone's house; but then concealment of private emotion and intention seems to have been a virtue.[123] In Lindau, in marked contrast to the case examined by Weissman, although it was considered an abuse to employ the platform or leverage afforded by public life to gain privately, a different (and the strongest) condemnation was reserved for those who dealt behind closed doors, who disguised their intentions and conducted themselves in an unforthright manner. In Lindau this constituted the real meaning of corruption.

Inevitably, this discourse was present in the contest over private confession: it was already there in the contraposition of 'private' and 'public' confession and it had long been incorporated into the competition for authority, both between the government and the ministry and within the ministry itself. For example, in 1624 Neukomm had complained that his colleagues were holding secret (*geheimen*) CSC meetings behind his back and claimed that he knew what was going on despite the fact that they were doing it in secret (*heimlich*).[124] In 1626 he similarly charged the other members of the CSC with obfuscation, berating them for 'fighting with masks and shadows'.[125] On the other hand, when Neukomm first mounted an opposition to private confession, the authorities publicly announced that to do so was to go against the public interest. Those who opposed the measure would be doing so for vain and selfish (i.e. private) reasons.[126] In the CSC Neukomm attacked private confession with an evocative pun: private confession was a 'private business' (*Privatwerckh*). He thereby undermined the legitimacy of any government (i.e. public) act which introduced it. Predictably, the CSC chairman demanded to know if Neukomm alone spoke with public authority (*publicus*).[127] Nevertheless, that particular configuration of the contested subject was very persistent. In late June Neukomm was reprimanded officially because he had appropriated authority (*Authoritet*) for personal (i.e. private) reasons and had opposed private confession both in private (*privatim*) and openly (*öffentlich*). Moreover he was still denouncing the measure as a 'private business', as if his approval alone constituted a public authorisation (*publicam Authoration*).[128]

For his part, Neukomm simply smote the government with the other edge of the sword. Not only did Lindau, like other estates, practise a public church discipline,[129] but one already had private confession. The planned introduction was, therefore, unnecessary – a mere *adiaphora*.[130] In Lindau, claimed Neukomm, private confession took place, appropriately, in the pastors' 'private houses' (*Privatheüser*).[131] Once again, this argument had first surfaced in Neukomm's dispute with the CSC, when he claimed that what some people did in their church (i.e. examine potential communicants) the Lindau pastors did in their houses. This domestic examination, claimed Neukomm, was 'private' confession.[132] Neukomm's multiple use of the private/public discourse completely outmanoeuvred the government . Their private confession was not legitimate because it was 'private' and Neukomm's practice of examining communicants in his house was legitimate because it was 'private' confession. All he had to do was draw on the arguments for private confession produced by the government. Ironically, of course, what the government had hoped to achieve was some control of the examinations conducted in the privacy of the pastors' houses, compared to which individual examinations in the city church were 'public'. If they had realised the utility of designations such as 'collective' or 'general' confession (*Gemeindebeichte, allgemeine Beichte*), they might have reserved 'public confession' for their plan and burdened Neukomm with the 'private' measure.[133] In fact the government apparently mounted a last-ditch effort in this direction. An official communication (*Decret*) issued to Neukomm on 25 October claimed that the CSC had long since prohibited pastors from hearing confession and granting absolution in their houses.[134] Moreover, the government actually threatened Neukomm, hinting that the common man would be very interested to hear that he, Neukomm, had himself once been a practitioner of private confession.

## VII

I have attempted to treat religion and politics in Lindau as indistinguishable in their common cultural constitution. Choosing this point of departure for an examination of private confession implies a rejection of common formulations such as 'religion and social control' or 'morality and the law'. In any study of early modern religion and politics, local or otherwise, it is no longer sufficient to subordinate the one to the other with evaluations of faith/cynicism, superstition/rationalism, etc.

Finally, a few comments on the fate of private confession after the uprising of 7 November. Despite their best efforts, the Lindau authorities were unable to prevent the Emperor from involving himself in Lindau affairs. In 1627–8 two Imperial Commissioners – the bishop of Constance and Count Hugo of Montfort – conducted an inquiry (*general Inquisition*) in Lindau.[135] Although the two had manifest interests in diminishing Lindau's autonomy, their stated objective was to negate any and all consequences of the uprising and of the government's capitulation. Ideally the whole episode was to be eradicated, as if it had never happened. All things were to be returned to the state they had been in on the eve of 7 November. There was one notable exception: private confession – ominously referred to as auricular confession – was finally to be introduced. The preamble of the commissioners' report had already lamented the difficulty of establishing precisely who had played what role in the uprising. Lindauers, the commissioners noted, were given to perjury and did not honour their witness oaths. It is hard to say to what extent practical considerations stimulated their resolve to introduce private confession; however, individuals much closer to the events of 7 November had similar ideas. The Lindau ministers expressly linked the unqualified resolution of conflict – and, indeed, the absolution of the rebels – to private confession.

On Friday 10 November the four pastors appealed to the Bürgermeister and the Privy Council for instructions on how to proceed in the execution of their office.[136] They were especially concerned with what would happen if those involved in the uprising wished to take communion; without private confession there was no way for a minister to know whether the rebels had, by recognition and regret of their sin, cleared their consciences. Furthermore, it was feared that if they went ahead and celebrated communion the ministers would be denounced as hypocrites; if they refused to give communion, then either there would simply be no celebration of the Eucharist in Lindau or Alexius Neukomm would celebrate it in their stead. This, it was argued, would not be fair to those who had taken no part in the uprising, particularly women.

The gist of the authorities' reply can be inferred from the ministers' letter to Dr Zaeman dated 11 November.[137] Evidently the provisional government had instructed the ministry that, because without private confession they lacked the means to distinguish the truly rueful from the unrepentant, they could not refuse communion to any of the rebels who wished to receive it. Furthermore, the ministers were instructed that, since many citizens remained in a state of sworn enmity towards the authorities, they would have to proceed with the utmost care to avoid further agitation of the citizens.

Such an admission of the precarious position of secular and spiritual authority in Lindau can be contrasted with the very early signs of the creation of a history which presented the uprising as the work of a tiny minority. The pastors' description of the crowd which carried Neukomm to the church on the morning of 7 November claims that some citizens were swept along by the Neukomm party and did not necessarily know what they were doing. The real 'hard-cases', who were intent on upholding their treasonous oath and showed no sign of penitence or regret of their sin against God or their crime against the *Obrigkeit*, were now distinguished from the many who had, supposedly against their will, been forced to participate in the unrest.

The process of exonerating the vast majority of the citizens and ultimately blaming one individual for the uprising is delineated in the correspondence between the Lindau ministers and the theologians of other cities. In a sense, convincing the outside consultants was the top priority because, ultimately, only the corroboration of other imperial cities could legitimate the Lindavian version of events and vindicate the Lindau authorities.

In his letter of 15 November to the Lindau ministry Dr Zaeman set the blame for what he called a 'tumult, rebellion or sedition' squarely on the shoulders of Alexius Neukomm.[138] It was repeatedly intoned that Neukomm was the root cause of everything, the '*Urstiffter*'. On the other hand, Zaeman pragmatically allowed that, to prevent further trouble, one might make some provisional concessions to the commune.

The pastors received a similar letter (dated 16 November) from Dr Dietrich, and on 20 November they replied to Ulm. They once more claimed to be bothered by the following dilemma: while they did not want those who were unrepentant of the sins committed in the *tumult* to take communion, without private confession they could not distinguish this minority from the vast majority who had not approved of, or had taken no interest in, the uprising; these included the women and peasants of the Lindau jurisdiction. Of course, ascribing an improbable innocence to the many also necessitated exaggerating the knowledge of the few. Hence Neukomm was presented, on the basis of assumptions only, as the unlikely hub of a premeditated treasonous conspiracy.[139] The groundwork was thus being laid for what amounted to a complete social and political expurgation and reconstitution, a Lindavian 'hour zero'.[140]

# 8.  A Lübeck Prophet in Local and Lutheran Context

JÜRGEN BEYER

On the evening of 10 April 1629, the Friday after Easter, the pastor at the cathedral church in Lübeck, Bernhard Blume, M.A., received an unexpected visitor at his home. One of his parishioners, David Frese, a humble citizen of Lübeck, had already called at four o'clock when the minister was out, but now he was finally able to tell of his experience at lunchtime. He had been on his way back from Grönau. On coming to the heath where the border between the territories of Lübeck and Sachsen-Lauenburg was located, near the white stone that had fallen down, he became full of fear and thought about returning when he heard somebody say, 'Listen, I want to tell you something!' Then he saw an old grey man, dressed in white, sitting on the fallen stone. Two white doves were perched on his right shoulder, and one on his left. All three doves where drenched all over, and tears were flowing from their eyes. The old man began to speak and asked why it was that the dead in Lübeck were not allowed to rest? The church of St George should remain standing. Enough sin had already been committed by tearing down another church earlier. On the contrary, every week two days of prayer should be celebrated at St George's; if this was not done, they would see what was going to befall them. This he should tell the pastors in Lübeck. Then the old man said: 'Go away now and do not look back!' Still very fearful, Frese walked away until he came to the Grönau toll-bar where he sat down for a while. Even while telling his story to the minister, he continued to be afraid. His heart was racing and he could neither eat nor drink.

Pastor Blume asked him if other people had requested him to put forward this account. David Frese replied that, on his life and as God was his judge, the event had taken place as recounted. His heart, however, already felt somewhat relieved, since he had delivered his message.

A short while after leaving Pastor Blume's house, he came back saying that he had forgotten one thing: the old man had said that a child had been born in this town to serve as a mirror for everyone, but that this had been obscured.[1]

Pastor Blume concluded his report about David Frese's statement by saying that the man was sound in mind and not intoxicated but simple and plain. Therefore there was no reason for suspecting fraud. Albert Reimarus, M.A., minister at the cathedral church, and Franciscus Greier were present during the interview.

The following day the entire clergy of Lübeck was assembled to discuss the case. They sent a letter to the town council, followed by Pastor Blume's report and a theological judgement on the case, concluding that the old man could not have been a messenger from God.[2]

Unfortunately, it is not possible to say anything about the reaction of the town council.[3]

Besides a few customary expressions in Latin, all the documents are written in High German. There is, however, one exception: on the two occasions when the old man is quoted in direct speech, the language switches to Low German.[4] Low German was doubtless the language spoken in the streets. It was probably still used to some degree in church services, but the administration had already used High German for a long time.[5] The ministers Blume and Reimarus were born in Lübeck and were therefore almost certainly native speakers of Low German.[6] Inserting a Low German quotation adds an authentic flavour to the account but this need not be more than a literary device.[7]

Nothing is known about David Frese's age, occupation, or his degree of literacy. His abode, however, 'in der Hartigsgruben in Hans Bueren gange' indicates a backyard dwelling.[8]

David Frese was a citizen (*Bürger*). Less than half the population had this status. In order to take up the civic rights (*Bürgberrecht*), applicants had to pay a certain amount of money (*Bürgergeld*) and to be at least twenty-five years old. The status of citizen was necessary to set up house or to employ staff. Even after an economic failure, a citizen would retain his civic rights. David Frese's status as citizen therefore does not tell us very much about his social standing. He was probably not povertystricken but it is quite unlikely that he belonged to the wealthy classes with influence in the town council.[9]

## LUTHERAN POPULAR PROPHETS

What was this case about? David Frese's was not an isolated example; more than 150 similar cases are known from the Lutheran parts of early modern Germany, and, beyond the scope of this book, more than 50 from Lutheran Scandinavia. The comparative material in this chapter will to some extent be taken from the larger hinterland of Lübeck, although prophets are known from a much wider area.

These prophets[10] seem to be an almost exclusively Lutheran phenomenon.[11] Medieval apparitions and apparitions in contemporary Catholic countries would be more likely to take the form of a saint appearing and urging the community to do penance and to erect a shrine in honour of the saint in question in order to avoid God's punishment.[12] This was one of the roots of the Lutheran prophets. After the Reformation, however, the tradition had to be adjusted to the new theological frame of reference if prophets were to have any success with ecclesiastical and secular authorities. They now operated within Lutheran definitions of repentance (see below), and saints were exchanged for angels, who were usually dressed in white.

A rather telling example is to be found in the records concerning the recatholicisation of the Upper Palatinate after 1620, when Catholic authorities took over and started the Counter-Reformation. For the remainder of the century there are numerous reports about the appearances of saints which led to the founding of shrines. However, from the whole period there are traces of only one popular prophet meeting an angel: this prophet was a Lutheran.[13]

Common to the Lutheran prophets was the fact that they received a supernatural revelation asking them to admonish their contemporaries to repent. Often, as in the case of David Frese, they were to inform the minister, who in turn was to preach the message to the congregation. At least until the Thirty Years' War, many pastors accepted the prophets' message as divine. The principal sin in the prophets' eyes was pride (often specified as luxuriousness in dress); other points of criticism were usury, avarice, or fornication. If people did not repent, God's punishment would arrive shortly; often this was described in the apocalyptic terms of plague, war, and famine (cf. Rev. 6: 1–8). The impending punishment was not specified in David Frese's account.

Almost all prophets can be called unlettered. Although a number of them were capable of reading and even writing, hardly any of them had received a formal (Latin) education. Only a fraction of them were nobles. Prophets were to be found in all occupations, in all age groups, in all types of settlements (from large cities such as Lübeck down to hamlets and the pastures of roaming shepherds), and among both sexes.

The stories about prophets were well known and – when related in pamphlets and sermons – standardised to a certain degree. It can be assumed that most people had heard about contemporary angelic apparitions. Regardless of whether one chooses to view an apparition story as genuinely divine, as a diabolic illusion, as a case of melancholy, or as fraud (the options available to contemporary theologians), tales about angelic apparitions enabled common people to speak out on local politics – and to be heard.[14] With a view to explaining the background of a multitude of apparitions in early modern Germany and Scandinavia, I shall try to contextualise David Frese's case in the following pages.


## LÜBECK IN APRIL 1629

Several prophets made their appearance at a time of crisis, preaching under the conditions of plague, war, or famine.[15]

In 1629, times were not good in Lübeck. The Thirty Years' War had been going on for more than ten years. More troublesome for Lübeck, the Danish involvement in the war since 1625 had led to Catholic troops marching through Schleswig-Holstein right into Jutland. Troops of both sides had touched Lübeck's territory. Lübeck, although Lutheran, had maintained a neutral position during the war but was nevertheless severely handicapped by the fighting. Denmark had organised a blockade of the Trave, the river connecting Lübeck to the Baltic ocean. The general warfare had severely impeded normal trade. It goes without saying that this was very detrimental to the prosperity of a trading town like Lübeck. By the time of David Frese's apparition, an end to this part of the war was drawing near. On 12 May 1629, peace was concluded in Lübeck between the emperor's and the Danish king's delegates.[16]

In April 1629, the world must have seemed out of joint to David Frese. Although negotiations were taking place in Lübeck, there was no guarantee that they would end by concluding peace. On the contrary, a contemporary pamphlet suggests that at the end of March the prospects for peace were meagre. It was only in the second half of April that the parties started to reach agreement.[17] Around the time of his apparition, an unusually large number of violent deaths were recorded in Lübeck.[18] Food prices were high.[19] Large numbers of refugees from the neighbouring territories had come to Lübeck, seeking a haven from the warfare at home.[20] The plague had last visited the city in 1625, leaving 7,000 Lübeckers dead.[21] In 1628, outbreaks of plague were reported from several towns in Schleswig-Holstein. In Hamburg, a town also crowded with refugees, the plague was continuing to ravage. In 1629, the plague came to Schleswig-Holstein again, though probably after April, reaching the town of Travemünde within Lübeck territory and even Lübeck itself.[22]

The war troubles made the town council push on with older plans to extend the city's fortifications. The church of St George was located in the area designated for the extension, quite close to one of the gates (*Mühlentor*). On approaching Lübeck from Grönau, one would pass this church. It was attached to a hospital catering for a number of lepers (*Seken*) and served by ministers of the nearby cathedral church. On 16 March 1629, Albert Reimarus (who was present when David Frese told his story to Pastor Blume) held the last sermon in the church. A short while later the destruction of the building was begun. On 20 March, the town council discussed what to do with the lepers inhabiting the hospital. It was resolved that the churchwardens should investigate where to find a place for them. Near the hospital, there was a cemetery used for the deceased inmates of the poorhouse and other poor folks. Because of the intended earthworks, this cemetery was to be moved. The corpses buried there were transferred to a new site further away from the town. The erection of a new church and a new hospital took some years, the new church being finally consecrated on 31 August 1646.[23]

The removal of a church, graveyard, and hospital was not a new occurrence in Lübeck. Already in 1622, the chapel of St Gertrude, a cemetery and the smallpox hospital outside one of the other gates (*Burgtor*) had had to give way for fortifications. Unlike the cemetery and the hospital, the chapel was not later re-established at another place. It is probably to this demolition that the old man was referring. In this case as well, the works had led to popular discontent ('wovon da das gemeine Volck sehr übel redete') and even members of the clergy had privately and publicly expressed negative opinions. This led the town council to instruct the clergy about the necessity and lawfulness of the new fortifications. After the works had started, the clergy were to persuade the parishioners of the usefulness of the measures.[24] The memory of this reprimand probably caused the clergy's cautious reaction in 1629.

By taking up the matter of the transfer of the corpses, David Frese was voicing a common concern. In their letter to the town council, the clergy related that the news about the apparition had spread quickly among the parishioners, who had expressed diverse views on it. It was to be feared that those who did not want to see their dead being moved would soon take up the issue and misinterpret ('mißdeuten') it. Although the clergy did not think there was any reason to stop the ongoing works, they nevertheless asked the town council to see that the workers transferring the corpses treated them with due reverence ('ebarlich vnd bescheidentlich'), since an obvious discontent could be observed among the parishioners.[25]

In their judgement, the Lübeck clergy offered four possible interpretations of David Frese's apparition: (1) it could be a diabolic illusion leading to spiritual and maybe also to political troubles; (2) it could be a fraud organised by papists in order to tempt the congregation dangerously; (3) it could be the fantasy of someone whose dead were buried in the graveyard and who did not want to see them exhumed; (4) it could also have been arranged by those who wished to prevent the fortification works.

These four points seem very plausible, some more under contemporary circumstances, some even today. The first point was probably influenced by the memory of the disagreement in 1622 about the first chapel to be torn down. Furthermore, a standard argument in discussions about popular visions was that accepting them as divine would undermine the authority of the ordained clergy. The second point is not only commonplace, in that Catholics could be suspected of anything evil, but recalls the fact that there were a few Catholics, even priests, resident in Lübeck. A year earlier the clergy had had some difficulties in preventing a former schoolmaster's conversion to Catholicism.[26] The third argument seems to be the most plausible, but then the apparition was also about the destruction of the church. Concerning the fourth point, the citizens were obliged to participate in the defence and to pay a special tax to finance the fortifications (*Grabengeld*).[27] Maybe the extensions were viewed by some as an unnecessary, or at least cumbersome work.

## THE SPIRITS OF THE DEAD

David Frese saw the apparition on the Grönau heath. This uncultivated stretch of land might have had a reputation of being the abode of weird spirits.[28]

The clergy's judgement states quite correctly that there was no indication whether the old man should be taken for God, for a man, for a good or for an evil spirit, nor whether he was sent by God or by someone else.

According to the clergy, the doves 'are probably supposed to be the *manes* or souls whose corpses are resting in St George's cemetery. They are crying about the bad treatment of their bodies (*daß es ihren Leibern so vbel gehe*).' The theologians rejected this concept as an expression of paganism or papistry.

The apparition of souls from purgatory was indeed frequently recorded in Catholic countries. A Catholic author in 1618 reasoned that the tormented souls in hell were not allowed to leave their place of torture, whilst the rejoicing souls in heaven did not want to leave their blissful abode. Revenants were therefore a clear proof of the existence of purgatory.[29] In Lutheranism, with the rejection of purgatory, there was no possibility for souls to appear after death.

In the account of David Frese's apparition, no explanation was given for the three doves drenched with tears. There are possible associations with the Holy Trinity, in particular with the Holy Spirit. The clergy's interpretation could very well be nothing more than a learned construction, using the Roman concept of *manes*. On the other hand, three ministers had talked to David Frese, probably for much longer than a perusal of Pastor Blume's account would indicate, and they were also aware of the gossip in the streets. If the clergy's interpretation reflected popular notions we can here catch a glimpse of a much more varied world of spiritual beings than Lutheran orthodoxy would have accepted.

Apart from the Holy Trinity, all spirits active on earth could either be classed as good or as evil angels (i.e. devils). Good angels acted as guardian angels[30] and occasionally served as messengers (ἄγγελοι) to humans. All supernatural beings besides good angels were demonised even though they were not necessarily harmful in popular belief. Some of these beings survived underground until the nineteenth century, the age of collecting folklore from oral sources, for example the pixies, or Little People (*Unnerêrsche* or *Unterirdische*).[31] Very little is known about these characters' behaviour and function in early modern times. I shall restrict myself to two examples which do not match very well with nineteenth-century accounts.

In the 1570s, a girl from a Neumark village claimed to have been fed by the Little People for almost four years. She did not consume any ordinary food during this period. The Little People, however, were not only her benefactors but hurt her as well. When the girl was brought to town, she claimed that these country spirits had no power in an urban environment.[32]

In the 1730s, a woman in Lutheran Sweden was apparently communicating with several spirits. Of various kinds, these existed in great numbers within human beings. The number of vital spirits (*Lebensgeister*) increased with age. There were good ones and bad ones, and even spirits in-between which were not yet damned but were still hoping for salvation and were therefore more good than evil. These spirits had been created at the same time as the angels. At one point in the records, the woman seems to have suggested the existence of certain earth-spirits dwelling underground. She claimed to have divine authority to evoke in the name of God whatever vital spirits she wished from other people present, and not just evil spirits. She even claimed to be able to despatch one of her own vital spirits to absent persons in order to bring the vital spirit of someone else to her. She claimed that, in the presence of many people, this spirit clearly answered all her questions whenever she inquired about a person's condition and illness, the spirit speaking through her own throat without moving her tongue and lips.[33]

Comparable to a shaman, but in a Christian context, she could even send her spirits to God: 'One of the spirits assigned to her after intensive prayer goes to God, not leaving Him until its request (for an answer) is fulfilled. This takes about a day and a half.' A Pietist account reduced her range of spirits to a simple distinction between good and bad angels.[34]

This case raises the question of the role of the Lutheran pastors who wrote down the majority of the sources. To what degree were their reports pressed into the stereotypes of good and evil angels? An apparition story recounted by a Lutheran pastor might very well have covered up non-Christian concepts of the spiritual world or remnants or medieval practices. Some otherwise quite Lutheran angels, for example, still showed traits of the medieval apparition of saints in so far as they promised intercessory prayer.[35]

Returning to David Frese, it is difficult to say if the spirits of the dead (if the doves were such) were of a good or an evil nature. Being white in colour, they were probably meant to be good. Popular culture seems to have been rather unaware that Satan could transform himself into an angel of light (2 Cor.11:14).

It is very clear, though, that there was a desire to have the graves undisturbed. On the one hand, this is very understandable, especially if one's relatives were newly buried (as might have been the case with David Frese); on the other hand, there could be a connection with the hope for bodily resurrection on the Day of Judgement. This event was depicted graphically in prints and in church art, for example on the pulpit of the cathedral church in Lübeck.[36] The Easter Sermon, a few days before David Frese's apparition, might have mentioned it as well.

A few gravestones in Lübeck's churches request that the grave not be opened until the Day of Judgement.[37] This kind of inscription, however, is rather exceptional,[38] probably in part owing to the expense. The clergy's judgement on David Frese's case pointed out that almost all graves were disturbed anyway on the occasion of later burials, 'which would be difficult to change, due to the lack of space'.

## REPENTANCE

According to two Dominicans who spent four days in Lübeck on a secret papal mission in 1622, the Lübeckers adhered warmly to their Lutheran faith. Even weekday sermons were preached to overcrowded churches.[39]

The old man demanded that every week two days of prayer should be held at St George's. Public days of prayer were very common, being held both regularly and in times of crisis. They were usually decreed by the secular authorities. In Lübeck, they were held regularly on Tuesday and Thursday mornings, but apparently only in the major churches in town.[40]

What is repentance?[41] In Lutheranism, repentance no longer meant – as it had in medieval times – specific exercises of penance for example prayers, fasts and alms) for specific sins, but rather an inner conversion that should last one's whole life; i.e. man should constantly be aware of his sinful life and should live repentantly.

Divine punishment could be averted by showing repentance and by living in a manner agreeable to God.[42] The Lutheran prophets were true to official teaching on this point. By way of repentance one could gain influence over plague, war, and famine. The prophets offered the people a remedy for those threats over which they had no actual control.

Within the framework of the Lutheran theology of repentance, the prophets emphasised one thing: God's punishment would only be averted if *everyone* recognised their sins and repented. People (town, region, Christendom) were all collectively responsible before God. The good could no longer – as in the Middle Ages – do penance for other people's sins, but the evil people could bring calamities on the community from which the good would also suffer. The predicted horrors (such as plagues or earthquakes) were of such a nature that they did not strike individual sinners but whole communities.

The prophets' criticism of sin was modelled on the Ten Commandments and on Martin Luther's explanation of them in

the *Shorter Catechism*, but the prophets attached special importance to the sin of pride. In their view pride manifested itself
mainly in dress. This point of view was supported by the authorities issuing countless sumptuary edicts forbidding people to dress
more richly than their order permitted.[43]

A proud person was neither open to teaching nor willing to
convert. He either did not care about his salvation or felt sure
about it and was therefore not open to the Lutheran concept of
repentance.

Leaving the theological distinctions aside, what made days of
prayer attractive for common people? Was it, on a very profane
level, the fact that all work was forbidden? The Lübeck clergy
feared that the townspeople would superstitiously attend the prayer
services at St George's because they considered them to be in
higher esteem with God ('für Gott höher vnd krafftiger geachtet').
The Lübeckers thought that the days of prayer 'will deliver the
town from danger' ('die Stadt aus gefahr erretten werden').

Were these days of prayer meant as 'a kind of collective rite of
exorcism' or would it 'be too easy to look at Keil's [a prophet in
1648] notion of penance – a notion that all one has to do is to
show remorse in order for God to heap his blessings on the population – mechanically, or as a kind of magic'?[44]

From a theological point of view, it was not possible to obtain
God's blessing *ex opere operato*:

It is not enough to go to church every day and act like the
Pharisees but we should change our life to the better. We shall
not only sing the litany but arrange our conduct in such a way
in the faith in Christ that the prayer might leave an impression
with His Father ('daß das Gebet bey seinen [sic] Vater hafften
möge').[45]

I would suggest that the majority of prophets (though not
necessarily all of their followers) held the same view. They used
the established institution of days of prayer in order to achieve
their aim. Participation was compulsory. When the congregation
was assembled, there was a chance of everyone becoming aware of
his sins and repenting. The *collectivity* would show itself as
repentant and thus urge God to end the present suffering and
divert impending calamities.

Collective prayer in church was thought to be more powerful ('mit mehrer Krafft allgemeinen Gebeths') than individual prayer at home. This view was also expressed in a detailed edict of 27 March 1629, issued for the duchies of Schleswig and Holstein, admonishing the subjects to lead a Christian life. In general, it was not enough to show 'outward church-going, the external use of the sacraments, singing, prayer, etc.' if God's punishment was to be avoided.[46] Maybe David Frese had heard about this edict, which was valid in the immediate vicinity of Lübeck, and wished for similar action to be taken by the Lübeck town council. His message to the clergy was much more specific, though, asking for days of prayer to be held. There is no record of a Lübeck edict following David Frese's apparition. The preamble of a Lübeck edict issued in conjunction with the plague later in the year, however, stressed repentance as a remedy against the plague, together with God's mercy and sanitary measures – but this kind of statement was commonplace at the time.[47]

## MODELS FOR DAVID FRESE'S APPARITION

David Frese had probably heard of angelic apparitions before. Numerous pamphlets telling of popular prophets were printed, in Lübeck as elsewhere.[48] Angelic apparitions were mentioned in sermons; oral communication provided further information.[49] Lübeck was well placed in the communications network, being located between Hamburg and the countries surrounding the Baltic.

David Frese felt relieved after delivering his message. Pastor Blume had not dismissed his story outright. David Frese had now carried out an important task for the salvation of his community. Several other prophets who were hesitant in forwarding the message were repeatedly reminded of their duty by their angel and even threatened with personal punishment.[50]

In two cases, the prophets even needed written proof that they had carried out their job. In Thuringia in 1575, a girl was asked to obtain a certificate ('ein Zeddel vnd Bekendnus') confirming that she had delivered the message. She was to take this along with her into Life Everlasting.[51] In 1582, a man entered the town hall in

Nuremberg, asked for the burgomaster and told him that he had orders to announce to this and many other towns that a great punishment would come over them if they did not repent. Afterwards, he asked for a written testimony that he had informed this town. The burgomaster conferred with the town council and it was resolved that the man should first go to the other towns he had talked about. If he produced testimonies from them, he would get one from Nuremberg as well. A short time later, he was ordered to leave the town.[52]

After his apparition, David Frese could neither eat nor drink. Many prophets showed bodily signs, demonstrating that God controlled not only their words but also their bodies. They would fall into ecstasy, fast, fall ill, or become mute for a time, only to speak out with greater authority afterwards.[53]

At the end of his vision, David Frese was told to go away and not look back. This might allude to Lot and the destruction of Sodom and Gomorrah (Gen. 11), reminding the Lübeckers of the fate of towns disobedient to God. This was not just a biblical story. News about towns vanishing from the face of the earth was often reported.[54] Folk-tales localised similar disasters in the area of the narrators.[55]

Like most angels encountered by Lutheran prophets, the old man was dressed in white. The stone that had fallen down and the doves were of the same colour, normally indicating goodness. The significance of the stone is not clear. Sacred stones are known from all over the world but their 'symbolic meaning ... is not fixed'. The white stone was without doubt a well-known landmark, maybe denoting the actual border line.[56] The border control points, the toll-bar, was the place where David Frese rested after the apparition. His vision had, after all, meant a transgression of the normal limits of experience.

The Danish delegates at the peace negotiations were representing a king who was known to have seen Christ some three years earlier. On that occasion, however, Christ had not said anything to Christian IV. Reports about his vision were spread in pamphlets.[57]

Although there seem to be no records of Lutheran popular prophets in Lübeck before 1629, David Frese might have known about other popular prophetic figures visiting the town earlier, who, however, can hardly be termed Lutheran.

In June 1624, the tailor Johann Bannier of Havelberg (Brandenburg) arrived in Lübeck, coming from Elsinore in Denmark. He approached the printer Valentin Schmalhertz to have a book printed. Following the regulations, the printer gave the manuscript to the superintendent, Nicolaus Hunnius, who was in charge of censorship. Hunnius quickly realised that Bannier's writings were not in agreement with Lutheran orthodoxy. Among other things, Bannier held that all procreation was sinful and demanded abstention from matrimony. In a debate with three Lübeck pastors in January 1625, it became evident that Bannier was not willing to revoke his teachings. As the basis of his teachings he named not only Scripture, which he interpreted in an allegorical way, but also divine inspiration. He had earlier spread similar views in Sweden and Denmark.[58] The town council expelled him from Lübeck.

In 1616, a woman by the name of Anna Walcker had troubled the Lübeck clergy with her private revelations and predictions of the Second (but not the Last) Coming of Christ in 1621. She had been born in Denmark, grown up in Lübeck, moved back to Denmark, lived and married in England, and stayed in Holland. After spreading her prophecies in Hamburg, she passed through Lübeck on her way to Denmark.[59]

David Frese differed from these two prophets on two main points. Although Anna Walcker and Johann Bannier had not received any university education either, they put their views forward in writing. Furthermore, they were separating themselves from the established church through their own interpretation of the Bible and by criticising the clergy.

Maybe the recent examples had made David Frese aware that he could not expect any success by attacking the clergy or official dogmatics. Although the clergy did not follow David Frese's call, at no point did they discredit him personally as a heretic. The Lutheran prophets as a whole tried to achieve a general improvement within the existing church, not only for tactical reasons but also because they were convinced of the truth of its teachings.

The Lübeck clergy did not know what to make of David Frese's statement concerning the child born to serve as a penitential mirror (*Bußspiegel*) for all, since he had not indicated where the child was to be found. They suggested that the horrible

devastation of towns and countries was a sufficient mirror of
God's wrath (*Gottes ... Zornspiegel*).

There are several possible interpretations of David Frese's statement. One would be to view the newborn child either as a
Messianic figure or as the Antichrist, whose birth was frequently announced in pamphlets.[60] David Frese might also have been
influenced by another cheap-print genre, the tale of the birth of
three miraculous children, predicting plague, war, and famine.[61]
The more likely interpretation, though, is that the statement refers
to a monstrous birth. Maybe the parents had obscured the fact,
fearing that the abnormality of the child might be blamed on the
immorality of the parents, as some preferred to judge in these
cases.[62] Monstrous births were a favourite topic of theological commentators. If the deformities looked like fashionable garments,
they expressed God's dislike of these luxuries.[63] A more abstract
way of interpretation was to see the misshapen child as a mirror
showing the shortcomings of the body of the Christian church: misshapen eyes indicated blindness in spiritual things, abnormal ears,
deafness towards God's Word, and so on.[64] There is no record of a
monstrous birth in Lübeck for the year 1629, but at other times
they seem to have been as frequent there as elsewhere.[65]

## PROPHETS AS BAROMETERS OF POPULAR OPINION

There were several cases where the established cultural pattern of
a Lutheran popular prophet was used for fraudulent purposes. At
the end of the sixteenth century, a man in Dithmarschen made a
living by acting as a penitential preacher.[66] Much more similar to
David Frese, however, are cases where prophets tried to make a
local political point.

In 1659, a cowherd in the Palatinate admitted to having invented his apparitions after noticing that angelic apparitions generally were being accepted benevolently. His aim was to scare the
district officials (*Ampt-Leut*) who were oppressing the subjects –
probably without the knowledge of their superiors – and force
them to behave more mildly in the future.[67]

In the 1580s, a number of clergymen and members of the town
council in Danzig openly showed Calvinist sympathies. This led to

discontent among the parishioners. In 1587, pasquinades
(*Dräuzedul, Paßquillen*) were posted in the town at night. The town
council tried to quench this expression of discontent by promising 100 thaler for the name of a libeller. This curbed the libels to
a degree, but not the popular discontent. The wife of a schoolmaster appeared in public, claimed to have had revelations, and
warned the inhabitants against the Calvinists. She demanded to
be heard by the town council, promising to reveal many miraculous things. When she was admitted, she talked against the
Calvinists, and claimed to have seen one of the leaders of the
clergy's Calvinist faction and some members of the town council
burning in hell. This is rather early evidence of confessional identity at a popular level.[68]

Whether this was conscious fraud or not, Lutheran popular
prophets can in many ways be used as indicators of popular
beliefs and views, as in the way that David Frese's case can tell us
something about the range of spiritual beings beyond the sharp
theological divisions between demons and angels. By using the established cultural pattern of Lutheran popular prophets, ordinary
people could speak out, and their words were recorded. In most
cases, however, their message was mediated by the learned, normally by pastors.[69]

On the other hand, by using the established pattern, people
acting as popular prophets had to fulfil the expectations of their
listeners, for example by acting as spiritual advisors or living in an
exemplary manner. People came hurrying from far away in order
to profit – often financially – from their knowledge of and connection with divine power. Some prophets did not comment on
local politics, but rather on the state of grace of individuals in the
community. This cultural pattern was, after all, primarily determined by its religious content.[70]

Sometimes the prophets seemed to be more credible spiritual
authorities than the ministers. This was probably due not merely
to their bodily signs (ecstasy, fasts, muteness) but also to their
language. They only spoke the vernacular and they were not
capable of mixing it with Latin terms. Their performance could
be much more vivid than that of ordinary preachers. It will
suffice here to quote a report about a prophet in Stralsund
in 1558/59, preaching 'with a terrible face, laughing [?]
(*gry[ff]laggen*) and strange gestures, by shaking the head,

clapping hands in lamentation, distortion of the whole body'.[71]

The prophets stood in an ambivalent relation to the ministers. They were dependent on the ministers' acceptance to a certain degree in order not to be proclaimed heretics. On the other hand they assumed some of the ministers' functions but without dissociating themselves from the clergy.

The prophets tried to lead their contemporaries to the Christian life which they themselves wanted to live. The prophets' activity suggests not only that laymen listened passively to the long sermons in church but that they also processed them actively. Theological reasoning was not only to be found in the clerical world. It concerned the prophets and their audiences as well, although the accentuation might differ; at any rate, common people's conceptions of the sacred were not restricted to magical beliefs. A magical worldview was certainly common, but at the time this did not exclude Christian belief. This applied to pastors as well.

The prophets offer fascinating insights into the interplay between learned theology and popular religion. Lutheran sermons not only contained biblical exegesis but drew just as much on collections of *exempla* and recent miracles in the neighbourhood in order to incite the listeners to repentance.[72] Pastors preached about prophets, whilst prophets retold the pastors' sermons, adapting them to their universe, and enabling us to look into it.


## EPILOGUE

David Frese was not the last prophet with whom the Lübeck clergy had to deal. Indeed, Lübeck pastors later came to play a prominent role in the theological debates about prophets.[73]

Although David Frese's demands were rejected at the time, his effort was not totally in vain. The use of the poorhouse's 'old graveyard' seems to have continued after the Thirty Years' War. In 1967, it was referred to as being still in use.[74] After all, the plague of 1629 had proved David Frese's unspecified prediction of calamities to be correct even though similar disasters could have struck at any moment in those troubled times.

# 9. Blood, Tears and Xavier-Water: Jesuit Missionaries and Popular Religion in the Eighteenth-Century Upper Palatinate

TREVOR JOHNSON

## I

At first glance, associating the Jesuits with popular religion might appear paradoxical. Given their background, training, ecclesiastical power and political influence, the Jesuits constituted an elite within German Catholic society in the era of the Counter-Reformation. At the same time, their ministry was principally directed towards that society's other elite groups. Jesuit priests, or *patres*, were prominent, for example, in an educational role, as instructors of the secular and regular clergy in the universities, or as tutors to the sons of nobility and patricians in their imposing urban colleges. Similarly the order's significant political influence derived from the frequent occupation by Jesuits of posts as confessors to Catholic princely dynasties. Jesuits too trod the boards of high culture as artistic and literary patrons and practitioners. Such were the elevated circles in which they appear to have moved most comfortably. Unsurprisingly, historians of the Society of Jesus in Germany have chosen to focus their studies on those Jesuit activities and institutions which best reflect these themes, from theology to court politics, from Marian Sodalities to school drama.[1] But what of the rest of society and, in particular, of its largest constituency, the rural peasantry: were the non-elite ignored completely by the *patres*?

The order owed its origin to the missionary zeal of its founder, Ignatius Loyola, and the promotion of Catholic Christianity overseas was a major feature of Jesuit activity from the first generation onwards. In time, the lessons of missionary work in the New World came to be applied closer to home, as, like their rivals among some of the other religious orders, the Jesuits stepped out of their cosy urban environment into the cultural *terra incognita* of the European rural world. In Germany, hit-and-run evangelising tours of the countryside by small groups of Jesuits, tours which were later termed *Volksmissionen* or 'missions to the people', began to take place from the early seventeenth century. If there was an arena of cultural encounter between the Jesuit elite and popular religion, it was here.

By way of a case study, I propose to look at three such rural missions conducted between 1716 and 1722 in the Upper Palatinate, a former province of the Palatine Electorate which had been incorporated into the duchy of Bavaria during the Thirty Years' War. The sources are reports written by the missionaries themselves for their Jesuit superiors and, in the case of the first of the three missions, for the local secular authorities. From these triumphalist Jesuit accounts alone it is impossible to assess the impact of the missions and such an assessment will not be attempted. Instead, I shall try to use the reports as a mode of entry into the internal culture of the Jesuit order and concentrate on what they can tell us about the Jesuits' strategies.

How did the missionaries approach the popular religious culture which they encountered on their tours? The historiography of rural missions in other parts of Catholic Europe during the period has tended to highlight the dramatic penitential tone and emotional intensity of these events, symbolised by streams of flagellant blood and terrifying hellfire sermons calculated to reduce to tears even the sturdiest peasant. The Jesuit attitude to popular religious culture is seen to be, at best, negative, at worst, violently hostile. With such a focus, the missions can be, and have been, readily fitted into interpretations of the Counter-Reformation which represent the movement as, in the best-known formulations, an attempted acculturation of the rural world, a campaign of Christianisation, or a general reform of popular culture finding vivid expression in the contemporary image of the battle between Carnival and Lent.[2] As will be described below, the reports from the Upper Palatinate echo these themes and the missionaries there certainly placed great value on penitential performance and copious tears. They appear to have regarded their dramatic expiatory liturgies as a vital adjunct to more formal modes of indoctrination and reform, such as the sermon and the catechism. The objective of this short, sharp spiritual shock was individual and collective conversion, conversion here in the sense of moral reformation, but also in the sense of confessional change, of recatholicisation. To an extent, both forms of conversion could be said to have involved an attack on popular religion, but another aspect of the mission revealed a different side to the Jesuits' approach. The missionaries enthusiastically promoted their own 'sacramental' or blessing, a form of holy water known as Xavier-Water, which was credited with curative properties. The *patres* eagerly collected accounts of the miraculous benefits resulting from the water's application. This way of harnessing the power of the sacred for material as well as spiritual ends chimed with a fundamental aspect of traditional peasant religious culture, a culture suffused with a bewildering variety of prayers, charms, talismans and blessed objects. In their promotion of what one might call a form of ecclesiastical magic, however framed its distribution might have been by the penitential and catechetical content of the mission, the Jesuits appear to have compromised to a degree with this culture. In their accommodation of popular demand for devices with which to manipulate the sacred, we can see the Jesuit missionaries in a more nuanced light, responsive to popular religion, rather than unequivocally hostile towards it. To an extent, indeed, one can speak of a shared religious culture, which might be termed a culture of the miraculous. Before exploring these twin themes of conversion and accommodation in more detail, I shall give a brief account of the introduction of the Jesuit rural mission into Bavaria.

## II

Although Peter Canisius, who had introduced the Society into Germany in the mid-sixteenth century, could be regarded as the region's first Jesuit missionary, the structured and systematic rural mission, designed to implant the Counter-Reformation in the countryside, was a seventeenth-century development. Missions of this type were undertaken by Jesuits in the Rhineland from the late 1670s.[3] In the Upper German province, which included Bavaria and the Upper Palatinate, they arrived somewhat later, transplanted directly from Italy by Fulvio Fontana, a disciple of the leading Italian Jesuit missionary, Paolo Segneri the Elder. Accompanied by a Tyrolean Jesuit, Georg Loferer, Fontana conducted missions in Catholic Switzerland, the Tyrol and Austria between 1705 and 1710. When he returned to Italy, Loferer went, as well, to receive further coaching in the Italian missionary method from the younger Segneri. Missionary work was regarded as a specialist skill to be acquired through a form of apprenticeship based on personal contacts and the sharing of practical experience of years of travel and missionising in varied regions. By 1715, Loferer was back in Germany, leading missions in the Palatinate and other Catholic territories in the Rhineland. His assistant was Conrad Herdegen, former rector of the Jesuit college at Trent. In the following years, aided by a handful of German Jesuits, Loferer and Herdegen ranged across the Society's Rhenish and Upper German provinces. Bavaria, including the Upper Palatinate, was the last big domino to fall to this missionary wave. When the idea of a Bavarian mission was first mooted in 1718, the Elector, Max Emanuel, was sceptical and it was two years before Herdegen could begin work in Bavaria, with two new companions, Andreas Proesl and Joachim Ernst. The latter took charge of the Bavarian mission after Herdegen's death in 1726.[4]

In Bavaria, the typical rural mission spent from a week to nine days in each location and was conducted by a team of two or three *patres*. A model timetable for a mission involving three Jesuits, drawn up in the period after Herdegen's death, survives in the Munich archive.[5] On their first evening in a host village the Jesuits would receive a welcome from the parish priest, hold a short procession, perform the ceremony of Benediction and preach a sermon on the purpose and content of the mission. Over the following eight days, the mornings would be occupied with instruction on the sacraments followed by Mass and sermons devoted to the Ten Commandments, sin, infernal punishment and related topics. The afternoon sessions were taken up with catechism classes, further sermons, acts of contrition and examinations of conscience. The week also included public recitations of the Rosary, prayer in front of the Blessed Sacrament, and individual confession. The climax of the affair was the erection of a large mission-cross, accompanied by the administration of general communion and a blessing.[6]

The delay in the introduction of the rural mission into Bavaria has been attributed to opposition to another of its components, the so-called 'Italian method'. Loferer and Herdegen had borrowed from Segneri and Fontana the idea of enhancing the dramatic impact of their missions by staging public penitential processions, often at night. Congregations were encouraged to flagellate themselves or perform other acts of corporal mortification. Appropriate procedures included walking barefoot, wrapping iron chains round the ankles, wearing crowns of thorns, carrying large wooden crosses and placing heavy stones on the head. Not that the missionaries expected the people to perform acts to which they were unwilling to subject themselves. During a mission to Jülich in May 1715, for example, one of the Jesuits was said to have held his hand in the flames of a torch for longer than the time it took to say an Our Father. Both Loferer and Herdegen bared their backs and whipped themselves, telling their audience that they were great sinners and had to be punished. The tactic was designed to arouse compassion, guilt and emulation and appears to have succeeded. In tears at the spectacle of the Jesuits' ruthlessly self-inflicted pain, the crowd began to flagellate themselves or lie on the ground with outstretched arms, while Herdegen began a sermon with the words: 'Blood, blood, dear Christians!' Subsequently the people flocked to the confessionals.[7]

The Italian method attracted widespread criticism from both secular and ecclesiastical authorities. The sources of such opposition remain obscure and require further investigation, but a major factor seems to have been a fear that the frenzied missionary antics would threaten public order. This apprehension combined with a more general suspicion on the part of the authorities that the missions distracted entire village populations away from the source of their livelihood, their work on the land, particularly during the harvest or the vintage, and were therefore counterproductive. In turn, there was opposition from nervous local Jesuit superiors, who feared repercussions against the order after the missionaries had moved on.[8] In Bavaria, the Elector, having been won round eventually to the acceptability of the mission, accompanied his permits to the missionaries with specific bans on penitential processions and works of public penance. A similar tone was adopted by lesser sponsors and benefactors of the *Volksmissionen*. The dean of Vilshofen, for example, who donated 8,000 gulden to the Jesuit college at Straubing for the Bavarian mission, stipulated that no public penitential processions should take place; instead everything was to be done 'gently and without a din'.[9]

<h1 style="text-align:center">III</h1>

The bewildering series of confessional shifts which dominates the religious history of the Upper Palatinate in the century or so after 1550 provides a text-book illustration of the practical implications of the theory of *cuius regio eius religio*: the right of the prince to determine the religion of his subjects. Before the Thirty Years' War, the area lay under the rule of the Palatine Electors, who exercised their authority through a governor residing at Amberg. From the mid-sixteenth century successive Electors imposed first Lutheranism and then Calvinism on the territory. A brief return to Lutheranism in the late 1570s was followed by a longer spell of Calvinist rule. The seventy-year period of official Protestantism in the Upper Palatinate came to an end with Elector Frederick V's defeat at the battle of the White Mountain in November 1620.[10] The following year, the Upper Palatinate was invaded by the Catholic Duke Maximilian I of Bavaria and by degrees formally annexed to his duchy. In 1628, an *annus horribilis* for the Upper Palatinate's Protestants, Maximilian gave the entire population a six-month deadline to convert to Catholicism or emigrate.[11] From the start, the Society of Jesus played a crucial role in the recatholicisation: appropriately enough, the first Catholic clergy to say Mass in the territory after the seventy-year Reformation *caesura* were Jesuit chaplains ministering to the Bavarian soldiery.[12] Given the lack of diocesan clergy during the early years of the recatholicisation, the Jesuits, along with members of other religious orders, were often forced to assume parochial responsibilities, filling the posts left vacant by the expulsion of Protestant pastors. The Society swiftly established a number of outposts in the region, but it was in Amberg that its presence was most strongly felt. Beginning in the 1630s, an entire housing district was demolished and a town-gate repositioned to make room for the Jesuits' new, fortress-like college.[13] Through their college school, the Jesuits soon had a hold on the education of the region's social elite, while through their confraternities, or Marian Sodalities, they played an increasingly important role in the spiritual and moral formation of the capital's burghers.

The first new-style Jesuit rural mission to be held in the Upper Palatinate seems to have taken place in the winter of 1716/17. The Jesuits were called in by the Bavarian Elector, Max Emanuel, to help recatholicise the district of Rothenberg, a tiny enclave of territory surrounded by lands belonging to the great Lutheran imperial city of Nuremberg. During the recent War of the Spanish Succession the city of Nuremberg had briefly gained control of the district and many of the inhabitants had accepted Protestantism. In December 1716, the Jesuits Joseph Mayer and Caspar Rieger undertook a series of nine-day missions in the district's parishes. Their subsequent report to the Electoral government details how they promoted the Rosary and other devotions, taught the people Catholic hymns, catechised adults as well as children and preached against such Protestant abuses as eating meat on fast days. In the villages the missionaries conducted house-to-house searches for Protestant books and, after imposing a fine for each offending volume found, publicly burnt them all. In return they disseminated their own literature. With only two families still unconverted, the missionaries left.

When, however, under the influence of two local nobles, the district's inhabitants relapsed into Protestantism, the Elector immediately ordered the Jesuits back for a second strike. In January 1717, Mayer returned to repeat the mission, this time accompanied by another Jesuit, Maximilian Thor, along with a detachment of troops. Confident of having succeeded at the second attempt, the missionaries finally departed, leaving behind a twenty-five foot high mission-cross inscribed with the message 'Do not forget!'[14]

The next Jesuit missionary foray was on a much larger scale, intended to embrace virtually the whole of the Upper Palatinate. On 24 March 1721, the Elector informed the regional authorities in Amberg that he had given permission for three Jesuits from Straubing to hold a mission in the Upper Palatinate. As with other missions within his territories, he decreed that the tours be conducted 'without employing public processions or the corporal penitential acts that usually accompany them'.[15] On their first tour the Jesuits covered the eastern and north-eastern parts of the territory, venturing into the mountainous terrain of the Bavarian Forest on the Bohemian border. The following year they covered the western districts. Lengthy manuscript reports in Latin of both missions are preserved amongst other Jesuit material in the Bavarian State Archive at Munich.[16]

The Elector's decree opened doors for the Jesuits by requiring that the secular authorities cooperate in facilitating the mission. When the three *patres* arrived in Amberg, for example, the government declared a holiday and turned out the garrison to help steward the missionary events. At the same time, decrees from the bishops of Regensburg, Eichstätt and Bamberg were similarly designed to ensure the cooperation of the local clergy. The Jesuits were relying on parish priests not only to give advance warning from their pulpits of the forthcoming mission but also to help bring their flocks from outlying parishes into the small towns that had been selected as missionary centres. In their reports the Jesuits often singled out individual parish priests for praise, but they were aware that the ordinary parish clergy could resent the missionaries as apparently self-appointed ecclesiastical troubleshooters, and they were conscious too that they might be seen in the role of diocesan visitors, on the look out for clerical laxity. They detected, as they put it,

> a false suspicion that ... the missions had been introduced not so much for the sake of the ignorant and illiterate as for the parish priests themselves, as if they lacked the ability to educate the people with their sermons, or were failing in their task of catechising the young.[17]

The *patres* gauged the impact of the missions, and their degree of success or failure, in the first place in terms of their crowd-pulling popularity. Numbers counted, and the Jesuits duly counted numbers. The generally triumphalist tone of the reports is nowhere more manifest than in this aspect. If we can believe them, however, it would seem that large crowds certainly did appear, although judging their motivation is another matter. As the missions gradually progressed through the region, news of them spread and they acquired what the Jesuits termed *fama* or reputation. The start of the 1721 mission augured well, with a crowd of 10,000 people attending the Jesuits' sermons, including so many people from the district of Wörth that, according to the reports, the villages there appeared deserted, apart from the presence of the old women who had been left behind to look after the houses. In the Bavarian Forest, the missionaries attracted a contingent of people from Pilsen in Bohemia, who had been walking in the rain across difficult country for sixteen hours. In the Fichtelgebirge, the missionaries estimated the crowd, which contained many Lutherans from Wunsiedel in the Margravate of Bayreuth, as numbering 16,000.[18] In 1722, they claimed that 'the entire town of Forchheim' and many people from Bamberg had travelled to hear them in Auerbach. The Jesuits also boasted that the rural clergy were suddenly discovering that they could muster over seven or eight hundred of their parishioners to attend the missions, whereas previously, 'even in times of communal emergency', they had been unable to attract more than sixty people to their own processions.[19]

In addition to sheer numbers, the missionaries gauged their success by the 'fruits', or results, that they perceived. These were described in the central section of their reports and reveal the Jesuits' objectives. In the Upper Palatinate in 1721 and 1722, as previously in 1716 and 1717, an important aim was to combat heresy and if possible bring about the conversion of Protestants. The Jesuits took careful note of the response of the large number of foreign Protestants who crossed into the territory to attend the missions. This preoccupation helps to explain the apparent concentration of their efforts on the Upper Palatinate's border parishes, especially in the north, where they could hope both to extend some Catholic influence into Protestant regions and to counteract any reciprocal influence from outside upon the Elector's own subjects. With evident pleasure, therefore, the Jesuits noted the impact of their sermons on the group of Lutherans from Wunsiedel who had attended the mission in 1721:

> They were unable to hold back their tears. Their ferocious spirits were calmed, the hatred, which they had felt since child-

hood, was extinguished and they approached us with great ad-
miration and reverence. Having returned home, their friends
and neighbours asked them what they had gained from the
mission and the same response was heard from everyone: the
missionaries did not appear nearly as black or perverse as their
own pastors had depicted them![20]

The Lutherans appeared to be as moved as the Catholics by the
missionaries' sermons and the Jesuits afterwards observed 'men,
and Lutherans at that, prostrate at the feet of their parents,
begging pardon for their errors with much sobbing and wailing'.[21]
When the missionaries were in Schnaittach, Lutherans flocked
from Nuremberg to hear them. The Jesuits conceded that the
motives of some of them may originally have been dubious, but
even these doubters were swayed by their moving oratory:

> Weeping, wailing and loud lamentations were heard from the
> audience. Women, noblemen and priests alike were drenched
> in tears, and it was noticeable that the non-Catholics who had
> come in order to make fun and sport were actually the first to
> break into public weeping and lamentation.[22]

From such individuals, the Jesuits tried to extract not merely
tears but formal conversion to Catholicism as well. For their
reports they singled out examples of conversions by members of
the nobility. Among a number of such cases in 1722, a young noblewoman of the Ehrenstein family, who had 'for a long time
doubted the truth of her sect', came along to the missionaries to
be instructed in the Catholic faith. Having denounced the errors
of Lutheranism and handed over her Protestant books for
burning, she was publicly received into the Church. Another
woman, who had been born to Catholic parents but had aposta-
tised in order to secure a favourable marriage, confessed her
error and was welcomed back into the Church, promising to have
her child instructed in the Catholic faith.[23]

The anti-heretical drive made the rural missions in the Upper
Palatinate, as in other German territories which had been recently
recatholicised or which lay on the confessional front line, somewhat different from those conducted in the heartlands of Catholic
Europe, where popular ignorance, superstition and loose morals

were the chief targets. This aspect also gave the eighteenth-century missions a tone reminiscent of the period of militant recatholic-isation of the previous century. This is not to say, however, that the other, more conventional, 'fruits' were not desired too. The reports contain lengthy sections on the efficacy of repentance and confession, emphasising the reformatory content of the missions and the individual and collective conversions to a better life which accompanied them. Of importance here was the fact that, despite the Elector's ban on public flagellation, the *patres* succeeded in injecting a large penitential dose into their missions, with blood-curdling, tear-jerking sermons, carefully stage-managed expiatory ceremonies, and active audience participation. The best descrip-tion of their tactics is to be found in the report of the Rothenberg mission. On their return to the district in January 1717, after the disappointing results of their first tour, the Jesuits resolved to adopt what they called a 'new practice', consisting of 'the public performance of total repentance and contrition for all one's sins'. In fact this was simply a more moderate and less sanguinary version of the Italian method: a ritual designed to shock, but stop-ping short of public flagellation. In the choir of the parish church at Schnaittach the Jesuits set up a stage covered with black cloth and supporting a small table, on which they placed a large crucifix, a candle and a skull from the local ossuary. To the strains of a penitential hymn the missionaries made their way through dense crowds to the stage. Then, as they later reported,

> one of the *patres* took hold of the large crucifix and spoke movingly of the necessity of total repentance and contrition for all one's sins. Whereupon the other *pater*, who had been kneel-ing with a rope around his neck, like a poor sinner, in front of the table with the skull on it, stood up. Holding up the skull in his hand, he showed the people the end that the sinner could expect, the wretched extinction of all of the pleasures of this world. He then moved on to the act of repentance and con-trition itself. He threw himself down before the cross, which the first *pater* held out in front of him, and then turned to the con-gregation and asked them if they wanted to wound again such a loving God, to which everyone shouted back 'No!', and began to sigh and wail so loudly and furiously that the *patres* had to stop speaking.[24]

Again the Jesuits were inflicting public humiliation, if not physical pain, on themselves in order to inflame their congregation's pangs of guilt. On the later missions they noted that the people were prepared to emulate them. In Auerbach in 1722, for example, the Jesuits especially commended one of the rural priests for his imagination and 'excelling fervour' in orchestrating penitential devotions for his parishioners. Not content with imitating the Jesuit preaching style, he had encouraged the people to manufacture rough wooden crosses, which they then carried during their barefoot and hatless journey through the pouring rain, all the while singing hymns and weeping.[25] Descriptions of these collective responses alternate with reports of individual moral conversions, particularly of prominent figures, such as local nobility or clergy. In 1721, for example, after an evening sermon, the priest of Neunburg vorm Wald clutched the hand of the missionary as he descended from the pulpit, groaning and begging forgiveness for neglecting his parochial responsibilities. Even if this was pre-planned, the rare spectacle of the humbling of local notables must have added further to the mission's crowd-pulling *fama*.[26]

Whether the impact lingered beyond the mission's eight days is of course a different matter. The doctrines and devotions promoted during the mission could well have constituted merely superficial and temporary grafts, particularly in the absence of mechanisms which might have institutionalised them, such as confraternities, of the foundation of which there is no mention for the three missions here described. It is difficult to see how even the impact on the rural clergy, let alone the laity, could be guaranteed to persist outside the charged atmosphere of the mission. Stiffened backbones could easily recover their slouch. Perhaps the only answer was to hold more frequent missions. In the course of the eighteenth century this appears to have happened. But, again, the reports reviewed here can only really tell us something about the missionaries' aims and strategies, not their results. In those strategies, we see a stress not just on formal indoctrination through religious instruction but also on collective performance and ritual as a means of effecting conversion. The Society was quite prepared to fight on a 'semiotic battleground'[27] and attempt to persuade through vivid symbols as well as dry indoctrination. While the blood might have been only symbolic,

thanks to the Elector's decree, the other penitential per-
formances were real enough. The tears too were real, an example
of what William Christian has termed 'provoked religious
weeping', an act which was part of a rich, popular ritual and ges-
tural repertoire.[28] For the Jesuits an emotional response, rather
than an intellectual one, was clearly the objective. The volume of
tears therefore became a measure of the success of the mission,
hence the continual repetition in the reports of the phrase 'with
weeping and wailing' to describe the popular reception of the
missionary set pieces. Blood and tears, however, did not exhaust
the Jesuits' armoury.

## IV

The chronicles of the 1721 and 1722 tours end with sections
headed 'Benefits obtained by Xavier-Water'. These list cases of
miraculous cures which had taken place during the missions. The
agent was a type of holy water: using a special formula of prayers,
the Jesuits consecrated a quantity of water, immersing in it relics
or medals of St Francis Xavier, the Jesuit missionary to the Orient
who had been canonised a century earlier. The resulting 'Xavier-
Water' was then applied, externally or internally, to the patient. It
is an example of a sacramental, an object blessed by the clergy,
but then used, generally as a protective or medicinal talisman, by
the laity.[29] Its consecration by the eighteenth-century missionaries
illustrates how the Counter-Reformation both preserved the many
medieval sacramentals and actually expanded on them with additional types dedicated to its new saints. But its promotion during
the mission in the Upper Palatinate also reveals a more subtle and
less confrontational approach to popular religious culture on the
part of the Jesuits than their reformatory, penitential strategies,
described above, might suggest.

First the cures, of which in 1721 the Jesuits reported half a
dozen successful cases. At Haibach, for example, an entire family
was cured of fever by 'water touched with a relic of Xavier'. At
Neukirchen a peasant who had tried many remedies for fever
without success finally drank some Xavier-Water and promptly recovered. A pregnant noblewoman experiencing difficulty in

labour drank Xavier-Water and was safely delivered of a son. In Mitterfeld a man with a lame foot who was too poor to consult physicians was urged by his wife and sons to try a dose of Xavier-Water. On being dipped in the water the foot was healed and the miracle became the talk of the town. In Moosbach the parish priest testified in writing concerning a young boy who was suffering great pain in his limbs and appeared to be incurably lame:

> despairing of help or advice, his parents used Xavier-Water, on one occasion mixing it with his food, on another washing his body with it. And behold! The child recovered. He was able to stand firmly on his feet and to take a step, and was whole and well ... in gratitude for such a benefit, they paid for some wax candles for the altar, a minor thing in that they did not give anything luxurious, but they discharged their vow more with devotion than with pomp.[30]

For 1722, a further half dozen cures testified to the potency of the water. At Weissenohe another young boy, a lame, two-year old orphan, was healed when his paralysed legs were bathed in Xavier-Water. The Jesuits wrote that they had seen him walking unaided around the cloister of the monastery. A woman with poor eyesight, unable to read even capital letters easily, washed her eyes with Xavier-Water and was cured. The liquid was, so the Jesuit chronicler claimed,

> the only sound remedy against many fevers. One witness to this is a student from Amberg, who, having tried various remedies in vain, was immediately cured when he drank water consecrated with St Xavier's relics. Then there is one of the servants of the monks at Weissenohe who was plagued repeatedly for months by unknown pains and fevers and lost so much weight that he could barely keep alive. Persuaded by the monks, he decided in great faith to drink the salutary Xavier-Water: in a few days the illness departed and he recovered, so that very soon he was sufficiently fit to return to work.[31]

Fevers, blindness, paralysis and the complications of pregnancy: for all of these, Xavier-Water was presented as the wonder cure (the Jesuits of course tended only to report successes: we can never know how many resorted to the sacramental in vain). The saint whose intercession was sought and in whose honour the water was blessed was evidently regarded as a powerful, all-round performer of miracles, rather than as a specialist helper in any single brand of human sickness or emergency. In this respect Xavier's role paralleled that of the other great Jesuit saint, Ignatius Loyola. Ignatius-Water, blessed in the same way as Xavier-Water, was promoted by Jesuit missionaries elsewhere in Germany and, although Loyola does seem to have acquired a particular reputation for his efficacy against fevers and the plague and as a protector of women in labour, he too was invoked as an all-purpose helper. During a Jesuit mission in the Eifel in 1736, for example, the peasantry sprinkled Ignatius-Water on their fields in order to exterminate a plague of caterpillars. In many regions of Catholic Germany stables and cowsheds were asperged with the sacramental to protect the cattle and horses.[32] Not surprisingly, the cult of Ignatius was promoted by Jesuits in the Upper Palatinate too. For example, in Amberg the Society kept a piece of the soutane of Ignatius Loyola, which was lent out in cases of difficult childbirth. The scrap of material was kept inside a small metal capsule suspended from a silken cord which was hung around the neck of the mother.[33] In their report of the Rothenberg mission of 1716 the *patres* linked the miraculous application of an Ignatian relic (possibly the same one) to the experience of conversion from heresy. The pregnant wife of the innkeeper of Neunkirchen, one of the district's parishes, had become Lutheran during the period of Nuremberg control over the region. The Jesuits exhorted her to return to the Catholic fold, but she replied that, when she had married two years previously, the pastor from Nuremberg had made her swear a solemn oath that she would keep to the Lutheran faith all her life and as a result she was afraid to convert. The Jesuits assured her that she had been deceived by the Protestant minister and that her oath was invalid. The 'good soul' promptly confessed and was publicly received into the Church. Returning to her house she was suddenly seized with severe labour pains. The missionaries immediately sent her the relic of Ignatius and she was safely delivered after a few hours.[34]

The 'benefits' achieved through the use of Xavier-Water and the relics of Jesuit saints were by no means the only miraculous ingredient of the missions. The Jesuits' reports indeed are filled with references to the immanence of the sacred realm and its manifestation in wonders and miracles. Right at the start of the 1721 mission, for example, as the Jesuits entered the Bavarian Forest, they heard that people had reported strange lights in the sky 'illuminating the forest with a pleasant and serene light at night'. This was taken to be a God-sent portent of the success of the mission, or, as the Jesuits put it, a symbol of their own efforts whereby 'the new light of truth would enlighten the dull minds of men'.[35] Similarly, later in the same report, the Jesuits claimed that one of the factors attracting large crowds to the mission was the fact that many people had made a vow to attend in return for the miraculous deliverance of their communities from epidemic.[36]

The attention given by the Jesuits to sacramentals and other miraculous agents, both during the missions and then again in their reports, suggests that they were seen as an important means of achieving *fama* and drawing the crowds. But why should such a strategy have been popular? The answer would seem to lie in the fact that, through their sacramentals, the Jesuits were tapping into a vast reservoir of popular religious culture. Prayers, charms, conjurations, blessings and exorcisms were a vital ingredient of popular techniques of protection against disease, disaster and sorcery. Like Xavier-Water and other sacramentals, such rituals of consecration could be performed by the clergy according to canonical formulae and would consequently be considered orthodox by the ecclesiastical authorities (Xavier-Water and Ignatius-Water, for example, could in theory only be blessed by a Jesuit or else by a priest especially licensed by the Jesuit General). At the same time, many other techniques were lay inventions: contravening the claim of the Church to monopolise access to sacred power, they were therefore branded as superstitious by the ecclesiastical authorities. At the level of popular perception, however, it was not the orthodoxy but the efficacy of the techniques which seems to have been stressed, with canonical and unorthodox rituals alike taking their place within a common, composite religious culture which has been termed the 'system of the sacred'.[37] Within this system the position of the scaramental, as an orthodox device which could be taken home and used by the laity for their own purposes, was perhaps uniquely ambiguous, representing an interface between the norms of the ecclesiastical elites and popular religious culture. The perceived efficacy of a resource like Xavier-Water, freely supplied by the Jesuits, would have played a large role in attracting large numbers to the missions. Indeed it is probable that, in so far as the Jesuits were popularly welcomed to the Upper-Palatinate countryside, it was as medical missionaries rather than as evangelical zealots. Interestingly, in this region at least, the promotion of ecclesiastical remedies does not seem to have been accompanied by a negative campaign against unorthodox or superstitious techniques. The result, if not the strategy, seems to have been one of compromise with or accommodation of popular religious culture.

A similar pattern of accommodation can be detected in many of the Society's other activities. In parallel, for example, with their eager distribution of sacramentals to effect miraculous cures on the missions, the Jesuits were in the forefront of the foundation and administration of the Upper Palatinate's pilgrimage shrines, which one might describe as permanent centres of miraculous healing. During the period of Protestant control, frustrated Lutheran and Calvinist clergy and magistrates had lamented the populace's continued addiction to pilgrimages to the region's many pre-Reformation shrines, in violation of repeated official prohibitions. After the wonder-working relics and images had been destroyed and even after some of the chapels themselves had actually been demolished, people continued to visit the sites seeking cures or fulfilling vows made *in extremis*. During the re-catholicisation of the region in the 1620s these old centres were re-activated and new ones began to be established, with the Jesuits responsible for half of the foundations or revivals in the area in the seventeenth century. The most notable new example was the Marian shrine on the Mariahilfberg outside Amberg, which was set up by the Jesuit rector during an outbreak of plague in the capital in 1634. The dozens of short tales which accompanied the *ex-votos* at this and other shrines were reminiscent of the individual reports of cures attributed to Xavier-Water in the mission reports.[38] Given this Jesuit preoccupation with the promotion of pilgrimage, it was no accident that in 1721 the missionaries should include in their tour the shrine of the Virgin at Neukirchen Heilig Blut. In so doing they were associating their mission with the flow of miraculous power which emanated from the shrine.[39]

If the sacred could, in a special way, touch rituals and places connected with the Society, it was also seen on occasion to touch individuals among its membership. In southern Germany in the sixteenth and seventeenth centuries a number of Jesuits acquired reputations for sanctity, of which corroboration was apparently provided by miraculous manifestations of the sacred. A striking example is the Ingolstadt Jesuit visionary Jakob Rem (1546–1618), who had introduced the Marian Congregations into Germany and who famously levitated in April 1604 during a recitation of the Litany of Loreto in front of an icon of the Virgin. Other wonders were attributed to Rem, including the gift of prophecy, whilst his prayers were said to be especially efficacious in releasing Holy Souls from the torments of Purgatory.[40] Exorcism of those possessed by the Devil seems to have been another area in which individual German Jesuits readily engaged and in which they were considered especially effective. In 1570 Peter Canisius himself exorcised Anna von Bernhausen, a lady-in-waiting to the Fugger family. The exorcisms took place both in Augsburg and at the Bavarian shrine of Altötting, where again miraculous rituals and the saintly charisma of Canisius could be associated with an established sacred centre.[41] Chronologically and geographically closer to the Upper-Palatinate missions, in 1664 the Straubing Jesuits exorcised a local noblewoman called Anna de la Haye. Her liberation from possession by four demons was attributed to the miraculous intervention and intercession of St Francis Xavier, who had appeared to her in her dreams.[42] Accounts of successful exorcisms, of the wondrous exploits of Jesuit saints and of miracles imputed to the use by Jesuits of varied sacramentals fill the pages of the official history of the Society's Upper German province, the first volume of which was published in 1727.[43] In this context, the strategy of accommodation with popular religious culture through the promotion of Xavier-Water which seems to have been pursued by the missionaries in the Upper Palatinate in the 1720s is very much in keeping with the whole style of the Jesuits in early modern Germany. Decades later, the Jesuit sacramentals would come under the spotlight of enlightenment parody and the order itself would be lampooned for having apparently sunk from its position on the intellectual cutting edge in the sixteenth century to the level of peasant superstition in the eighteenth. The Jesuits were chided for sharing or colluding in the ignorance of the peasantry rather than attempting to reform it.[44] Yet their very reluctance to attack popular culture may have

been one of the key factors in the Jesuits' success in preserving
the confessional identity not just of Catholic bastions but also of
the recently recatholicised areas of Germany. Ultimately, as
Günter Lottes has suggested, it made for better social control.[45]

V

Taking the three Jesuit reports as evidence, not of the impact of
the Upper-Palatinate missions, but of the objectives and strategies
of the missionaries, two tendencies can be distinguished. On the
one hand are the aspects for which such rural missions are
perhaps best known: the drive to reform, convert and indoctri-
nate, accompanied by the device of hellfire sermons and penitential histrionics. The strategy here echoed the blood and the tears
of the Italian method, even if the latter did not reach the Upper
Palatinate in its extreme form. The grim expiatory spectacles
seem the antithesis of the festal aspects of popular culture, of the
inverted, licentious, flatulent world of Carnival, and appear to
mark the victory, even if only temporary, of Lent and the triumph
of the moral economy of the Jesuit elite. Yet even in this aspect,
the colourful mission rituals might well have been popularly received as a welcome diversion from the greyness of rural life, a
brief escape from the boredom of the peasant *Alltag*. The mission
could have become a spectacle to look forward to, enjoy and then
forget, until the next one came along, like any other festival of the
rural calendar. Hoping to assimilate peasant culture into their
moralising framework through strategies of engagement, the
Jesuits and their missions might well have ended up being themselves assimilated into peasant culture.[46]

The potential for such a reverse assimilation seems all the
greater when we turn to the second tendency evidenced by the
Upper-Palatinate *Volksmissionen*: the promotion of sacramentals,
particularly Xavier-Water, as a form of missionary propaganda.
Far from attempting to eradicate the magical aspects of popular
religion, a strategy that had been pursued unsuccessfully by their
Calvinist predecessors in the territory, the Jesuits actively supported them. Not only did they decline to wage war on superstition, they also imported their own magical goods. This strategy of

accommodation could be seen as an exercise in cynical manipulation, its subtlety designed to achieve greater success in the long run than the antagonistic techniques of the Protestant reformers. However, the fact that their sacramental's spectacular effects were celebrated in their reports, which were internal documents, would suggest that the Jesuits themselves shared with the people what might be termed a culture of the miraculous. Such an overlap of attitudes provides a reminder that varied cultures cannot be distinguished simply by their ingredients or products alone, but by how such ingredients are used. The lubricants of the Jesuit missions, blood, tears and Xavier-Water, should make us wary of rigid taxonomies of elite and popular religion.

# Bibliography

There are no recent extended surveys of the general theme of 'popular religion' for Germany. Brief discussion of major themes is provided in Robert W. Scribner, 'Elements of Popular Belief', in Thomas A. Brady, Heiko A. Oberman and James D. Tracey (eds), *Handbook of European History, 1400–1600: Late Middle Ages, Renaissance and Reformation* (Leiden, 1994), vol. 1: *Structures and Assertions*, pp. 231–62, and Robert W. Scribner, 'The Reformation and the Religion of the Common People', in *Die Reformation in Deuetschland und Europa: Interpretationen und Debatten, Archiv für Reformationgeschichte, Sonderband* (Gütersloh, 1993) pp. 221–42. Wider theses of significance for understanding popular religion can be found in John Bossy, *Christianity in the West, 1400–1700* (Oxford, 1985), and J. Delumeau, *Sin and Fear: The Emergence of a Western Guilt Culture, 13th–18th Centuries* (New York, 1990). Kaspar von Greyerz (ed.), *Religion and Society in Early Modern Europe, 1500–1800* (London, 1984), and R. Po-Chia Hsia (ed.), *The German People and the Reformation* (Cornell, 1988) both contain several essays of immediate relevance, while Pieter H. Vriihof and Jacques Waardenburg (eds), *Official and Popular Religion: Analysis of a Theme for Religious Studies* (The Hague, 1979) raises some important conceptual issues. Some stimulating interpretative ideas are offered by John van Engen, 'The Christian Middle Ages as an Historiographical Problem', *American Historical Review*, 91 (1986) pp. 519–32, and John van Engen, 'Faith as a Concept of Order in Medieval Christendom', in Thomas Kselman (ed.), *Belief in History: Innovative Approaches to European and American Religion* (Notre Dame, Ill. 1991) pp. 19–67.

For religion before the Reformation, as well as the above items, see also Kathleen Ashley and Pamela Scheingorn (eds), *Interpreting Cultural Symbols: St Anne in Late Medieval Society* (Athens, Ga., 1990); Miri Rubin, *Corpus Christi: The Eucharist in Late Medieval Culture* (Cambridge, 1991); Richard Wunderli, *Peasant Fires: The Drummer of Niklashausen* (Bloomington, Ind. 1992), especially useful for situating belief within peasant culture. Broad themes of importance are touched upon by individual essays in Peter Biller and Anne Hudson (eds), *Heresy and Literacy, 1000–1530* (Cambridge, 1994), esp. chs 1, 15–16. Charles Zika, 'Hosts, Processions and Miracles: Controlling the Sacred in Fifteenth-century Germany', *Past & Present*, 18 (1988) pp. 25–64, is essential reading for understanding late-medieval criticisms of popular religion, as is Peter A. Dykema and Heiko A. Oberman (eds), *Anticlericalism in Late Medieval and Early Modern Europe* (Leiden, 1993). Euan Cameron, *The European Reformation* (Oxford, 1991) part 1, pp. 9–93, is an excellent and balanced survey which makes many stimulating and original suggestions.

Controversial and unconvincing in its central thesis, but very useful for certain aspects of popular religion, is Lionel Rothkrug, 'Religious Practices and Collective Perceptions: Hidden Homologies in the Renaissance and Reformation', *Historical Reflections*, 7 (1980); a slightly different version appeared in L. Rothkrug, 'Popular Religion and Holy Shrines: their Influence on the Origins of the German Reformation and their Role in German Cultural Development', in J. Obelkevich (ed.), *Religion and the People, 800–1700* (Chapel Hill, N.C., 1979) pp. 20–86. The author's views are restated more emphatically in 'Holy Shrines, Religious Dissonance and Satan in the Origins of the German Reformation', *Historical Reflections*, 14 (1987) pp. 143–286. In general, Rothkrug's essays have been poorly received by other scholars of the period and have been accorded no critical scrutiny. The theme of healing shrines has also been discussed by Steven D. Sargent, 'Miracle Books and Pilgrimage Shrines in Late Medieval Bavaria', *Historical Reflections*, 13 (1986).

The important issue of confession is discussed in L. Duggan, 'Fear and Confession on the Eve of the Reformation', *Archiv für Reformationsgeschichte*, 75 (1984) pp. 153–75; and in John Bossy, 'The Social History of Confession in the Age of the Reformation', *Transactions of the Royal Historical Society*, 5th series, vol. 25 (1975) pp. 21–38, while Thomas N. Tentler, *Sin and Confession on the Eve of the Reformation* (Princeton, N.J., 1978) is still indispensable reading for the theme.

On female piety in particular, Merry E. Wiesner, *Women and Gender in Early Modern Europe* (Cambridge, 1993) provides the best discussion locating female religion within wider issues of gender. Essential reading for this theme are three works by Caroline Walker Bynum: *Jesus as Mother: Studies in the Spirituality of the High Middle Ages* (Berkeley, Cal., 1982); *Holy Feast and Holy Fast: The Religious Significance of Food to Medieval Women* (Berkeley, Cal., 1987); *Fragmentation and Redemption: Essays on Gender and the Human Body on Medieval Religion* (New York, 1991). The gendered features of male piety compared with female piety are usefully discussed by Richard Kieckhefer, 'Holiness and the Culture of Devotion: Remarks on Some Late Medieval Male Saints', in Renate Blumenfeld-Kosinski and Timea Szell (eds), *Images of Sainthood in Medieval Europe* (Ithaca, N.Y., 1991) pp. 288–305. Female asceticism is also discussed in Rudolf M. Bell, *Holy Anorexia* (Chicago and London, 1985), while pious representations of Christ's body are discussed controversially by Leo Steinberg, *The Sexuality of Christ in Renaissance Art and in Modern Oblivion* (London, 1983); an extensive critique of Steinberg's interpretation is provided by Caroline Walker Bynum, 'The Body of Christ in the Later Middle Ages: A Reply to Leo Steinberg' in her *Fragmentation and Redemption*, pp. 79–118.

The writings of Margarethe Ebner can be sampled in *Margaret Ebner: Major Works*, trans. and ed. Leonard P. Hindsley, The Classics of Western Spirituality (New York, 1993). For women's pious reading and writing, see Elizabeth A. Petroff, *Medieval Women's Visionary Literature* (New York, 1986) and Susan Groag Bell, 'Medieval Women Book Owners: Arbiters of Lay Piety and Ambassadors of Culture', in Mary Erler and Maryanne Kowaleski (eds), *Women and Power in the Middle Ages* (Athens, Ga., 1988) pp. 149–87. There has been no discussion of holy dolls for Germany, but for a wider comparison see Christine Klapisch-Zuber, *Women, Family and Ritual in Renaissance Italy* (Chicago, 1985) pp. 310–29. The important issue of images and piety is discussed in Jeffrey Hamburger, 'The Visual and the Visionary: the Image in Late Medieval Monastic Devotions', *Viator*, 20 (1989) pp. 162–82, and also his 'The Use of Images in the Pastoral Care of Nuns: the Case of Heinrich Suso and the Dominicans', *Art Bulletin*, 1 (1989) pp. 20–45. For an illuminating discussion of the pious image in relation to a theology of images, see Lee Palmer Wandel, *Voracious Idols and Violent Hands: Iconoclasm in Reformation Zurich, Strasbourg and Basel* (Cambridge, 1995) pp. 1–51.

The Hussites and Hussite Religion, as well as the wider context, are covered in the following, which provide both basic orientation and detailed discussion: Thomas A. Fudge, 'Myth, Heresy and Propaganda in the Radical Hussite Movement, 1409–37' (Cambridge University Ph.D. thesis, 1992); Thomas A Fudge, 'Art and Propaganda in Hussite Bohemia', *Religio*, 1 (1993) pp. 135–53; Frederick G. Hyman, *John Zizka and the Hussite Revolution* (New York, 1969); Howard Kaminsky, *A History of the Hussite Revolution* (Berkeley, Cal., 1967); Frantisek Kavka, 'Bohemia', in Bob Scribner, Roy Porter and Mikulas Teich (eds), *The Reformation in National Context* (Cambridge, 1993) pp. 131–54; John M. Klassen, *The Nobility and the Making of the Hussite Revolution* (New York, 1978); Josef Macek, *The Hussite Movement in Bohemia* (London, 1965); Frantisek Smahel, 'The Hussite Critique of the Clergy's Civil Dominion', in Heiko A. Oberman and Peter Dykema (eds), *Anticlericalism in Late Medieval and Early Modern Europe* (New York, 1993); Frantisek Smahel, 'Literacy and Heresy in Hussite Bohemia', in Biller and Hudson (ed.), *Heresy and Literacy*, pp. 237–54.

On popular attitudes towards the Jews, see R. Po-Chia Hsia, *The Myth of Ritual Murder: Jews and Magic in Reformation Germany* (New Haven, Conn., 1988); R. Po-Chia Hsia, *Trent 1475: Stories of a Ritual Murder Trial* (New Haven, Conn., 1992); Heiko A. Oberman, *The Roots of Anti-Semitism* (Philadelphia, Penn., 1981); E. M. Safran, 'The Iconography of Antisemitism: a study in the Representation of the Jews in the Visual Arts of Europe, 1400–1600' (Ph.D. dissertation, New York University, 1973); J. Trachtenberg, *The Devil and the Jews: The Medieval Conception of the Jews and its Relation to Modern Antisemitism* (2nd edn, New York, 1966). For good background details, see G. Kisch, *The Jews in Medieval Germany* (2nd edn, New York, 1970) and for the wider context of Jewish–Christian relations, see John Edwards, *The Jews in Christian Europe, 1400–1700* (London, 1988).

On witchcraft and the origins of the witchcraze, the best overall introduction is B. Levack, *The Witch-hunt in Early Modern Europe* (London, 1987), while G. Scarre, *Witchcraft and Magic in Sixteenth- and Seventeenth-Century Europe* (London, 1987) provides a useful brief orientation to the wider literature. An essential background to popular magic is provided by Richard Kieckhefer, *Magic in the Middle Ages* (Cambridge, 1990), while Carlo Ginzburg, *Ecstasies: Deciphering the Witches' Sabbath* (London, 1990), despite its over-blown wider thesis and dubious methodology, is very useful on the evolution of the witchcraze and witch paradigm. The recent overviews of the witchcraft problem can be found in B. Ankarloo and G. Henningsen (eds), *Early Modern Witchcraft: Centres and Peripheries* (Oxford, 1990) and Jonathan Barry, Marianne Hester and Gareth Roberts (eds), *Witchcraft in Early Modern Europe: Studies in Culture and Belief* (Cambridge, 1995). Gabor Klaniczay, *The Uses of Supernatural Power: The Transformation of Popular Religion in Medieval and Early-Modern Europe* (Cambridge, 1990), chs 8–10, provides valuable insights from an Eastern European perspective. Lyndal Roper, *Oedipus and the Devil: Witchcraft, Sexuality and Religion in Early Modern Europe* (London, 1994) offers highly original and often controversial interpretations of great importance for the future development of the subject.

Important articles which tell us much about attitudes towards witchcraft are Stuart Clark, 'Protestant Demonology: Sin, Superstition and Society (*c.*1520-*c.*1630)' in Ankarloo and Henningsen, *Early Modern Witchcraft*, pp. 45–81; H. C. E. Midelfort, 'The Devil and the German People: Reflections on the Popularity of Demonic Possession in Sixteenth-century Germany', in S. E. Ozment (ed.), *Religion and Culture in the Renaissance and Reformation*, Sixteenth-Century Essays and Studies 11 (Kirksville, Miss., 1989) pp. 99–119; Lyndal Roper, 'Witchcraft and Fantasy in Early Modern Germany', *History Workshop Journal*, 32 (1991) 19–43, now reprinted in her *Oedipus and the Devil*, pp. 199–225; Bob Scribner, 'Witchcraft and Judgment in Reformation Germany', *History Today*, April 1990, pp. 12–19; R. W. Scribner, 'Sorcery, Superstition and Society: The Witch of Urach 1529', in *Popular Culture and Popular Movements*, pp. 257–76; Charles Zika, 'The Devil's Hoodwink: Seeing and Believing in the World of Sixteenth-Century Witchcraft', in Charles Zika (ed.), *No Gods Except Me: Orthodoxy and Religious Practice in Europe* (Melbourne, 1991) pp. 153–98.

On implementation of the Reformation and the tribulations of the Protestant clergy, see C. Scott Dixon, 'Rural Resistance, the Lutheran Pastor and the Territorial Church in Brandenburg Ansbach-Kulmbach, 1528–1603', in Andrew Pettegree (ed.), *The Reformation of the Parishes: The Ministry and the Reformation in Town and Country* (Manchester, 1993) pp. 85–112, as well as R. W. Scribner, 'Pastoral Care and the Reformation in Germany', in James Kirk (ed.), *Humanism and Reform: The Church in Europe, England and Scotland, 1400–1643. Essays in Honour of James K. Cameron* (Oxford, 1991) pp. 77–98. R. Po-Chia Hsia, *Social Discipline in the Reformation: Central Europe, 1550–1750* (London, 1989) provides a broader background and some valuable insights. Although it does not deal directly with popular religion, Heinz Schilling, *Religion, Political Culture and the Emergence of Early Modern Society: Essays in German and Dutch History* (Leiden, 1992), esp. chs 5, 7–8, has broader implications for an understanding of the theme, especially in terms of his 'confessionalisation' thesis. An important study of an example central to the collision between 'confessionalisation' and popular belief is Bodo Nischau, *Prince,*

*People and Confession: The Second Reformation in Brandenburg* (Philadelphia, Penn., 1994).

On continuity in popular belief, see different aspects of the problem discussed by David W. Sabean, *Power in the Blood: Popular Culture and Village Discourse in Early Modern Germany* (Cambridge, 1984); Susan Karant-Nunn, 'A Women's Rite: Churching and the Reformation of Ritual', in R. Po-Chia Hsia and R. W. Scribner (eds), *Problems in the Historical Anthropology of Early Modern Europe* (Wolfenbüttel, forthcoming) and in essays by Scribner, 'Incombustible Luther: the Image of the Reformer in Early Modern Germany', in *Popular Culture and Popular Movements*, pp. 301–22; 'Luther Myth – a Popular Historiography of the Reformer', in *Popular Culture and Popular Movements*, pp. 324–54; 'The Impact of the Reformation on Daily Life', in *Mensch und Objekt im Mittelalter und in der frühen Neuzeit. Leben–Alltag–Kultur*, Veröffentlichungen des Instituts für Realienkunde, Österreichische Akademie der Wissenschaften, vol. 568 (Vienna, 1990) pp. 315–43; 'Symbolising Boundaries: Defining Social Space in the Daily Life of Early Modern Germany', in G. Blaschwitz *et al.* (eds), *Symbole des Alltags–Alltag der Symbole. Festschrift für Harry Kühnl* (Graz, 1992) pp. 821–41. See also Paul Barber, *Vampires, Burial and Death: Folklore and Reality* (New Haven, Conn., 1988) for perspectives on the 'dangerous dead'.

Important for understanding Protestant popular prophecy and holy figures in relation to orthodox Lutheranism are R. B. Barnes, *Prophecy and Gnosis: Apocalypticism in the Wake of the Lutheran Reformation* (Stanford, Cal., 1988), and Robert Kolb, *For All the Saints: Changing Perceptions of Martyrdom and Sainthood in the Lutheran Reformation* (Macon, Ga., 1987).

Recent work on the Counter-Reformation and popular religion in Germany has been sparse in anglophone scholarship. The direction of recent interpretations has been set by Jean Delumeau, *Catholicism between Luther and Voltaire: A New View of the Counter-Reformation* (London, 1977), and to a lesser extent by Bossy, *Christianity in the West*, although neither has much to say about Germany. The best overview of trends is Hsia, *Social Discipline in the Reformation*, pp. 39–52 passim. R. Po-Chia Hsia, *Society and Religion in Münster, 1535–1618* (New Haven, Conn., 1984) is an exemplary study. The most stimulating recent work has been by Marc Forster, *The Counter-Reformation in the Villages: Religion and Reform in the Bishopric of Speyer* (Ithaca, N.Y., 1992) and Philip M. Soergel, *Wondrous in his Saints: Counter-Reformation Propaganda in Bavaria* (Berkeley, Cal., 1993), both of which show the direction future research will take. Badly needed for Catholic Germany in the sixteenth and seventeenth centuries is research such as that by James Melton, 'From Image to Word: Cultural Reform and the Rise of Literate Culture in Eighteenth-Century Austria', *Journal of Modern History*, 58 (1986) pp. 95–124, reprinted in his *Absolutism and the Eighteenth-Century Origins of Contemporary Schooling in Prussia and Austria* (Cambridge, 1988) pp. 60–90.

# Notes and References

INTRODUCTION     *Bob Scribner*

1. For an overview of recent approaches and issues, see Robert W. Scribner, 'Elements of Popular Belief', in Thomas A. Brady, Heiko A. Oberman and James D. Tracey (eds), *Handbook of European History* (Leiden, 1995); for recent German work, see Richard van Dülmen, 'Volksfrömmigkeit und konfessionelles Christentum im 16. und 17. Jht', in Wolfgang Schieder (ed.), *Volksreligiosität in der modernen Sozialgeschichte* (Göttingen, 1986) pp. 14–30; Richard van Dülmen (ed.), *Arbeit, Frömmigkeit und Eigensinn: Studien zur historischen Kulturforschung II* (Frankfurt a. M., 1990).

2. For an overview of these polarities, see R. W. Scribner, 'Volksglaube und Volksfrömmigkeit: Begriffe und Historiographie', in H. Molitor and H. Smolinsky (eds), *Volksfrömmigkeit in der Frühneuzeit* (Münster, 1994) pp. 121–38.

3. For 'culture as appropriation', Roger Chartier, 'Culture as Appropriation', in S. L. Kaplan (ed.), *Understanding Popular Culture* (Berlin, New York, Amsterdam, 1984) pp. 229–53.

4. R. W. Scribner, 'Is a History of Popular Culture Possible?', *History of European Ideas*, 10 (1989) pp. 175–91, esp. 179.

5. Gananath Obeyesekere, 'British Cannibals: Reflections on the Death and Resurrection of the Explorer James Cook', *Critical Inquiry*, 18 (1992) pp. 630–54.

6. See also Johannes Wolfart, 'Political Culture and Religion in Lindau 1520–1628', Cambridge University Ph.D. dissertation, 1994.

7. See Marc Forster, *The Counter-Reformation in the Villages: Religion and Reform in the Bishopric of Speyer, 1560–1720* (Ithaca, NY, 1992); Étienne François, *Die unsichtbare Grenze: Protestanten und Katholiken in Augsburg 1648–1806* (Abhandlungen zur Geschichte der Stadt Augsburg, 33, Sigmaringen, 1991).

8. See Thomas A. Fudge, 'Myth, Heresy and Propaganda in the Radical Hussite Movement, 1409–1437', Cambridge University Ph.D. dissertation, 1992; for the broader tradition connecting the first Bohemian Reformation to the Reformations of the sixteenth century, Frantisek Kavka, 'Bohemia', in Bob Scribner, Roy Porter and Mikulas Teich (eds), *The Reformation in National Context* (Cambridge, 1994) pp. 131–54.

9. On these issues, see R. W. Scribner, 'The Reformation, Popular Magic and the "Disenchantment of the World"', *Journal of Interdisciplinary History*, 23 (1993) pp. 475–94; on 'providentialism' see especially Kaspar von Greyerz, *Vorsehungsglaube und Kosmologie: Studien zu englischen Selbstzeugnissen des 17. Jhts* (Göttingen, 1990), which although focussed on England has considerable parallels in the German context.

10. For the Catholic campaign, Philip M. Soergel, *Wondrous in his Saints. Counter-Reformation Propaganda in Bavaria* (Berkeley, Cal., 1993); the cult of St Luther in R. W. Scribner, '"Incombustible Luther": the Image of the Reformer in Early Modern Germany' and 'Luther Myth – A Popular Historiography of the Reformer', both in *Popular Culture and Popular Movements in Reformation Germany* (London, 1987) pp. 301–55; for Protestant attitudes towards sainthood, Robert Kolb, *For All the Saints: Changing Perceptions of Martyrdom and Sainthood in the Lutheran Reformation* (Macon, Ga, 1987).

11. On this point, see the important discussion in Soergel, *Wondrous in his Saints*, pp. 131–216.

12. I have discussed these subjects in 'The Impact of the Reformation on Daily Life', in *Mensch und Objekt im Mittelalter und in der frühen Neuzeit. Leben – Alltag – Kultur*, Veröffentlichung des Instituts für Realienkunde des Mittelalters und der frühen Neuzeit, vol. 13, Sitzungsberichte der Österreichischen Akademie der Wissenschaften, phil.-hist. Klasse, vol. 568 (Vienna, 1990) pp. 315–43, esp. 334–40; 'Symbolising Boundaries: Defining Social Space in the Daily Life of Early Modern Germany', in G.Blaschitz *et al.* (eds), *Symbole des Alltags – Alltag der Symbole. Festschrift für Harry Kühnl* (Graz, 1992) pp. 821–41, esp. 831–2. On the 'dangerous dead' see Thomas Schürmann, *Nachzehrglauben in Mitteleuropa* (Marburg, 1990) and Paul Barber, *Vampires, Burial and Death: Folklore and Reality* (New Haven, 1988).

13. There is a substantial body of documentation on this case in Hauptstaatsarchiv Stuttgart, A206, Bü. 3619. It will be discussed in detail in Jürgen Beyer's forthcoming dissertation.

14. The classic statement of this view is that of Jean Delumeau, *Catholicism between Luther and Voltaire: A New View of the Counter-Reformation* (London, 1977), with his 'christianisation' thesis, an interpretation that now looks increasingly implausible on both sides of the Reformation divide. For a recent sketch of the wider historiographical tradition here, see Forster, *The Counter-Reformation in the Villages.*

15. Louis Châtellier, *The Europe of the Devout: The Catholic Reformation and the Formation of a New Society* (Cambridge, 1989); Louis Châtellier, *La religion des pauvres: Les sources du christianisme moderne xvi$^e$–xix$^e$ siècles* (Paris, 1992); Forster, *The Counter-Reformation in the Villages*; David Gentilcore, *From Bishop to Witch: The System of the Sacred in Early Modern Terra d'Otranto* (Manchester, 1992); Soergel, *Wondrous in his Saints.*

16. For a fuller view of Johnson's work, see Trevor R. Johnson, 'The Recatholicisation of the Upper Palatinate 1621–c.1700', Cambridge University Ph.D. dissertation, 1992.

17. R. Po-Chia Hsia, *The Myth of Ritual Murder: Jews and Magic in Reformation Germany* (New Haven, Conn., 1988).

18. Caroline Walker Bynum, *Jesus as Mother: Studies in the Spirituality of the High Middle Ages* (Berkeley, Cal., 1982); *Fragmentation and Redemption: Essays on Gender and the Human Body in Medieval Religion* (New York, 1991).

210                          *Notes and References*

19. L. Roper, 'Witchcraft and Fantasy in Early Modern Germany', *History Workshop Journal*, 32 (1991) pp. 19–43.

20. Besides the recent work of Obeyesekere, 'British Cannibals' and his *The Apotheosis of Captain Cook* (Princeton, N.J., 1992), see the remarks by Hans Medick, '"Missionare im Ruderboot"? Ethnologische Erkenntnisweisen als Herausforderung an die Sozialgeschichte', *Geschichte und Gesellschaft*, 10 (1984) pp. 295–319.

1.    FEMALE SPIRITUALITY AND THE INFANT JESUS IN LATE MEDIEVAL DOMINICAN CONVENTS    *Ulinka Rublack*

1. I wish to thank Lyndal Roper for her translation of all German quotations and for important suggestions, and Vic Gatrell for clarifying discussions, and for turning this into a readable English article.

2. Otto Engelhardt, 'Kloster Maria Medingen und seine Votivtafeln', *Schwäbische Heimat*, 21 (1971) pp. 18–24. For similar seventeenth-century pilgrimages see B. Rothemund and J. Packett, *Gnadenreiche Jesulein. Jesuskindwallfahrtsorte: Enstehung – Geschichte – Brauchtum* (Autenried, 1982).

3. Peter Dinzelbacher, *Visionen und Visionsliteratur im Mittelalter* (Stuttgart, 1981); Siegfried Ringler, *Viten- und Offenbarungsliteratur im Mittelalter* (Munich, 1980); Ernst Benz, *Die Vision: Erfahrungsform und Bilderwelt* (Stuttgart, 1969); Ursula Peters, 'Vita religiosa und spirituelles Erleben: Frauenmystik und frauenmystische Literatur im 15. und 16. Jahrhundert', in Gisela Brinkler-Gabler (ed.), *Deutsche Literatur von Frauen* (Munich, 1988) vol. 1, pp. 88–112; Alois Maria Haas, *Geistliches Mittelalter* (Freiburg, 1984) esp. pp. 373–92.

4. Caroline Walker Bynum, *Holy Feast and Holy Fast: The Religious Significance of Food to Medieval Women* (Berkeley, Cal., 1987) p. 18; Rosemarie Rode, *Studien zu den mittelalterlichen Kind-Jesu-Visionen* (Diss. Frankfurt a. M., 1957); Ringler, *Viten- und Offenbarungsliteratur*, p. 187.

5. On this see especially Jeffrey F. Hamburger's recent articles, 'The Visual and the Visionary: the Image in Late Medieval Monastic Devotions', *Viator*, 20 (1989) pp. 161–82, and 'The Use of Images in the Pastoral Care of Nuns: the Case of Heinrich Suso and the Dominicans', *Art Bulletin*, 1 (March 1989) pp. 20–45.

6. Elisabeth Vavra, 'Bildmotiv und Frauenmystik', in P. Dinzelbacher and D. Bauer (eds), *Frauenmystik im Mittelalter* (Stuttgart, 1985) pp. 201–30.

7. Herbert Grundmann, *Religiöse Bewegungen im Mittelalter* (Berlin, 1935) p. 414.

8. Christiane Klapisch-Zuber, 'Holy Dolls: Play and Piety in Florence in the Quattrocento', in *Women, Family, and Ritual in Renaissance Italy* (Chicago, 1985) pp. 310–31 and p. 326.

9. Klapisch-Zuber, 'Holy Dolls', p. 327; Klapisch-Zuber analyses the function of these dolls, which formed part of the trousseaux of middle-class women, as 'toys' of adult women 'delivered up to a spouse' (p. 317).

On the other hand, she analyses the experiences nuns had with the infant Jesus as showing 'that the husband so desperately absent was hidden in the baby of their dreams' (p. 326).

10. Siegfried Ringler, 'Gnadenviten aus süddeutschen Frauenklöstern des 14. Jahrhunderts – Vitenbeschreibung als mystische Lehre', in Dietrich Schmidtke (ed.), '*Minnichlichiu gotes erkennusse': Studien zur frühen abendländischen Mystiktradition. Heidelberger Mystiksymposium vom 16. January 1989* (Stuttgart, 1990) pp. 89–104, esp. 103.

11. This close analysis has been most successful with the writings of religious women as a source. See in particular Clarissa W. Atkinson, *Mystic and Pilgrim: The Book and the World of Margery Kempe* (Ithaca and London, 1983); Elizabeth Alvilda Petroff, *Medieval Women's Visionary Literature* (New York and Oxford, 1986), and Bynum, *Holy Feast and Holy Fast.*

12. Phillip Strauch (ed.), *Heinrich von Nördlingen und Margaretha von Ebner. Ein Beitrag zur Geschichte der deutschen Mystik* (Freiburg i. Br., 1882) p. 1. For a detailed account of Margaretha's life see Manfred Weitlauff, '"dein got redender munt machet mich redenlosz..." Margaretha von Ebner und Heinrich von Nördlingen', in P. Dinzelbacher and D. Bauer (eds), *Religiöse Frauenbewegung und mystische Frömmigkeit im Mittelalter* (Vienna, 1988) pp. 303–51.

13. Dictating and not writing in Latin both partly account for a more immediate style closer to oral thought, which makes this kind of writing different from men's. See C. W. Bynum, *Fragmentation and Redemption: Essays on Gender and the Human Body in Medieval Religion* (New York, 1991) p. 196.

14. Strauch, *Heinrich von Nördlingen*, p. 87.

15. Ibid., p. 81.

16. Ibid., pp. 89, 50.

17. Ibid., p. 147.

18. O. W. Oslo (ed.), *Gertrude von Helfta, ein botte der götlichen miltekeit* (Ottobensen, 1973) p. 127.

19. Anton Gabele (ed.), *Deutsche Schriften von Heinrich Seuse* (Leipzig, 1924) pp. 27–9.

20. Strauch, *Heinrich von Nördlingen*, p. 233.

21. Ringler, *Viten- und Offenbarungsliteratur*, p. 414. Sunder's *Gnadenleben* was posthumously compiled by nuns under the supervision of Konrad of Füssen.

22. Ringler, *Viten- und Offenbarungsliteratur*, pp. 415ff.

23. Ibid., p. 414.

24. Ibid., p. 416.

25. Ibid., p. 414.

26. Bynum, *Fragmentation and Redemption*, p. 235.

27. On infant Jesus dolls see H. Wentzel, 'Christkind', *Reallexikon der Kirchengeschichte*, vol. III, pp. 590–608; 'Christkind-Bilder aus alter Zeit', *Die Kunst und das schöne Heim*, 60 (1962/3) pp. 93–7; 'Ad infantem Christi. Zur Kindheit unseres Herrn', in *Festschrift für Hubert Schrade* (Stuttgart, 1960) pp. 134–60.

28. 'On St Stephen's day my lord gave me a loving gift of my desire, for he sent me a loving statue from Vienna. It was a Jesus doll in a cradle and four golden angels waited upon him', in Strauch, *Heinrich von Nördlingen*, p. 90.

29. Otto Kastner, 'Die Gottesmutter und das Kind mit dem Vögelein', *Alte und moderne Kunst* (1961/2) pp. 10–15; on Italian infant Jesus figures see Ursula Schlegel, 'The Christchild as Devotional Image in Medieval Italian Sculpture', *Art Bulletin*, 52 (1970) pp. 1–10.

30. Wentzel, 'Christkind', pp. 590–608; for examples in Dominican convents see Hironymus Wilms, *Das Beten der Mystikerinnen, dargestellt nach den Chroniken der Dominikanerinnen-Klöster zu Adelshausen, Diessenhofen, Engelthal, Kirchberg, Oetenbach, Töß und Unterlinden* (Leipzig, 1916) esp. pp. 155–9, and Francis Rapp, 'Zur Spiritualität in Elsässischen Frauenklöstern am Ende des Mittelalters', in P. Dinzelbacher and D. Bauer (eds), *Frauenmystik im Mittelalter* (Stuttgart, 1985) esp. pp. 354–7.

31. Valentin Lötscher (ed.), *Felix Platter. Tagebuch (Lebensbeschreibungen) 1536–1567* (Basel and Stuttgart, 1976) p. 373.

32. Strauch, *Heinrich von Nördlingen*, p. 90.

33. Rode, *Kind-Jesu-Visionen*, p. 86.

34. Strauch, *Heinrich von Nördlingen*, p. 87.

35. Ibid., p. 90.

36. Ferdinand Vetter (ed.), *Das Leben der Schwestern zu Töß beschrieben von Elsbeth Stagel* (Berlin, 1906) p. 52.

37. In a vision Sunder saw himself receiving the same care as the infant. Mary offered to become both the child's and his soul's nurse in order to give them 'the spiritual things they both needed: bedding, bathing, suckling and other things one does with natural children physically'. But again this described a spiritual experience. Ringler, *Viten- und Offenbarungsliteratur*, p. 416.

38. Strauch, *Heinrich von Nördlingen*, p. 69.

39. W. Schleussner (ed.), *Mechthild von Magdeburg, Das fliessende Licht der Gottheit* (Mainz, 1929) p. 40; Engl. transl. Christine Mesch Galvani (ed.), *Mechthild von Magdeburg, Flowing Light of the Divinity* (New York and London, 1991).

40. Vetter, *Das Leben der Schwestern zu Töß*, p. 39. For an almost identical account see Karl Bihlmeyer (ed.), 'Mystisches Leben in dem Dominikanerinnenkloster Weiler bei Eßlingen im 13. und 14. Jahrhundert', in *Württembergische Vierteljahreshefte für Landesgeschichte* (1916) p. 84.

41. On popular door-knocking customs and spiritual exercises in convents see Hans Moser, 'Zur Geschichte der Klöpfelnachtbräuche, ihrer Formen und ihrer Deutungen', in Hans Moser, *Volksbräuche im geschichtlichen Wandel* (Munich, 1985) pp. 1–28, esp. p. 6.

42. F. W. E. Roth (ed.), 'Aufzeichnungen über das mystische Leben der Nonnen von Kirchberg bei Sulz Predigerordens während des XIV. und XV. Jahrhunderts', in *Alemannia*, 21 (1893) pp. 145.

43. J. König (ed.), 'Die Chronik der Anna von Munzingen', in *Freiburger Diözesan-Archiv*, 13 (1880) p. 176.

44. Ibid., p. 171.
45. Strauch, *Heinrich von Nördlingen*, p. 89.
46. Vetter, *Das Leben der Schwestern zu Töß*, p. 52.
47. Strauch, *Heinrich von Nördlingen*, p. 78.
48. Ibid., p. 87. Her imagined answer refers to Matthew 12: 46–50, where Mary and Jesus's brothers want to talk with him while he is speaking to the people, and he replies that he counts his disciple who follows God's will as his brother, sister, and mother.
49. Strauch, *Heinrich von Nördlingen*, p. 88.
50. Bohemia was under the interdict, because Ludwig fought for the free elevation of the king. In 1338 he ordered the Bohemians to ignore the interdict, so that conflicts developed in the convents. Von Nördlingen supported the pope, but Margaretha was loyal to the popular Ludwig.
51. Nuns helping her felt something alive in her body. The vision resulted in her desire to pronounce the name 'Jesus Christ' over and over again. Strauch, *Heinrich von Nördlingen*, p. 134, pp. 119ff.
52. On this belief see J. de Coo, '"In Josephs Hosen Jhesus gewordem wert". Ein Weihnachtsmotiv in Literatur und Kunst', *Aachner Kunstblätter*, no. 30.
53. Strauch, *Heinrich von Nördlingen*, p. 91.
54. Ibid., p. 31.
55. Ibid., p. 42.
56. Ibid., p. 135.
57. Ibid., p. 171.
58. Bernhard von Clairvaux, *Ansprachen auf die kirchlichen Zeiten* (Wittich, 1934) vol. 1, pp. 187–96.
59. See Leo Steinberg, *The Sexuality of Christ in Renaissance Art and in Modern Oblivion* (London, 1983) pp. 50–65.
60. Ulrich Köpf, 'Bernhard von Clairvaux in der Frauenmystik', in P. Dinzelbauer and D. Bauer (eds), *Frauenmystik im Mittelalter* (Stuttgart, 1985) p. 69.
61. Bynum, *Holy Feast and Holy Fast*, p. 246.
62. Cited in Rode, *Kind-Jesu-Visionen*, n. 22, p. 111.
63. See Marianne Schuller, 'Hysterie als Artefaktum. Zum literarischen und visuellen Archiv der Hysterie um 1900', in Marianne Schuller, *Im Unterschied. Lesen/Korrespondieren/Adressieren* (Frankfurt a. M., 1990) pp. 81–94.
64. Jean Martin Charcot's and Paul Richer's *Les démoniaques dans l'art* was published in 1887. I quote from the German reprint, Manfred Schneider (ed.), *Die Besessenen in der Kunst* (Göttingen, 1988) p. 135.
65. Oscar Pfister, 'Hysterie und Mystik bei Margaretha von Ebner', *Zentralblatt für Psychoanalyse*, 1 (1911) p. 468.
66. Ibid., p. 478.
67. Ibid., p. 482.
68. Joseph Breuer, Sigmund Freud, *Studien über Hysterie*, 3rd edn (Berlin/Leipzig, 1916) pp. 89, 141, 162; Renate Schlesier, *Konstruktionen der Weiblichkeit bei Sigmund Freud* (Frankfurt a. M., 1981) pp. 61–74.

69. See note 9.
70. Adolf Spamer, *Weihnachten in alter und neuer Zeit* (Jena, 1937) p. 32.
71. British Library Add. MS 11,430, fols. 103, 118.


2.  THE 'CROWN AND THE 'RED GOWN': HUSSITE POPULAR RELIGION
*Thomas A. Fudge*


1. Jaroslav Šůla (ed.), *Kronika velmi pěkná o Janovi Žižkovi, Čeledína Krále Vácslava* [The Very Pretty Chronicle of Jan Žižka, the Servant of King Václav] (Hradec Králové, 1979) pp. 28–9.
2. A prohibition issued by the Council of Constance, article 17, session 44, 1418, directed against the Bohemian reform movement. Johannes D. Mansi (ed.), *Sacrorum Conciliorum Nova, et Amplissima Collectio ...*, vol. 27 (Venice, 1784) col. 1197.
3. Robert W. Scribner, *Popular Culture and Popular Movements in Reformation Germany* (London and Ronceverte, 1987) p. 44.
4. *Výklad na evangelium Svatý Lukáše* [Commentary on the Gospel of St Luke], Prague, National and University Library MS. XVII D 21, fol. 432ᵛ.
5. Vavřinec of Březová, *Historia Hussitica*, in Jaroslav Goll (ed.), *Fontes rerum bohemicarum*, vol. 5, (Prague, 1893) p. 416.
6. This would include the communal experiments in south Bohemia around 1420 as well as the compact between Hussite gentry in 1417 wherein the collateral of personal private property was juxtaposed to the promotion of free preaching and utraquism. In other words, those signing the agreement pledged to promote Hussitism or lose their property to the other co-signers. This latter text has been published in John M. Klassen, *The Nobility and the Making of the Hussite Revolution* (New York, 1978) pp. 152–3.
7. For example, a Hussite priest captured near the east Bohemian town of Hradec Králové was carrying an umbilical cord in his bag in the belief that it would save him from a cruel death. Cited in František Šmahel, 'Silnější než víra: magie, pověry a kouzla husitského věku' [Stronger than Religious Faith: Magic and Superstitions in the Hussite Age], *Sborník vlastivědných prací z Podblanicka*, 30, no. 2 (1990) p. 43.
8. Gábor Klaniczay, *The Uses of Supernatural Power. The Transformation of Popular Religion in Medieval and Early-Modern Europe*, translated by Susan Singerman and edited by Karen Margolis (Cambridge, 1990) p. 47.
9. See especially Želivský's sermons for 17 April and 8 June 1419, in Amedeo Molnár (ed.), in *Jan Želivský Dochovaná kázání z roku 1419* [Jan Želivský's Sermons Preserved from the Year 1419] (Prague, 1953) pp. 29 and 181. Molnár's edition is based upon Prague, National and University Library MSS. IV F 23 and V G 3, both of which I have checked.
10. This is Želivský's term for himself. See Amedeo Molnár, Želivský, prédicateur de la révolution', *Communio Viatorum*, 2 (Winter 1959) p. 327. A number of scholars of Hussitism have acquiesced in the acceptability of the assumption. See František Graus, *Chudina městská v době předhusitské* [The Poor in the Cities in the Pre-Hussite Age] (Prague, 1949) p. 25.

Notable for his exception to the idea is Miloslav Ransdorf, *Kapitoly z geneze husitské ideologie* [A Chapter from the Early Hussite Ideology] (Prague, 1986) p. 202, who thinks the designation is inaccurate and misleading apropos of Želivský's true function.

11. See the trial records of interrogations involving Jerome in Hermann von der Hardt (ed.), *Magnum oecumenicum constantiense concilium*, vol. 4 (Frankfurt and Leipzig, 1699) cols 674–5.

12. František Mareš (ed.), *Popravčí kniha pánův z Rožmberka* [The Executioners' Book of Lords of Rožmberk], in *Abhandlungen der königlichen böhmischen Gesellschaft der Wissenschaften*, vol. 9 (Prague, 1878) pp. 36–7.

13. *Traktát Mistra Ondřeje z Brodu o původu husitů. Visiones Ioannis, Archiepiscopi pragensis, et earundem explicaciones (alias Tractatus de origine hussitarum)*, ed. Jaroslav Kadlec (Tábor, 1980) p. 19.

14. Molnár (ed.), *Jan Želivský Dochovaná kázání z roku 1419*, p. 79.

15. Vavřinec of Březová, *Historia Hussitica*, p. 449. The translation is Howard Kaminsky's *A History of the Hussite Revolution* (Berkeley and Los Angeles, 1967) p. 411.

16. Vavřinec of Březová, *Historia Hussitica*, p. 389. Koranda's title '... *proprie et insane mentis presbiter*' reflects the growing apprehension within 'official' Hussite religion towards the popular appropriation of that religion.

17. Vavřinec of Březová, *Historia Hussitica*, p. 413.

18. 'Epistola ad Hussitas', in Bernard Pez (ed.), *Thesaurus anecdotorum novissimus seu veterum monumentorum*, vol. 4 (Augsburg, 1723) part 2, col. 519.

19. *Tractatus de origine hussitarum*, ed., Kadlec, p. 11.

20. Václav Nebeský, 'Verše na Husity [Verses on the Hussites], Dvé staré satyry' [Two Old Satires], *Časopis českého museum*, 26 (1852) p. 149.

21. The figure is probably exaggerated. See Vavřinec of Březová, *Historia Hussitica*, p. 345 and also the Anonymous, '*de Origine Taboritarum*', in Konstantin von Höfler (ed.), *Geschichtsschreiber der Hussitischen Bewegung in Böhmen*, vol. 1 and *Fontes rerum austriacarum*, vol. 2 (Vienna, 1856) p. 528.

22. Vavřinec of Březová, *Historia Hussitica*, pp. 344–5.

23. See the excellent analysis in Howard Kaminsky, 'The Prague Insurrection of 30 July 1419', *Medievalia et Humanistica*, 17 (1966) pp. 106–26, as well as thorough references to the primary sources.

24. Dated 17 September 1419, in Amedeo Molnár (ed.), *Husitské manifesty* [Hussite Manifestos] (Prague, 1986) p. 61.

25. František Palacký (ed.), *Staří letopisové čeští od r. 1378 do 1527* [Old Czech Annalists from 1378 to 1527] in *Scriptores rerum bohemicarum*, vol. 3 (Prague, 1829) p. 30.

26. See Howard Kaminsky, 'The Religion of Hussite Tabor', in *The Czechoslovak Contribution to World Culture*, Miloslav Rechcigl, Jr ed. (The Hague, London and Paris, 1964) pp. 210–23. Kaminsky's work is valid and valuable, but he deals more with ideas and theological concepts and

does not investigate the interpretation of those ideas and concepts at the popular level.

27. On this see Thomas A. Fudge, 'Myth, Heresy and Propaganda in the Radical Hussite Movement, 1409–1437', unpublished Ph.D. dissertation, University of Cambridge, 1992, pp. 109–67.

28. Kaminsky, *A History of the Hussite Revolution*, p. 249.

29. 'Contra Andream Brodam pro communione plebis sub utraque specie', in von der Hardt (ed.), *Magnum oecumenicum constantiense concilium*, vol. 3, p. 472.

30. Palacký (ed.), *Staří letopisové čeští*, in *Scriptores rerum bohemicarum*, vol. 3, p. 472.

31. See the printed excerpts in František M. Bartoš, *Husitství a cizina* [Hussitism and Foreign Countries] (Prague, 1931) pp. 84–5.

32. The opinion of F. M. Bartoš and cited with approval in Enrico C. S. Molnar, 'Anglo-Czech Reformation Contacts', unpublished Th.D. dissertation, The Iliff School of Theology, 1953, p. 134.

33. See Příbram's 'Tractate Against all the Errors of the Heretics' [*Cum ab inicio*], Prague Castle Archive MS. D 47, fols 1$^r$–40$^r$. He refers to 'the naked law (or Scripture) alone' on fol. 1$^r$.

34. Frederick G. Heymann, *John Žižka and the Hussite Revolution* (New York, 1969) p. 11, n. 9.

35. 'Místo Mikuláše z Drážďan v raném reformačním myšlení' [The Place of Nicholas of Dresden in Early Reformation Thought], *Rozpravy Československé akademie věd*, vol. 77, no. 16 (Prague, 1967) pp. 15, 49–50.

36. For example, the protest of the Bohemian and Moravian nobles against the burning of Hus promised to defend the Law of God to the end. The sole extant copy of the protest is kept in Scotland under the signature Edinburgh, University Library MS. P.C. 73.

37. Prague, National and University Library MS. V G 3, fol. 46$^v$.

38. *Dějiny husitského zpěvu* [History of the Hussite Songs], vol. 4 (Prague, 1955) pp. 249ff.

39. For the foregoing see Vavřinec of Březová, *Historia Hussitica*, pp. 406–7. For the note about women see ibid., p. 498.

40. For a thorough-going critique of the Táborite communion ceremony see Jan Příbram, *Apologia cereminiarum missae contra Taboritas*, Prague Castle Archive MS. 0 17, fols 145$^r$–172$^r$,

41. Vavřinec of Březová, *Historia Hussitica*, pp. 470–1.

42. Ibid., p. 474.

43. Article 63 of the *Articulos Hussitarum Hungarium*, Rome, Vatican Library MS. Vat. Lat. 7307, fol. 24$^v$.

44. Cited in Josef Macek (ed.), *Ktož jsú boží bojovníci. Čtení o Táboře v husitském revolučnim hnutí* [Ye Warriors of God. Readings About Tábor in the Hussite Revolutionary Movement] (Prague, 1951) pp. 59, 61.

45. Vavřinec of Březová, *Historia Hussitica*, pp. 355–6.

46. For the establishment of communal chests see Vavřinec of Březová, ibid., p. 438 and František Šimek (ed.), *Staré letopisy české z vratislavského rukopisu* [Old Bohemian Chronicles from the Wratislav Manuscript] (Prague, 1937) pp. 27–8.

Notes and References 217

47. Jan Příbram, 'Život kněži táborských' [The Lives of the Priests of Tábor], in Josef Macek (ed.), *Ktož jsú boží bojovníci*, p. 265.

48. I have treated this subject at length elsewhere, '"Neither Mine Nor Thine": Communist Experiments in Hussite Bohemia', forthcoming.

49. See Rudolf Urbánek, *Věk poděbradský* [The Age of Poděbrady], vol. 3 (Prague, 1930) p. 722.

50. Gerald Christiansen, *Cesarini: The Conciliar Cardinal, The Basel Years, 1431–1438* (St Ottilien, 1979) p. 205.

51. Cited in Christiansen, *Cesarini*, p. 80.

52. For example, Master Martin Talayero, King Sigismund's representative, wrote in April 1421 to Wladyslaw Jagiello, King of Poland, along these lines. The letter has been published in Jaroslav Kadlec, 'Magister Martin Talayero aus Tortosa im Kampf gegen die Hussiten', *Annuarium historiae conciliorum*, 12, no. 1/2 (1980) pp. 297–308.

53. Palacký (ed.), *Staří letopisové čeští*, in *Scriptores rerum bohemicarum*, vol. 3, p. 13.

54. Vavřinec of Březová, *Historia Hussitica*, p. 354.

55. See Heymann, *John Žižka and the Hussite Revolution*, pp. 218–19.

56. Jaroslav Šůla (ed.), *Kronika velmi pěkná o Janovi Žižkovi*, p. xxiii.

57. Heymann, *John Žižka and the Hussite Revolution*, p. 362.

58. 'De sancto Iohanne Hus cum sociis', in *Fontes rerum bohemicarum*, vol. 8 (Prague, 1932) p. cxxviii.

59. Mansi (ed.), *Sacrorum Conciliorum Nova, et Amplissima Collectio*, vol. 27, col. 786.

60. Cited in Josef Krása, 'Studie o rukopisech husitské doby' [Studies on Manuscripts from the Hussite Age], *Umění*, 22, no. 1 (1974) p. 20.

61. Vavřinec of Březová, *Historia Hussitica*, p. 416.

62. The relevant document has been published by Josef Macek, 'K počátkům táborství v Písku' [On the Beginning of Táboritism in Písek], *Jihočeský sborník historický*, 22 (1953) pp. 113–24.

63. Ludolf of Sagan, *De longevo schismate*, ed., Johann Loserth, in *Archiv für österreichische Geschichte*, 60 (1980) p. 450.

64. *Articulos Hussitarum Hungarium*, Rome, Vatican Library, Codex Vat. Lat. 7307, fol. 24ᵛ.

65. Estergom, Metropolitical Library MS. I. 313, pp. 501–11. Holeton has published part of the text. See his 'The Office of Jan Hus: An Unrecorded Antiphonary in the Metropolitical Library of Estergom', in J. Neil Alexander (ed.), *Time and Community* [Festschrift for Thomas J. Talley] (Washington DC, 1990) pp. 137–52.

66. Prague, National and University Library MS. IV H 12. My reasons for making this assumption have been discussed in detail in 'Myth, Heresy and Propaganda in the Radical Hussite Movement, 1409–1437', pp. 116–17.

67. See the brief description in Thomas J.Talley, 'A Hussite Latin Gradual of the XV Century', *Bulletin of the General Theological Seminary*, 48 (1962) pp. 8–13.

68. The Rackovsky Kancionale, 'De sancto Johanne Hus', Prague, National and University MS. VI C 20ᵃ, fols. 88ʳ–98ᵛ.

69. The Smiškovský Graduále, Vienna, Österreichische National-bibliothek suppl. mus. sam. MS. 14592, fol. 285ʳ and Prague, National Museum Library MS. IV B 9, fols. 25ʳ, 170ᵛ–171ᵛ, 172ʳ et al.

70. *Malostranská Graduále*, Prague, National and University Library MS. XVII A 3, fol. 363ʳ.

71. A similar idea is prepared in a Czech woodcut in Berlin, Staatsbibliothek Handschriftenabteilung YA 872. The Protestant 'canonisation' of Hus has recently been reviewed by Robert Kolb, '"Saint John Hus" and "Jerome Savonarola, Confessor of God". The Lutheran "Canonization" of Late Medieval Martyrs', *Concordia Journal*, 17 (October 1991) pp. 404–18.

72. Terezín, Regional Archives MS. IV C 1, fol. 244ᵛ. The codex has been deposited in Litoměřice, General Regional Museum.

73. According to the eyewitness account of Petr of Mladoňovice, 'the paper crown was round, almost eighteen inches high, and on it were shown three horrible devils about to seize a soul and to tear it among themselves with claws. The inscription on that crown describing his guilt read: "This is a heresiarch"'. '*Relatio de Mag. Ioannis Hus causa*', trans. and ed. Matthew Spinka, *John Hus at the Council of Constance* (New York, 1965) p. 231.

74. Martin Luther, 'Sermons on the Sermon on the Mount', in *Luther's Works*, vol. 21, ed. and trans., Jaroslav Pelikan (St Louis: Concordia Publishing House, 1956) p. 165

75. Martin Luther, 'Concerning the Answer of the Goat in Leipzig', trans. Eric W. and Ruth C. Gritsch, in Eric W. Gritsch (ed)., *Luther's Works*, vol. 39 (Philadelphia: Fortress Press, 1970) p. 134.

76. Von Höfler (ed.), *Geschichtsschreiber der Hussitischen Bewegung in Böhmen*, vol. 2, p. 203.

77. Paul de Vooght, 'Jan Hus: Heretic or Martyr?', trans. W. H. Zawadzki, *The Tablet*, 223 (1 February 1969) p. 100. See also my 'Myth, Heresy and Propaganda in the Radical Hussite Movement, 1409–1437', pp. 223–45.

78. Michel Vovelle, *Ideologies and Mentalities*, trans. Eamon O'Flaherty (Cambridge, 1990) p. 91.

79. See R. A. Houston, *Literacy in Early Modern Europe. Culture and Education 1500–1800* (London and New York, 1988) p. 226, and Robert W. Scribner, 'Oral Culture and the Diffusion of Reformation Ideas', *History of European Ideas*, 5, no. 3 (1984) p. 245.

80. Jiří Daňhelka, *Husitské písně* [Hussite Songs] (Prague, 1952) p. 140.

81. Ibid., p. 142. See especially lines 1–19. Anticlericalism within Hussite popular religion took a number of forms. See most recently František Šmahel, 'The Hussite Critique of the Clergy's Civil Dominion', in Heiko A. Oberman and Peter A. Dykema (eds), *Anticlericalism in Late Medieval and Early Modern Europe* (Leiden and New York, 1993) pp. 83–90.

82. Daňhelka, *Husitské písně*, p. 143.

83. Ibid., p. 133.

84. Jistebnický kancionál, Prague, National Museum Library MS. II C 7, pp. 87–8. This translation is in Josef Macek, *The Hussite Movement in*

*Bohemia*, trans. Vilém Fried and Ian Milner (Prague and London, 1965) pp. 116–17.

85. Bohuslav Havránek, Josef Hrabák and Jiří Daňhelka (eds), *Výbor z české literatury doby husitské* [A Selection of Czech Literature from the Hussite Age], vol. 1 (Prague, 1963) p. 327. Translated by Frederick G. Heymann, *John Žižka and the Hussite Revolution*, p. 140.

86. Zdeněk Nejedlý, *Dějiny husitského zpěvu*, vol. 3, pp. 442–3.

87. Prague, National and University Library MS. III G 16, fol. 18ʳ.

88. Nejedlý, *Dějiny husitského zpěvu*, vol. 6, p. 259.

89. Ibid., pp. 231–2.

90. I have treated Hussite popular songs in greater detail in my 'Myth, Heresy and Propaganda in the Radical Hussite Movement, 1409–1437', pp. 258–90.

91. See the *Anonymi invectiva contra husitas*, in Höfler (ed.), *Geschichtsschreiber der Hussitischen Bewegung in Böhmen*, vol. 1, p. 624.

92. See the description of this event in 'The Article Against Jerome of Prague', in Hermann von der Hardt (ed.), *Magnum oecumenicum constantiense concilium* vol. 4, cols 672–3.

93. *Expositio decalogi*, in Václav Flajšhans (ed.), *Spisy M. Jana Husi* [The Collected Works of Jan Hus] (Prague, 1903) vol. 1, pp. 7–8.

94. See my 'Learn it on the Wall – Images of Dissent', in 'Myth, Heresy and Propaganda in the Radical Hussite Movement, 1409–1437', pp. 303–26 and my 'Art and Propaganda in Hussite Bohemia', *Religio*, 1 (1993) pp. 135–53.

95. *Tabulae novi et veteris coloris*. There is a critical edition. Howard Kaminsky, Dean Loy Bilderback, Imre Boda, and Patricia N. Rosenberg (eds), 'Master Nicholas of Dresden: The Old Color and the New. Selected Works Contrasting the Primitive Church and the Roman Church', *Transactions of the American Philosophical Society*, 55 (March 1965) pp. 5–88.

96. Kaminsky, *A History of the Hussite Revolution*, p. 40.

97. Leipzig, Universitätsbibliothek MS. 181. See also František M. Bartoš, 'Po stopách obrazů v Betlemské kapli z doby Husovy' [An Investigation of the Symbols of the Bethlehem Chapel from the Time of Hus], *Jihočeský sborník historický*, 20 (1951) pp. 121–7.

98. S. Harrison Thomson (ed.), *Magistri Johannis Hus Tractatus de ecclesia* (Cambridge and Boulder, 1956) p. 217.

99. *Martinická bible* [Martinic Bible], Prague, National and University Library MS. no signature, fol. 11ᵛ.

100. Prague, National and University Library MS. XVII A 34, fol. 115ʳ. See also the Zámojských Bible, Prague, National and University Library MS. XVII C 56, fol. 95ᵛ, from *c.* 1440.

101. *Krumlovský sborník*, Prague, National Museum Library MS. III B 10, fol. 20ᵛ.

102. For example, see the Jistebnický gradual, Prague, National Museum Library MS. XII F 14, fol. 61ʳ.

103. Jena Codex, Prague, National Museum Library MS. IV B 24 and Göttingen, Universitätsbibliothek MS. Theol 182.

104. Jena Codex, fols 67ᵛ–68ʳ and Göttingen, Universitätsbibliothek MS. Theol 182, pp. 18–19.
105. Jena Codex, fols 76ᵛ–77ʳ and Göttingen, Universitätsbibliothek MS. Theol 182, pp. 76–7.
106. Jena Codex, fols 78ᵛ–79ʳ.
107. Göttingen, Universitätsbibliothek MS. Theol 182, pp. 80–1.
108. Jena Codex, fol. 25ʳ, Göttingen, Universitätsbibliothek MS. Theol 182, p. 59.
109. Mladá Boleslav, Regional Museum MS. 1/70ᵃ olim II A 1, fol. 115ᵛ.
110. See the description in Ferdinand Hrejsa, *Dějiny křest'anství v Československu* [History of Christianity in Czechoslovakia], vol. 4 (Prague, 1948) p. 171.
111. Jena Codex, fol. 93ʳ.
112. Latin gradual, Mladá Boleslav, Regional Museum MS. 1/70ᵃ olim II A 1, fol. 109ᵛ.
113. Such is the term used to describe the glory of the Hussite movement in Palacký (ed.), *Staří letopisové čeští od r. 1378 do 1527*, vol. 3, p. 79.
114. Jena Codex, fol. 76ʳ, Göttingen, Universitätsbibliothek MS. Theol 182, p. 75.
115. Jena Codex, fol. 5ᵛ.
116. This derogatory term for Žižka, *snöden man*, appears in the contemporary biography of King Sigismund by Eberhard Windecke, *Denkwürdigkeiten zur Geschichte des Zeitalters Kaiser Sigmunds*, ed., Wilhelm Altmann (Berlin, 1893) p. 197.
117. Latin gradual, Mladá Boleslav, Regional Museum MS. 1/70ᵃ olim II A 1 fol. 200ᵛ.
118. Zoroslava Drobná, *Gothic Drawing*, trans., Jean Layton (Prague, n.d.) p. 57.

3. *JUDENGASSE* TO CHRISTIAN QUARTER: THE PHENOMENON OF THE CONVERTED SYNAGOGUE IN THE LATE MEDIEVAL AND EARLY MODERN HOLY ROMAN EMPIRE   *J. M. Minty*

1. R. Straus, *Urkunden und Aktenstücke zur Geschichte der Juden in Regensburg 1453–1738* (Munich, 1960) no. 1052. Upon the death of Emperor Maximilian, long-standing tensions between the emperor and the town of Regensburg about the Regensburg community – much worsened by the aggressive anti-Jewish activities of the cathedral preacher Balthasar Hubmaier from 1516 on – exploded. For a brief outline of escalating tensions over the Regensburg Jews from the mid-fifteenth century to 1519, see A. Angerstorfer, 'Von Judensiedlung zum Ghetto in der mittelalterlichen Reichsstadt Regensburg', in M. Treml and J. Kirmeier (eds), *Geschichte und Kultur der Juden in Bayern*, Veröffentlichungen zur Bayerischen Geschichte und Kultur, no. 17/88 (Munich, 1988) pp. 166–9.

2. J. and M. Guillard (eds), *Altdorfer and Fantastic Realism in German Art* (Paris, 1985) p. 275.

3. Straus, *Urkunden*, no. 1040, p. 386.

4. Christoph Hofmann (ostrofrankus), a member of the Benedictine order of St Emmeram, Regensburg, at this time, remarks the destruction of thirty Jewish houses; see Straus, *Urkunden*, no. 1040, p. 385.

5. Straus, *Urkunden*, no. 109, p. 416. Permission was officially granted by Pope Leo X on 13 June 1520.

6. This has been remarked by R. Dollinger, *Das Evangelium in Regensburg* (Regensburg, 1959) p. 99; E. M. Zafran, 'The Iconography of Antisemitism: A Study in the Representation of Jews in the Visual Arts of Europe, 1400–1600' (Ph.D dissertation, New York University, 1973) p. 97.

7. For scholarship on these images, among others, see W. Hofmann (ed.), *Luther und Die Folgen für die Kunst* (Munich, 1983) pp. 132–3.

8. For instance, the Brühl synagogue and adjacent houses were razed and replaced by a house of Strict Franciscan Observants; in 1480, following the Poppelsdorf disputation, the archbishop of Cologne ordered the expulsion of Jews from Brühl and in 1491 Landgrave Hermann, archbishop of Cologne, erected the home; see C. Brisch, *Geschichte der Juden in Cöln und Umgebung aus ältester Zeit bis auf die Gegenwart*, 2 vols (Cologne, 1882; rpt. Walluf bei Weisbaden, 1973) vol. II, p. 60. The convert Viktor von Carben discusses the event in his tract entitled 'Dem durchleuchtigsten... Heir inne wirt gelesen wie Her Victor von Carben, Welicher eyn Rabi der Juden gewest ist zu Christlichen glawbn komen' (1508) fol. e6$^v$–f$^v$, as cited in H. M. Kirn, *Das Bild vom Juden im Deutschland des frühen 16. Jahrhunderts* (Tübingen, 1989) p. 89, n. 159.

9. Burned and destroyed synagogues include those in Görlitz (1390) and Hallein (1404); see A. Maimon (ed.), *Germania Judaica*, vol. III/I (Tübingen, 1987) pp. 445, 508; Austria (1420s), see C. H. Krinsky, *Synagogues of Europe: Architecture, History, Meaning* (Cambridge, Mass., 1985) p. 187; Vienna (1420s), see S. Krauss, *Die Wiener Geserah vom Jahre 1421* (Vienna, 1920) p. 124, who notes an entry in the University records dated 21 December 1420, entered by the superintendent Master Johannes Aygl, the duke's doctor, stating that the Vienna synagogue had been demolished, and the stone given to the university at the end of 1421.

10. The Tülln synagogue was given by Duke Albrecht V to the provost and convent of St Dorothea in Vienna on 10 May 1422; see J. E. Scherer, *Die Rechtsverhältnisse der Juden in den deutschösterreichischen Ländern* (Leipzig, 1901) p. 416. By 1437, the house which had functioned as the Mödeling synagogue was being used by Christians; see Krinsky, *Synagogues of Europe*, p. 142, who includes a late nineteenth-century drawing showing a crucifix in the interior of the building. The Miltenberg synagogue was confiscated and placed in private hands in 1429; see H. Eschwege, *Die Synagoge in der deutschen Geschichte: eine Dokumentation* (Dresden, 1981) p. 63. In Krems in 1430, a house situated near the hospital, apparently once used as a synagogue, was sold for 120 pounds following an expulsion; see Krauss, *Die Wiener Geserah*, p. 812. The Augsburg, Bachrach and

Glatz synagogues became privately owned; see Maimon (ed.), *Germania Judaica*, vol. III/I, pp. 49, 70, 43. In 1467, Emperor Friedrich III gave Erfurt and Halle synagogues to one Niclas Pflug; see Dr M. Wiener (ed.), *Regesten zur Geschichte der Juden in Deutschland während des Mittelalters* (Hannover, 1862) p. 90, no. 78. In 1454 in Brunn, following an expulsion, King Wenceslaus gave the city Jewish properties for the purpose of building living quarters for Christians; see Dr H. G. Gengler (ed.), *Codex Juris Municipalis Germaniae*, vol. 1 (Erlangen, 1863) p. 424, no. 38. The Bockenem synagogue was sold to a burgher in 1487; see Maimon (ed.), *Germania Judaica*, vol. III/I, p. 133. In 1490, Emperor Friedrich III authorised the selling of the synagogues in towns including Heilbronn, where the town council purchased the synagogue, additional buildings and the cemetery for 250 gulden; see Dr Moritz von Rauch *Urkundenbuch der Stadt Heilbronn*, (ed.), 2 vols (Stuttgart, 1913) vol. II, pp. 470–1. When in 1498 Nuremberg secured permission from Emperor Maximilian to expel its Jewish community, the city council, which first offered to pay 4,000 gulden for immovable Jewish properties, eventually made the accepted offer of 8,000 gulden for the rights to the Jews. Following expulsion, which was officially decreed to begin and end between 6 November 1498 and 2 February 1499, on 20 February 1499 the mayor of Nuremberg gave the houses, synagogue and cemetery to the town council; see M. Toch, 'Umb Gemeyns Nutz und Nottdurff Willen', *Zeitschrift für historische Forschung*, 11 (1984) pp. 2–6. They were then put on the open market.

11. Basel synagogue (*c.*1350); see W. P. Eckert, 'Die Juden in Zeitalter Karl IV', in F. Seibt (ed.), *Kaiser Karl IV, Staatsmann und Mäzen* (Munich, 1978) p. 127.

12. Freiburg synagogue (*c.*1350); see Eckert, 'Die Juden in Zeitalter Karl IV', p. 127.

13. Korneuburg synagogue (*c.*1420s); see Krinsky, *Synagogues of Europe*, p. 141, and Maimon (ed.), *Germania Judaica*, vol. III/I, p. 674.

14. A. Thorbecke, *Die älteste Zeit der Universität Heidelberg (1386–1449)* (Heidelberg, 1866) p. 23, n. 41. King Rupert II (1390–8) decreed the expulsion of Palatinate Jews in February 1391, and a number of synagogues were converted during the 1390s. The Heidelberg synagogue was turned into a Marian chapel.

15. Expulsion resulted in the destruction of the Amberg synagogue; see Maimon (ed.), *Germania Judaica*, vol. III/I, p. 14. In a document dated 5 September 1398, King Rupert II mentions that the Amberg Lady Chapel had once been a synagogue; see D. Gotschmann, 'Die Juden in Amberg während des Mittelalters', in K-O. Ambronn, A. Fuchs and H. Wanderwitz (eds), *Amberg 1034–1984 aus tausend Jahren Stadtgeschichte* (Amberg, 1984) pp. 103–4.

16. The conversion of the Ingolstadt synagogue to a chapel dedicated to the Virgin of Mercy ('Cappellan unnser lieben Frauwen der Schütter') is mentioned in a letter dated 1397 in the Ingolstadt privilege book cited in A. Friedmann, *Die Geschichte der Juden in Ingolstadt (1300–1900)* (Ingolstadt a D., 1900) pp. 21–2.

17. In 1404 in Rothenburg ob der Tauber, when the *Judengasse* was moved as a result of the implementation of a fourteenth-century plan to enlarge the town, the synagogue was transformed into a Marian chapel; see H. Künzl, 'A Recently Discovered MIQWEH in Rothenburg ob der Tauber: Preliminary Report', *Jewish Art*, 14 (1988) p. 28.

18. By 1426 in Linz, Austria, in the aftermath of the persecution and expulsion of 1420–21, Hahnengasse no. 6, a private house which had served as a synagogue, had been converted to a chapel dedicated to All Saints and the Trinity; see V. Kurrein, 'Die Juden in Linz – Festschrift anlässlich des fünfzigjährigen Bestandes des Linzer Tempels', *Jüdische Kultgemeinde in Linz* (Linz, 1922) pp. 6–7.

19. Following Duke Albert V of Austria's expulsion of the Jews from Iglau in 1426 (G. Bondy and F. Dworsky (eds), *Zur Geschichte der Juden in Böhmen, Mähren und Schlesien von 906 bis 1620*, 2 vols (Prague, 1906) vol. 1, p. 101, no. 218), the synagogue was consecrated as the Fronleichnams Kapelle; see Maimon (ed.), *Germania Judaica*, vol. III/I, p. 580.

20. Due to expulsion in 1424, the Cologne synagogue was consecrated as a Marian chapel in 1426; see Dr T. J. Lacomblet (ed.), *Urkundenbuch für die Geschichte des Niederrheins*, 4 vols (Düsseldorf, 1858) vol. 4, p. 210, no. 177.

21. The Deutz synagogue was turned into a Marian chapel; see Brisch, *Geschichte der Juden in Cöln und Umgebung*, vol. II, p. 52.

22. In 1430, after expulsion by King Sigmund, the Eger synagogue was converted to the Church of the Ascension of Mary; see Bondy and Dworsky (eds), *Geschichte der Juden*, vol. 1, p. 102, no. 220.

23. In 1438, the city of Jauer, Silesia, secured permission from Emperor Albert II to convert the synagogue to a church, which he obliged them to dedicate to Saint Adalbert; see J. F. Böhmer (ed.), *Regesta Imperii* (Innsbruck, 1877; rpt. Hildesheim, 1966) vol. XII, p. 17, no. 37. It had sat abandoned since the expulsion of 1420; see Dr I. A. Grotte, '"Synagogen"-Kirchen in Schlesien', *Denkmalpflege und Heimatschutz*, 31 (1929) p. 38.

24. In Graz, where expulsion had occurred in 1420, the synagogue was converted to a chapel; see Maimon (ed.), *Germania Judaica*, vol. III/I, pp. 464–9.

25. Expulsion in Munich in 1442 resulted in the conversion of the synagogue to 'Unsere Liebe Frau in der Gruft' between 1442 and 1447; see Dr F. Solleder, *München in Mittelalter* (Munich 1938; rpt. Aalen, 1982) pp. 346–7, 523. The synagogue was located on the north side of the Grufstrasse on the corner of the Weinstrasse.

26. In Mainz, following an expulsion decree issued on St Michael's day in 1438 (S. Simonsohn, *The Apostolic See and the Jews*, 6 vols (Toronto, 1988–9) vol. 2, p. 861), in 1441 the synagogue was turned into a chapel dedicated to Mary and All Saints (Capella Omnium Sanctorum); see S. Simonsohn, *Apostolic See and the Jews*, vol. 2, pp. 860–1, no. 735.

27. Expulsion resulted in the transformation of the Coburg synagogue into a church in 1447; see Maimon (ed.), *Germania Judaica*, vol. III/I, p. 213.

28. Two years after an expulsion, the Landshut synagogue was transformed in 1452; see Maimon (ed.), *Germania Judaica*, vol. III/I, p. 714.

29. One consequence of the 1453 host desecration charge in Breslau was an expulsion decree aimed at all Silesian Jews. By 1455, the Schweidnitz synagogue had become the Fronleichnamskirche; see Grotte, '"Synagogen"-Kirchen in Schlesien', p. 35, n. 4.

30. Expulsion resulted in the transformation of the Striegau synagogue into St Barbara's Church; see Grotte, '"Synagogen"-Kirchen in Schlesien', p. 37.

31. In Bamberg, a synagogue had been converted to a Marian chapel in the fourteenth century and expulsion in the 1470s prompted the replacement of this now dilapidated chapel with an elaborate Marian church; see D. A. Eckstein, *Geschichte der Juden in ehemaligen Fürstbistum Bamberg* (Bamberg, 1893) p. 99.

32. In the aftermath of the ritual murder charges of 1475, the Trent synagogue was converted to a church (c.1475); see M. J. Wenninger, *Man bedarf keiner Juden mehr. Ursachen und Hintergründe ihrer Vertreibung aus den deutschen Reichsstädten im 15. Jahrhundert* (Vienna, 1981) p. 101, n. 128.

33. In the aftermath of the host desecration charge of 1478, the Passau synagogue was razed and replaced by the Church of St Salvator, 1479–1484; see W. M. Schmid, 'Zur Geschichte der Juden in Passau', *Zeitschrift für die Geschichte der Juden in Deutschland*, 1/2 (1929), p. 135.

34. In 1479 an Erfurt synagogue was converted to a church; see Wenninger, *Man bedarf keiner Juden mehr*, p. 101.

35. In Magdeburg following the 1493 expulsion of the Jews of Judendorf, Sudenburg (G. Hertel (ed.), *Die Wüstungen im Nordthuringgau* (Halle, 1899) p. 209), the synagogue was converted to a church; see Dr I. A. Grotte, *Deutsche, böhmische und polnische Synagogentypen von XI. bis Anfang des XIX. Jahrhunderts* (Berlin, 1915) p. 27.,

36. Due to expulsion in Steiermark in 1496 (Dr A. Rosenberg, *Beiträge zur Geschichte der Juden in Steiermark* (Leipzig, 1914) p. 101), the Wiener-Neustadt synagogue was converted to the Allerheiligen Kirche; see F. C. Böheim, *Chronik von Wiener-Neustadt* (Vienna, 1830) p. 196.

37. After expulsion in 1506 the Budweis synagogue was destroyed and replaced by a chapel dedicated to St Margaret; see Maimon (ed.), *Germania Judaica*, vol. III/I, pp. 189–91.

38. To my knowledge, to date, this is the most well known and comprehensively discussed synagogue conversion; see notes 1, 48.

39. In 1520, in Rothenburg ob der Tauber, following expulsion the synagogue was converted to a Marian chapel; see A. Schnitzlein, 'Zur Geschichte der Vertreibung der Juden in Rothenburg ob der Tauber 1519/20', *Monatschrift für Geschichte und Wissenschaft des Judentums*, 61 (1917) pp. 263–84. Also see Kirn, *Das Bild vom Juden*, p. 88, n. 158. It was, however, destroyed soon afterwards in 1525; see Künzl, 'A Recently Discovered MIQWEH', p. 30.

40. Grotte, *Deutsche, böhmische und polnische Synagogentypen*, p. 27.
W. Volkert, 'Die Juden in der Oberpfalz im 14. Jahrhundert', *Zeitschrift für bayerische Landesgeschichte*, 30 (1967) p. 174, notes fourteenth-century synagogue conversions in Germanic areas.

41. Wiener, *Regesten zur Geschichte der Juden in Deutschland*, p. 129, no. 198. Also see A. Müller, *Geschichte der Juden in Nürnberg 1146–1945* (Nuremberg, 1968) pp. 36–7.

42. Wiener, *Regesten zur Geschichte der Juden in Deutschland*, p. 130, no. 206.

43. Ibid., p. 128, no. 193.

44. Volkert, 'Die Juden in der Oberpfalz im 14. Jahrhundert', p. 174.

45. G. Spitzlberger, 'Die judische Siedlung im mittelalterlichen Landshut', in M. Freml and J. Kirmeier (eds), *Geschichte und Kultur der Juden in Bayern*, pp. 135–6.

46. K. Trüdinger, *Stadt und Kirche im spätmittelalterlichen Würzburg* (Stuttgart, 1978) p. 128, n. 35.

47. Volkert, 'Die Juden in der Oberpfalz im 14. Jahrhundert', p. 174, notes this.

48. For scholarship on this event, among others, see Dollinger, *Das Evangelium in Regensburg*, pp. 95–101; G. Stahl, 'Die Wallfahrt zur schönen Maria in Regensburg', *Beiträge zur Geschichte des Bistums Regensburg*, vol. 2 (1968) pp. 1–281.

49. This phenomenon in German territories has been noted in scholarship; it has not been systematically studied. Volkert, 'Die Juden in der Oberpfalz im 14. Jahrhundert', pp. 174–5, lists eleven examples without discussing them in detail. Schniztlein, 'Zur Geschichte der Vertreibung der Juden in Rothenburg ob der Tauber 1519/20', pp. 263–84, discusses the case of Rothenburg ob der Tauber. A. Grotte, '"Synagogen"–Kirchen in Schlesien', pp. 35–8, discusses three Silesian examples. The phenomenon is very briefly remarked in the following scholarship: O. Stobbe, *Die Juden in Deutschland während des Mittelalters* (Berlin, 1923; rpt. 1968) pp. 168–9; P. Browe, 'Die religiöse Duldung der Juden im Mittelalter', *Archiv für katholisches Kirchenrecht*, 118 (1938) pp. 1–76, 19; R. Bauerreiss, *Geschichte der Kirchengeschichte Baierns*, 6 vols (St Ottilien, 1949) vol. 6, p. 109; Zafran, 'The Iconography of Antisemitism', p. 200, n. 26; L. Rothkrug, 'Religious Practices and Collective Perceptions: Hidden Homologies in the Renaissance and Reformation', *Historical Reflections*, 7/1 (Waterloo, Ontario, 1980) pp. 63–6; Trüdinger, *Stadt und Kirche*, pp. 127–30; Dr Z. Asaria (ed.), *Die Juden in Köln von den ältesten Zeiten bis zur Gegenwart* (Cologne, 1959) p. 139, no. 35a; Künzl, 'A Recently Discovered MIQWEH', p. 30; Kirn, *Das Bild vom Juden*, pp. 88–9; C. Meckseper, 'Zur Lage des Judenviertels in der deutschen Stadt des Mittelalters', in D. Dolgner (ed.), *Stadtbaukunst im Mittelalter* (Berlin, 1990) p. 218; Wenninger, *Man bedarf keiner Juden mehr*, pp. 28, 101; G. Zimmermann, 'Patrozinienwahl und Frömmigkeitswandel im Mittelalter', I, II, in *WDGB*, 20 (1958) pp. 24–126; 21 (1959) pp. 5–124; H. J. Böker, 'Die Nikolaikapelle zu Soest. Irrwege einer Symbolinterpretation', *Soester Zeitschrift*, 104 (1992) p. 32.

50.  The present discussion is drawn from chapter 5 of my dissertation 'Images of Conversion and the Converted Jew in Fifteenth- and Early Sixteenth-Century Germany, 1400–1515', in preparation for Cambridge University.

51.  Exploration of the Jewish response is beyond the scope of the present chapter.

52.  See the lists of expulsions in: A. D. von Brincken, 'Das Rechtsfertigungsschreiben der Stadt Köln wegen der Ausweisung der Juden im Jahre 1424. Zur Motivierung spätmittelalterlicher Juden-Vertreibungen in West- und Mitteleuropa', *Mitteilungen aus dem Stadtarchiv Köln*, 60 (1971) pp. 307–11; P. N. Bebb, 'Jewish Policy in Sixteenth-Century Nürnberg', *Occasional Papers of the American Society for Reformation Research*, 1 (1977) p. 132; H. Veitshans, 'Die Judensiedlungen der schwäbischen Reichstädte und der würtembergischen Landstädte im Mittelalter', in *Arbeiten zum historischen Atlas von Südwestdeutschland*, 5 (Stuttgart, 1970) p. 38. Also see the maps in Wenninger, *Man bedarf keiner Juden mehr*, pp. 248–9. H. A. Oberman, *The Roots of Anti-Semitism*, trans. J. I. Porter (Philadelphia, 1981) p. 43, notes that in the German empire, after 1520, 'only a handful of towns issued expulsion decrees'. Apparently, the causes of the majority of these expulsions have yet to be individually scrutinised. To my knowledge, the most comprehensive and recent analyses of fifteenth-century expulsions are those by H. Horburger, *Judenvertreibung im Spätmittelalter* (Frankfurt, 1981), and Wenninger, *Man bedarf keiner Juden mehr*. These two studies examine pre-expulsion conditions in Basel, Freiburg im Breisgau, Cologne, Constance, Augsburg, Nuremberg, Nördlingen, Regensburg, and Frankfurt am Main. Both concentrate on the political and economic causes of expulsions. A. D. von Brincken, 'Das Rechtsfertigungsschreiben der Stadt Köln', pp. 305–39, analyses the Cologne expulsion in detail. The economic and political factors of the Nuremberg expulsions of 1499 have also been explored in some detail: among others, see: Wenninger, *Man bedarf keiner Juden mehr*, pp. 135–54; M. Toch, 'Umb Gemeyns Nutz und Nottdurfft Willen', *Zeitschrift für historische Forschung*, 11 (1984) pp 1–21.

53.  Bebb, 'Jewish Policy in Sixteenth Century Nürnberg', p. 132.

54.  Amberg, Heidelberg, Ingolstadt, Eger, Cologne, Deutz, Munich, Mainz, Coburg, Landshut, Erfurt, Magdeburg, Wiener-Neustadt, Budweis, Regensburg, Rothenburg ob der Tauber, Graz, Jauer, Linz, Iglau, Schweidnitz, Striegau.

55.  Prague (1194), and mid-fourteenth-century Nuremberg, Bamberg, Würzburg, Werthheim, Rothenburg ob der Tauber, and Landshut.

56.  Nuremberg (1350–55), Landshut (c.1350–1410), Rothenburg ob der Tauber (1404), Cologne (1424).

57.  Trent, 1475.

58.  Passau, 1478.

59.  For examples of medieval *Judengassen* situated near town walls see A. Pinthus, 'Studien über die bauliche Entwicklung der Judengassen in den deutschen Städten', *Zeitschrift für die Geschichte der Juden in Deutschland*, II (1930) pp.101–30, 108–20, who lists those in: Bingen,

Cologne, Mannheim, Rufach, Worms, Marburg (Steiermark), Rothenburg ob der Tauber, Einbeck, Budweis, Leitmeritz, Berlin, and Frankfurt
a.O., Mittenwalde.

60. For examples of *Judengassen* situated near or outside town limits
see Pinthus, 'Studien über die bauliche Entwicklung der Judengassen in
den deutschen Städten', pp. 108–20, who lists those in: Parchim, Halle,
Magdeburg, Meissen, Guben, Prenzlau, Spandau, Breslau, and Görlitz.

61. Künzl, 'A Recently Discovered MIQWEH', p. 28.

62. 1201, according to Pinthus, 'Studien über die bauliche
Entwicklung der Judengassen in den deutschen Städten', p. 114.

63. Ibid., p. 114.

64. Among others, see: E. Mummenhoff, 'Studien zur Geschichte und
Topographie des Nürnberger Markplatzes und seiner Umgebung',
*Aufsätze und Vorträge zur Nürnberger Ortsgeschichte* (Nuremberg, 1931);
G. Bräutigam, 'Gmünd-Prag-Nürnberg. Die Nürnberger Frauenkirche
und der Prager Paarlerstil vor 1360', *Jahrbuch der Berliner Museen*, n.s. 3
(1961) pp. 38–75, and 'Die Nürnberger Frauenkirche Idee und Herkunft
ihrer Architecktur', in *Festschrift für Peter Metz* (Berlin, 1965) pp. 170–97;
G. Michelfelder, 'Die wirtschaftliche Tätigkeit der Juden Nürnbergs
im Spätmittelalter', in *Stadtarchiv Nürnberg* (ed.), *Beiträge zur
Wirtschaftsgeschichte*, vol. 1 (Nuremberg, 1967) pp. 236–60; W. F. von
Stromer, 'Die Metropole im Aufstand gegen König Karl IV – Nürnberg
zwischen Wittelsbach und Luxemburg, Juni 1348 September 1349. Mit
einer Beilage "Das hochmittelalterliche Judenviertel Nürnbergs", eine
topographische Rekonstruktion von Karl Kohn', in *Festschrift des Vereins
für Geschichte der Stadt Nürnberg zur Feier seines hundertjährigen Bestehens
1878–1978* (Nuremberg, 1978) pp. 55–90; Toch, 'Umb Gemeyns Nutz
und Nottdurfft Willen', pp. 5–8; H. Maué, 'Nuremberg's Cityscape and
Architecture', in J. P. O'Neill and E. Schulz (eds), *Gothic and Renaissance
Art in Nuremberg 1300–1550*, trans. R. M. Stocknow (New York, 1986)
pp. 27–50; K. Ulshöfer, 'Zur Situation der Juden in mittelalterlichen
Nürnberg', in M. Freml and J. Kirmeier (eds), *Geschichte und Kultur der
Juden in Bayern*, pp. 147–160.

65. Ulshöfer, 'Zur Situation der Juden im mittelalterlichen Nürnberg',
p. 153. This left the Burggrafen and bishop of Bamberg the huge sum of
13,000 lb hl. Also see Stromer, 'Die Metropole im Aufstand gegen König
Karl I', p. 80.

66. At least five months before the pogrom, Charles IV gave houses in
the Nuremberg Judengasse to Schützherren; see J. Kirmeier, 'Aufnahme,
Verfolgung und Vertreibung. Zur Judenpolitik bayerischer Herzöge im
Mittelalter', in M. Freml and J. Kirmeier (eds), *Geschichte und Kultur der
Juden in Bayern*, p. 98.

67. Ulshöfer, 'Zur Situation der Juden im mittelalterlichen Nürnberg',
p. 159, n. 31.

68. Maué, 'Nuremberg's Cityscape and Architecture', p. 34, notes that
Nuremberg merchants had had the right to run a market since the
eleventh century, and the first known market was located below the
castle, north of St Sebald's church.

69. Bräutigam, 'Die Nürnberger Frauenkirche', p. 170. Wenninger, *Man bedarf keiner Juden mehr*, who, p. 135, notes that the new unwalled Judengasse was moved to the periphery of the city where the old cemetery had been.

70. Wenninger, *Man bedarf keiner Juden mehr*, p. 136.

71. Bräutigam, 'Gmünd-Prag-Nürnberg', p. 39, n. 2.

72. Müllner, *Die Annalen der Reichsstadt Nürnberg*, vol. II, p. 10. For more recent scholarship on topographical changes to Nuremberg at this time, among others, see above, n. 64.

73. Maué, 'Nuremberg's Cityscape and Architecture', p. 35.

74. Müllner, *Die Annalen der Reichsstadt Nürnberg*, vol. II, p. 10. For scholarship on the Frauenkirche, see especially the studies of G. Bräutigam listed above in n. 64.

75. G. Bräutigam, 'Gmünd-Prag-Nürnberg', p. 44, n. 13.

76. Müllner, *Die Annalen der Reichsstadt Nürnberg*, vol. II, p. 10, and Maué, 'Nuremberg's Cityscape and Architecture', p. 34, who also notes that Emperor Charles IV 'pardoned the city in advance for any harm that might come to the Jews under his protection'.

77. Pinthus, 'Studien über die bauliche Entwicklung der Judengassen in den deutschen Städten', p. 112.

78. Spitzlberger, 'Die judische Siedlung im mittelalterlichen Landshut', p. 143.

79. For scholarship on the Cologne expulsion, see above, n. 52.

80. H. Künzl, 'Die Architektur der mittelalterlichen Synagogen und rituellen Bäde', in K. Schubert (ed.), *Judentum im Mittelalter* (Eisenstadt, 1978) p. 50.

81. Pinthus, 'Studien über die bauliche Entwicklung der Judengassen in den deutschen Städten', p. 109. Pinthus, pp. 197–301, also notes that synagogues in Nördlingen, Erfurt, Braunschweig, Duderstadt, Lüneburg, and Osterode were located near town halls.

82. Since at least 1180; see E. Schirmacher, *Stadtvorstellungen: die Gestalt der mittelalterlichen Städte, Erhaltung und Planendes und Handeln* (Zurich, 1988) p. 97.

83. Wenninger, *Man bedarf keiner Juden mehr*, pp. 75, 220.

84. Stobbe, *Die Juden in Deutschland*, pp. 94–5.

85. 'Unter der Rathaushalle durfen sie [the Jews] nicht gehen, stehen, noch sitzen, es sei denn, wie sie vom Rathe dahin geheischet werden; auf dem Rathausplatz durfen sie nicht versammeln, die weil der Rath auf dem Rathause ist, in und aus der Synagogue durfen sie nur zwei und drei gehen'; cited in Brisch, *Geschichte der Juden in Cöln und Umgebung*, vol. II, pp. 28–9.

86. On the resettlement of Jewish communities following the ravages of the Black Death, among others, see Pinthus, 'Studien über die bauliche Entwicklung der Judengassen in den deutschen Städten', *Zeitschrift für die Geschichte der Juden in Deutschland*, p. 104. Also see this chapter, below, n. 104.

87. That is for Rothenburg ob der Tauber; see Pinthus, 'Studien über die bauliche Entwicklung der Judengassen in den deutschen Städten',

pp. 206–8; for Wurzburg (1349), see S. Jenks, 'Judenverschuldung und Verfolgung von Juden im 14. Jahrhundert: Franken bis 1349', *Vierteljahrschrift für Sozial- und Wirtschaftsgeschichte*, 65 (1978) p. 350, n. 73.
88. G. Kisch, *The Jews in Medieval Germany*, 2nd edn (New York, 1970) p. 129.
89. Kisch, *The Jews in Medieval Germany*, pp. 129–32.
90. A late fourteenth-century alphabetical register of medieval German law arranged according to subject matter (Regulae iuris 'Ad decus'), cited in Kisch, *The Jews in Medieval Germany*, p. 361.
91. To my knowledge, there are no systematic studies of the ownership of individual medieval Ashkenazi synagogues, or cemeteries for that matter. On the question of ownership, Kisch, *The Jews in Medieval Germany*, p. 184, notes that synagogues and cemeteries were considered communal property in Saxon lands, and, p. 209, states that the protection against violation which the law extended to both synagogues and cemeteries (which he elaborates on; see Kisch, pp. 184–5) suggests that these places of worship and sanctity 'seem to have been legally their property'. Kisch, *The Jews in Medieval Germany*, p. 448, n. 26, notes that Richard Krautheimer does not discuss synagogue ownership in his pioneering study *Mittelalterliche Synagogen* (Berlin, 1927), and synagogue ownership is not a focus in one of the most recent studies of the European synagogue, Krinsky, *Synagogues of Europe*. Krinsky, *Synagogues of Europe*, pp. 41, 116, n. 29, relies on Kisch to state that although it was not necessarily the case in fifteenth-century Germany, 'many governments prevented the Jews from owning the land on which their synagogues stood'. Krinsky, *Synagogues of Europe*, p. 113, notes cases of synagogues being owned by Christians where Jews could not own real property; i.e., Haguenau Alsace (12th–14th centuries).
92. In Bamberg (1349), as King Charles IV had pawned the Judensteuer to the bishop of Bamberg, ownership of the synagogue and other Jewish properties was therefore first transferred to the bishop; see Eckstein, *Geschichte der Juden*, p. 99; Krautheimer, *Mittelalterliche Synagogen*, pp. 181–8; H. Mayer, *Die Kunst im alten Hochstift Bamberg*, 2 vols (Bamberg, 1955) vol. I, p. 265; *Encyclopaedia Judaica*, 16 vols (Jerusalem, 1971–2) vol. 3, col. 1012. The case of Nuremberg, which had also come under the jurisdiction of the bishop of Bamberg, is discussed above on p. 66. In Würzburg (1349), following the pogrom, King Charles IV turned over private and communal Jewish belongings to Bischof Albrecht II von Hohelohe; see R. Flade, '"Jene, einem rebenreichen Weinstock verglichene Gemeinde." Zur Situation der Juden im mittelalterlichen Würzburg', in M. Freml and J. Kirmeier (eds), *Geschichte und Kultur der Juden in Bayern*, p. 178. In Heidelberg (1390s), King Rupert II reclaimed the houses and synagogues, before giving the Heidelberg synagogue to the university; see Thorbecke, *Die älteste Zeit der Universität Heidelberg*, p. 23, n. 41. In Ingolstadt (late 1390s), Duke Stephan der Knäuffel confiscated the synagogue before giving it to the town; see Friedmann, *Geschichte der Juden in Ingolstadt*, p. 21. In Rothenburg ob der Tauber (1350s), in 1353 Charles IV had given the synagogue, cemetery and

private houses of the Jews to the town of Rothenburg, which was responsible for the Jews; see Künzl, 'A Recently Discovered MIQWEH', p. 28. In Austria (1420s), Duke Albert V seized Jewish properties, see above, n. 10. In Cologne (1424), the town initially took over the synagogue because of outstanding taxes, while the mayor and town council proposed the conversion soon after, and two years later, on 7 September 1426, the provost and archdeacon of Cologne, Gerhard von Berg, gave the magistrate permission to erect a chapel and employ a chaplain; see Lacomblet (ed.), *Urkundenbuch*, vol. 4, p. 210, no. 177. In Eger (1430), King Sigmund ordered the conversion; see Bondy and Dworsky (eds), *Die Geschichte der Juden in Böhmen, Mähren und Schlesien*, vol. 1, p. 103, no. 220. In Jauer (Jower) (1438), the town had to request permission from Emperor Albert II to alter the abandoned building before the conversion could take place; see Böhmer, *Regesti Imperii*, vol. XII, p. 17, no. 37. In Munich (1440s), in 1442 Duke Albert III gave the synagogue to his son-in-law, Dr Johann Hartlieb; see A. F. von Oefele, *Rerum Boicarum Scriptores nusquam antehac editi, quibus vicinarum quoque gentium nec non Germaniae universae historiae ex monumentis genuinis historicis et diplomaticis plurimum illustrantur*, 2 vols (Munich, 1763) vol. II, p. 231. In Mainz (1441), the papacy authorised the synagogue conversion, upon the town's request; see Simonsohn, *The Apostolic See and the Jews*, vol. 2, pp. 897–8, no. 755. In 1462, this chapel was taken by the Elector Adolf; see Maimon (ed.), *Germania Judaica*, vol. III/I, p. 366. In Coburg (1447), Duke Wilhelm von Sachs ordered the conversion of the synagogue; see Maimon (ed.), *Germania Judaica*, vol. III/I, p. 214. In Landshut (1452), the synagogue was first claimed by Duke Ludwig the Rich in 1459, who then sold it to the town; see Spitzlberger, 'Die judische Siedlung im mittelalterlichen Landshut', p. 137. In Striegau (Strzegom) (1454), King Ladislaus, age fourteen, ordered the conversion; see Grotte, '"Synagogen" – Kirchen in Schlesien', p. 37. In Iglau (1426), the town was given the synagogue – probably by Duke Albrecht V, see above, n. 19 – and then obtained permission from Pope Pius II to convert it; see Maimon (ed.), *Germania Judaica*, vol. III/I, p. 580. In Magdeburg (1493), Maximilian gave the synagogue to the town; see Böheim, *Chronik von Wiener-Neustadt*, p. 406. In the 1490s, Emperor Frederich III repossessed Jewish properties before selling them; see above, n. 10. After expulsions in Steiermark and Nuremberg in the 1490s, there was a flurry of selling as Christians bought up Jewish houses in *Judengassen*; see this above, n. 10. In Wiener-Neustadt (late 1490s), Maximilian I gave the synagogue and some surrounding houses to the town; see Böheim, *Chronik von Wiener-Neustadt*, p. 106. In Rothenburg ob der Tauber (1520), the city scribe writes that as soon as the Jews had been expelled, the city council secured the right to the synagogue and began proceedings to gain permission to convert it to a Marian chapel by sending a letter to the bishop of Würzburg; see Schnizlein, 'Zur Geschichte der Vertreibung der Juden in Rothenburg ob der Tauber 1519/20', p. 272.

   93. See the previous note for the cases of Coberg and Striegau, and above p. 66 for the case of Nuremberg 1350.

94. See notes 8, 33, 92.
95. Krinsky, *Synagogues of Europe*, p. 15.
96. See the plan and photographs of the church of St Barbara provided in Grotte, '"Synagogen" – Kirchen in Schlesien', pp. 36–7, figs 3, 5, 6 and 7.
97. For additional examples, see n. 92.
98. See below, n. 108.
99. Mayer, 'Die Gründung von St Salvator in Passau – Geschichte und Legende', p. 258.
100. See above, n. 23. It may also be noted that the dispersal of movable Jewish property also contributed to the business-like mood which governed the organising of most of these conversions. In some cases, it has been established that confiscated Jewish wealth was used to pay for building costs and/or decorations of a number of these chapels and churches. For example: in Nuremberg in 1349, the city council, which had acquired the rights to the Jews five months before the pogrom of 5 December, seized the estates of the 562 murdered Jews, and most of it was used to pay for building costs for King Charles IV's special building project in the former *Judengasse*, the Frauenkirche (see above, p. 66); in Heidelberg in the 1390s, the university took possession of two of the synagogue's candelabra; see Maimon (ed.), *Germania Judaica*, vol. III/I, p. 528, n. 59; in Bamberg in the 1470s it seems probable that funds seized from the Bamberg Jews, expelled by Baron Georg von Schaumberg in the 1470s (see Eckstein, *Geschichte der Juden*, p. 100, and Mayer, *Die Kunst im alten Hochstift Bamberg*, vol. I, p. 265), aided the refurbishing of the choir and adjacent sacristy of the Marian chapel which had replaced the synagogue at Judenstrasse no. 1 in the mid-fourteenth century; see G. G. Dehio, *Handbuch der deutschen Kunstdenkmaler*, 13 vols (Berlin, 1964) vol. 1, p. 99.
101. It is important to note that the meaning of the synagogue for Jews is rather different from the meaning of the church for Christians. While a church is sited on consecrated ground, a synagogue is not. On the meaning of the synagogue for Jews, see Krinsky, *The Synagogue of Europe: Architecture, History, Meaning*, p. 5: 'The community is so central to the idea of a synagogue that any location in which the Jewish men gather for prayer may serve as a synagogue. The quorum, ten rather than the building itself constitutes the building in its most fundamental sense', and p. 8: 'Because a synagogue's sanctity comes from the activity pursued within it, the congregation may sell the building and move elsewhere.'
102. Kisch, *The Jews in Medieval Germany*, pp. 283–4.
103. Ibid., pp. 184, 209.
104. On medieval legislation restricting the height of synagogues, see Browe, 'Die religiöse Duldung der Juden im Mittelalter', p. 17. There was much legislation about the synagogue building. For an excellent overview of early Christian attitudes to and legislation on synagogue buildings still pertinent in the medieval period, see J. Juster, *Les Juifs dans l'Empire Roman*, 2 vols (Paris, 1914) vol. I, pp. 456–72. For discussions of medieval Christian legislation on the synagogues see: J. W. Parkes, *The Jew in the*

*Medieval Community* (London, 1938) p. 12; Scherer, *Die Rechtsverhältnisse der Juden*, p. 334; Browe, 'Die religiöse Duldung der Juden im Mittelalter', pp. 9–20; Baron, *A Social and Religious History of the Jews*, vol. XI, pp. 42–9. Canon law had long prohibited the building of new synagogues, or the enlargement of existing ones, in particular, increasing the height of the synagogue or adding costly decoration. Restrictive legislation passed in the medieval Holy Roman Empire includes that passed in late thirteenth-century Salzburg at the Synod of Archbishop Wladislaus, which banned the building of new synagogues and the enlargement of existing ones; in Nuremberg in 1404, the Jews were prevented from building a new synagogue (Müllner, *Die Annalen der Reichsstadt Nürnberg*, p. 195); in the treatise *Tractatus Judeorum* (*c.*1475), London, British Library, BL 37229, the 'Quartum Avisamentum' (unpaginated) states that Jews are not permitted to build new synagogues nor to enlarge existing ones, and cited are the rulings of Popes Gregory IX and Alexander III. However, evidence suggests that restrictive synagogue legislation was enforced erratically or not at all: a new synagogue was built in Bamberg following consecration of the existing synagogue in 1350; see Eckstein, *Geschichte der Juden*, p. 100; in Nuremberg although, as noted above, in 1404 they were prevented from building a new synagogue, in 1355 they had been able to set one up; see Krautheimer, *Mittelalterliche Synagogen*, p. 250; in 1406 in Rothenburg ob der Tauber, a synagogue was erected in the newly situated *Judengasse*; see Künzl, 'A Recently Discovered MIQWEH', p. 30; following the wave of expulsions and pogroms in Austria in the 1420s, Pope Martin V issued a bull permitting the Jews to return to every place from which they had been expelled by Duke Albert V, which included granting them the right to build new synagogues; see M. Stern, *Urkundliche Beiträge über die Stellung der Päpste zu den Juden* (Kiel, 1893) p. 54, no. 49); in 1440, though Pope Eugene IV approved a petition by Mainz to bar the return of the Jews, he stipulated that if they did return, they were to be provided with a new synagogue; see S. Simonsohn, *Apostolic See and the Jews*, pp. 862–3, no. 737; in fifteenth-century Erfurt, Jews evidently obtained permission to have more than one synagogue, for there is record of five synagogues in 1452; see J. Hofer, *Johannes Kapistran: ein Leben im Kampf um die Reform der Kirche*, 2 vols (Heidelberg, 1964–5) vol. I, p. 423); in Speyer, an ordinance of 1486 prohibited the building of a new synagogue without the bishop's permission; see K. Schilling (ed.), *Monumenta Judaica*, 2 vols (Cologne, 1963) Katalog B, pp. 315–16.

105. Revelations 2:9; 3:9. J. Trachtenberg, *The Devil and the Jews: The Medieval Conception of the Jews and its Relations to Modern Antisemitism* (2nd edn, New York, 1966) p. 21, cites John of Chrysostum's description of the synagogues of the Jews as 'the homes of idolatry and the devils'. For Chrysostum's passages on the synagogue, see R. R. Ruether, *Faith and Fratricide: The Theological Roots of Anti-Semitism* (New York, 1974) pp. 175–9. Peter the Venerable mentions 'the Synagogue of Satan' in his 'Tractatus contra Judaeos'; see J. P. Migne (ed.), *Patrologia Latina*, vol. 189, p. 549.

106. Among others, see: Trachtenberg, *The Devil and the Jews*, pp. 210, 214, J. B. Russell, *Witchcraft in the Middle Ages* (London, 1972), pp. 130–3.
107. See chapter 4 of my dissertation (see above, n. 50), for Munich (1285) and Trent (1475).
108. See chapter 4, ibid., for Passau (1478).
109. See chapter 4, ibid., for Breslau (1453); Passau (1478); Sternberg (1492).
110. See chapter 4, ibid., for Mainz (1096), and numerous examples for 1298, 1349.
111. See chapter 4, ibid., for Munich (1285), and numerous examples from 1298, 1349.
112. Eckstein, *Geschichte der Juden*, p. 99.
113. Ibid., p. 99. Grotte, '"Synagogen"-Kirchen in Schlesien', p. 35, also notes that a synagogue in Oels converted at a later date (1695), St Salvator, became known as the Judenkirche.
114. To my knowledge, of this group, only the synagogues of Nuremberg (1349), Würzburg (1349), Amberg (1390s), Passau (1478), Budweis (1506), and Regensburg (1519) were razed.
115. Oberman, *The Roots of Anti-semitism*, p. 90, n. 46, states that Teuschlein came to Rothenburg ob der Tauber in 1512.
116. Schnizlein, 'Zur Geschichte der Vertreibung der Juden in Rothenburg ob der Tauber 1519/20', p. 277.
117. Ibid., p. 277.
118. Ibid., p. 277.
119. Ibid., p. 273.
120. Trüdinger, *Stadt und Kirche*, pp. 62–8.
121. Ibid., p. 128.
122. See above, n. 92.
123. Wiener, *Regesten zur Geschichte der Juden in Deutschland*, p. 176, no. 495.
124. Pinthus, 'Studien über die bauliche Entwicklung der Judengassen in den deutschen Städten', p. 111.
125. Solleder, *München in Mittelalter*, p. 523. The papal legate was Cardinal Alexander, the Patriarch of Aquila.
126. Mummenhoff, 'Studien zur Geschichte und Topographie des Nürnberger Marktplatzes und seiner Umgebung', pp. 228–31.
127. For a more extensive discussion of this point, see chapter 5 of my dissertation (see above, n. 50). It was not here possible to discuss and reproduce the full range of imagery generated by the event of a conversion; this will be done in a forthcoming book.
128. 'Et ecce mirum, Synagoga veteris legis in scholam virtutum novae legis mirabiliter transmutatur', cited in Dr I. Schwarz, *Das Wiener Ghetto: seine Hauser und seine Bewohner*, 2 vols (Vienna, 1909) vol. 1, p. 46. Also see above, n. 9.
129. Lacomblet (ed.), *Urkundenbuch*, vol. 4, p. 210, no. 177.
130. 'Colner Jahrbucher des 14 und 15 Jahrhundert', in *Die Chroniken der deutschen Städte vom 14. bis ins 16. Jahrhundert*, (ed.) Die historische Commission bei der königlichen Akademie der Wissenschaften (Leipzig,

1862–1929; rpt. Göttingen, 1965) vol. 13, p. 156: 'Dat die Joedenschole zu Coellen geweit wart.'

131. 'Cölner Jahrbücher des 14 und 15 Jahrhundert', in *Die Chroniken der deutschen Städte vom 14. bis ins 16. Jahrhundert*, vol. 13, p. 156; 'Koelhoffische Chronik' (1499), in *Die Chroniken der deutschen Städte vom 14. bis ins 16. Jahrhundert*, vol. 13, p. 762: 'Dese Joedenschole hadde gestanden in der Joeden hant 400 ind 14 jair, alias.'

132. Letter of Pope Eugene IV; see S. Simonsohn, *The Apostolic See and the Jews*, vol. 2, pp. 860–1, no. 735.

133. S. Simonsohn, *The Apostolic See and the Jews*, vol. 2, p. 1040, no. 847, dated 1458: 'Ante paucos annos sinagoga Iudeorum fuit, et postea per dilectum filium nobilem virum Ludovicum, comitem palatinum reni et Bavarie ducem, in domum Dei erecta extitit'. On the chapel, see Spitzlberger, 'Die judische Siedlung im mittelalterlichen Landshut', pp. 135–6.

134. Fritz Fellhainer, 'Von den Juden zu Passau' (*c.*1490) published in R. von Liliencron (ed.), *Die historischen Volkslieder der Deutschen vom 13. bis 16. Jahrhundert*, 4 vols (Leipzig, 1865–6; rpt. Hildesheim, 1966) vol. II, p. 145: 'An dem end, da der ofen stat, / da man das hochwirdig sacramentgeworfen hat, / da tut man ain schons gotshaus zu pawen; / vil säliger mess werden verpracht / und loblicher amt mit groszer andachtdem leiden gots und unser lieben / frawen.

135. '... in loco, quo antehac blasphema, usuraria ac cruenta Judaeae fecis synagoga erat ...'; see Straus, *Urkunden*, p. 389.

136. L. H. Stookey, 'The Gothic Cathedral as Heavenly Jerusalem: Liturgical and Theological Sources', *Gesta*, VII/I (1969) p. 35.

137. Stookey, 'The Gothic Cathedral as Heavenly Jerusalem', p. 37.

138. The researching of the consecration liturgies and ceremonies of these thirty-two examples has yet to be undertaken. According to recent scholarship on the European synagogue, Krinsky, *Synagogues of Europe*, p. 109, n. 50, there is little scholarship on liturgy used especially for the conversion of synagogues. J. W. Parkes, *The Conflict of the Church and the Synagogue: A Study in the Origins of Antisemitism* (London, 1934) p. 401, cites prayers specified for the consecration of converted synagogues found in the 'Liber Sacramentorum Romanae Ecclesiae'. Juster, *Les Juifs dans l'Empire Roman*, vol. 1, p. 468, n. 1, cites a prayer included in the Gelasian Sacramentary which, he remarks, is missing from the Gregorian Sacramentary: 'Orationes et preces in Dedicatione loci illius ubi prius fuit synagoga: Deus ... respice super hanc basilicam in honore beati illius nomini tuo dicatam; ut vestutate Iudaici erroris expulsa, huic loco sancti Spiritus novitatem ecclesiae conferas veritatem.... Omnipotens sempiterne Deus, qui hunc locum, Iudaicae superstitionis foeditate detersa, in honore beati illius ecclesiae ...'.

139. To my knowledge, this was first noted by Parkes, *The Conflict of the Church and the Synagogue*; see previous note.

140. Parkes, *The Conflict of the Church and Synagogue*, p. 401. Pope Innocent III (1198–1216) had described French chapels and churches of this origin as places 'divested of the blind Jewish perversion of Faith'; see

letter of 23 March 1204 to the Dean and canons of St Croix in Étampe, published in S. Grayzel, *The Church and the Jews in the XIIIth century* (2nd edn, New York, 1966) p. 105.

141. Parkes, *The Conflict of the Church and Synagogue*, p. 401. 'Ad populum: A plebe tua, quaesumus, Domine, spirituales nequitiae repellantur, et aerearum discedat malignitas Potestatem ...'.

142. 'Jahrbücher des 15. Jahrhunderts', in *Die Chroniken der deutschen Städte vom 14. bis ins 16. Jahrhundert*, vol. 4, p. 124. Also see Müllner, *Annalen der Reichstadt Nürnberg*, p. 10.

143. Sigmund Meisterlin, 'Die Chronik der Reichstadt Nürnberg' (1488), in *Die Chroniken der deutschen Städte vom 14. bis ins 16., Jahrhundert*, vol. 3, p. 160, n. 2.

144. Mummenhoff, 'Studien zur Geschichte und Topographie des Nürnberger Marktplatzes und seiner Umgebung', p. 335.

145. For sources, see: Thorbecke, *Die älteste Zeit der Universität Heidelberg*, p. 23, n. 41; Volkert, 'Die Juden in der Oberpfalz im 14. Jahrhundert', p. 183.

146. Thorbecke, *Die älteste Zeit der Universität Heidelberg*, p. 23, n. 42.

147. G. Ritter, *Die Heidelberger Universität*, 2 vols (Heidelberg, 1936) p. 136.

148. 'Koelhoffsche Chronik' (1499), in *Die Chroniken der deutschen Städte vom 14. bis ins 16. Jahrhundert*, vol. 13, p. 762.

149. 'Cölner Jahrbücher des 14. und 15. Jahrhundert', in *Die Chroniken der deutschen Städte vom 14. bis ins 16. Jahrhundert*, vol. 13, p. 156, n. 3.

150. Ibid., p. 156, n. 3.

151. Brisch, *Geschichte der Juden in Cöln und Umgebung*, vol. II, p. 46.

152. Ibid., p. 46.

153. That is, Adalbert (Jauer, 1438), Barbara, Streigau (1454), All Saints, Mainz (1471) and St Margaret, Budweis (1506). In his stimulating study of Marian shrines, *Religious Practices and Collective Perceptions*, Lionel Rothkrug, p. 68, stated that *all* chapels and churches built in synagogue sites and in the ruins of *Judengassen* were dedicated to the 'Queen of Heaven' (later known as Siegerin aller Gottes Schlachten, Lady Victor of all God's battles).'

154. Nuremberg, Bamberg, Würzburg.

155. Heidelberg, Amberg, Ingolstadt, Rothenburg ob der Tauber (1404, 1520), Cologne, Deutz, Eger, Munich, Mainz, Regensburg. Volkert, 'Die Juden in der Oberpfalz im 14. Jahrhundert', p. 174, remarks the Marian dedications of consecrated syngagogues, as do Zafran, "The Iconography of Antisemitism', p. 200, n. 26, who cites the example of Regensburg, and Künzl, 'A Recently Discovered MIQWEH', p. 30, n. 1, who cites the examples of Cologne, Würzburg, Nuremberg and Heidelberg.

156. Volkert, 'Die Juden in der Oberpfalz im 14. Jahrhundert', p. 174. On the symbolism of Mary as the new Eve, among others, see P. Bloch, 'Nachwirkungen des Alten Bundes in der christlichen Kunst', in *Monumenta Judaica*, E. K. Schilling (ed.), Handbuch, p. 745. An apple is the usual attribute of Mary represented as the new Eve.

157. Volkert, 'Die Juden in der Oberpfalz im 14. Jahrhundert', p. 175. For the transformation of Mary into Ecclesia, and artistic representations of Mary as Ecclesia, among others, see: E. Kirschbaum (ed.), *Lexikon der christlichen Ikonographie*, 8 vols (Rome, 1968–76) vol. I, col. 994; vol. III, cols 562–3; W. Seiferth, *Synagogue and Church in the Middle Ages*, trans. L. Chadeayne and P. Gottwald (New York, 1970) pp. 136, 138, 146, 156, who, p. 138, stresses that in art they appear interchangeable.

158. Volkert, 'Die Juden in der Oberpfalz im 14. Jahrhundert', p. 174. Rothkrug, *Religious Practices and Collective Perceptions*. It is important to stress that scholarship on the history of the Marian cult in the medieval Holy Roman Empire remains under-studied; the most comprehensive study of the cult of Mary in late medieval Germany remains the early twentieth-century work of S. Beissel, *Geschichte der Verehrung Marias in Deutschland während des Mittelalters* (Freiburg, 1909). Also see Rothkrug, *Religious Practices and Collective Perceptions*.

159. Rothkrug, *Religious Practices and Collective Perceptions*, pp. 68, 87. Like Rothkrug, Wenninger, *Man bedarf Keiner Juden mehr*, p. 28, views the celebration of Mary on these sites as retaliation for her dreadful persecution by the Jews.

160. Volkert, 'Die Juden in der Oberpfalz im 14. Jahrhundert', p. 174. For scholarship on this type of Marian statuary, among others, see: *Schöne Madonnen 1350–1450*, Exhibition Catalogue, Salzburg, 1965. E. G. Grimme, *Deutsche Madonnen* (Cologne, 1966) pp. 105, 106, 108. Volkert, 'Die Juden in der Oberpfalz im 14. Jahrhundert', p. 174. Zimmermann, 'Patrozinienwahl und Frömmigkeitswandel im Mittelalter', p. 89.

161. Rothkrug, *Religious Practices and Collective Perceptions*, p. 91.

162. Mary was proclaimed supreme symbol of the Bavarian church in the thirteenth century by Louis IV (1287–1347), Duke of Bavaria, who founded the monastery of Ettal in her honour; see Rothkrug, *Religious Practices and Collective Perceptions*, p. 63.

163. Ibid., p. 63.

164. Ibid., p. 68.

165. Ibid., p. 87.

166. K. Trüdinger, *Stadt und Kirche*, p. 128; J. Dünninger, 'Processio peregrinationis. Volkskundliche Untersuchungen zu einer Geschichte des Wallfahrtswesen in Gebiet der heutigen Diözese Würzburg I, II', in *Würzburger Diözesangeschichtsblätter*, 23 (1961), pp. 53–176, and 24 (1962), pp. 52–188, I, p. 145.

167. Trüdinger, *Stadt und Kirche*, p. 128, n. 36.

168. As Seiferth, *Synagogue and Church*, p. 127, states: 'Ecclesia did not need to feel ashamed of either her pagan or Jewish ancestry'.

169. For scholarship on Capistrano, among others, see J. Hofer, *Johannes Kapistran*.

170. 'Chronik von Heinrich Deichsler bis 1487', in *Die Chroniken der deutschen Städte vom 14. bis ins 16. Jahrhundert*, XI, pp. 190–91. Also see Hofer, *Johannes Kapistran*, vol. II, p. 153.

171. Cited in Hofer, *Johannes Kapistran*, vol. II, p. 154. 'To my knowledge, medieval German views of Mary and Christ's Jewish origins remain

unstudied. There are many other examples. For instance, the deeply entrenched medieval iconographies of 'Tree of Jesse' and 'Holy Kinship' scenes vividly emphasise Mary and Christ's Jewish origins. On the iconography of the first, among others, see: Bloch, 'Nachwirkungen des Alten Bundes in der christlichen Kunst', pp. 737–41, who briefly comments on German examples dating from 1086 to 1536; G. Schiller, *The Iconography of Christian Art*, vol. 1, pp. 15–17. On the iconography of the second, see Schiller, *The Iconography of Christian Art*, vol. 1, pp. 15–17. For an intriguing late fifteenth-century German example featuring the bell-shaped *Judenhut*, see Bernard Strigel's painting of this scene. Mention of Mary's Jewish origins begins the account of her birth in the widely disseminated *Legenda Aurea*; see R. Cruel, *Geschichte der deutschen Predigt im Mittelalter* (Detmold, 1879; rpt. Hildesheim, 1966) p. 483. The Dominican Heroldt preached that the patriarchs, prophets, apostles and Christ were all Jews; see Cruel, *Geschichte der deutschen Predigt*, p. 483. Near the beginning of the 1515 tract entitled *Enterung und schmach, der bildung Marie von de jude bewissen, und zu ewiger gedichtnüss durch Maximilianum den römische keyser zu male verschaffet in der löbliche stat kolmer. Vo danen sy ouch ewig vertriben syndt* (1515), the theme of which is alleged Jewish atrocities, Mary's Jewish origins are stressed: '... Von irem stam erboren wardt / Maria schon die reyn und zart, Durch die alss heyll uff erden kam; / das ist hie von dem iüdishen stam ...'; cited in A. Klassert (ed.), 'Entehrung Maria durch die Juden. Eine antisemitische Dichtung Thomas Murners', in *Jahrbuch für Geschichte, Sprache und Literatur Elsass-Lothringens*, 21 (1905) p. 110.

172. Sigmund Meisterlin, 'Die Chronik der Reichstadt Nürnberg' (1488), in *Die Chroniken der deutschen Städte vom 14. bis ins 16. Jahrhundert*, vol. 3, p. 158: 'Es was ein groszer mangel zu Nurenberg, dass die kaiserin der himmel, die gottes gebererin, die edel junkfrawe Maria kein eigen kirchen hett in der stat. ich mein, dass die mutter des gekreutzigten fluhe das mörderisch geschlechte, das ir liebes kint getöttet hett, und wolt nit besonder wesen haben, do ir so vil woneten.'

173. Friedmann, *Die Geschichte der Juden in Ingolstadt*, p. 21: 'Die ob ihrer Vertreibung wütigen Juden stahlen aus der Kapelle, welche an Stelle ihrer Synagogue enstand, das wunderreiche Gnadenbild, insgemein die Schuttermuttergottes genannt, und versteckten es, nachdem sie ihm den Knopf abgeschitten, die Donau aufwärts an einem heimlichen Ort am Gestade. Nach nicht langer Zeit aber, siehe, da schwamm des Muttersgottesbild mit abgeschittenem Kopfe von freien Stücken die Donau herab, in die Schutter hinein, sich nächst an die Kapelle anlegend. Darob enstand ein jubelgeschrei in der ganzen Stadt.'

174. A stone mason by the name of Jacob Kern. See Dollinger, *Das Evangelium in Regensburg*, p. 97.

175. *In dysem buchlein seind begriffen die wunderbarlich zaychen beschehen zu Regensburg zu der Schönen Maria der Mutter gottes*, Tübingen, Sonderforschungsbereich, no. 3160 (Regensburg, *c.*1519); unpaginated: see second page under the heading 'das Vierdt zaichen'.

176. Tübingen, Sonderforschungsbereich, no. 3160 (Regensburg *c.*1519). Unpaginated; see first page, 'das erst zaichen', and second page, 'das vierdt zaichen'.

177. *In dysem buchlein seind begriffen die wunderbarlichen zaychen beschehen zu Regensburg zu der Schönen Maria der Mutter gottes* (1519), Tübingen, Sonderforschungsbereich, no. 3160. Unpaginated; see page immediately following frontispiece: ... auch ir Synagogue / in der sy teglichen unsern herrn Jesum Christum / auch seyn lobsame muter / die hochgelobten kunigin / die schonen Mariam / geschent / geschmeht und schwerlichen gelestert / zersprochen / nydergelegt / und den pflaster gleich gemacht / und der orten ein loblich gotzhaus zu erheben und zu pawen angefangen / in der eren der yetz benanten Junckfrawen der Schonen Maria / da auch grosse wunderbarliche zaichen beschehen sein ...'.

178. Von Liencron, *Historische Volkslieder*, vol. III, p. 356: 'Da man die Juden treib hin dann, / die mann und auch die frauwen, / da fingen die von Rottenburg an, / ein capel da zu pawen / in der eer der rein Maria gut, / die mit der hilf irs kindes / da grosse zeichen thut.'

179. A Rossi, *The Architecture of the City*, trans D. Ghirardo and J. Ockman (New York, 1982) p. 130; also see his discussion of the 'City as History', pp. 127–30.

180. Kisch, *The Jews in Medieval Germany*, p. 184, on the Meissener Rechtsbuch and Roman law. It is significant that he notes: 'There is no record, however, of any actual violations which were prosecuted in local courts and submitted for decision to the Oberhof of Magdeburg.'

181. That is, the Vorstadt Gumpendorf, Vienna (1421), see Schwarz, *Das Weiner Ghetto*, p. 55; Regensburg (1519). Apparently about 4,200 grave stones were removed between 16 and 20 March; see Andreas Raselius, 'Chronicon de civitate Ratisbonensis', as summarised in Dollinger, *Das Evangelium in Regensburg*, pp. 97–8, and Angerstorfer, 'Von Judensiedlung zum Ghetto in der mittelalterlichen Reichsstadt Regensburg', p. 168, who says that they were also immured in houses in Mangolding, Mintraching, Tegernheim, Wolkering.

182. For example, city walls in Liegnitz and Breslau (1345); see Baron, *A Social and Religious History of the Jews*, vol. XI, p. 51: 'In 1345 Dukes Wenceslaus and Louis granted the Liegnitz burghers "full authority and license" to use Jewish tombstones in building their city walls, King John of Bohemia in 1345 gave similar permission to the Breslau burghers "regardless of any objections raised by Jews or anyone else."'

183. For example, Salzturmebrücke, Speyer; see T. Kwasmann, 'Jüdische Grabsteine', in M. Treml, J. Kirmeier (eds), *Geschichte und Kultur der Juden in Bayern*, pp. 39–50, p. 48, n. 8.

184. For example, Kriegshaber, Pfersee, Steppach (*c.*1449), all small towns in the vicinity of Augsburg; see Wenninger, *Man bedarf Keiner Juden mehr*, p. 133.

185. Hebrew-inscribed tombstones, one dating from 1302, were immured in the tower (*c.*1350) of St Lamberti Church in Münster; see H. J. Böker, *Die Marktpfarrkirche St Lamberti zu Münster* (Bonn, 1989) p. 30. Jewish tombstones became steps in the spiral staircase of the south

tower (1352) of the Lorenzkirche in Nuremberg; see Müllner, *Die Annalen der Reichsstadt Nürnberg*, vol. II, p. 88, and Stromer, 'Die Metropole im Aufstand gegen König Karl IV', p. 80. They were incorporated into a Würzburg church (*c.*1349); see Flade, '"Jene, einem rebenreichen Weinstock verglichene Gemeinde." Zur Situation der Juden im mittelalterlichen Würzburg', p. 178. They were also incorporated into the converted Landshut synagogue (*c.*1452), the Trinity chapel; see Maimon (ed.), *Germania Judaica*, III, p. 716, n. 77, and the lavish stone version of the Schöne Maria church in Regensburg (1520); see Eschwege, *Die Synagogue in der deutschen Geschichte*, p. 60.

186. R. W. Scribner, *For the Sake of the Simple Folk: Popular Propaganda for the German Reformation* (Cambridge, 1981) p. 85.

4. INSTITORIS AT INNSBRUCK: HEINRICH INSTITORIS, THE *SUMMIS DESIDERANTES* AND THE BRIXEN WITCH-TRIAL OF 1485    Eric Wilson

1. Joseph Hansen, *Zauberwahn, Inquisition und Hexenprozess im Mittelalter und die Entstehung der Grossen Hexenverfolgung* (Historische Bibliothek, 12, Munich, 1900) pp. 467–75; W. T. Soldan and H. Heppe, *Geschichte der Hexenprozesse I* (Hanau, no date) pp. 245–70.

2. For a collection of such documents, see Joseph Hansen, *Quellen und Untersuchungen zur Geschichte des Hexenwahns und der Hexenverfolgung im Mittelalter* (Hildesheim, 1963) pp. 1–37. The judicial and diplomatic status of these *Fakultäten* are discussed at length by Ernst Pitz in his 'Diplomatisches Studien zu den Papstlichen Erlassen über das Zauber- und Hexenwesen', pp. 23–69 in Peter Segl (ed.) *Der Hexenhammer: Entstehung und Umfeld des Malleus Maleficarum von 1487* (Bayreuther Historische Kolloquien, 2, Cologne 1988).

3. Russell Hope Robbins, *The Encyclopedia of Witchcraft and Demonology* (New York, 1981) pp. 263–6.

4. 'Witchcraft' is referred to only as *haeretica pravitas*. Innocent does, however, explicitly mention *maleficium* in his epistle to Archduke Sigismund of 18 June 1485. Hansen, *Quellen*, p. 28.

5. 27 February 1318, 22 August 1320, 1326–7, 4 November 1330, 12 April 1331. Cf. Hansen, *Quellen* pp. 2–8. John is most concerned with homeopathic magic and ritualistic court sorcery. Sigmund von Riezler, *Geschichte der Hexenprozesse in Bayern, im Lichte der allgemeinen Entwicklung dargestellt* (Stuttgart, 1896) p. 84.

6. 24 February 1434, 1437, 23 March 1440, 17 July 1445. Reprinted in Hansen, *Quellen*, pp. 17–18. Eugenius cites as examples of *crimen magicum* adoration of the Devil, the demonic pact, the demonic infliction of illness, the raising of tempests, and diabolic divination. Riezler, *Die Geschichte der Hexenprozesse*, p. 85.

7. Edward Peters, *The Magician, the Witch and the Law* (Brighton, 1978) pp. 172–3. Heinrich Institoris frequently laments the opposition he has encountered from ignorant or perverse laymen and clerics. 'Sequiter modus praedicandi, contra quinque argumenta laicorum, quibus probare videntur sparim quod Deus non permittat tantum potestatem

Diabolo, et maleficis, circa huiusmodi; maleficia inferenda' (Heinrich Institoris, *Malleus Maleficarum, Maleficas et Earum haeresim framea conterens, ex Variis Auctoribus Compilatus, in quatuor Tomos iuste distributus. Tomus Primus*) (Lyon, 1669) I, Q. 18).

8. Pitz, 'Diplomatische Studien', p. 56.

9. The text of the *Summis Desiderantes* is reprinted in J. R. Schmidt (ed.), *Jakob Sprenger, Heinrich Institoris: Der Hexenhammer* (*Malleus Maleficarum*) (Berlin, 1960) pp. xxxii–xxxvi. 'Fidem praetera ipsam, quam in sacri suspectione baptismi susceperunt, ore sainlego abregere, aliaque quam plurima nefarda, excessus et crimina instigante humani generis inimico committere et perpetrare non verentur, in animarum suarum periculum, divinae Maiestatis offensum ac perniciosum exemplam ac scandalam plurimorum.'

10. It is important to note that the Bull neither presents any 'sophisticated' account of witchcraft nor even appears to consider witchcraft as a separate category of supernatural transgression clearly separable from the more traditional forms of heretical devil-worship.

11. Peters, *The Witch, the Magician and the Law*, p. 172.

12. These 'literas apostolicas deputati fuerint' could have included a formal episcopal letter from Bishop Kaspar zu Rhein of Basel, composed in September 1482, that invested Institoris with full inquisitorial authority within the diocese; and the *Ad comprimendam quorundam*, a bull issued on 28 October 1485 by Sixtus IV that officially cited Institoris to combat conciliarist heretics. See Eric Wilson, 'The Text and Context of the Malleus Maleficarum (1487)' (unpublished Ph.D. dissertation, University of Cambridge, 1990) chapter 2.

13. 'Tamen nonnulli clerici et laici illorum partium, quaerentes plus sapere quam oporteat, pro eo quod in literas deputationis huiusmodi provinciae, civitates dioceses, terrae et alia loca praedicta illarumque personae ac excessus huiusmodi noministum et specifice expressa non fuerunt, illa sub eisdem portibus minime contineri et propterea praefatis inquisitoribus in provinciis, civitatibus, diocesibus, terris et locis praedictis huiusmodi; inquisitionis officium exequi non licere et ad personarum earundem super excessibus et animinibus antedictis punitionem, incarcerationem et correctionem admitti non debere, pertinaciter assere non erubescunt.'

14. 'Eisdem inquisitoribus in illis officium huiusmode; exequi licere et ad personarum earundem super excessibus et animibus praedictis correctionem, incarcerationem et punitionem admitti debere, perinde in omnibus et per omnia ac si in literis predictis provinciae, civitates, dioceses, terrae et loca ac personae et excessus huiusmodi nominatione et specifice expressa forent, auctoritate apostolica tenmore praesentium statuimus.'

15. 'Praedictis contra quascumque personas, cuiuscumque conditionis et praeeminentiae fuerint, huiusmodi inquisitionis officium exequi ipsaque personas, quas in praemisis culpabiles reperint, iuxta earum demerita corrigere, incarcere, punire et mutilare, necnon in singulis provinciarum huiusmodi parochialibus ecclesiis verbam dei fideli populo

quotiens expederit ac eis visum fuerit, proponere et praedicare, omni-
aque alia et singula in praemissis et circa ea necessaria et opportuna
facere et similiter exequi libere et licite valeant, plenam ac liberam
eadem auctoritate de novo concedimus facultatem.'

16. Pitz, 'Diplomatische Studien', p. 55.

17. The designation of Bishop Albrecht as custodian would appear to
have less to do with any involvement of the bishop in witchcraft trials or
with an exceptionally high rate of alleged malefic activity within
Strassburg, but rather with the fact that Institoris himself was the *ordinis
praedicator* of the diocese – a consideration which indirectly attests to
Institoris's personal involvement in obtaining the promulgation of the
*Summis*.

18. 'Non permittat eos per quoscumque super hoc contra praedicato-
rum et praesentium literanum tenorem quavis auctoritate molestari seu
alias quomodolibet impediri, molestatores et impedientes et contra-
dictores quoslibet et rebelles, cuiuscumque dignitatis, status, gradus,
praeeminentiae, nobilitatis et excellentiae aut conditionis fuerint et
quocumque exemtionis privilegio sunt muniti, per excommunicationis,
suspensionis et interdicti ac alias etiam formidabiliores, de quibus sibi
videbitur, sententias, censuras et poenas, omni appelatione post posita,
compesenda, et etiam legitimis super his per eam servandis processibus,
sententias ipsas, quoties opus fuerit, aggravare et reaggravare auctoritate nostra procuret, invocato ad hoc, si opus fuerit, auxilio brachii.'

19. Riezler, *Die Geschichte der Hexenprozesse*, p. 86.

20. Ibid., p. 87.

21. Cf. Institoris, *Malleus Maleficarum*, II, Q. 1, c. 4, p. 95.

22. The only primary documentation we possess concerning the
Ravensburg trial is a series of *Urfehden* held in the town archive, U. 1116,
1119, 1129, and 1131. This paucity of corroborating material has also
caused me to restrict any discussion to the events at Brixen. For a comprehensive discussion of the Ravensburg trial and its relationship to the
composition of the *Malleus Maleficarum*, see Wilson, 'Text and Context',
chapter 3, and Karl Otto Müller, 'Heinrich Institoris, der Verfasser des
Hexenhammers, und seine Tätigkeit als Hexeninquisitor in Ravensburg
im Herbst 1484', *Württembergische Vierteljahrshefte für Landesgeschichte* (New
Ser., 19, 1970) pp. 397–417.

23. Müller, 'Heinrich Institoris, der Verfasser des Hexenhammers',
p. 409.

24. Institoris, *Malleus Maleficarum*, II, Q. 1, c. 12, p. 151.

25. Wilhelm Baum, *Sigmund der Münzreiche* (Bozen, 1987) pp. 440–1.

26. Hansen, *Quellen*, pp. 28–30. Abbot Johann also received a similar
letter from the Pope, likewise dated 18 June 1485.

27. Ludwig Rapp, *Die Hexenprozesse und ihre Gegner in Tirol: Ein Beitrag
zur Kulturgeschichte* (Innsbruck, 1874) p. 9; Riezler, *Die Geschichte der
Hexenprozesse*, p. 95.

28. Ulrich Molitor, *Tractatus Vitilis et Necessarius, per Viam Dialogi, de
Pythonicis Mulieribus*, in Institoris, *Malleus Maleficarum. Tomi Secundi Pars*
(Lyon, 1669) pp. 17–45. In a moment of amazing sobriety, Sigismund

himself touches upon the potentially distorting effect of inquisitorial procedure: 'Facile enim dictum sequitur vulgus, nec confessione tortuali satiabor, cum mentu tormentorum quis inducitur quandoque ad confitendum id quod in rerum natura non est' (Molitor, *Tractutus*, p. 19).

29. 'Si ea quae in uro dumtaxat oppido illius diocesis repenta sunt, inferenda essent, liber integer foret conficiendus, conscripta autem et reposita sunt apud eundem Episcopum Brixen et utique stupenda et maudita, ut testis idem existit' (Institoris, *Malleus Maleficarum*, II, Q. 1, c. I, pp. 103–4).

30. See Wilson, 'Text and Context', Appendix 1, pp. 409–410.

31. Hartman Amman, 'Der Innsbrucker Hexenprozess von 1485', *Zeitschrift des Ferdinandeums für Tirol und Vorarlberg* (Ser. 3, 34, 1890) p. 79. This article contains the transcription and critical summaries of the extant trial records of the Innsbruck trials held at the Fürstbischöfliches Hofarchiv at Brixen, the only known source of documentation. I have acquired my own copy of the trial records and have noted no serious discrepancy between Amman's transcription and the original sources. As the transcripts are unpaginated, I have followed Amman's notation.

32. Wolfgang Ziegeler, *Möglichkeiten der Kritik am Hexen- und Zauberwesen im ausgehenden Mittelalter: zeitgenössische Stimmen und ihre soziale Zugehörigkeit* (Vienna, 1973) p. 84.

33. A duty he performed with apparently uneven results. One of the accused witches at Brixen, Helena Scheuberin, was brought before the inquisitor after it had been reported that she had been heard to mutter: 'Pfei dich, du Sneder minch, daz dich das fullend uebel in deinen grauwen Scheitel sol! Wan fiert der Duefel den Muench enweg er bredigt nuest dan Ketzerei.' Amman, 'Der Innsbrucker Hexenprozess von 1485', pp. 35–6, 40.

34. The two accused men were Andree Fierer from the parish of Ambos, who was suspected of divining the location of lost objects, and an unnamed 'Schulmeister' who, aided by his wife Dorothea, was alleged to have obtained stolen goods by necromantic practices! Amman, 'Der Innsbrucker Hexenprozess von 1485', pp. 13, 22.

35. Ibid, pp. 9–25; Riezler, *Geschichte der Hexenprozesse*, p. 90.

36. Amman, 'Der Innsbrucker Hexenprozess von 1485', p. 8. The only other communities explicitly cited are Ammeros, Hal and Kemten, p. 22.

37. Ibid., p. 25. Cf. Institoris, *Malleus Maleficarum*, II, Q. 1, c. 12, *passim*.

38. 'Wo ain inquisitor von des heiligen stuels au Rom wegen chumpt, sein wir schuldig mitsambt dem inquisitor darinn zu handeln und unsern gewalt in auch lassen gebrauchen' (Amman, 'Der Innsbrucker Hexenprozess von 1485', p. 80).

39. '… moecht E. G. mit willen derselben doctor erlangen, oder ob in das auch guet bedunckchen wolt, das die groessern sach als die uner und lestrung gottes mit gayseln und nadeln stechen der gepildnuss, auch wo durch die zawbery die lewdt umb das leben sein choemen und desgleichen strengklich mit urtail fuergenomen und gestrafft' (Amman, 'Der Innsbrucker Hexenprozess von 1485', pp. 80–1).

40. Perhaps as a result of his experience at Brixen, Institoris insists in the *Malleus Maleficarum*, III, Q. 9, p. 234, that this procedure be waived. 'Sed an Iudex teneatur eo deponentes manifestere, nec ad conspectum eius praesentare. Hic advertat Iudex, quod nullum illorum tenetur facere, nec nomina manifestare, nec ad conspectum praesentare, nisi deponentes per se et sponte ad hoc se offerunt, ut videlicet eorum aspectibus praesententur, et ea quae deposuerunt eis in faciem oblicere. Quod autem non tenetur Iudex et hoc propter periculum deponentium probatur.'

41. 'Scribimus dicto illustrissimo principi, quatenus favore fidei orthodoxe et pro obedientia apostolice sedi V. P. in executione ofitii inquisitionis requisitur iuxta P. V. invocationem assistere ac auxilium ferre et manutenere dignetur, ut huiusmodi gravia peccate evitentur ac emendentur et secundum sacras sanctiones super potestatibus secularibus editas vestris tamquam inquisitoris heretice pravitatis invocationibus satisfaciat et factis vestri acquiescat et ab aliis serenitati sue subiectis hoc idem fieri committat' (Amman, 'Der Innsbrucker Hexenprozess von 1485', p. 82).

42. Ibid., pp. 54, 56.

43. Ibid., pp. 35–9, 43–64.

44. Ibid., p. 32.

45. Ibid., p. 31.

46. Ibid., pp. 83–4.

47. Rapp, *Die Hexenprozesse und ihre Gegner in Tirol*, p. 6.

48. Ziegeler, *Möglichkeiten der Kritik am Hexen- und Zauberwesen*, p. 89.

49. Amman, 'Der Innsbrucker Hexenprozess von 1485', p. 37.

50. Institoris apparently selected these representatives from a short-list of those Dominicans who had previously aided him in the interrogation of suspects – Wilhelm Behringer, Wolfgang of Basel, Caspar of Freiburg, and Magister Johann of Resback. Amman, 'Der Innsbrucker Hexenprozess von 1485', p. 66.

51. Ibid., p. 65.

52. Ibid., p. 67.

53. Ibid., pp. 67–9.

54. Ibid., p. 69.

55. Ibid., pp. 69–71.

56. 'Quia aliquorum animos exasperatos intellexi contra vestram paternitatem, ideo visum est omnio paternitatem vestram avizare debere, ut a loco isto discedatis pro hoc temporum conditione et dequanto cicius tanto comodius. Plures defatigati sunt et processum paternitatis vestre estimant insolitum seu graviter ferunt. Ideo tamquam is, qui scandala et pericula debet quomodo submovere seu intercipere, avizo paternitatem vestram, ut se conferat ad locum solite residentie et non manere in hoc loco: id conducit plurimum (scio quid scribo). Nequaquam scribo sine misterio aut leviter. Ideo in meliorem partem accipere scripta mea dignetur paternitas vestra, quam cupio bene valere' (Amman, 'Der Innsbrucker Hexenprozess von 1485', pp. 84–5).

57. 'Ich find in des babst bullen, das es bey vil baebsten ist vor inquisitor gewesen, er bedunckt mich aber propter senium gantz chindisch sein

244 *Notes and References*

worden, als ich in hie zu Brichsen gehoert hab cum capitulo .... Ich meuss ex officio ordinario derinn handeln und bedarff sein gar nit der zue' (Amman, 'Der Innsbrucker Hexenprozess von 1485', p. 69).

58. 'Venerabilis doctor. Miror valde, quod manetis in diocesi mea et in loco it vicino curie, in qual errores sunt sommissi et perventum ad dissensiones ne dicam scandalu. Gratiosissimus dominus archidux honorifice dotavit vos, ut sic recederetis in pace. Non videtur accomodum, quod intromittat se paternitas vestra de illis personis, sed onus incumbit mihi. Usque modo non fuit datum loqui cum domino principe de hac materia, sed adhoc faciam attento quod mihil fructuose fieri posset sine sue excellentie assistentia. Verendum est, ne mariti mulierum vel amici possent paternitatem vestram offendere. Non indigos in agendo presentia vestra, que plus posset impedire quam conferre; ego autoritate ordinaria faciam que videbuntur expedire. Certe paternitas vestra declinare deberet ad suum monasterium sicut prius peruasi. Non deberetis aliis esse molestus. Sepe dixi paternitati vestre, quod nihil faceretis in diocese, pro hac temporum conditione sed exiretis. Ita etiam putabam vis diu recessisse' (Amman, 'Der Innsbrucker Hexenprozess von 1485', p. 87).

59. Müller, 'Heinrich Institoris, der Verfasser des *Hexenhammers*', p. 409.

60. Ziegeler, *Möglichkeiten der Kritik am Hexen- und Zauberwesen*, p. 96.

61. One certainly cannot go as far as Wolfgang Ziegeler in viewing the bishop as a proto-enlightenment representative of early modern rationalism, purportedly the result of his humanistic education at the University of Vienna, coupled with the legacy bequeathed by Nicholas of Cusa, Golser's predecessor as bishop of Brixen. Ziegeler, *Möglichkeiten der Kritik am Hexen- und Zauberwesen*, p. 110. Ironically, Nicholas himself expressly sanctioned the prosecution of two women on charges of *maleficium*. Andreas Blauert, *Frühe Hexenverfolgungen: Ketzer, Zauberer und Hexenprozesse des 15. Jahrhunderts* (Hamburg, 1989) p. 35.

62. For a discussion of the sceptical tradition associated with the *Canon Episcopi*, cf. Wilson, 'Text and Context', Chapter 6.

63. Man könnte daraus folgern, daß er [Golser] möglicherweise – unter dem Eindruck der Bulle und ihrer päpstlichen Autorität – schon eine Verbindung zwischen Zauberei und Ketzerei sah bzw. nicht prinzipiell ausschloß. Seine Strafvorstellungen bezüglich Zauberei widersprechen dem allerdings; sie bewegten deutlich einen Unterschied zwischen Zauberei und Ketzerei.... Für Zaubereivergehen wünschte er offensichtlich, soweit rechtlich irgend möglich, Milde walten zu lassen. Umsomehr mußte er sich an den rigorosen Vorgehen des Inquisitors stoßen. Die große Anzahl der Verdächtigen scheint bei dem bedachtsamen Bischof aber auch Zweifel ausgelöst zu haben, ob die angeblichen Verbrechen überhaupt geschehen seien. Jedenfalls hielt er den Ketzerrichter für höchst überflüssig. Dies könnte andeuten, daß des Institoris Praxis für ihn vielleicht nur der Vorwand war, ihn fortzuschicken, ohne sich den Vorwurf loyalen Verhaltens gegenüber dem Papst zuzuziehen' (Ziegeler, *Möglichkeiten der Kritik am Hexen- und Zauberwesen*, p. 95).

64. Amman, 'Der Innsbrucker Hexenprozess von 1485', p. 68.
65. 'Die Niederlage in Innsbruck dürfte seinen Wunsch nach einem umfassenden Handbuch aller theoretischen und praktischen Belange der Hexenverfolgung so verstärkt haben, daß der Inquisitor innerhalb kurzer Zeit all seine Vorarbeiten zu dem systematisch geordneten *Hexenhammer* vereinigte.' Heide Dienst, 'Magische Vorstellungen und Hexenverfolgungen in den Österreichischer Ländern 15. bis 18. Jahrhundert', E. Zöllner (ed.), *Wellen der Verfolgung in der Österreichischen Geschichte* (Vienna, 1986) pp. 78–9.
66. Institoris, *Malleus Maleficarum*, II, Q. 1, c. 12, pp. 148–51.
67. For an extensive discussion of the diabology of the *Malleus* cf. Wilson, 'Text and Context', Chapters 4–7.

5. WITCHCRAFT AND POPULAR RELIGION IN EARLY MODERN ROTHENBURG OB DER TAUBER    *Alison Rowlands*

1. The author wishes to thank the following for their help in the preparation of this chapter: Bob Scribner, Brian Ward and all those who attended and offered helpful comments on an earlier version of this paper at the 2 June 1993 meeting of the Institute of Historical Research Seminar series on 'Evil'. Clark's article appears in *Early Modern European Witchcraft*, ed. B. Ankarloo and G. Henningsen (paperback edition, Oxford, 1993). See especially pp. 59–60, 69–70, 73–4, 77.
2. 1630 was chosen to end the period of study to correspond with Clark's final date and because the last of my nine witchcraft cases is from 1629 (see note 6). Most sources used are from Rothenburg's Stadtarchiv (hereafter RStA); the rest from Nuremberg's Staatsarchiv (hereafter NStaatsA Ro. Rep.).
3. K. Borchardt, *Die geistlichen Institutionen in der Reichsstadt Rothenburg ob der Tauber und dem Zugehörigen Landgebiet von den Anfängen bis zur Reformation* (Neustadt/Aisch, 1988) vol. I, p. 15; P. Schattenmann, *Die Einführung der Reformation in der ehemaligen Reichsstadt Rothenburg ob der Tauber (1520–1580)* (Gunzenhausen, 1928) pp. 124–9; H. W. Bensen, *Historische Untersuchungen über die ehemalige Reichsstadt Rothenburg* (Nuremberg, 1837) chs 22–4.
4. See appendix for a list of these cases with full references.
5. See, for example, the Franconian prince-bishoprics of Bamberg and Würzburg in the late sixteenth/early seventeenth centuries, F. Merzbacher, *Die Hexenprozesse in Franken* (Schriftenreihe zur bayerischen Landesgeschichte, vol. 56, Munich, 1957) pp. 30–6; H. H. Kunstmann, *Zauberwahn und Hexenprozeß in der Reichsstadt Nürnberg* (Schriftenreihe des Stadtarchivs Nürnberg, Nuremberg, 1970) p. 17.
6. The case of Magdalena Dürrin, who was beheaded – the usual punishment for infanticide in Rothenburg at this time – then her body burned on 12 January 1629 (See appendix). She *had* freely confessed to acts of witchcraft as well as to killing her baby, but her interrogators had

been bemused rather than intrigued by these confessions and had shown little interest in pursuing them further.

7. RStA A875, fols 187$^r$–7$^v$, 202$^v$ (Seitzin's claims); 211$^v$, 221$^v$–2$^r$ (jurists' comments). On witchcraft as a diabolic illusion, see C. Zika, 'The Devil's Hoodwink: Seeing and Believing in the World of Sixteenth-Century Witchcraft', in C. Zika (ed.), *No Gods Except Me* (University of Melbourne, 1991), pp. 153–98.

8. RStA A886, fols 283$^r$–3$^v$, 284$^v$. Zyrlein's first category corresponds entirely with the exorcists, diviners, healers and conjurors condemned in the Protestant demonology identified by Clark; see 'Protestant Demonology', pp. 62–9.

9. It is hard to say with certainty which came first in Rothenburg, the scrupulous legal approach or the particular Lutheran perception of witches. The first two witchcraft cases of 1561 and 1563 were both characterised by these two legal features, yet contained no mention of witchcraft as diabolic illusion, while other defamation cases showed the same degree of scrupulousness and concern for the good name of the accused as did those involving suspicions of witchcraft. It is thus perhaps most useful to see the legal approach and Lutheran perception of wtiches as part of a general elite mentality and as mutually reinforcing.

10. As suggested by C. Larner in 'Crimen Exceptum?: the Crime of Witchcraft in Europe', V. A. C. Gatrell *et al.* (eds), *The Social History of Crime in Western Europe since 1500* (London, 1980) pp. 49–75, and by H. C. E. Midelfort in 'Heartland of the Witchcraze: Central and Northern Europe', *History Today* (February 1981) pp. 27–31.

11. J. H. Langbein, *Prosecuting Crime in the Renaissance* (Harvard, 1974) pp. 180–1.

12. See clauses 30 and 44 of the *Carolina*, translated and printed in Langbein, *Prosecuting Crime*, pp. 275, 279.

13. See clauses 25 and 30 of the *Carolina*, Langbein, *Prosecuting Crime*, pp. 274, 275.

14. While men and women featured in Rothenburg's records as users and purveyors of beneficent magic, it was only ever women who were called witches (*Unhuld* or *Trute*). The moderate treatment of witches in Rothenburg may thus have saved many women from the torture-chamber and stake.

15. As a woman, Seitzin could not provide sufficient testimony, especially in a capital case, RStA A875, fols 212$^r$–12$^v$.

16. RStA A739, fol. 472$^r$. This dictum was linked to two others cited by the jurist ('one man is no man' – i.e. one witness is no witness – and 'an honourable man should not say what he cannot prove'), both of which were crucial to the council's treatment of witchcraft rumours and accusations.

17. RStA A875, fols 192$^v$–93$^r$, 195$^r$, 198$^r$. The ability to transport themselves or others through the air was one of the talents attributed to Rothenburg witches.

18. RStA A875, fols 222$^v$, 212$^v$–213$^r$.

19. In the Barbara Brosam case of 1561, rumours that her parents- and brother-in-law worked magic had circulated since the Peasants' War, RStA A858, fol. 29$^v$. In the Brandt case of 1602, one of the women he accused of being a witch had had an ill-fame to that effect for about six years, RStA A739, fol. 449$^r$. (See appendix for full case details.)

20. RStA A875, fol. 209$^v$.

21. RStA A875, fol. 223$^r$. For an account of the Wiesensteig hunt, see H. C. E. Midelfort, *Witch-hunting in Southwestern Germany, 1562–1684* (Stanford, Cal., 1972) pp. 88–90.

22. RStA A875, fols 212$^v$, 221$^v$. This explanation was put forward first by Oberstetten's pastor, and other villagers also stated that Seitzin often drank to excess at her mother's, which was where she had been drinking on the night of her 'strange' experience.

23. RStA A886, fols 291$^r$–292$^r$, 301$^r$.

24. RStA A886, fols 269(a)$^r$–9(a)$^v$.

25. For the jurists' advice, see RStA A886, fols 275$^v$, 277$^r$–78$^r$.

26. Torture was only used in the Kellnerin, Gackstattin and Dürrin cases. (See appendix for full references.)

27. RStA A877, fols 572$^r$–73$^v$.

28. RStA A877, fols 579$^v$ ('... dieweil man Ja vf kein gewissen grund komen, vnd die Warheit nit erfaren könne[n] ...').

29. There were hunts in Bamberg, Würzburg, Bad Windsheim and Nördlingen, see note 4; Kunstmann, *Zauberwahn und Hexenprozeß*, pp. 23–4; C. W. Schirmer, *Geschichte Windsheims und seiner Nachbarorte* (Nuremberg, 1848) pp. 151–2.

30. The cases in which Barbara Brosam (1561), the Kellnerins (1563) and the five women of Steinach unter Endsee (1602) were accused of being witches. See appendix.

31. These were the cases involving Barbara Brosam (1561), the Kellnerins (1563), Seitzin (1582), Brandt (1602), Röestin (1628–9) and Härterin (1629). See appendix.

32. By which the accuser was liable to a charge of false accusation if the accused proved his innocence, see B. P. Levack, *The Witch-Hunt in Early Modern Europe* (London, 1987) p. 149. Punishments for making false accusations of witchcraft could be harsh in Rothenburg: pillory and banishment (Hans Lautenbach, 1561, RStA A846, fols 438$^v$–441$^v$); banishment (Barbara Röestin, 1629, RStA B665, fols 21$^r$–23$^v$); flogging and banishment (Margareta Härterin, 1629, RStA, fols 618$^r$–619$^v$).

33. On the importance of honour to the inhabitants of Rothenburg and its hinterland, see ch. 1 of my 'Women, Gender and Power in Rothenburg ob der Tauber and its Rural Environs, 1500–c.1618' (Cambridge University Ph.D. dissertation, 1994).

34. RStA A888, fols 601$^r$, 603$^r$–3$^v$, 609$^r$–612$^r$, 614$^r$–616$^v$. See note 32 for Härterin's punishment.

35. For examples of ordinances, see L. Schnurrer, *Die Rechtssatzungen der Reichsstadt Rothenburg ob der Tauber* (Rothenburg, 1988) nos. 400, 440, 464, 478, 503, 525, 528, 569, 626, 641, 695, 730, 724, 743, 762 etc. These ordinances aimed chiefly to ensure that people went to church, stopped

swearing, going to the pub on Sunday afternoons and other sorts of impious behaviour, and that weddings and christenings were celebrated within prescribed limits. For visitation records, see RStA A1426, fols 27ʳ–37ʳ; NStaatsA Ro. Rep. 2089, fols 38ʳ–57ʳ.

36. H.-P. Ziegler, *Die Dorfordnungen im Gebiet der Reichsstadt Rothenburg* (Rothenburg, 1977) pp. 122–3; H. Woltering, *Die Reichsstadt Rothenburg ob der Tauber und ihre Landschaft über die Landwehr*, vol. 2, (Rothenburg, 1971) pp. 52–8.

37. RStA A888, fols 596ᵛ–97ʳ, 601ʳ, 603ʳ–3ᵛ, 609ʳ–12ʳ.

38. RStA A877, fols 547ᵛ–49ᵛ.

39. RStA A877, fols 547ᵛ–548ʳ.

40. RStA A877, fol. 548ʳ.

41. RStA A877, fols 548ᵛ–49ʳ.

42. See below, note 60.

43. RStA A877, fol. 551ʳ.

44. RStA A844, fols 56ʳ–7ʳ.

45. RStA A875, fols 221ᵛ–22ʳ, 223ᵛ.

46. RStA A886, fols 299ᵛ–300ʳ. For the report on the shepherd, see fol. 287ʳ.

47. See above, note 8.

48. RStA A363, fols 48ʳ–50ʳ, see fols 49ᵛ–50ʳ.

49. For full case records, see RStA A874, fols 24ʳ–30ᵛ, 31ʳ–2ʳ, 33ʳ–3ᵛ, 34ʳ–47ᵛ, 49ʳ–50ᵛ, 51ʳ–4ᵛ (interrogations); B331, fols 8ʳ–11ᵛ (verdict).

50. For full case records, see RStA A873, fols 296ʳ–305ᵛ, 306ʳ–21ᵛ, 322ʳ–3ᵛ, 325ʳ–6ᵛ, 334ʳ–8ᵛ, 340ʳ–3ᵛ, 351ʳ–7ᵛ, 362ʳ–76ᵛ, 378ʳ–87ᵛ, 388ʳ–95ᵛ, 399ʳ–9ᵛ (interrogations); B331, fols 3ʳ–6ᵛ (verdict).

51. There is an ordinance identical to the 1612 one in the Rothenburg archive; see RStA A362, fols 284ʳ–8ʳ. However, as it is undated and full of amendments it is safe to conclude that is a rough draft of the 1612 ordinance, which is dated Wednesday 23 September. Moreover: (1) there is no mention of any earlier ordinance in sixteenth-century visitation records, and (2) a list of notorious users and purveyors of magic which can be dated to the late sixteenth/early seventeenth century noted that 'these people were found trafficking in magic *before* the edict against magic was published' (my emphasis), see NStaatsA Ro. Rep. 2089, fols 101ʳ–1ᵛ.

52. RStA A1426, fols 34ʳ–5ᵛ, 25ᵛ–6ʳ (1560 and 1558).

53. See RStA B331, fols 8ʳ–11ᵛ (Kissling); 220ʳ–2ʳ (Geüder, who was beheaded).

54. RStA A873, fols 313ᵛ, 389ʳ.

55. Gebhartin's crime was defined as fraud (Betrug), RStA B331, fols 3ʳ–6ᵛ. Branding with a cross had earlier been connected with the crimes of magic and blasphemy; branding the cheeks, with fraud, see K.-P. Herzog, 'Das Strafensystem der Stadt Rothenburg ob der Tauber im Spätmittelalter' (Ph.D. dissertation, Würzburg, 1971) p. 107. However, by the second half of the sixteenth century branding a cross was used in cases just of fraud, see for example RStA B330, fols 83ʳ–5ʳ (1569).

56. So they had to act selectively. See also G. Schwerhoff, *Köln im Kreuzverhör* (Bonn/Berlin, 1991) p. 27.

57. See RStA B331, fols 9ᵛ and 220ᵛ.

58. For example, NStaatsA Ro. Rep. 2089, fols 38ᵛ, 72ʳ–2ᵛ, 80ᵛ.

59. Supporting the idea that the Lutheran Reformation had failed to reform popular belief, see G. Strauss, 'Success and Failure in the German Reformation', *Past and Present*, 67 (1975) pp. 30–63; H.-C. Rublack, 'Success and Failure of the Reformation', in A. C. Fix and S. C. Karant-Nunn (eds), in *Germania Illustrata* (Kirksville, 1992) pp. 141–65.

60. Described by Kissling under interrogation, RStA A874, fol. 29ᵛ. For Ursula and her nails, see above, note 43.

61. RStA A874, fols 29ᵛ, 30ʳ.

62. For examples, see NStaatsA Ro. Rep. 2089, fols 38ᵛ, 72ᵛ.

63. RStA A1426, fols 25ᵛ–6ʳ.

64. RStA A874, fols 28ᵛ–9ʳ.

65. In 1578 Hans Bruderson of Oberstetten went to a soothsayer after his wife deserted him, NStaatsA Ro. Rep. 2089, fols 52ᵛ–3ʳ; in 1581 Jorg Bauer's daughter paid Anna Gebhartin six gulden to make the man who had got her with child return, RStA A873, fols 315ʳ–5ᵛ, 363ᵛ–4ᵛ.

66. For the smiths, see notes 49 and 53; for the herdsman of Gammesfeld, see NStaatsA Ro. Rep. 2090, fol. 109ᵛ; for Els, see NStaatsA Ro. Re. 2089, fol. 80ᵛ.

67. For Fronhöfer, see NStaatsA Ro. Rep. 2089, fol. 108ʳ; for the magicians of Aib and Feuchtwangen, NStaatsA Ro. Rep. 2089, fols 101ʳ–1ᵛ; for Müllerlin, RStA 363, fols 279ʳ–282ʳ, see fol. 280ʳ.

68. RStA A874, fols 35ᵛ, 36ᵛ, 41ʳ.

69. RStA A1426, fols 25ᵛ–26ʳ.

70. RStA A865, fols 575ʳ–6ᵛ, see especially 576ʳ.

71. NStaatsA Ro. Rep. 2090, fols 97ʳ, 99ᵛ.s

6.   POPULAR BELIEFS AND THE REFORMATION      *C. Scott Dixon*

1. Jacob Graeter, *Hexen oder Vnholden Predigten. Darinnen zu zweyen vnderschiedlichen Predigten, auff das kürtzest vnnd ordenlichest angezeight würdt, was in disen allgemeinen Landklagen, vber die Hexen und Vnholden, von selbigen warhafftig vnnd Gott seeliglich zuhalten* (Tübingen, 1589) p. Diiⱽ.

2. Roger Chartier (trans. Lydia G. Cochrane), *Cultural History: Between Practices and Representations* (Oxford, 1988); Peter Burke, *Popular Culture in Early Modern Europe* (London, 1978); Bob Scribner, 'Is a History of Popular Culture Possible?', *History of European Ideas*, 10 (1989) pp. 175–91; Michel Vovelle (trans. Eamon O' Flaherty), *Ideologies and Mentalities* (London, 1990) pp. 81–113.

3. Otto Clemen, 'Joh. Moninger, Poet, Historiker, Arzt, Apotheker und Archivar', *Zeitschrift für bayerische Kirchengeschichte*, 13 (1938) pp. 215–23.

4. Landeskirchliches Archiv Nürnberg (hereafter LKAN); Markgräfliches Dekanat Hof (hereafter MDH), XX, 2, nos 1–4 (1581). 'Nun ist aber zu Baÿerngrun Im Ampt Schaüenstein eine Zaüber vettel,

wonhafft, welche sich nicht allein von Urinis (ea reverentia zu reden) villeicht dürch Cristallen zu Jüdicirn und Artzney zugeben, sundern auch von gestolnen und verlornnen dingen. Auch con verzauberniß und (wie es der gemainen Mann Pflegt zunennen) vorgethenen sachen responsa und oracüla pÿthonica zugeben ... derhalben auch zü ir ein lange Zeitt hero, ein unglaüblich groß gelaüff, von nahe und ferne gewesen, und leider noch ist Und derowegen vil Clag in den Visitationis fürkommen, Aber gleichwol noch biß hero nicht ohne viler gotsfuerchtiger leutt seufftzen, unabgeschaft geblieben.'

5. LKAN, Markgräfliches Dekanat Kulmbach (hereafter MSK), 352, 28 January 1584.

6. LKAN, MSK, 157, Schaüenstein 1580, *Querelae pastoris*.

7. Staatsarchiv Bamberg (hereafter StaB), C2 1827, fol. 11 (1589). 'Es wird die fraw zü Beÿersgrün schir von menniglich darfür gehalten und angelauffen, alß könne sie in allerleÿ leibs gebrechen rathen und helffen, darümb wie an andern orthen also [aüch] hie ohne zweifel Ihr gar vil sind, die sich raths beÿ Ihr erholen.'

8. StaB, C2 1827, fol. 108 (1589).

9. StaB, C2 3240, 16 February 1603.

10. Fr. Spanuth, 'Die Grubenhagenische Kirchenvisitation von 1579 durch Superintendent Schellhammer', *Jahrbuch der Gesellschaft für niedersächsische Kirchengeschichte*, 52 (1954) p. 117.

11. LKAN, MSK, 157, *Beschwerüng und Ergernüs* (1578) Point 2. They claimed that they had learned it from the Jews.

12. Staatsarchiv Nürnberg (hereafter StaN), *Ansbacher Neues Generalrepertorium*, no. 49, rep. no. 103e, fols 16, 59; LKAN, *Markgräfliches Dekanat Uffenheim*, 8, Equarhofen 1587; Walmersbach 1573. LKAN, Markgräfliches Dekanat Gunzenhausen (hereafter MDG), 71, fols 37, 43, 45; LKAN, MSK, 157, *Bericht der spetial Visitation, In der Süperintendentz Beÿrreüth A[nn]o 1572*, fol. 14 (my pagination); *Executio Visitationis Anno 1574 vorrichtett, fol. 2 (my pagination)*. StaB, C2 1827, fol. 147.

13. LKAN, MSK, 157, *Beschwerüng und Ergenüs* (1578) Point 2.

14. LKAN, MSK, 157, *Beschwerüng und Ergenüs* (1578) Point 2. Even when their magic is proved faulty, observed the visitor, their reputations remain intact.

15. StaB, C2 1826, fol. 4.

16. StaB, C2 3235, fol. 5.

17. StaB, 3237, 28 February 1592.

18. LKAN, MDG, 71, fol. 43 (1572).

19. LKAN, Markgräfliches Dekanat Schwabach, 122, T.1, 3 March 1575.

20. StaB, 1223, fol. 149 (1568).

21. StaN, *Ansbacher Neues Generalrepertorium*, no. 49, rep. no. 103e, fol. 61.

22. Bob Scribner, 'Magic and the Formation of Protestant Popular Culture in Germany' (unpublished MS, forthcoming) p. 1.

23. LKAN, MSK, 157 (Drosenfeld, 8 September 1575). 'Est ist das Zaübern und zü den warsager[n] laüffen gar gemein worden, von wegen

der diebereÿ, daraüs erfolget das aüch etliche in ihren Kranckeytten za-
überey braüchen, und Warsager zü sich holen lassen, dieselben teüffels
banner leren die leütt mancherley ergerliche kunste, zu ihrem vihe
Narüng, und gesündtheytt, machen oftmals unschüldige leütt verdechtig,
und leren anders wie sie den leütten sollen oder konte den tott thün.'
24. See Keith Thomas, *Religion and the Decline of Magic* (London, 1985)
pp. 209–332; Richard Kieckhefer, *Magic in the Middle Ages* (Cambridge,
1990); Valerie I. J. Flint, *The Rise of Magic in Early Medieval Europe*
(Oxford, 1991); Richard Cavendish, *A History of Magic* (New York, 1977);
Lynn Thorndike, *The History of Magic and Experiemental Science* (New York,
1934) vol. 4, pp. 274–307.
25. StaB, C2 3238, fols 9–10, 4 May 1592.
26. For example, LKAN, MDG, 71, fol. 83 (1579). A prayer led by the
visitors; StaB, C3 1223, fol. 138 (1568). The pastor of Neudrossenfeld
told his parishioners that the Devil 'im Landt zw Mechelbürg ein weib
sichtbarlich hinwegk gefürht' in an effort to elicit greater piety.
27. As late as 1705 the margrave was dispatching mandates against'
Segensprechen und andere aberglaubische Dinge' – though by this late
date, as the research into witchcraft has evidenced, there was also a
concern with the 'Satanischen Wesen' of such practices. *Von Gottes
Gnaden / Wir Wilhelm Fride / rich, Marggraf zu Branden / burg, in Preussen ...
Onolzbach den 2. Martii Anno 1705*, in LKAN, Markgräfliches Dekanat
Schwabach, 29.
28. Johann Wierus (Weyer), *De Lamiis: Von Teuffelsgespenst Zauberern
und Gifftbereytern ...* (Frankfurt, 1586) pp. 17–18, 22, 33; *Von verzeuberun-
gen, verblendungen, auch sonst viel und mancherley gepler des Teuffels und seines
gantzen Heer ...* (Basel, 1565) p. 302. On Weyer, see Rudolph van Nahl,
*Zauberglaube und Hexenwahn im Gebiet von Rhein und Maas* (Rheinisches
Archiv, 116, Bonn, 1983) pp. 37–78. Van Nahl doubts that Weyer was
Protestant, despite the claims of some scholars.
29. StaB, C2 3235, fol. 82.
30. Emil Sehling (ed.), *Die evangelischen Kirchenordnungen des XVI.
Jahrhunderts* (Tübingen, 1961) 11:1 (Bayern: Franken) p. 160.
31. Robert Muchembled (trans. Lydia Cochrane), *Popular Culture and
Elite Culture in France 1400–1750* (Chapel Hill, 1985).
32. Robert Muchembled, 'The Witches of the Cambrésis: the
Acculturation of the Rural World in the Sixteenth and Seventeenth
Centuries', in James Obelkevich (ed.), *Religion and the People, 800–1700*
(Chapel Hill, 1979) pp. 221–76.
33. Jean Delumeau, *Catholicism between Luther and Voltaire: A New View of
the Counter-Reformation* (London, 1977).
34. See Richard van Dülmen, 'Reformation und Neuzeit. Ein Versuch',
*Zeitschrift für historische Forschung*, 14, 1 (1987) pp. 1–25.
35. Sehling, pp. 321, 352.
36. Copy of the *Brandenburgische Halßgerichtsordnung* (1516) in StaN,
Ansbacher Generalakten, 23, 1582 edition in *Corpus Constitutionum
Brandenburgico-Culmbacensium* (1748).
37. StaB, C2 1827, fol. 11, Hof 8, 9, 10 December 1589.

38. Stuart Clark, 'Protestant Demonology: Sin, Superstition, and Society (*c.*1520–*c.*1630)', in Bengt Ankarloo and Gustav Henningsen (eds), *Early Modern Witchcraft: Centres and Peripheries* (Oxford, 1990) pp. 45–81.

39. Reinhardus Lutz, *Wahrhaftigge Zeitung* (1571) P. Bi^V. 'Erstlich, darmit er die fromen und Gottsfürchtigen in ihrem Glauben probier, ob sie gleich so wol in trübsal als glückseligkeit bestendig beliben wollen.'

40. Andreas Althamer, *Eyn Predig von dem Teüffel, das er alles Unglück in der Welt anrichte* (Nuremberg, 1532) Aiii.

41. Charles Zika, 'The Devil's Hoodwink: Seeing and Believing in the World of Sixteenth-Century Witchcraft', in Charles Zika (ed.), *No Gods Except Me: Orthodoxy and Religious Practice in Europe* (Melbourne, 1991) pp. 153–98.

42. StaN, *Ansbacher Neues Generalrepertorium*, no. 49, rep. no. 103e, fols. 55, 120; LKAN, MSK, 157, Lentzendorff, 11 October 1586.

43. StaB, C2 1827, fol. 31 (1589); LKAN, Markgräfliches Dekanat Leutershausen, Kirchberg, 16 October 1594.

44. StaN, *Ansbacher Neues Generalrepertorium*, no. 49, rep. no. 103e, fol. 16.

45. LKAN, Markgräfliches Dekanat Uffenheim, 8 Mönchsondheim, 20 September 1571.

46. Fritz Heeger, 'Volksmedizinisches aus fränkischen Hexenprozeßakten', *Mainfränkisches Jahrbuch für Geschichte und Kunst*, 9 (1957) p. 204, '… dem Pfaffen nix darvon sagen, auch nit beichten und communicieren, sonst helfe seine kunst nichts'.

47. Magical practices had always been explicitly condemned by the church. As Valerie I. J. Flint has demonstrated in *The Rise of Magic in Early Medieval Europe*, the interplay between the church and medieval parish culture was intimate enough for a communication between the two traditions to take place and a strain of 'tolerated' magical beliefs was the result. But the type of surveillance introduced by the Reformation was more comprehensive than the medieval system and accelerated and facilitated intervention at the parish level.

48. See Perez Zagorin, *Ways of Lying: Dissimulation, Persecution and Conformity in Early Modern Europe* (London, 1990).

49. Scribner, 'Is a History of Popular Culture Possible?', pp. 178–81.

50. Carlo Ginzburg (trans. Raymond Rosenthal), *Ecstasies: Deciphering the Witches' Sabbath* (London, 1990) p. 11.

51. Friedrich Merzbacher, *Die Hexenprozesse in Franken* (Schriftenreihe zur bayerischen Landesgeschichte, 56, Munich, 1957) pp. 44–6; Wolfgang Behringer (ed.), *Hexen und Hexenprozesse* (Munich, 1988) pp. 223–4; 374–9.

52. Aside from the occasional mention, the only large-scale treatment of this case known to me is by Karl Lory, 'Hexenprozesse im Gebiete des ehemaligen Markgrafenlandes', in *Festgabe Karl Theodor von Heigel* (Munich, 1903) pp. 290–304. The following analysis is based upon the archive materials, StaB, C2, 3235.

53. StaB, C2, 3235, fols 1–4, 7 April 1569.

54. StaB, C2, 3235, fols 5–6, 5 April 1569.

55. StaB, C2, 3235, fols 5–6, 19–20. The verse she employed is transcribed on fol. 20. it ends with the line: 'Das seÿ dir Hans zür Büeß getzeldt, Im namen vatters, sohn und des hailigen gaist. Amen.'

56. StaB, C2, 3235, fol. 6, '... daran etliche gleisende stain gehangen sein, am hals gehenckt, hatt kirchnerin die angegrieffen und gesagen, in diesen steinen kons sie baß sehen, was sünd oder nicht sünd seÿ, dan ein preister in den Büch'.

57. StaB, C2, 3235, fols 7–8.

58. For rural witchcraft in Germany, see Walter Rummel, *Bauern, Herren und Hexen* (Kritische Studien zur Geschichtswissenschaft, 94, 1991) pp. 259–315; Eva Labouvie, *Zauberei und Hexenwerk* (Frankfurt, 1992) pp. 57–94; 202–19.

59. StaB, C2, 3235, fol. 10, 'Es müste der Raü ein Kunst gebraücht haben, das sie Ihn in Ihrn stein nit ferner sehen konnen.'

60. StaB, C2, 3235, fols 10–12; 11.

61. StaB, C2, 3235, fols 15–16, 15 April 1569.

62. See Brian Levack, *The Witch-Hunt in Early Modern Europe* (London, 1987) pp. 25–62; 93–115.

63. StaB, C2, 3235, Questions fols 13–14; Answers fols 17–22.

64. StaB, C2, 3235, fol. 29.

65. StaB, C2, 3235, fols 27–8, 19 April 1569, '... so achten wir doch das solches aus verblendung des bosen feindts ... [der] ... die armen weibs personen leichtlich verfüren kahn ...'

66. Lory, p. 292.

67. StaB, C2, 3235, fol. 30.

68. StaB, C2, 3235, fol. 31.

69. StaB, C2, 3235, fol. 38.

70. StaB, C2, 3235, fol. 38, 'Sihe Katherina hastü nicht gewüst das dü Eine Teüfels bannerin bist gewesen, mußen wir dich mit deiner künst selbs uberweisen.'

71. StaB, C2, 3235, fols 43–4.

72. StaB, C2, 3235, fol. 60. In Franconia, a session of torture was to last no longer than half an hour, Merzbacher (1957) p. 118.

73. StaB, C2, 3235, fols 54–5. 'Nachdem ich umb schweres vordachts willen, durch einem bürger Georg Brebitzern zü Creüssen gefenglichen eingetzogen, nit allein sieben wochen lang Ihnen gelegen, Sondern mit Schwehrer hefftiger tortür und peinligkeit dürch denn [Nachricter] befraget worden, das ich also (umbesümner) weiß, umb des grosen schmertzen bekennet und angeitzeigt, wie dan ich mit dem Bösenfeindt, hete vormischung gepfleget ...'

74. StaB, C2, 3235, fols 56–7.

75. On witchcraft, see the comments and literature in Eva Labouvie, *Zauberei und Hexenwerk*; Norman Cohn, *Europe's Inner Demons* (London, 1975); Gábor Klaniczay (trans. Susan Singerman), *The Uses of Supernatural Power* (Oxford 1990) pp. 151–67; 230–1.

76. Serge Gruzinski (trans. Eileen Corrigan), *Man-Gods in the Mexican Highlands* (Stanford, Cal., 1989) p. 5.

77. StaB, C2, 3235, fol. 11.

78. StaB, C2, 3235, fol. 46, 'Zaig an, wo N. ist, was Im fellet, wie es Ihm gehett, oder gehen soll oder wo ehr ist so wahr als er getaufft ist, Im namen das vatters sohns und es hailigen gaistes.'

79. StaB, C2, 3235, fols 29–30.

80. StaB, C2, 3235, fol. 40.

81. StaB, C2, 3235, fols 34–5.

82. StaB, C2, 3235, fol. 47.

83. See Roger Chartier, 'Intellectual History or Sociocultural History? The French Trajectories', in Dominick LaCapra and Steven L. Kaplan (eds), *Modern European Intellectual History* (London, 1982) pp. 13–46; Peter Burke, 'Strengths and Weaknesses in the History of Mentalities', *History of European Ideas*, 75, (1986) pp. 439–51.

84. Fredrik Barth, *Cosmologies in the Making: A Generative Approach to Cultural Variation in Inner New Guinea* (Cambridge, 1987); G. E. R. Lloyd, *Demystifying Mentalities* (Cambridge, 1990).

85. Compare Carlo Ginzburg, *The Night Battles* (London, 1985).

86. Fernando Cervantes, 'The Devil in Colonial Mexico: Cultural Interaction and Intellectual Change (1521–1767)' (Cambridge University Ph.D. dissertation, 1989) pp. 52–97; Serge Gruzinski, *Man-Gods in the Mexican Highlands*; Nathan Wachtel (trans. Ben and Siân Reynolds), *The Vision of the Vanquished: The Spanish Conquest of Peru through Indian Eyes 1530–1570* (Sussex, 1977) pp. 150–165; Amos Megged, 'Conversion and Identity in Early Colonial Perspectives: Friars and Indians in Mesoamerica 1545–1670' (Cambridge University Ph.D. dissertation, 1988) pp. 153–89.

87. Bob Scribner, 'Magic and the Formation of Protestant Popular Culture'.

88. Dr Jäger, 'Geschichte des Hexenbrennens in Franken im siebzehnten Jahrhundert aus Original-Prozeß-Akten', *Archiv des historischen Vereins für den Untermainkreis*, 2, 3 (1834) pp. 10–12.

89. Heinrich Heppe (ed.), *Soldan's Geschichte der Hexenprozesse* (Stuttgart, 1880) vol. 2, p. 128, no. 2.

90. The categories of magic and religion, as they have been defined by scholars in different disciplines, are investigated in Stanley Jeyaraja Tambiah, *Magic, Science, and the Scope of Rationality* (Cambridge, 1990).

### 7.   WHY WAS PRIVATE CONFESSION SO CONTENTIOUS IN EARLY SEVENTEENTH-CENTURY LINDAU?   *J. C. Wolfart*

1. The mechanics of auricular confession are covered in H. C. Lea, *A History of Auricular Confession and Indulgences in the Latin Church* (Philadelphia and London, 1896) 3 vols; more recently H.-P. Arendt, *Bußsakrament und Einzelbeichte: Die tridentinischen Lehraussagen über das Sündenbekenntnis und ihre Verbindlichkeit für die Reform des Bußsacramentes* (Freiburg/Basel/Vienna, 1981) esp. chapters 3 and 8. Interesting interpretative perspectives in J. Bossy, 'The Social History of Confession in the Age of the Reformation', *Transactions of the Royal Historical Society*, ser. 5,

vol. 25 (1975) pp. 21–38, and J. Delumeau, *L'aveu et le pardon: Les difficultés de la confession XIII^e–XVII^e siècle* (Paris, 1990). For critical responses to Bossy's thesis – that the change from the public confession to a private act in a confessional signifies a shift from public piety to private devotion – see L. Duggan, 'Fear and Confession on the Eve of the Reformation', *Archiv für Reformationsgeschichte*, 75 (1984) pp. 153–75, and W. de Boer, "Ad audiendi non vivendi commoditatem". Note sull' introduzione del confessionale soprattutto in Italia', *Quaderni Storici*, n.s. 77 (1991) pp. 543–72.

2. K. Wolfart, *Die Geschichte der Stadt Lindau in Bodensee* (Lindau, 1909) vol. I.i, p. 118.

3. In Lindau, as in other parts of south Germany, the danger of receiving the sacrament in a state of 'unworthiness' was established with reference to St Paul's first letter to the Corinthians (I Cor. XI: 26–9). According to L. Rothkrug, this insistence on the worthy reception of the eucharist distinguished south German from north German churches. L. Rothkrug, 'Popular Religion and Holy Shrines: Their Influence on the Origins of the German Reformation and their Role in German Cultural Development', in: J. Obelkevich (ed.), *Religion and the People, 800–1700* (Chapel Hill, N.C., 1979) pp. 20–86; D. W. Sabean, *Power in the Blood: Popular Culture and Village Discourse in Early Modern Germany* (Cambridge, 1984) p. 44; E. Sehling (ed.), *Die evangelischen Kirchenordnungen des XVI. Jahrhunderts*, Teil Bayern: Schwaben (Tübingen, 1963) vol. XII.ii, p. 207.

4. K. Wolfart, *Stadtgeschichte*, vol. I.i, p. 304.

5. Ibid., p. 389. The formula was repeated twice, once right at the start of a service and again, without step (iii), immediately prior to celebrating the Eucharist.

6. According to E. Sehling the confession formula described in the Lindau Church Constitution of 1573 drew heavily on the Württemberg equivalent of 1553, except that the Lindauers did not provide for the individual examination of communicants. Sehling, *Kirchenordnungen*, vol. XII.ii, pp. 206–7.

7. 'Dreyßig Christliche Fragen mit ihrer Antwort für die Kinder und einfältige so zum hl. Abendmahl gehen wollen'; K. Wolfart, *Stadtgeschichte*, vol. II, p. 179.

8. 'Von der Beicht, ob der Papst macht habe die zu gebieten' (1521). *D. Martin Luthers Werke* (Weimar, 1889) vol. VIII, pp. 138–85.

9. Here I accept the thesis of K. Aland. One of the major pillars of his argument is Melanchthon's 'Unterricht der Visitatoren an die Pfarrherrn im Kurfürstentum zu Sachsen' (1528), which is also one of the few tracts cited by Lindauers in 1626. Kurt Aland, 'Die Privatbeichte im Luthertum von ihren Anfängen bis zu ihrer Auflösung', in Kurt Aland, *Kirchengeschichtliche Entwürfe: Alte Kirche, Reformation und Luthertum, Pietismus und Erweckungsbewegung* (Gütersloh, 1960) pp. 452–519.

10. Aland, 'Privatbeichte', p. 453; *Die Augsburgische Confession oder Bekenntnis des Glaubens etlicher Fürsten und Städte, überantwortet Kais. Majestät zu Augsburg. Anno 1530*, Tübinger Nottexte (Tübingen, 1948) p. 10. The Tetrapolitan Confession, by contrast, emphasised the volun-

tary nature of the entire practice of confession. R. Stupperich (ed.), *Martin Bucers deutsche Schriften III. Confessio Tetrapolitana und die Schriften des Jahres 1531* (Gütersloh, 1969) pp. 143–5.

11. E. Roth, *Die Privatbeichte und Schlüsselgewalt in der Theologie der Reformatoren* (Gütersloh, 1952) pp. 15, 114.

12. Ibid., pp. 114–18.

13. Ibid., pp. 129–30.

14. Ibid., p. 13; C. Klein, *Die Beichte in der evangelisch-sächsischen Kirche Siebenbürgens* (Göttingen, 1980) p. 18.

15. Although, as a tool for historical analysis, it is far from fool-proof. Hence the disagreement between Klein and Roth over whether the early Reformation in Siebenbürgen was 'Zwinglian' or 'early Lutheran'.

16. Roth, *Privatbeichte*, p. 150

17. Klein, *Beichte*, pp. 83–5.

18. *Stadtarchiv Lindau, Reichstädtische Akten* (henceforth: StAL Ra) 65, 7/A, Summary of Augustin Müller's suit against Alexius Neukomm, October 1626; StAL Ra 65, 3/A, Council reprimand (*Decret*) of Neukomm, 25 October 1626.

19. StAL Ra 68, 3, Petition of four Lindau ministers (11 February 1603); StAL Ra 68, 3, Recommendations of Dr Daniel Heider, City Syndic, concerning the four ministers' petition.

20. For example, on 5 April 1626 the Council decided to double the fine for adultery and appointed a committee to deliberate an anti-swearing ordinance. StAL *Ratsprotokolle* (henceforth: Rp) 1626, p. 281.

21. K. Wolfart, *Stadtgeschichte*, vol. I.ii, p. 33.

22. StAL Ra 65, 5/A, 'Extract Kirchen- und Schuelrhats Protocollß', 4/27 April and 29 May 1626.

23. StAL Ra 65, 5/A, Council reprimand (*Decret*) to Neukomm, 13 August 1625.

24. Roth, *Privatbeichte*, p. 132.

25. For a discussion of this concept see H. Schilling (ed.), *Die reformierte Konfessionalisierung in Deutschland – das Problem der 'Zweiten Reformation'* (Gütersloh, 1986); for an English survey of recent work on 'social discipline' and 'confessionalisation', see R. Po-Chia Hsia, *Social Discipline in the Reformation: Central Europe 1550–1750* (London, 1989).

26. StAL Ra 65, 7/E, a catalogue of incidents, in Neukomm's own hand, covering the years 1600–1623; also the more official 'Vita Neukomii Sincere delineata weil er im Predig Ampt'.

27. The centrepieces of this particularly bitter conflict were a sermon delivered by Neukomm on St Bartholomew's Day 1624 and the response of the advocates, 'Beschlließliche Resolution Dr Daniel Heyders and Dr Johann Ulrich Funckhens ... ' (25 September 1624), StAL Ra 65, 1.

28. A very interesting indictment of the legal profession is provided in an unsigned, updated narrative and analysis of Lindau politics in 1626 (probably the work of a Bürgermeister), StAL Ra 65, 6/C. For an overview of early modern German anti-clericalism, see P. Dykema and H. Oberman (eds), *Anticlericalism in late medieval and early modern Europe* (Leiden and New York, 1992).

29. Both contemporary and modern observers have overemphasised the reforms' importance. Charles V hoped to undermine the guilds, thereby denying evangelical movements what he perceived to be their ideological and numerical base in the cities. See L. Fürstenwerth, 'Die Verfassungsänderung in den oberdeutschen Reichsstädten zur Zeit Karl V'. (dissertation, Göttingen, 1893) and E. Naujoks (ed.) *Kaiser Karl V. und die Zunftverfassung: ausgewählte Aktenstücke zu den Verfassungsänderungen in den oberdeutschen Reichsstädten 1547–1556* (Stuttgart, 1985). For Lindau, P. Eitel has represented these reforms as a cataclysmic end to a whole epoch: P. Eitel, *Die oberschwäbischen Reichsstädte im Zeitalter der Zunftherrschaft: Untersuchungen zu ihrer politischen und sozialen Struktur unter besonderer Berücksichtigung der Städte Lindau, Memmingen, Ravensburg und Überlingen* (Stuttgart, 1970).

30. The choice of terms is of some importance. I follow Schilling in favouring 'republicanism' over P. Blickle's 'communalism', especially in the context of the free cities. P. Blickle, 'Kommunalismus und Republikanismus in Oberdeutschland' and H. Schilling, 'Gab es im späten Mittelalter und zu Beginn der Neuzeit in Deutschland einen städtischen "Republikanismus"?' in H. G. Koenigsberger (ed.), *Republiken und Republikanismus in der frühen Neuzeit* (Munich, 1989) pp. 57–75 and 101–43.

31. The published literature on the uprising is slim. H. Löwe, *Der Prediger Alexius Neukomm und der Lindauer Kirchenhandel des Jahres 1626*. Forschungen zur Geschichte Bayerns (Munich, 1906/1907) gives a good overview, as does Löwe's chapter in K. Wolfart, *Stadtgeschichte*, vol. I.ii, pp. 28–44. A shorter account, but one which is rather more sympathetic to Neukomm's position, is found in H. Jordan, 'Der Neukomm-Handel', in: *Bodensee Heimatschau*, vol. 11, issue 24 (December 1931).

32. Christopher Friedrichs has recently re-examined seventeenth-century German urban revolts, concluding that the political culture, rather than social and economic factors, determined the occurrence and character of these revolts. C. Friedrichs, 'Urban Politics and Urban Social Structure in Seventeenth-Century Germany', *European History Quarterly*, 22 (1992) pp. 187–216.

33. StAL Ra 39, 8, undated anonymous report on 1626, and StAL Ra 65, 6/B, 'Corrigierter Vertrag ...' (late 1626) mention it; StAL Ra 39, 8, Mezler's report and StAL Ra 65, 6/C, an unsigned analysis (Bürgermeister Miller's ?) do not.

34. Early modern Lindauers apparently used the terms *Kirchenordnung* and *Kirchenagend* interchangeably. Because these defined structure, described doctrine and partially established the relationship of the Lindau church to other civic bodies and offices, I have chosen to translate both of the above terms as 'church constitution'.

35. Only Mezler's report (StAL Ra 39, 8) completely skirts the issue. Official reports (StAL Ra 38, 8; 65, 5/B; 65, 5/C), a 'Protocoll' on negotiations with the guilds (StAL Ra 65, 4) and a letter from Alexius Neukomm to his brother-in-law (StAL 65, 1/B) all implicate private confession in some way.

36. StAL Ra 65, 7/C, 'Verlorne Protocoll'; StAL Rp 1626, p. 410.
37. StAL Ra 65, 5/A, 'Extract ...'
38. StAL Rp 1626, p. 282.
39. StAL Ra 65, 7/C, 'Verlorne Protocoll'.
40. StAL Ra 65, 5/A, 'Extract ...'
41. Sehling, *Kirchenordnungen*, vol. XII.ii, pp. 206–7.
42. Samuel Lyns, *Communicanten-Büchlein für die Schulen der Stadt Lindau* (Lindau, 1598).
43. StAL Ra 65, 5/B, 'Information über herr M. Newkhomms schrifftlich resolution vomm 26. Octobr. 1626'.
44. StAL Ra 65, 5/A, 'Extract ...'
45. Matthew 7:6. 'Give not that which is holy unto the dogs, neither cast ye your pearls before swine.'
46. StAL Ra 65, 5/A, 'Extract ...'
47. For example, the Luther pamphlet 'Von der Beicht, ob die der Bapst macht habe zu gepieten' (1521). In the CSC session of 4 April a 'Wahrnungschrifft D. Lutheri ann die zu Franckhfurt' was cited. This is almost certainly the letter 'Den Erbarn und fursichtigen, Dem Rat und Gemeine der Stad Franckfort am Meyn, meinen günstigen herrn und freunden' (1533), printed in 1561 as 'Wahrnungschrifft, D. Martini Lutheri, an die zu Franckfurt am Meyn ...' The church ordinances of Lower Saxony, along with advice to the visitors there, as well as an opinion of the theological faculty of Rostock (1568), are also mentioned. StAL Ra 65, 5/B 'Extract ...'; StAL Ra 65, 5/B 'Memorial wegen der Privatbeicht'.
48. StAL Ra 65, 5, reports on Alexius Neukomm's sermon of 5 November 1626 by M. Matthias Hager, M. Martin Müller, Melchior Beyer, D. Abraham Räm, D. Ulrich Funk, D. Daniel Heider, Heinrich Felß, David Felß, Calixt Rietman, one anonymous witness. The passage in question was referred to both as 'Matthew 15' and as 'Matthew 18'; Neukomm almost certainly cited Matthew 18:15, 'Moreover if thy brother shall trespass against thee, go and tell him his fault between thee and him alone.'
49. StAL Ra 65, 4/B, 'Summarischer Kurzer Begriff ...' (issued to Dr Jelin). As early as 1616 the Council was receiving reports on the activities of a 'gang', the core of which was identified as several younger Neukomms, StAL Rp 1616, p. 850. By 1626, the documents identify an unofficial party referred to as 'his [Neukomm's] faction' or simply as 'die Neukommischen'. StAL Ra 65, 3/B, 'Missiva An herrn D. Georgium Zaeman'.
50. StAL Ra 65, 5/A, 'Extract ...'; StAL Ra 65, 5/B 'Fürhalt der Burger- und Baurschafft' (11 June); StAL Ra 65, 3/A Council reprimand (*Decret*) of Neukomm, 25 October); StAL Ra 65, 4, 'Protocoll' (on negotiations to reach a permanent settlement).
51. StAL Ra 39, 8, anonymous account of the 7 November uprising from early 1627.
52. StAL Ra 65, 4, 'Protocoll' (on negotiations to reach a permanent settlement).
53. StAL Ra 39, 8, Mezler's report; StAL Ra 65, 7, 'Verlorne Protocoll'.

54. StAL Ra 45, 7, 'Copia der Straff Urthel ...'; StAL *Literalien* (henceforth: Lit) 14, 'Amts- und Dienstleute der Stadt Lindau, 1588–1799'.

55. StAL Ra 39, 8, Mezler's report; StAL Ra 65, 4, 'Summarischer Kurzer Begriff ...' (issued to Dr Jelin); StAL Ra 65, 3/B, Lindau pastors to Dr Zaeman (11 November) and to Superintendent Dr Dietrich (20 November).

56. StAL Ra 65, 1, Dr Jacob Jenisch to Lindau, 2 October 1624.

57. StAL Ra 65, 1/B, 'Extract aus Herrn Marx Zangmeisters ... Schrift'.

58. StAL Ra 65, 1/B, 'Beschließliche Resolution Dr Daniel Heyders und Dr Johann Ulrich Funckhens ...' (submitted to Council, 25 September 1624).

59. StAL Ra 65, 3/A, Neukomm's suit against Magister Hursich, Hans Heinrich Buchschor and son-in-law, and Augustin Miller.

60. StAL Ra 65, 5/A, 'Extract ...'

61. StAL Ra 65, 5/B, Zaeman to the Lindau Council, 30 November 1626.

62. StAL Ra 65, 5/B, Neukomm to Council, received 13 October 1626.

63. Alexius Neukomm himself recorded the tense atmosphere in Lindau in terse commentary on the suffering of Lindauers due to inflation and frequent troop movements. StAL Lit 25, 'Neukomm'sche Chronik'.

64. On 13 October Heider returned from negotiations with the bishop of Constance and confirmed rumours that the Jesuit order had been granted use of the imperial armoury building in Lindau, StAL Rp 1626, p. 661.

65. StAL Ra 65, 4, 'Protocoll' of deliberations on a plan to permanently reconcile the government and the citizenry.

66. That is, compulsory private confession to an ordained priest as established, in theory at least, by Lateran IV.

67. Presumably, old people cost more because, in the many years that Lindau had been without private confession, they had amassed considerably more sins than the young. In fact, confession fees were a vexation in other churches which reintroduced private confession. For example, in 1587 the Weikersheim Superintendent, Johannes Assum, had confronted ministers who persisted in taking the confession penny. In 1588 the issue remained unresolved and Count Wolfgang of Hohenlohe ordered Assum to redouble his efforts to eradicate the practice. E. Sehling (G. Franz), *Die evangelischen Kirchenordnungen des XVI. Jahrhundert*, Teil Württemberg: Hohenlohe (Tübingen, 1977) vol. XV, pp. 533, 549.

68. StAL Ra 65, 5/A, 'Extract ...'; StAL Ra 65, 5/B, 'Fürhalt der Bürger- und Baurschaft', 11 June.

69. StAL Ra 65, 5/B, various reports on Neukomm's sermon of 5 November.

70. StAL Ra 65, 1/B, Neukomm to his brother-in-law, 22 November. Although this letter was composed after the fact, Neukomm had expressed the same position, although not so evocatively, prior to 7 November.

71. J. D. Marte, *Die ausswärtige Politik Lindaus, 1530–1532* (Heidelberg, 1904).

72. StAL Ra 65, 3, 'Copia Bedenckhenß Herrn Dr Georg Zeamannß', 1 August 1626. Zwingli had indeed pronounced: 'Non enim tuo verbo ipsum potes magis certum reddere, quam muscam elephantum facere, cum dixeris: Elephas es'. E. Egli, G. Finsler and W. Köhler (eds), *Huldreich Zwinglis sämtliche Werke*, III (Leipzig, 1914) p. 821.

73. K. Wolfart, *Stadtgeschichte*, vol. I.i. pp. 286–96.

74. Alexius Egger, one of the citizens who left Lindau during the Interim crisis, wrote an account of that episode, which Ulrich Neukomm reproduced in his chronicle, StAL Lit 25, 'Neukomm'sche Chronik'.

75. K. Wolfart, *Stadtgeschichte*, vol I.i, pp. 386–8.

76. StAL Ra 39, 8, anonymous analysis of 7 November from early 1627.

77. StAL Ra 65, 1/B, Neukomm to his brother-in-law, 22 November 1626.

78. StAL Ra 65, 5/A, 'Extract ...'

79. StAL Ra 65, 3/B, 'Memorial wegen der Privat Beicht'; StAL Ra 65, 5/B, 'Extract ...'

80. StAL Ra 65, 5/C, Excerpt of an unsigned, undated narrative.

81. StAL Ra 65, 5/A, 'Extract ...'

82. StAL Ra 65, 5/B, Zaeman to the Lindau, 30 November 1626.

83. Mack Walker, *German Hometowns: Community, State and General Estate, 1648–1871* (Ithaca, NY, 1971) remains an outstanding study. For a critical appraisal of Walker's work see Celia Applegate, *A Nation of Provincials: The German Idea of Heimat* (Berkeley, Cal., 1990).

84. StAL Ra 65, 5/B, 'Extract ...'

85. StAL Ra 65, 7/C, 'Verlorne Protocoll'.

86. StAL Ra 65, 5/B, Neukomm's report to the Council on his conversation with Dr Dietrich.

87. StAL Ra 65, 5/B, various reports on Neukomm's sermon of 5 November; StAL Ra 65, 5/B 'Concept Fürhalt' intended for 7 November.

88. StAL Ra 65, 5/B, 'Beschreibung ...' is the notable exception.

89. StAL Ra 39, 8, anonymous report dated late 1626; StAL Ra 65, 4 'Protocoll' of negotiations to extract the capitulation document; StAL Ra 65, 5/A, report on reconciliation process. There is no indication of how the guarantee to preserve the church constitution came to be qualified 'for the time being', but it is safe assumption that the rebels did not realise the concession. Since all of the above documents were generated as part of official 'information packets' for external consultants, it is possible that the qualification was an official face-saving device of which Lindauers were unaware.

90. StAL Ra 65, 5/B, 'Extract ...'

91. StAL Ra 65, 6/B, 'Information über herr M. Newkhomms schrifftliche resolution vomm 26. Octobr. 1626'. These changes had been designed to prevent Cryptocalvinists from attending the sacrament.

92. StAL Ra 65, 5/B, 'Extract ...'

93. Andreae had come to Lindau to participate in a colloquium on the doctrine of Matthias Flacius Illyricus, G. Karo, 'Das Lindauer

Gespräch: Ein Beitrag zur Geschichte der Concordienformel', *Zeitschrift für wissenschaftliche Theologie*, n.s. 10 (1902).

94. StAL Ra 65, 3, Neukomm's response to the Council, 26 October 1626.

95. StAL Ra 65, 5/B, various reports on Neukomm's sermon of 5 November.

96. For an interesting discussion of some of the ways in which various forms of piety might generate different connections between the living and the dead, see L. Rothkrug, 'Popular Religion and Holy Shrines: Their Influence on the Origins of the German Reformation and their Role in German Cultural Development', in J. Obelkevich (ed.), *Religion and the People, 800–1700* (Chapel Hill, N.C., 1979) pp. 20–86.

97. StAL Ra 65, 5/B, Neukomm's suspension from office.

98. StAL Ra 65, 5/B, 'Concept Fürhalt' intended for 7 November.

99. StAL Ra 65, 6/C, 'Protocoll' of negotiations between Lindauers and delegates from Ulm, Memmingen and Kempten. The opening address identified the delegates' primary concern: 'ob dieses [Lindau's] wesen also *componirt* daß dardurch kheine weitere gefahr zubesorgen und sonderlich auch die Oberkeitliche *Autoritet* erhalten worden'.

100. Surprisingly little work has been directed at the concept of *Obrigkeit* itself. Two good discussions can be found in E. Maschke, ' "Obrigkeit" im spätmittelalterlichen Speyer und in anderen Städten', in *E. Maschke, Städte und Menschen: Beiträge zur Geschichte der Stadt, der Wirtschaft und Gesellschaft, 1959–1977* (Wiesbaden, 1980) and E. Naujoks, *Obrigkeitsgedanke, Zunftverfassung und Reformation* (Stuttgart, 1958). In sixteenth-century Lindau it was argued – with specific reference to the jurisdictional claims of an aristocratic ladies' convent – that *Obrigkeit* existed in the performance of *obrigkeitliche* acts, such as the appointment of officials, the issuing of orders, etc. If you could not or did not behave as an *Obrigkeit*, then your *Obrigkeit* was lost or lapsed. StAL Ra 6, 110, 'Suplication uff den tag zu Franckfurt zu ubergeben des viscalischen furnemens halber 1536. Betreffend die Abstellung der Papistischen meß Im Closter hie'.

101. StAL Ra 65, 5/B, 'Extract ...'

102. StAL Ra 65, 1/B, Neukomm to his brother-in-law, 22 November 1526.

103. StAL Ra 65, 1, 'Protocoll Herrn M. Alexium Newkom betreffend', 9 February 1626.

104. StAL Ra 65, 5/A, 'Extract ...'

105. On 21 June the Council warned Neukomm that they would not permit him to turn the pastor's house into a tavern; on 30 June the Council ordered an official to curtail all ministerial wine retail. StAL Ra 65, 3/A, 'Herrn M. Alexio Newkhomen zubehändigen' (21 June 1626); StAL Rp 1626, p. 477.

106. StAL Ra 65, 5/B, various reports on Neukomm's sermon of 5 November.

107. StAL Ra 39, 8, Mezler's report.

108. StAL Ra 65, 5/B, 'Beschreibung ...'

109. StAL Ra 65, 5/C, Excerpt of an unsigned, undated narrative.

110. StAL Ra 65, 5/C, unsigned, undated narrative of pacification guild by guild in late 1626.

111. StAL Ra 39, 8, anonymous, undated analysis of 7 November, early 1627.

112. StAL Ra 65, 3/A, Neukomm's 'Nottrungenliche, warhaffte, verantwortung und Endtschuldigung'.

113. StAL Ra 65, 1/9, Council Decree issued to Neukomm, 3 September 1624; StAL Ra 65, 1/29, report of Ulrich Miller and Hans Heinrich Mezger, 1624.

114. StAL Ra 68, 3, Dr Heider's recommendations to the Council concerning the preachers' request of 11 February 1603.

115. StAL Rp 1617, pp. 691, 697, 720, 722.

116. StAL Ra 65, 5/B, 'Beschreibung ...'

117. StAL Ra 65, 1, 'Protocoll Herrn M. Alexium Neukom betreffend', 9 February 1626.

118. StAL Ra 65, 5/C, report on official deliberations, 18 December 1626.

119. For example, in Neukomm's requests for extended powers of coercion over his parishioners (see above, note 19). Also in his anonymously published criticism of the Lindau church and a chastisement of its congregation, StAL Ra 65, 2/D, 'Impietas et Ataxia Ecclesiae Lindaviensis'.

120. H. Schilling, 'Gab es im späten Mittelalter und zu Beginn der Neuzeit in Deutschland einen städtischen "Republikanismus"?', in: H. G. Koenigsberger (ed.), *Republiken und Republikanismus in der frühen Neuzeit* (Munich, 1989); also English translation in: H. Schilling, *Religion, Political Culture and the Emergence of Early Modern Society: Essays in German and Dutch History* (Leiden, 1992).

121. For example, in a contemporary marginal comment on the text 'Herrn M. Alexio Newkhomen zubehändigen ...', 21 June 1626, StAL Ra 65, 3/A. There is no entry for *heimlich* or *öffentlich* in J. Grimm, *Deutsche Rechts Altertümer*; if etymological dictionaries are anything to go by, this pairing in Lindau is extraordinary.

122. F. Kluge, *Etymologisches Wörterbuch der deutschen Sprache*, 22nd edn (Berlin, 1989): '*heimlich*: zum Haus gehörig ... von Anfang an auch zur Bezeichnung des damit verbundenen Aspekts: wer sich in das Heim zurückzieht, verbirgt sich vor anderen, vor Fremden, *öffentlich*: ... im Sinn von vor Augen liegend, erst spät im politischen Sinn ... Hierzu *öffentlichkeit* seit dem 18. Jh. als Ersatzwort für *Publizität*'.

123. R. F. E. Weissman, *Ritual Brotherhood in Renaissance Florence* (New York, 1982) pp. 32–5. It has been observed that for early modern south German rural society, while the threshold was significant, the interior front room was not an emphatically private space; private bedrooms, for example, appear to have developed in a later period, in tandem with an upper storey. H. Heidrich, 'Grenzübergänge: Das Haus und die Volkskultur', in: R. van Dülmen, *Kultur der einfachen Leute* (Munich, 1983) pp. 17–41.

124. StAL Ra 65, 1/B, 'Memoriale und wahrhaffte Relation ...', 27 September 1624.

125. StAL Ra 65, 5/A, 'Extract ...': 'das sie ... cum larvis & umbris luctieren'.

126. StAL Ra 65, 5/B, 'Fürhalt der Burger- und Baurschafft', 11 June 1626.

127. StAL Ra 65, 5/A, 'Extract ...'

128. STAL Ra 65, 3/A, Council reprimand issued to Neukomm, 21 June 1626.

129. StAL Ra 65, 3, 'Nottdrungliche, wahrhaffte, verantwortung und Endtschuldigung'.

130. StAL Ra 65, 5/A, 'Extract ...': here Neukomm is alluding to the 'doctrine of dispensible things', which had been hotly debated in Lindau in the previous century. Because it was part of the debate on the possibility of compromise with the Calvinists, the subject remained sensitive in Lindau. For example, it was prominent in a clash between Dr Peter Eggolt and Alexius Neukomm over whether or not the liturgy should be sung or spoken. StAL Ra 65, 1/A, copy of a letter from Dr Peter Eggolt to M. Michael Schnell.

131. StAL Ra 65, 1/B, Neukomm to his brother-in-law, 22 November 1626.

132. StAL Ra 65, 5/A, 'Extract ...'

133. This, for example, is what the clever compilers of the Württemberg *Kirchen- und Schulordnung* of 1582 did. While article 6 of that document established the practice of 'individual' and 'secret' (i.e. private) confession and absolution for all parishioners, it also prohibited pastors from hearing the said confession 'privately' (*privatim*), in their own homes. Instead it was twice intoned that the new private confession would take place in a 'public' (*öffentlich*) place, namely the church. E. Sehling (G. Franz), *Die evangelischen Kirchenordnungen des XVI, Jahrhundert*, Teil Württemberg: Hohenlohe (Tübingen, 1977) vol. XV, pp. 446–7.

134. StAL Ra 63, 3/A, Council reprimand (*Decret*) of Neukomm, 25 October 1626.

135. StAL Ra 45, 7, 'Copia der Straff Urthel ...'

136. StAL Ra 65, 3/B. This would appear to be the earliest dated Lindau document registering a response to the uprising of 7 November.

137. StAL Ra 65, 3/B, 'Missiva An herrn D. Georginn Zeaeman', 11 November 1626. It is significant that the writer of this document began by describing the events of 7 November as an 'insurrection/uprising' (*auffstand*), but subsequently deleted this, replacing it with the less specifically oppositional 'disorder/unrest' (*tumult*).

138. StAL Ra 65, 3/B, Zaeman to Lindau ministry, 15 November 1626. Zaeman and others who pursued this line were aided considerably by Neukomm's death, presumably from natural causes, on 26 February 1627. H. Löwe, *Der Prediger Alexius Neukomm und der Lindauer Kirchenhandel des Jahres 1626*, Forschungen zur Geschichte Bayerns (Munich, 1907) p. 65.

264     *Notes and References*

139. StAL Ra 65, 3/B, Dietrich to Lindau ministry, 16 November 1626; Lindau ministry to Dietrich, 20 November 1626.
140. The association of the 'Stunde Null' with private confession is not my own. Both E. Roth and K. Aland were very much aware of their own work's post-war context: each mentioned it in his preface. Aland went one step further, however, and related his interest in the subject of private confession to a movement afoot in the German Lutheran Church of the 1950s. According to Aland, these years saw an outpouring of writing on confession, most of which called for the reintroduction of private confession. The post-war advocates of private confession hoped that it would 'alleviate many of the damages in the life of the community (*Gemeinde*) and the church' (Aland, 'Privatbeichte', p. 452).

8.   A LÜBECK PROPHET IN LOCAL AND LUTHERAN
          CONTEXT    *Jürgen Beyer*

**Abbreviations**

AHL   Archiv der Hansestadt Lübeck
BKHL  Die Bau- und Kunstdenkmäler der (Freien und) Hansestadt Lübeck
BN    Bibliothèque Nationale, Paris
HAB   Herzog August Bibliothek, Wolfenbüttel
HDA   Handwörterbuch des deutschen Aberglaubens
MLGA  Mittheilungen des Vereins für Lübeckische Geschichte und Alterthumskunde
StBL  Stadtbibliothek, Lübeck
ZLGA  Zeitschrift des Vereins für Lübeckische Geschichte und Altert(h)umskunde
Unless otherwise stated, all pre-1800 books cited in this chapter are held by the Royal Library in Copenhagen (now including the university library's Fiolstræjde collection).

1. 'Zu dem Ende, daß sich ein ieder daran spiegeln solle, aber es were verdungkelt worden'.
2. The only source for this apparition story is preserved in AHL, Geistl. Ministerium, Tomus IV (1628–1642) fols 83$^r$–83$^v$: letter from the clergy to the town council (11 April 1629); fols 84$^r$–84$^v$: report by Pastor Blume (10 April 1629); fols 85$^v$–89$^r$: theological judgement (misbound). The case has been retold before by C. H. Starck, *Lubeca Lutherano-Evangelica, das ist, der ... Hanse- und Handel-Stadt Lübeck Kirchen-Historie ...* (Hamburg: Felginer, 1724) pp. 773–4. All later references to the case appear to be based on Starck's account: J. R. Becker, *Umständliche Geschichte der ... Stadt Lübeck*, vol. 2 (Lübeck: Green, 1784) p. 382; *Neue Lübeckische Blätter*, 4 (1838) p. 207; E. Deecke, *Lübische Geschichten und Sagen* (Lübeck, 1852) p. 370 (rewritten as a folk narrative (*Volkssage*) 'nach Privataufzeichnung'); A. Benda, 'Wolfsrachen. Berichtigung und

Nachtrag', *MLGA*, 4 (1889–90) pp. 191–2; H. Weimann, *Der 30 jährige Krieg im lübschen Raum zwischen Elbe und Fehmarn. Volkstümlich erzählt* (Türme, Masten, Schlote, H. 4) (Lübeck, 1954) pp. 34–6. There has been no attempt to put the case into its wider context.

3. The town council enjoyed the services of three keepers of the minutes, who were on duty on different days of the week. For that reason there are three series of records of which only one is preserved for the period in question (AHL, Ratsprotokolle bis 1813, I. Serie, 1629 (Friedr. Pöpping)). The preserved series does not mention David Frese's case. A letter copy-book was not kept. This study therefore has to rely on the drafts and copies in the ecclesiastical records.

I am grateful to Antjekathrin Graßmann of the AHL for giving me valuable guidance in the sources and literature concerning Lübeck.

4. 'Hore hir, Ich will die wat seggen – Gehe nu wegh vnd sehe di nicht vmb'. Given the liberal spelling conventions of the time, the differences from High German are very little. In Starck's account (cf. n. 2) normalised spelling emphasises the Low German character of the sentences. The preserved version of Blume's account is not written in his own hand. The scribe might or might not have been acquainted with writing Low German.

5. W. Jannasch, *Geschichte des lutherischen Gottesdienstes in Lübeck. Von den Anfängen der Reformation bis zum Ende des Niedersächsischen als gottesdienstlicher Sprache (1522–1633)* (Gotha, 1928) pp. 137–54; W. Heinsohn, *Das Eindringen der neuhochdeutschen Schriftsprache in Lübeck während des 16. und 17. Jahrhunderts* (= Veröffentlichungen zur Geschichte der Freien und Hansestadt Lübeck, vol. 12) (Lübeck, 1933) pp. 149–60 and 180–3.

6. Starck, *Lubeca Lutherano-Evangelica*, pp. 780–2 and 864–5. There seems to be no biographical information available about Franciscus Greier.

7. In Deecke's version (cf. n. 2), the Low German parts have been enlarged to comprise the old man's entire message.

8. The evidence of the parish registers in inconclusive. The *Hartigsgrube* (today *Hartengrube*) belonged to the parish of the cathedral church. A David Frese had children baptised there on 26 August 1627, on 11 December 1628, and on 13 June 1633 (AHL, Dom, Taufen 1618–30, 1627, no. 148, and 1628, no. 228, Taufen 1631–48, 1633, p. 136, no. 107). For the first two dates, the place of residence is not indicated, whilst the father's occupation is given as 'workman' (*arbeits[man]*) in 1627, as *Linentrecker* (*Leinezieher* – a man employed in towing ships) in 1628, and as *Arbeitsman in der Danckw[arts]gruben beÿ Johan Rölfs* in 1633. In the last case, though, the address probably refers to the place of work. According to the index at the AHL, a David Frese is only mentioned on two other occasions in the surviving pre-1800 parish registers: on 12 October 1634, a David Frese had a son baptised in another parish church (AHL, St Aegidien, Taufen 1633–44, 1634, no. 125). No abode or occupation is given. On 10 August 1637, David Frese, *ein Boßman* (sailor) *in der Beckergrube in [Rüters]gange,* had a child baptised in yet another church (AHL, St Jacobi, Taufen 1636–41, p. 70). Although it is possible that all

266  *Notes and References*

entries refer to the David Frese who had the apparition, there cannot be any certainty. None of the occupations mentioned, however, are very high on the social scale.

9. Cf. J. Asch, *Rat und Bürgerschaft in Lübeck, 1598–1669* (= Veröffentlichungen zur Geschichte der Hansestadt Lübeck, vol. 17) (Lübeck, 1961) pp. 18–20; A. Graßmann, 'Lübeck im 17. Jahrhundert: Wahrung des Erreichten', in A. Graßmann (ed.), *Lübeckische Geschichte* (Lübeck, 1989) pp. 435–88, here pp. 443–4 and 464.

10. The word 'prophet' perhaps arouses associations with Mohammed or the prophets of the Old Testament, but even contemporaries called some of these figures 'New Prophets'. See, for example, the title of a 1585 broadsheet in W. L. Strauss, *The German Single-Leaf Woodcut 1550–1600* (New York, 1975) p. 941 and *Newe Prophetin. Von Schönebeche ... Aus dem Latein ins Deutsche bracht, Durch M. Simonem Musæaejnium, Luchouianum* ... (Eisleben: Petri, 1580) (reprint [Lübeck:] Balhorn, 1580); the Latin original of this pamphlet bears the title *Nova de Sibylla Marchica* ... 1580).

11. A number of prophets made their appearance during the English Civil War but they belonged to sects and not to the state church. Only rarely did they claim to have angelic apparitions (P. Mack, 'The Prophet and Her Audience: Gender and Knowledge in The World Turned Upside Down', in G. Eley and W. Hunt (eds), *Reviving the English Revolution. Reflections and Elaborations on the Work of Christopher Hill* (London and New York, 1988) pp. 139–52). Only one case from France has come to my knowledge (*Apparition merveilleuse de trois phantosmes dans la forest de Montargis, a vn bourgois de la mesme ville* (Paris 1649) (BN); for the preceding period, no comparable title is mentioned in J.-P. Seguin, *L'information en France avant le périodique. 517 canards imprimés entre 1529 et 1631* (Paris, 1964). Later, however, there were the well-known Camisard prophets (bibliography in B. Plongeron and P. Lerou (eds), *La piété populaire en France. Répertoire bibliographique*, vol. 5 (Turnhout, 1988) pp. 156–8). The Italian prophets date from before 1530 (O. Niccoli, *Profeti e popolo nell' Italia del rinascimento* (= Biblioteca di Cultura Moderna, Bd. 947) (Bari, 1987)). In the Netherlands, though, some pamphlets on comparable prophets were published, for example *Een Vvarachtighe geschiedenisse van eenen stomme / ghenaemt Michiel Saeckes ... de welcke wonderlijcke teeckenen heeft beschreven / die hem geopenbaert syn ... 1609)* (Royal Library, The Hague).

12. W. A. Christian, *Apparitions in Late Medieval and Renaissance Spain* (Princeton, 1981); R. Habermas, *Wallfahrt und Aufruhr. Zur Geschichte des Wunderglaubens in der frühen Neuzeit* (= Historische Studien, vol. 5) (Frankfurt a. M and New York, 1991).

13. The 1627 case of Anna Rumpfin at Amberg is to be found in Staatsarchiv Amberg, Subdelegierte Registratur, no. 217. I am grateful to Trevor Johnson for this reference.

14. A general study of Lutheran popular prophets in Germany, Scandinavia, and the Baltic states will be presented in my Ph.D. thesis. Some aspects have been treated in J. Beyer, 'Lutherske folkelige profeter

som åndelige autoriteter', in B. P. McGuire (ed.), *Autoritet i Middelalderen* (Copenhagen, 1991) pp. 157–81; Beyer, 'Lutherische Propheten in Deutschland und Skandinavien im 16. und 17. Jahrhundert Entstehung und Ausbreitung eines Kulturmusters zwischen Mündlichkeit und Schriftlichkeit', in *Europa in Scandinavia. Kulturelle Dialoge während der frühen Neuzeit. 1520–1720* (working title) (= Studia Septentrionalia, vol. 2) (Frankfurt a. M.), and Beyer, 'Hellige kvinder og mænd i de lutherske lande, ca. 1550 til 1700', *Chaos. Dansk–norsk tidskrift for religionshistoriske studier*, 20 (1993) pp. 101–13. These prophets have so far received scant attention in historical research. The most important studies on German prophets are: K. Kayser, 'Hannoversche Enthusiasten des siebzehnten Jahrhunderts', *Zeitschrift der Gesellschaft für niedersächsische Kirchengeschichte*, 10 (1905) pp. 1–72; W. -E. Peuckert, articles in *HDA*, vol. 7 (1935–6) pp. 338–66; vol. 9, 1 (1938–41) pp. 358–87; vol. 9, 2 (1941) pp. 66–100; D. W. Sabean, 'A prophet in the Thirty Years' War: Penance as a social metaphor', in his *Power in the Blood. Popular Culture and Village Discourse in Early Modern Germany* (Cambridge, 1984) pp. 61–93 (cf. also the comment on this article by N. Haag, 'Frömmigkeit und sozialer Protest: Hans Keil, der Prophet von Gerlingen', *Zeitschrift für Württembergische Landesgeschichte*, 48 (1989) pp. 127–41).

15. For example, *Nova de Sibylla Marchica*, fol. A2ʳ; H. F. Rørdam (ed.), 'Mestermanden i Viborg som Profet', *Kirkehistoriske Samlinger*, 6 (1867–8) pp. 181–90, here p. 186 (the main document is in German, the prophet being a German soldier who stayed at Viborg after the war in Jutland was over. He worked as a hangman at the time of his apparitions in 1630. The edition by Rørdam is not always to be trusted; for the original of the German text see: Rigsarkivet Copenhagen, K. U., 12.01.15, no. 3-3-573).

16. For background reading on Lübeck see Graßmann 'Lübeck im 17. Jahrhundert'; W.-D. Hauschild, *Kirchengeschichte Lübecks* (Lübeck, 1981). On the Thirty Years' War see T. Hach, 'Nachrichten zur Geschichte Lübecks im 30jähr. Kriege ...', *MLGA*, 7 (1895–6) pp. 122–5; Weimann, *Der 30jährige Krieg*; J. O. Opel, *Der niedersächsisch-dänische Krieg*, vol. 3 (Magdeburg, 1894) pp. 195 and 475–83.

17. E. Wilmanns, *Der Lübecker Friede 1629* (diss. Bonn) (Bonn, 1904) pp. 37–48 and 64–70; *Abdruck dessen / Was zu Lübeck / so wol zwischen den Käyserl... Commissarijs / als auch denen Königl. Dennemarchkischen ... Commissarijs newlich abgehandelt ... worden ... 1629).* The last document is dated 21 March 1629.

18. M. Sirckes, *Justitiæ et miseracordiæ dei temperamentum zwo Christliche Predigten Vom Krieg vnd Frieden / Für den Hochansehnlichen Königlichen Herrn Abgesandten / nach beschlossenen vnd publicirten Friede / auff dero Begehren zu Lübeck gehalten ...* (Lübeck: Schmalhertz/Embß, 1629) p. 22.

19. C. Kuß, *Jahrbuch denkwürdiger Naturereignisse in den Herzogthümern Schleswig und Holstein ...*, vol. 1 (Altona, 1825) p. 146 (for prices in neighbouring Schleswig-Holstein).

20. *Kurtzer Bericht / Wie man sich in werender Pestilentz ... verhalten soll / Beneben der Taxa der Artzneyen / so auff den Apotheken verordnet ... Mit ange- hengtem Eines Ehrbaren Raths Mandat vnd Verordnung auff diese Zeit gerichtet*

(Lübeck: Jauchen S. Erben, 1629) fols B2ᵛ–B3ʳ (BL); Weimann, *Der 30jährige Krieg*, pp. 16 and 41.

21. [K. v. Hövelen], *Der Kaiserl: Freien Reichs-Stadt Lübeck ... Herrligkeit ...* (Lübeck: Smalherzische Druckerey/Volk, 1666) p. 40.

22. Kuß, *Jahrbuch*, p. 142–5; [J. G.] Gallois, *Hamburgische Chronik ...* vol. 3 (Hamburg, 1870) p. 65; Becker, *Umständliche Geschichte*, p. 383; *Kurtzer Bericht*, fols A1ᵛ and B2ᵛ; AHL, Altes Senatsarchiv, Interna, Pest 1/5: Vorschlag der Bader wegen des Betriebs der Badestuben bei Pestgefahr, dated 9 October 1629.

23. AHL, Ratsprotokolle bis 1813, I. Serie, 1629 (Friedr. Pöpping) fol. 57ᵛ; [H. Lebermann], *Die Beglückte und Geschmückte Stadt Lübeck ...* (Lübeck: Krüger, 1697) p. 29; J. Hilmers, *Die von Gott gewürdigte Lob-Eck ...* (Lübeck: Böckmann and Ratzeburg: Hartz, 1716) p. 101–2; O. Pelc (ed.), *Gründliche Nachricht des St Annen Armen- und Werck-Hauses in Lübeck von 1735* (= Kleine Hefte zur Stadtgeschichte, hg. v. AHL, H. 7) (Lübeck, 1990) p. 20; W. Brehmer, 'Die Befestigungswerke Lübecks', *ZLGA*, 7 (1898) pp. 341–488, here pp. 423–4; *BKHL*, vol. 4 (1928) 389–93 (p. 392 a reproduction of a painting of 1597 showing the church and the *Mühlentor*); *BKHL*, vol. 1, 1 (1939) p. 85.

24. v. Hövelen, *Der Kaiserl: Reichs-Stadt*, p. 40; Starck, *Lubeca Lutherano-Evangelica*, pp. 606, 737 (quotation), and 774; W. Brehmer, 'Die Befestigungswerke Lübecks', pp. 413–4; *BKHL*, vol. 1, 1 (1939) p. 82. According to Brehmer, the town council promised in 1624 that the cemetery would not be touched; according to v. Hövelen, 'the new ditch was laid through the graveyard' in 1622.

25. 'die weil nicht geringe Klagen vnd murren darüber gehöret werden' (the first draft had: ' ... darüber getrieben wirdt').

26. Graßmann, 'Lübeck im 17. Jahrhundert', p. 467; J. P. Wieselgren, 'Itinerarium Danicum. Lübeck im Reisebericht zweier Dominikaner von 1622', *ZLGA*, 42 (1962) pp. 115–17, at p. 117; Starck, *Lubeca Lutherano-Evangelica*, pp. 766–7.

27. Graßmann, 'Lübeck im 17. Jahrhundert', p. 448.

28. According to nineteenth-century folk-tales, it was a place to which evil spirits were fixed by a spell (Deecke, *Lübische Geschichten und Sagen*, pp. 178 and 393).

29. *Histoire remarouable d'vne femme decedee depvis cino ans en ca, laquelle est reuenuë trouuer son mary & parler à luy aux faux bourgs S. Marcel lez Paris ...* (Paris: Alexandre, 1618) pp. 5–7 and 15–16.

30. I. Franck, *Mikaelidagens predikan* (= Bibliotheca theologiae practicae, vol. 31) (diss. Uppsala) (Lund, 1973) pp. 120–5.

31. For Lübeck, see Deecke, *Lübische Geschichten und Sagen*, pp. 174–6, and also O. Mensing, *Schleswig-Holsteinisches Wörterbuch*, vol. 5 (Neumünster, 1935) pp. 329–31.

32. A. Angelus, *WiderNatur vnd Wunderbuch ...* (Frankfurt a. M.: Collitz/Brachfeld, 1597) pp. 206–[210] (HAB); this case is dealt with by H. C. E. Midelfort, 'The Devil and the German People: Reflections on the Popularity of Demon Possession in Sixteenth-Century Germany', in S. Ozment (ed.), *Religion and Culture in the Renaissance and Reformation*

(= Sixteenth-Century Essays and Studies, vol. 11) (Kirksville, 1989) pp. 99–119, here pp. 99–100. Two similar cases from Lutheran Iceland in 1638 are described by Gísli Oddsson, 'De mirabilibus Islandiae', ed. by H. Hermannsson, *Islandica*, 10 (1917) pp. 31–84, here pp. 75–6.

33. C.-M. Edsman, *A Swedish Female Folk Healer from the Beginning of the 18th Century* (= Skrifter utg. av religionshistoriska institutionen i Uppsala (hum. fak.), vol. 4) (Uppsala, 1967) p. 85; the translation from the German is partly adapted from Edsman's paraphrase (p. 122–3).

34. Edsman, *A Swedish Female Folk Healer*, p. 89; English translation by Edsman (p. 125).

35. O. Tschirch, 'Ein Niederlausitzer Geisterseher', *Niederlausitzer Mitteilungen*, 4 (1895) pp. 150–67, here pp. 159 and 166; *Ein new wunder Gesicht: Welchs im Ertzstifft Magdeburgk / hart bei Wolmerstedt ... einem Megdlein von achzehen Jahren am hellen liechten Tage erschienen ist ...* (Magdeburg: Francke [1596]) fol. A2ᵛ (StBL); there is also a shortened Low German translation: *Ein Nye Wunder Gesicht ... 1597*) fol. A2ʳ, cf. also n. 12.

36. *BKHL*, vol. 3 (1919–20) p. 151; other Lübeck examples pp. 406, 493, and *BKHL*, vol. 4 (1928) p. 120; cf. also G. Spiekerkötter, *Die Darstellung des Weltgerichtes von 1500–1800 in Deutschland* (diss. Berlin) (Düsseldorf, 1939) pp. 32–3, 61, 74.

37. F. Techen, 'Die Grabsteine der Lübeckischen Kirchen', *ZLGA*, 8 (1900) pp. 54–168, here p. 105, no. 73, p. 136, no. 131 (two stones from 1611 and 1638). Later inscriptions are printed on pp. 135–6, no. 127 [1709], p. 90, no. 24 [1716], p. 92, no. 37 [1796], p. 91, no. 24G [n. d.]; F. Techen, 'Die Grabsteine des Doms zu Lübeck', *ZLGA*, 7 (1898) pp. 52–107, here pp. 64–5, n. 35b [1753], p. 78, no. 138 [1809].

38. Techen, 'Grabsteine des Doms', p. 57, n. 22; 'Grabsteine der Lüberckischen Kirchen', p. 59.

39. Wieselgren, 'Itinerarium Danicum'.

40. L. Schmidt, 'Kirchliche Buß- und Bettage', *TRE*, vol. 7 (1981) pp. 492–6; J. Hartwig, 'Zur Geschichte des Bußtages in Lübeck', *Nordelbingen*, 13 (1937) pp. 161–7; Jannasch (cf. n. 5) pp. 166, 122, and 159.

41. The Greek μετάνοια is rendered into Latin as *pœnitentia* and into German as *Buße* but none of these languages allow for the English distinctions between *penance, penitence,* and *repentance*. Some of the translations offered in this essay may therefore be arbitrary. The following argument is taken from Beyer, 'Lutherske folkelige profeter', pp. 167–8.

42. For an example from Lübeck, see M. Sirckes, *Justitiae et Miseracordiae*, p. 56.

43. For Lübeck see J. C. H. Dreyer, *Einleitung zur Kenntniß der ... [Lübecker] ... Verordnungen ...* (Lübeck: Donatius, 1769) pp. 568–70.

44. Sabean, 'A prophet in the Thirty Years' War', pp. 69 and 91. The author seems to have changed his mind in the course of writing the article. For some reason Sabean employs the medieval definitions of penance (*Buße*).

270     *Notes and References*

45. N. Heldvad, *Tractatus Physic[o]-theologicus, oder* ... *Bedencken / von den Er[d]biebungen* ... (Copenhagen, 1632) fols B2ᵛ–B3ʳ.

46. Published by E. Pontoppidan, *Annales ecclesiæ Danicæ diplomatici oder* ... *Kirchen-Historie Des Reichs Dännemarck,* vol. 3 (Copenhagen: Lynow, 1747) pp. 771–92, quotations pp. 789 and 772. Himself a Pietist, Pontoppidan very much approved of this earlier effort to improve church life.

47. *Kurtzer Bericht,* fol. B2ᵛ; cf. V. Gregorius, *Consilium antipestiferum* ... *Bedencken / vber die anjetzo grassirende gifftige Seuchen* ... (Halberstadt: Kolwaldt, 1636) pp. 23–4 (UL Copenhagen, 2nd div.); J. Schelius, *Kurtzer Bericht / Von der Pest* ... (Copenhagen: Martzan, 1636) fols A2ʳ–A2ᵛ.

48. C. Schlichtenberger, *Prophecey eines einfeltigen Bawren Tochter* ... (Lübeck: Balhorn, 1580), another edition printed in the same year in Lübeck by Kröger. The original was printed in 1580 in Danzig by Rodus (HAB). Another Lübeck reprint was *Newe Prophetin* (cf. n. 10). On Schlichtenberger's pamphlet, see also M. Tveitane, 'Henrykt til himmel og helvete – Folkelige visjoner og deres kulturhistoriske bakgrunn', *Tradisjon,* 2 (1972) pp. 38–48, here pp. 43–4.

49. Beyer, 'Lutherische Propheten'.

50. Rørdam (cf. n. 15), pp. 184–6, *Erschrecklike Vnerhorde / doch warhafftige Nye Tydinge / de sick tho Spandow* ... *hefft tho gedragen* (1594) fol. A4ᵛ.

51. *Warhafftige Geschichte / so sich zugetragen haben den 4. vnd den 19. Maij. Des jetzt 1575. Jahrs / Wie eine lange weisse Fraw zu einem Megdlein von 16. Jharen komen ist / zwischen Apfelstet vnd grossen Rettewich / vnd jhm befohlen / anzuzeigen alle Menschen / wie Gott der Herr sehr zornig were vber vnser Sünd / vnd so wir nicht Busse thun / würde er mit der Welt ein ende machen / Sölchs solte das Megdlein den Pfarherrn anzeigen / das Volck zur Busse zuvermanen* (1575) fol. A3ʳ (BL).

52. *Historische Nachricht Von* ... *Nürnberg* . . (Frankfurt and Leipzig: Bachmeyer, 1707) pp. 490–1.

53. Rørdam (cf. n. 15), pp. 184–7; L. Alardus, *Zeichen vnd Wunder-Predigt / Darinnen berichtet vnd mit satsamen Gründen bewiesen wird Wofür die Zeichen / so biß anhero bey vns / vnd in benachtbarter Gegend geschehen / zu achten* ... (Hamburg: Werner, 1636) pp. 13 and 18–19 (a girl in Dithmarschen); *Theatrum europæjum,* vol. 6 (Frankfurt a. M., 1663) pp. 632–3 (a shepherd near Hamburg in 1648).

54. On the destruction of Timişoara in Romania, see a 1576 broadsheet in Strauss, *The German Single-leaf Woodcut,* p. 122; on the destruction of Bergen in Norway in 1623, see N. Heldvad, *Sylva chronologica circuli Baltici, das ist: Historischer Wald / vnnd Vmbzirck deß Baltischen Meers ...,* vol. 2 (Hamburg: Carstens, 1624) pp. 320–1, and *Theatrum europæum,* vol. 1 (Frankfurt a. M., 1662) p. 787.

55. These legends are known from many places. The Schleswig-Holsteinian legend about the destruction of Rungholt can be traced back to at least 1623 (O. Hartz, 'Die Rungholtsage bei den nordfriesischen Chronisten', *Jahrbuch des Nordfriesischen Vereins für Heimatkunde und Heimatliebe,* 20 (1933) pp. 80–6); see also W.-E. Peuckert, 'Sodom und Gomorrah', in *HDA,* vol. 8 (1936–7) pp. 21–5.

56. C.-M. Edsman, 'Stones', in *The Encyclopedia of Religion*, vol. 14 (New York and London, 1987) pp. 49–53, quote p. 50; see also R. Hünnerkopf, Stein II., in HDA, vol. 8 (1936–7) pp. 390–401, and W. Müller-Bergström, Grenze, Rain; Grenzstein, in HDA, vol. 3 (1930–31) pp. 1137–57.

57. *Wolmeinende Erklerung dieses Bildes / Welches Königliche Maytt: zu Dennemar̂ck den 8. Decembris früh Morgens vmb 5. vhren abgewichenen 1625. Jahrs / zu Rodenburg ... erschienen* (n. d.); see also H. Rasmussen, 'Christian 4.s syn', *Fynske Minder* (1957) pp. 60–75.

58. Starck, *Lubeca Lutherano-Evangelica*, pp. 758–60 and 939–46; C. G. Gjörwell (ed.), *Svenska Magazinet* (1766) pp. 87–90; G. H. Goetzius (præjs) – C. H. v. Elßwich (resp.) *Dissertatio historico-theologica, errores, ovos Joh. Bannier ... proposuit, exhibens & refutans ...* (Lübeck: Vidua B. Schmalhertzii [1707] (StBL).

59. Starck, *Lubeca Lutherano-Evangelica*, pp. 593–5 and 720–9. Maybe Pontoppidan, *Annales Ecclesiae Danicoe*, p. 724, is referring to the same person when writing about a prophetess with an English background in Copenhagen in 1620, although her name is given as Anna Brusch.

60. To list but a selection: *Von dem Newgebornen Abgott zu Babel Ein Abschrifft* ... (1550) (BL); *Neuwe zeitung Von dem Newgebornen Antichrist* ... ([Cologne:] Röschlin, 1578) (Zentralbibl. Zürich); *Ein newe Zeittung / von eim wunderlichen Kindt / welchs geboren ist* ... (Cologne: Schreiber, 1591) [broadsheet] (BN).

61. See two broadsheets of 1629 and 1631 in D. Alexander and W. L. Strauss, *The German Single-Leaf Woodcut 1600–1700* (New York, 1977) pp. 176 and 709. In A. Belbeza, *Warhafftige Wundergeschicht ... Erstlichen Getruckt zu Prag in Böhem 1619. Jahr.*, fols A2ᵛ–A3ʳ (BL), a child of twelve weeks predicts calamities.

62. L. H. Munthe, *En Sandferdig Berentning / om nogle selsomme ... Fødseler ...* (Copenhagen: Sartorius, 1641) fol. A8ᵛ.

63. E. Holländer, *Wunder, Wundergeburt und Wundergestalt in Einblattdrucken ...* (Stuttgart, 1921) pp. 329–36.

64. Munthe, *En Sandferdig Beretning*, for an example of 1629, see C. Potinius, *Prognosticum Divinum. Das ist / Ein Göttlich Prognosticum darinnen Gott viel Wunders ankündiget. 1. In einem Wunderkinde. 2. Noch in einer Wundergebuhrt. 3. Als auch in sieben Wundergesichten ...* (Bremen: Martens [1629]) (UL Göttingen); on Potinius, see Kayser, 'Hannoversche Enthusiasten', pp. 34–6.

65. E. Hach, 'Aus den älteren Lübecker Kirchenbüchern', *MLGA*, 7 (1895–6) pp. 129–34, here p. 129.

66. F. C. Dahlmann (ed.), *Johann Adolfi's genannt Neocorus, Chronik des Landes Dithmarschen*, vol. 2 (Kiel, 1827) pp. 323 and 352.

67. B. Anhorn, *Magiologia. Christliche Warnung für dem Aberglauben vnd Zauberey ...* (Basel: Meyer, 1674) pp. 93–6 (BL). I owe this reference to Martin Gnann in Tübingen.

68. C. Hartknoch, *Preussische Kirchen-Historia ...* (Frankfurt a. M., Leipzig, and Danzig: Beckenstein, 1686) pp. 720–52, esp. pp. 745–6. Earlier, a linen-weaver had preached against the Interim ('Nachricht von einem Propheten der A. 1550. herumb gewandert', *Unschuldige Nachrichten*, [8] (1708) pp. 283–4).

69. Among the exceptions are: 'Hans Neuschels Leinwebers zu Hirschbergk Bericht an Herr Martinum Proserum ... geschrieben den 10. Sept. Ao. 1632', *Wanderer im Riesengebirge* (March 1903) p. 35; Hans Engelbrecht (cf. H. Reller in *Neue deutsche Biographie*, vol. 4 (Berlin, 1959) p. 511); Johann Warner/Werner (cf. R. Haase, *Das Problem des Chiliasmus und der Dreißigjährige Krieg* (diss. Leipzig) (Leipzig, 1933) pp. 70–8).
70. Beyer, 'Lutherske folkelige profeter', pp. 173–9.
71. C. H. Tamms, *Peter Suleke, ein Religionsschwärmer des 16. Jahrhunderts* ... (Stralsund, 1837) p. 14.
72. A typical example is Alardus, *Zeichen vnd Wunder-Predigt*, see also W. Brückner, 'Protestantische Exempelsammlungen', in *Enzyklopädie des Märchens*, vol. 4 (Berlin and New York, 1982–4) pp. 604–9.
73. G. H. Goetzius (præs.) – H. Bünckau (resp.), *Bibliothecam anti-fanaticam Lubecensem ... inspiciet ...* (Lübeck: Struck [1721]), and Starck, *Lubeca lutherano-Evangelica*.
74. Lebermann, *Die Beglückte und Geschmückte Stadt Lübeck*, p. 29.

9. BLOOD, TEARS AND XAVIER-WATER: JESUIT MISSIONARIES AND POPULAR RELIGION IN THE EIGHTEENTH-CENTURY UPPER PALATINATE    *Trevor Johnson*

1. B. Duhr, *Geschichte der Jesuiten in den Ländern Deutscher Zunge* (Freiburg, 1907–28), still the standard institutional history of the Society in Germany; K. Hengst, *Jesuiten an Universitäten und Jesuitenuniversitäten* (Paderborn, Munich, Vienna and Zurich, 1981); Hsia, R. Po-chia, *Society and Religion in Münster, 1535–1618* (New Haven and London, 1984); L. Châtellier, *L'Europe des Dévots* (Paris, 1987); E. M. Szarota, *Das Jesuitendrama im deutschen Sprachgebiet* (Munich, 1979/80). The Jesuits' predilection for a ministry to the elite has been contrasted with the more popular focus of other Counter-Reformation orders, such as the Capuchins. See, for example, B. Hubensteiner, *Vom Geist des Barock: Kultur und Frömmigkeit im alten Bayern* (second edition, Munich, 1978) pp. 81–9.
2. See, for example, J. Delumeau, *Catholicism between Luther and Voltaire* (London, 1977) especially pp. 189–94, and *Sin and Fear: The Emergence of a Western Guilt Culture, 13th–18th Centuries* (New York, 1990) especially pp. 329–47 and 480–90; R. Muchembled, *Culture populaire et culture des élites* (Paris, 1978) (English translation, *Popular Culture and Elite Culture in France, 1400–1750*, Baton Rouge, 1985) and 'The Witches of the Cambrésis. The Acculturation of the Rural World in the Sixteenth Century', in J. Obelkevich (ed.), *Religion and the People, 800–1700* (Chapel Hill, 1979) pp. 21–276; P. Burke, *Popular Culture in Early Modern Europe* (London, 1978).
3. B. Duhr, 'Zur Geschichte der deutschen Volksmissionen in der 2. Hälfte des 17. Jahrhunderts', *Historisches Jahrbuch*, 37 (1916) pp. 593–623.
4. B. Duhr, 'Die kurpfälzischen und kurbayerischen Volksmissionen im 18. Jahrhundert', *Historisch-politische Blätter für das katholische Deutschland*, 170 (1922) pp. 510–26, 565–80, 637–55.

5. Bayerisches Hauptstaatsarchiv München (hereafter BayHSTA), Jesuitica, 562, Ordo diurnus, materiarum ad dicendum, ac functionum reliquarum servatus in Missione Bavarica post obitum Patris Conradi Herdegen.

6. The structure was not inflexible. Accompanying this particular timetable is a list of suggestions which ring of experience in the field. Their author recommended, for example, an abbreviation of the afternoon sessions, 'for if the catechism is taught for half of the first hour, a sermon and an act of contrition take place in the second hour and then either an examination of conscience take place or a public procession is held in the fourth hour, the people are once again detained for several hours without a break. This seems to me to be too much, especially in very hot weather': BayHSTA, München, Jesuitica, 562, Quae in Missione Bavarica ..., fol. 3. The reference to the heat is a reminder that rural missions were normally held during the summer. In winter months the missionaries concentrated on conducting the Ignatian Spiritual Exercises for members of the Marian Congregations, either in the Society's urban colleges or, as occurred in Bavaria from the mid-eighteenth century, in purpose-built 'exercise-houses': Duhr, 'Die kurpfälzischen und kurbayerischen Volksmissionen', pp. 573, 578–9.

7. Ibid., pp. 519–22.

8. Ibid., pp. 567–8.

9. Ibid., p. 637.

10. On the Protestant period in the Upper Palatinate, see: J. B. Götz, *Die religiöse Bewegung in der Oberpfalz von 1520 bis 1560* (Freiburg im Breisgau,1914), *Die erste Einführung des Kalvinismus in der Oberpfalz 1559–1576* (Münster, 1933), and *Die religiösen Wirren in der Oberpfalz 1576–1620* (Münster, 1937); F. Lippert, *Die Reformation in Kirche, Sitte und Schule der Oberpfalz* (Rothenburg ob der Tauber, 1897); V. Press, *Calvinismus und Territorialstaat. Regierung und Zentralbehörden der Kurpfalz 1559–1619* (Kiel, 1970), and 'Das evangelische Amberg zwischen Reformation und Gegenreformation', in K.-O. Ambronn, A. Fuchs and H. Wanderwitz (eds), *Amberg 1034–1984: Aus tausend Jahren Stadtgeschichte* (Amberg, 1984) pp. 119–36; B. Vogler, 'Die Ausbildung des Konfessionsbewußtseins in den pfälzischen Territorien zwischen 1555 und 1619', in H. Rabe, H. Molitor and H.-C. Rublack (eds), *Festgabe für Ernst Walter Zeeden* (Münster, 1976) pp. 281–8.

11. On the period of recatholicisation and Counter-Reformation in the Upper Palatinate, see K.-O. Ambronn and A. Fuchs (eds), *Die Oberpfalz wird bayerisch. Die Jahre 1621 bis 1628 in Amberg und der Oberpfalz* (Amberg, 1978); M. Högl, *Die Bekehrung der Oberpfalz durch Kurfürst Maximillian I*, 2 vols (Regensburg, 1903); F. Lippert, *Geschichte der Gegenreformation in Staat, Kirche und Sitte der Oberpfalz-Kurpfalz zur Zeit des dreißigjährigen Krieges* (Freiburg im Breisgau, 1901); M. Popp, 'Kirchengeschichte Ambergs zwischen Rekatholisierung und Säkularisation', in K.-O. Ambronn, A. Fuchs and H. Wanderwitz (eds), *Amberg 1034–1984: Aus tausend Jahren Stadtgeschichte* (Amberg, 1984); A. Schosser, *Die Erneuerung der religiös-kirchlichen Lebens in der Oberpfalz nach*

*der Rekatholisierung (1630–1700)* (Düren, 1938); G. Schwaiger, *Kardinal Franz Wilhelm von Wartenberg als Bischof von Regensburg (1649–1661)* (Munich, 1954); A. Sperl, 'Der oberpfälzische Adel und die Gegenreformation', *Vierteljahrschrift für Wappenkunde,* 28 (1900) pp. 339–487; W. Ziegler, 'Die Rekatholisierung der Oberpfalz', in H. Glaser (ed.), *Wittelsbach und Bayern,* vol. 2, 1 (Munich, 1980) pp. 436–47.

12. Popp, 'Kirchengeschichte Ambergs', p. 137.

13. Ibid., pp. 137–40; Duhr, *Geschichte der Jesuiten,* vol. 2, pp. 242–4.

14. Staatsarchiv Amberg (hereafter STAA), Geistliche Sachen, 728/1.

15. Duhr, 'Die kurpfälzischen und kurbayerischen Volksmissionen', pp. 647–8.

16. BayHSTA, Jesuitica, 562, Relatio Missionum, quae per Palatinatum Superiorem obitae sunt, a Patribus Soc. Jesu, Ao. 1721; Relatio Missionum, quae in Palatinatu Superiori habitae sunt, Ao. 1722.

17. BayHSTA, Jesuitica, 562, Relatio Missionum ... 1722, fols 2, 3.

18. Ibid., 1721 fols 2, 6, 7 and 19.

19. Ibid., 1722 fols 7, 8 and 4, 5.

20. Ibid., 1721 fol. 16.

21. Ibid., fol. 16.

22. Ibid., 1722, fols 8, 9.

23. Ibid., fol. 16.

24. STAA, Geistliche Sachen, 728/1, fols 8ᵛ, 9ʳ.

25. BayHSTA, Jesuitica, 562, Relatio Missionum ... 1722, fols 5, 6.

26. Ibid., 1721, fol. 15.

27. G. Klaniczay, *The Uses of Supernatural Power. The Transformation of Popular Religion in Medieval and Early-Modern Europe* (Cambridge and Oxford, 1990) p. 1.

28. W. Christian, 'Provoked Religious Weeping in Early Modern Spain', in J. Davis (ed.), *Religious Organization and Religious Experience* (Association of Social Anthropologists, Series 21, London, 1982) pp. 97–114.

29. On sacramentals, see A. Franz, *Die kirchlichen Benediktionen im deutschen Mittelalter,* 2 vols (Freiburg, 1909), and the discussion in chapters 1 and 2 of R. W. Scribner, *Popular Culture and Popular Movements in Reformation Germany* (London and Ronceverte, 1987).

30. BayHSTA, Jesuitica, 562, Relatio Missionum ... 1721, fol. 39.

31. Ibid., 1722, fol. 23.

32. Schreiber, 'Heilige Wasser', pp. 205–6.

33. Lippert, *Geschichte der Gegenreformation,* p. 160. Similarly the relic of Loyola's soutane at Cologne, an important addition to that city's already massive inventory of relics, was touched with belts, which in turn became relics by virtue of their physical contact with the saint's robe and were then worn by women during pregnancy. In Trier, Emmerich and Hildesheim, paper bearing Loyola's signature was hung around the neck or placed on the body of a pregnant woman to ensure a safe delivery. Schreiber, 'Heilige Wasser', p. 203.

34. STAA, Geistliche Sachen, 728/1, fol. 6ʳ.

35. BayHSTA, Jesuitica, 562, Relatio Missionum ... 1721, fol. 4.

36. The missionaries compared this experience in the Upper Palatinate with similar events at Gundelfingen in Swabia, where the citizenry, despairing of any other remedy, had made a vow and gone in procession to the mission-cross in the nearby town of Lauingen, as a result of which there had been a speedy, universal recovery. BayHSTA, Jesuitica, 562, Relatio Missionum ... 1721, fol. 8.

37. For the most recent elaboration of this theme, drawing on evidence from southern Apulia, see D. Gentilcore, *From Bishop to Witch: The System of the Sacred in Early Modern Terra d'Otranto* (Manchester, 1992).

38. On pilgrimage shrines in the Upper Palatinate, see T. Gebhard, 'Zur Geschichte des Wallfahrtswesens in der Oberpfalz', *Verhandlungen des Historischen Vereins für Oberpfalz und Regensburg*, 112 (1972) pp. 311–24; W. Hartinger, 'Das Wallfahrtswesen und seine Entwicklung in der Oberpfalz', in *Wallfahrtswesen und Heimatpflege* (Kallmünz, 1983) pp. 3–24; H. Utz, *Wallfahrten im Bistum Regensburg* (Munich, 1981).

39. Neukirchen was similar to the many other pilgrimage centres which dotted the region, but it did possess two distinctive features. First, its location, virtually straddling the Bavarian/Bohemian border, meant that its catchment area extended into both regions. In visiting it the missionaries could be confident of spreading their *fama* into Bohemia. Secondly, an ancient legend linked Neukirchen's wonder-working image, a carving of the Madonna, to an iconoclastic attack by Hussite troops in the fifteenth century. The local iconography even depicted the statue of the Virgin with a Hussite sabre splitting her head. The easy association with the Calvinist iconoclasm of a later period made it a particularly dramatic site in which to engage in confessional point-scoring. On the history of the shrine, see W. Hartinger, 'Die Wallfahrt Neukirchen bei heilig Blut. Volkskundliche Untersuchung einer Gnadenstätte an der bayerisch-böhmischen Grenze', *Beiträge zur Geschichte des Bistums Regensburg*, 5 (1971) pp. 23–240.

40. On Rem, see G. Schwaiger, *Bavaria Sancta*, vol. 3 (Regensburg, 1973) pp. 312–20 and C. Schreiber (ed.), *Wallfahrten durchs deutsche Land Eine Pilgerfahrt zu Deutschlands heiligen Stätten* (Berlin, 1928) p. 88.

41. P. Soergel, *Wondrous in His Saints: Counter-Reformation Propaganda in Bavaria* (Berkeley, Los Angeles, London, 1993) pp. 122–6.

42. J. Keim, 'Ein vermeintlicher Exorzismus in Straubing', *Jahres-Bericht des Historischen Vereins für Straubing und Umgebung*, 73 (1970) pp. 60–4. Latin and German manuscript reports by the Jesuits of the Straubing exorcism survive in the Munich archive: BayHSTA, Jesuitica, 525.

43. I. Agricola, I. Flott and F. X. Kropf, *Historia Provinciae Societatis Iesu Germaniae Superioris*, 3 vols (Augsburg and Munich, 1727–54).

44. Schreiber, 'Heilige Wasser', pp. 207–9.

45. G. Lottes, 'Popular Culture and the Early Modern State in 16th Century Germany', in S. Kaplan (ed.), *Understanding Popular Culture* (Berlin, New York, Amsterdam, 1984) p. 180.

46. For French parallels, see R. Briggs, *Communities of Belief: Cultural and Social Tension in Early Modern France* (Oxford, 1989) especially pp. 267, 327–8.

# Notes on Contributors

JÜRGEN BEYER is currently a Research Fellow at Uppsala University, Sweden.

C. SCOTT DIXON is Lecturer in History at the Institute of European Studies, Queen's University, Belfast.

THOMAS A. FUDGE was Assistant Professor of Church History at Warner Pacific College, Oregon, and is now Lecturer in History, University of Canterbury, Christchurch, New Zealand.

TREVOR JOHNSON is Lecturer in History at the University of the West of England, Bristol.

J. M. MINTY teaches art history at McGill University, Montreal.

ALISON ROWLANDS is Lecturer in European History at the University of Essex.

ULINKA RUBLACK is a Research Fellow in History at St John's College, Cambridge.

BOB SCRIBNER is Reader in the Social History of Early Modern Europe, Cambridge University, and Fellow of Clare College, Cambridge.

ERIC WILSON has taught history at Mount Allison University, Sackville, New Brunswick, at Mount St Vincent University, Bedford, Nova Scotia, and at Dalhousie University, Halifax, Nova Scotia. He is currently training as a lawyer.

J. C. WOLFART was a Research Fellow at the University of Princeton and now Assistant Professor in Religious History at University of Toronto, Erindale.

# Index